THE MAN WHO PLAYS ALONE

THE MAN
WHO PLAYS ALONE

———

DANILO DOLCI

Translated from the Italian by
ANTONIA COWAN

MACGIBBON & KEE

Originally published by Giulio Einaudi, editore, Turin, 1966
as *Chi gioca solo*. New edition 1967
First published in English by MacGibbon & Kee Ltd 1968
Copyright © Giulio Einaudi, editore, 1966, 1967
English translation copyright © MacGibbon & Kee Ltd 1968
This translation is made from the second edition,
abridged by the author and the translator
Printed in Great Britain by Ebenezer Baylis & Son Ltd
The Trinity Press, Worcester and London

SBN: 261.62120.3

Contents

v

PART TWO

Contents

PART THREE

Illustrations

1*

Introduction

The politicians who compromise with the mafia in Sicily (and there are not a few of them) can be divided into four categories:

First, that of the unprincipled politicians who, particularly at election time, have rapid encounters and meetings at which they are not too careful about how they pick up votes and who they have dealings with: 'you scratch my back and I'll scratch yours'.

Second, that of the politicians who cold-bloodedly and systematically exploit the closed mafia group, opportunists who will resort to every possible kind of double dealing to suit the time and place: themselves systematically exploited in turn by the mafia.

Third, that of the actual mafiosi who manage to get themselves elected, sometimes even to positions of high responsibility: fortunately this is not the most numerous category.

Fourth, that of the young men who, though they may have opposed the system to begin with, have come to accept it and adapt themselves to it in order to get ahead.

What are the local conditions that for more than twenty years have permitted this exploitation of the mafia (and for a certain time even of the bandits) for electoral purposes?

Since the last war, the mafia has managed to have a hand in the government of Italy at every level, from the local Council to the Provincial administration, the Regional Government, and right up to the very highest levels.

How has all this been possible, as far as this area of Western Sicily is concerned?

A person looking at Palermo and the surrounding province will not need to be very observant to notice that the great majority of the population is discontented, often gravely discontented, bitter, in mourning. 'But why'—the observer may well wonder—'why can't this majority of discontented people become a majority that will press for change, stimulate progress: why can't they be a new political majority?'

Is this situation really as irrational and absurd as it often seems at first sight—or does it only seem so to someone who has difficulty in grasping all the inner connections? How far is it really like a motor in neutral, with its gears failing to connect so that the cogwheels go spinning round on themselves? To what extent are present conditions (being determined by particular history) inevitable? How far is the situation other than what it seems—and what is the real situation?

An essential part of the process of trying to grasp a problem is opening ourselves up to what is new, trying to see from a fresh point of view what we may previously have thought of as already known and of no interest, and noting carefully whatever we may come across: however, this apparently random activity is also bound to be partly determined by our own intuitions and aspirations, and by what we already know. This book is a collection of the notes made in the course of an attempt to elucidate what are the obstacles to group life and democratic organization in the city of Palermo and the surrounding area, my instrument being the primitive one of getting people to think and express themselves: I am more and more convinced that no study from the outside can equal the value of self-examination by a population.

I questioned quite a number of people, from various backgrounds, in such a way that their answers should give a sketch both of the situation and of the particular personality; the more thoughtful among them I met several times, in order that they should have the opportunity to consider the problem in greater depth. These are only a few—some of them documents, some no more than simple sketches, others quite thorough analyses of individual circumstances —among the many encounters possible; certainly not enough to give a complete picture, but useful, I think, for stimulating more concrete and active reflection, discussion, research, and projects for development.

In *Inchiesta a Palermo* I tried to clarify in particular the circumstances, the difficulties, the wasted potential of men without work; in *Spreco*, the waste of human and natural resources when the stimulating and co-ordinating force of planning is lacking; this book (parts of which have appeared in the Palermo newspaper *L'Ora* to encourage rethinking and popular discussion on the subject) is an attempt to clarify the difficulties and the waste involved in the failure to develop and make use of the open group—the indispensable medium between man and society, between individual commitment and democratic planning.

Since the very poor of this area, including the peasants, had already been represented in my previous books and in Lorenzo Barbera's excellent book *La Diga di Roccamena*,[1] it seemed to me necessary now to devote more attention to other sections of society, not forgetting Palermo as capital of the province and of Sicily.

As for the documentation directly concerning certain politicians—compiled with great attention to accuracy—I must point out, in case it isn't obvious, that I have no personal animosity towards them: I simply believe that their behaviour is a bad example and a hindrance and obstacle to the development of the region, and that any action so far taken by the bodies appointed to safeguard democracy has been gravely inadequate.

In order to devote maximum attention to the diagnosis, I have here deliberately avoided suggesting specific remedies: some of the meetings constituting Part Two of the book, which were attended by some of the most concerned and active people in the area, aimed at elaborating the diagnoses in greater detail in order to make clearer the kind of action needed, and the urgency with which it is needed. I am sure that the more careful observers will easily foresee how the next ten or twenty years cannot but confirm the essence of these self-analyses.

I would ask anyone who finds the book libellous to attack it only after having read it all and checked its truth; and I would also point out that it is difficult in every part of the world to form live, inter-communicating, productive groups: every part of the world has, in this respect too, its own particular difficulties, its own evils, its own particular forms of violence. And I must also confess at once, to anyone who finds the whole book provocative, that I shall consider it a mistake and a failure if it does not contribute—as far as a book can—towards provoking a substantial change in the situation: group work and group life are valuable only in so far as they are genuine revolutionary instruments, and not mere textbook moralizing.

[1] Laterza, Bari 1964.

I was often struck by the really impressive desire for truth that I found in the people I met—the people who are the real authors of this book. And in talking about their own experience and their own difficulties I believe they say things that are interesting and relevant far beyond the limits of this particular, relatively small, area. To all of them goes my warmest gratitude and also, I imagine, the gratitude of those who in the diligent pursuit of a new world will reflect on and (in the best sense) judge this book.

D.D.

NOTE TO THE SECOND EDITION

To this new edition (Italian) is added a third section which helps to document and clarify my conclusion to the first edition, which read as follows:

We have hundreds and hundreds of encounters and meetings in the area.

Thousands, tens of thousands, hundreds of thousands of people say more or less this: we all know, the scandals or potential scandals in Italy today are such and so many that if we attempted to cure them all at once, this State would just come to a standstill; at the moment, for example, the Parliamentary Antimafia Commission no doubt serves some purpose: but why does this Commission, which has it in its power officially to verify what is already plain to see in the area (as it ought to have succeeded in doing by now, if it had been working diligently)—why does it allow this situation to continue like this in danger of putrefaction? Who benefits by the delays if not the most cunning schemers, the most refined outlaws, and those most adept at profiting from the perpetuation of corruption and the old clientship system? How, once again, can people have any real faith in public bodies, in State and Parliamentary organizations at any level (and in consequence the desire to participate at all levels in the life of the nation), if the efforts of these organizations are fundamentally directed towards accommodating compromise rather than towards responsible plainness; as long as their efforts are directed mainly towards evading fundamental truths and therefore —under the unhealthy equivocation of reasons of State—denying the most elementary justice?

Many people, the more understanding and better informed, repeat: what sort of justice is this, which comes to a halt when faced with the power and officiality of certain people and certain groups? It is quite plain that no State in the world can win the trust and the participation of its people as long as it goes on—partisan by neglect —covering up falsehood and defending the parasitic abuse of power.

And, more explicitly, they insist: the social body will remain sluggish and diseased and no real progress can be made, as long as the representatives of the State go on trying at any cost to cover up for generals, chiefs of police, government ministers and under-secretaries involved in the mafia-clientship structure; as long as certain people continue to do their utmost to make everyone believe that it is the mafiosi who cajole the politician, and fail to criticize the favour reciprocated, the reciprocal exploitation that has been evident in the area for years now; until it is made clear just how far certain politicians are responsible for their own behaviour, and how far the government shares responsibility; as long as we can still come across people at the highest levels of responsibility—ministers, under-secretaries, magistrates—who admit in private to knowing that certain of their colleagues are men of the mafia (either actually belonging to it or at its disposal), but who don't care to come out into the open about it; as long as officialdom and government continue to expect of poor and defenceless people the courage which, in spite of being protected by their office, they themselves lack; until we overcome the slippery and ambiguous vagueness of those who try to cover up their own lack of courage by saying that everyone is equally corrupt; until every group, every party that calls itself democratic dares to break its links with the mafia-clientship system; as long as the majority of people go on behaving as if these problems were absolutely no concern of theirs: in other words, until people at every level of responsibility are willing to take risks for the sake of the truth—until they dare systematically to oppose organized violence and injustice wherever it may be.

What happened recently in Rome in the course of a trial concerning material of which the greater part is reproduced in this book is so revealing and symptomatic that (though it goes rather against the grain to recount what might appear to be mere wrangling rather than real conflict) I think it will be helpful to publish an account of the proceedings; this is drawn from the official records, from the minutes of the various agencies, and from the shorthand notes of Fabrizia Guglielmi, whom I thank most warmly.

D.D.

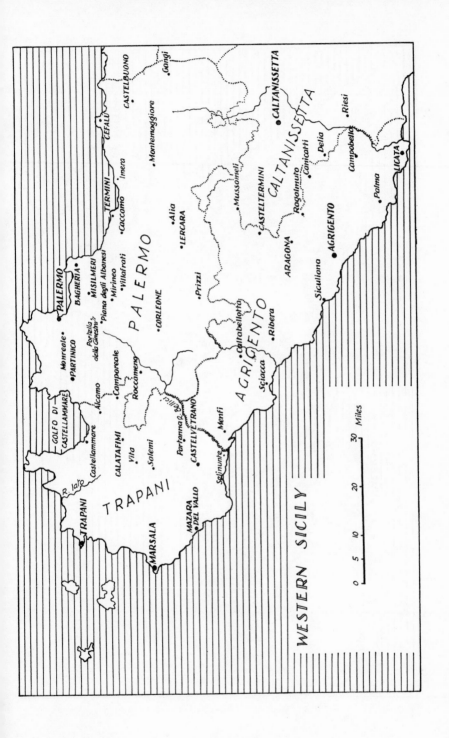

WESTERN SICILY

0 5 10 20 30 Miles

TRAPANI
PALERMO
AGRIGENTO
CALTANISSETTA

PALERMO
BAGHERIA
MISILMERI
Piana degli Albanesi
Mirineo
Villafrati
Monreale
PARTINICO
Portella
della Ginestra
Alia
LERCARA
Prizzi
CORLEONE
Roccameng
Comporeale
Alcamo
CASTELLAMMARE
GOLFO DI
CASTELLAMMARE
Castellammare
R. Iato
TRAPANI
MARSALA
CALATAFIMI
Vita
Solemi
MAZARA
DEL VALLO
CASTELVETRANO
Partanna
Gibellina
Menfi
Selinunte
Sciacca
Ribera
Caltabellotta
Mussomeli
CASTELTERMINI
ARAGONA
AGRIGENTO
Siculiana
Ragolmuto
Canicatti
Delia
Campobello
Palma
LICATA
Riesi
CALTANISSETTA
CASTELBUONO
Gangi
CEFALU
TERMINI
Montemaggiore
Imera
Coccamo

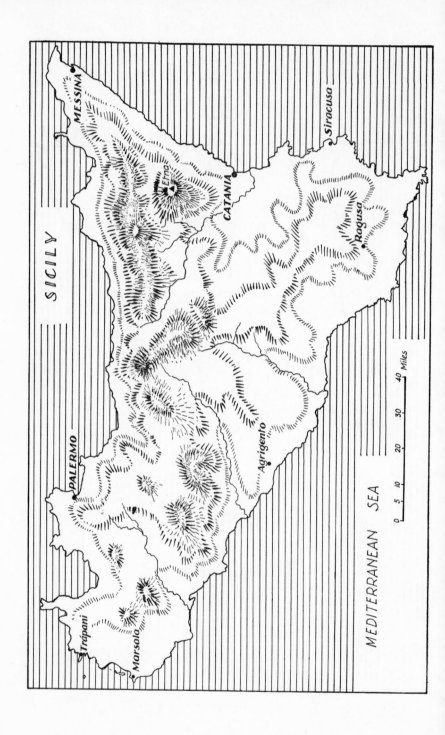

SICILY

MESSINA

Etna

CATANIA

Siracusa

Ragusa

PALERMO

Agrigento

Trapani

Marsala

MEDITERRANEAN   SEA

0 5 10   20   30   40 Miles

Translator's Notes

On political parties, Italian terms, abbreviations, etc., appearing in the text.

POLITICAL PARTIES

DC   *Democrazia Cristiana*—Christian Democrat Party: right-wing and Church.

PCI   *Partito Comunista Italiano*—Communist Party.

PSI   *Partito Socialista Italiano*—left-wing Socialist Party.

PSDI   *Partito Socialista Democratico Italiano*—right-wing Socialist Party.

PSU   *Partito Socialista Unificato*—United Socialist Party: PSI and PSDI combined.

PRI   *Partito Republicano Italiano*—Republican Party: small party mainly of the liberal intelligentsia.

PLI   *Partito Liberale Italiano*—'Liberal' Party: extreme right-wing.

PDIUM   *Partito Democratico Italiano di Unione Monarchica*—Monarchist Party.

MSI   *Movimento Sociale Italiano* ('*Missini*')—neo-Fascist Party.

PSIUP   *Partito Socialista Italiano di Unità Proletaria.*

USCS   (in Sicilian Regional elections): *Unione Siciliana Cristiano-Sociale.*

NEWSPAPERS

Giornale d'Italia—right-wing DC tendency.

Giornale de Sicilia—the Sicilian Establishment paper.

Il Tempo—Fascist tendency.

Il Popolo—DC official daily.

L'Unità—official Communist daily.

L'Ora—left-wing Palermo paper.

Paese Sera—left-wing daily.

TRADE UNION FEDERATIONS
(these are not officially affiliated to the political parties)

CGIL   *Confederazione Generale Italiana di Lavoro*—left-wing. The *Camera del Lavoro* is the local office of the CGIL.

xix

CISL *Confederazione Italiana Sindacati Liberi*—Christian Democrat.

UIL *Unione Italiana del Lavoro*—Social Democrat.

CISNAL *Confederazione Italiana Sindacati Nazionali Liberi*—extreme right-wing; neo-Fascist.

Other associations mentioned:

ACLI *Associazioni Cristiane dei Lavoratori Italiani*—Catholic Workers Societies.

FUCI *Federazione Universitaria Cattolica Italiana*—Catholic University Association.

Bobomiana—DC peasant association (called after l'Onorevole Bonomi).

STATE ORGANIZATIONS (National or Regional)

ERAS *Ente Riforma Agraria Siciliana*—Organization for Agrarian Reform in Sicily.

ESA *Ente Sviluppo Agricolo*—Agricultural Development Board (ERAS renamed).

IRFIS *Istituto Regionale per il Finanziamento alla Industria in Sicilia.*

SOFIS *Societa Finanziaria Siciliana.*

ENEL *Ente Nazionale* Energia Elettrica—National Electricity Board.

ECA *Ente Comunale Assistenza*—Municipal Public Assistance Board.

TITLES

Onorevole (Honourable)—Member of Parliament.

Ingegnere—graduate in engineering.

Avvocato—lawyer.

Ragioniere—accountant.

Commendatore—Knight of an order of chivalry.

MONEY VALUES

When the material for this book was collected, 1,000 lire was worth approximately 11s. 6d., i.e. about 1,750 lire to the Pound Sterling.

Part One

Two Emigrants back from Switzerland

——Have you ever been a member of any organization?

VITO: How d'you mean?

——Have you ever taken part in any organization, of any kind?

——I've always kept myself to myself.

——Why have you never belonged to an organization?

——I've always kept myself to myself—nobody's ever told *me* what to do. In Mussolini's day I was on the dole, that was the only time.

——Haven't you ever felt like joining a party?

——Being on the dole, wasn't that a party?

——What d'you think a party is?

——A party's like . . . well, like the father of a family, who can get certain jobs done.

——You've heard of communism, socialism, Christian Democracy? What do you think they are?

——They're parties, all at odds with each other.

——You've never felt like being a member of some religious group?

——No, never.

——Why?

——Because I've always kept myself to myself, nobody's ever told me what to do.

——How old are you?

——Forty-nine.

——Did you go to school?

——Only a few days. I'm illiterate.

——Would you say, then, that your family is your party?

——That's it, exactly.

——Your wife, your children, and who else?

——My brother; we're always close, our family.

——And how about other people?

——No, not close really. In fact, we keep our distance. It's habit. The proverb says, 'The man who goes his own road can never go wrong.' And 'The man who plays alone never loses.'

3

——Have you been abroad?

——To Squitzerland.

——How long?

——Two years.

——Did you like it there?

——How could I ever be happy there? Worrying about my family?

——How did you get on with other people there?

——The language was different, I couldn't understand a word. Someone else used to come and tell us what the boss had said, that sort of thing.

——Why d'you think Sicilian proverbs say things like that?

——If a man goes alone, he needn't get involved in any trouble. He goes his own way. He does whatever he pleases, he goes his own road. With other people, one says one thing, another says something else, and they can't agree.

——But when you come out in the evening, when you stand at your door to enjoy the fresh air, you have neighbours, don't you? You meet people?

——Yes, we say 'Good evening'—'Good evening'. '*Salutamu e cacciamu*', the old proverb says: we greet each other, then each goes his own way, each goes about his own business.

——How many are you in your house?

——Nine. And my mother-in-law, ten.

——What sort of relationship d'you have at home, with your wife and children?

——The children are absolutely obedient, and my wife even more so: before she does anything she always consults with me.

——And your mother-in-law?

——Just the same.

——D'you think the world can change?

——No one can say whether it can change or whether it can't. That's my opinion.

——D'you think it's possible to set up co-operatives?

——Yes—but they break down at once. The world's always been like that and it always will be. In all my years, wherever I've been, far and near, I've seen it's always just the same for us. We're born to work.

——Who d'you mean 'we'?

——The poor. Us poor are born to work.

——What impression did it make on you seeing things different in Switzerland?

——I looked from mouth to mouth and didn't understand a word that came out.

——When you came back to Sicily, did you feel changed in any way?

——When I came back to Italy, to Sicily, I took heart again. We were back in our own land. I felt better, we all talked the same. When you don't understand, it's a torture: you can't make out what they're saying, you're frightened of getting it wrong, you don't know what's wanted of you.

——Why d'you say, 'Us poor are born to work'?

——The poor are bound to work, the rich don't work.

——Do you think that's fair?

——Fair? I think . . . fair, fair—it's not fair. But someone who's poor is obliged to work—he has to, otherwise he won't eat.

——In your opinion, is it only the poor who stand alone, or the rich too?

——The poor are more alone than the rich: the rich always get together.

——Why?

——Why? Because they don't go to work, they spend their time in town, in the city. Whereas the poor man has to sweat away at work all the time.

——Are there more poor or more rich?

——Many more of us, many more poor.

——Then couldn't the poor all get together and agree, and change things, make a different world?

——How could they all agree to make a different world? I don't think they can ever agree.

SARIDDU: There are some farmers who make only two or three hundred thousand lire a year, at most, out of two or three or four thousand vines—the price is so low because of this mass of adulterated wine that's going about. And being as they couldn't live off the land any more, they've tried emigrating. Also, the various ways of scraping a living that people used to go in for ten years ago—gathering wild pot-herbs, catching frogs, collecting snails, picking up coal off the railway line, gleaning—nowadays nobody wants to do that sort of thing, so they try to emigrate. Today, as you know, all Italy is going abroad. The only ones who stick it out here living this wretched life are the ones who don't want to emigrate, or who can't because they haven't got a clean record or because they're not so young as they were.

About three years ago, though, things began to get difficult again, and there have been fewer jobs going. Before, if a man went to Palermo to look for a job as a builder's labourer, he'd find one: but today there isn't much new building going on. Some men are still emigrating, but even in, say, Switzerland there's less work going now.

If I have to leave this site, if the work here comes to a stop as it seems there's a risk now—where am I to go? Back to my old life. I'd have to go back to collecting snails, all on my own, collecting capers—back to the filthy life of misery and exhaustion day after day. That's what I'd do myself: but someone who hasn't even got that to fall back on will be out on the street again once his credit at the shop has run out—and what he has to do, he'll do: that's why we Sicilians are criminals. We're driven to it, it's our children's need that forces us into it. Over these last few years, as the number of destitute people on the streets diminished, there were fewer murders and robberies. If these jobs abroad give out, crimes will go up again. People's eyes have been opened now, and they're not going to want to go back to the kind of life they led before.

In the old days, I used to get up in the morning not knowing where I was going that day. But up there in Switzerland seeing them all friendly together at work, it seemed like an earthly Paradise. You get up in the morning and know where to go, and it's a pleasure working with other people, exchanging talk: your mind is opened and your wits are sharpened; you're in company, there's talk about what ought to happen in the future. Working out here on my own, I'm nothing but a block of wood, my eyes are shut, I don't know what might happen to me: but working in company, I began to pick up a word here, a word there—and that's the beginning of organization. The first few days, a man is still a bit suspicious because he's been a solitary for so long: he keeps looking behind him, and thinks the worst of everybody. My first few days I was unhappy because I hadn't got my family with me, and the life was so different—I felt very ill at ease, I'd never been on familiar terms with anyone before. Then I began to settle down a bit; I looked around, and I felt more cheerful: life seemed to be a game, and I very soon made friends and felt more secure. Everything was calm and settled around us, and we felt calm and settled too. But I missed my family terribly: I missed them so much that I had to come back.

And then I turned back into a block of wood: I felt I was in Hell. I was happy to be with my family again, but now I'd lost my friends and the sociable life I'd only just begun to know.

Come to think of it, I'd changed completely: before I went away, I was reconciled to having nothing but a bit of stale bread; but when I came back I'd quite forgotten what it had been like before, the bit of bread and the soup. When I arrived, my wife put a loaf on the table, and a few olives. As she put them down I looked at them, and I said to her: 'What's this then?' I'd forgotten all about the old days. My wife stared at me, and then she says: 'Why don't you eat?' And then deep down inside me I came to my senses again: in those five minutes I realized all at once that I was back in Sicily. I ate the stuff, but I felt I couldn't go on with that life any more.

Up there, when girls go past in the street you say hello—but here if you say anything you'll quite likely be clouted with a handbag. There were difficulties over the children, too: I'd seen how children there were brought up, and when I looked at my own children out on the street it really hurt me to see the way they were dressed; and I thought of how the other children who were going to school would have the chance to grow up better. And I felt a need to have a different house from what we had—one with a lavatory, too. Up there we even had a bath.

Before, I hadn't joined the *Camera del lavoro*[1]—I didn't feel this need to join in those days, and I was suspicious of organizations; but when I came back I thought that through the *Camera del lavoro* I might be able to get something done with the workers' union, and

[1] For explanations of Italian terms, initials, etc., that appear in the text, see notes on p. xix. (Tr.)

so I joined. Even though I could see there were some things we could never agree on—some people would say one thing and some another and it was impossible to come to an agreement—still, even that was better than staying on your own like a block of wood. Of course, when a man comes back and sees that things are still just the same here, he can't help thinking it's difficult to change anything: but it comes like a natural instinct to get together with other people and try and do something.

And what's happening now? The leader of an organization isn't listened to like he once was. Before, if the leader said: 'This is impossible', everyone else had to do as he said, even at the cost of things going badly, because he was the leader. But now it's not like that. Now people are beginning to understand: 'We created you, and we can destroy you.' In the old days a bloke would sit and listen like a silly great sheep, and not take in a word, and not know how to express his own feelings, and no one would think of trying to get him to talk. Not now. A man who's picked things up, who's taken in a word here, a word there, a word from someone else—if he thinks what the leader says is right, then he'll go along with it: if it's not right, then the rest of them will try to get the leader to understand it properly. A man wants his opinion to be heard, and if he disagrees he'll say so, and act accordingly.

Once upon a time if a man was strong then because he was strong he was automatically right, and everyone else just sat there like puddings: today, a thing can gain strength *because* it's just. A cause may be weak at first, but if it's just people know it's just, and it must win because it's just. Of course people must get together and work for it: it's through unity and organization that the just cause gets its strength. Even if at the beginning one person sees it one way and another another way, through the organization, chewing it over among themselves, among ourselves, in the end right comes out stronger.

When you get groups with different and opposing interests talking to each other, there's pandemonium. You have to try talking first, you have to try and reach an understanding through words; but when it becomes clear that however much you wrangle and chew over it nothing's going to come of it, then you have to find some form of organized struggle to arrive at your just objective.

This sort of thing's important—if you consider it, you can't help thinking it's important: it's like when you're a baby and don't know anything, but then as you grow up you find out more and more and come to understand the circumstances of life.

Two Illiterate Labourers

——Do you think it's possible in this region to work in groups, to have a group life?

PAOLINO: I would have said so, yes.

——What experience have you had so far of group work and group life?

——Well, as regards me personally, I started off as a peasant. I worked along with my father until I was twenty-one. After that, when I got married, I started working with two others (still on the land, this was)—my brother-in-law and my father-in-law; part of the land we rented and part we share-cropped, and we worked it ourselves. And at the same time, when we'd finished our own work we used to do a week here and a week there day-labouring for a big landowner.

Then after about eight years of that I worked for four years for a landowner, just me alone, paid by the day—there was nobody else. And after that—I've always liked work, you see—for about eight years I made baskets, always working on my own. Then I found that wasn't bringing in enough money, the market was slackening off, so I went back to work on the land—share-cropping, doing a stretch on the farm and then a stretch on the baskets at the right time of year.

So you see, I've never had the chance to work together with many people. But I think a man is happier working together with other people.

Before the last war, they used to work in groups on the land: the owner would keep a group of men on his land the whole year round, to do the hoeing, and prune the vines, and stake them and train them—all the work, right round to harvest time. That was the way then. Since the war, though, that system has gone out, because the landowner cultivates his vines with a horse and plough now to save money; and so you don't often get peasants working regularly for one landowner, but only at the busiest time when he really needs them like the harvest and the olive-picking.

——Do you think it's possible to have new forms of group work and group life different from those we've always had?

——To have different forms? The old way was to have, say, ten peasants on a job, and if the landowner was a peasant himself then he'd work along with the men too; if the owner was very rich, though, he'd stay indoors and send messages through some trusted man of his.

——Do you think things could be different?

——I think it's unlikely. How can anything be changed? There's a Sicilian proverb which says: 'Do you want to learn how to grow poor? Send the men out but don't go yourself.' I'll tell you what happens: a man sends out so many labourers, and pays them, and if these men instead of hacking deep with the hoe just skim over the top, then the vines will suffer, and the owner will notice—and so he'll either have to come out himself or send someone else along to keep an eye on the men.

——What would be the best sort of group to have, do you think?

——The best group for farm work, you mean?

——In any field.

——Well, let's say I'm making baskets: instead of working on my own, it would be better to be combined in a group, even a small group of, say, four of the same trade. 'Unity is strength', the saying goes: one man could go on deliveries, one would be on communications, while the other two would be working—there'd be united help. And then every month we'd do the accounts and say: 'We've made 100,000 lire, so we'll put thirty aside towards our fund, and the rest will go towards our families.' And it's the fund that makes them strong, because it ensures the growth of their business.

But I think it's too difficult.

——And on the land?

——The right sort of group on the land, when it's someone else's property—I can't think how this could be changed.

——You've never belonged to any union or party or other organization?

——No.

——Why not?

——I've never bothered. And in any case I didn't know what they were like, so I can't say if it would have been better to have joined or not.

We have a saying: "Every man hoes his own furrow", meaning that he minds his own business and doesn't meddle in other things, in the affairs of people who are nothing to do with him.

——Then if everyone ought to mind their own business, are you right to think of taking part in other groups, or forming new ones?

——Here's what I say: a man should mind his own business—but if it's a question of making peace between two others and being helpful, then he can step in. Once, about eighteen years ago, a friend of mine bullied me into joining the Catholic Association; this is what I said to him: 'To be a Christian,' I said, 'there's no need to join the Association: what matters is being an honest man.' But in the end he made me go. I only stayed in it a few days, though, because they talked about politics (and before the war there was no such thing as politics), saying things against Fascism, against Stalin, and so I told my friends: 'I'm not coming here any more, because I don't want to listen to this sort of stuff.' And I wouldn't go any more.

——Could it be that you don't really trust trades unions, parties, organizations?

——If I don't know about a thing I can't just say, 'I don't trust this.' "The man who plays alone never loses", that's what we say. If a kid plays with another kid, they may start to quarrel, and he'll get hurt: but if he plays on his own, then there's no one to hit him and make him cry. And it's the same for grown men too—in general it's true about everything: proverbs are never wrong. When a man's on his own he's at peace, you see. But if there are two or three or four together, then sooner or later there'll be a disagreement, a quarrel, and then there's a risk that it'll end in trouble. To be really safe it's best not to have contacts. When someone keeps company with men of bad faith—and there are many too many of them—then they'll lead him along the road to ruin: that's why the proverb says, "The man who plays alone never loses." That's it exactly. And that doesn't just mean playing cards—it applies to everything. It's a proverb that can be proved. The old sayings are never wrong.

SALVATORE: First I used to work on the land. Then I told my father I didn't want to go on with that any longer. I wanted to become a bricklayer. The first thing I learnt was to mix lime, then I learnt how to hold the trowel, and do plastering and whitewashing houses. Then unluckily I had an accident: I fell down off the top of a building—I fell on my back, and I was so badly injured that my mates thought I'd only another half hour to live. But some of them said: 'No, let's take him to Palermo: if he doesn't live, then we'll just have to bring him home again, but at least let's do our duty first and take him to Palermo.' I was a month inside the hospital.

I sent a message to my wife (I was married—we'd run away together not long before)—I sent to tell her I wasn't coming home that night because I'd found a job somewhere else. But one night she dreamt I was in hospital, and she started crying; and while she was crying, I arrived, and told her the whole story.

When I went back to work, I didn't go out on the top of buildings any more, it made me giddy. And then I happened on another job on the railway. Then there were a lot of dismissals, because the work had to stop. But since we all of us have a way of turning one *soldo* into two for love of the family, for the sake of building up the home, by that time I'd managed to put by two hundred thousand lire. For three months I went backwards and forwards every day to Palermo without finding any job—a little over two years ago, that was, when there was a lot of unemployment. At one place they'd tell me: 'We can't start just yet'; and the next place: 'We can't start for the moment, but let's see how things are in a month or two.' Then at last I found a job in Termini Imerese, about forty kilometres out on the other side of Palermo. That lasted three months. When the job was finished, I was dismissed again. And so I came back to working on the land, and now I work partly on the land and partly at bricklaying.

——What do you think a co-operative is?

——It's a society for being all combined . . . I don't know how to explain it.

——Did you go to school?

——When I was little, but I went to work on the land when I was nine—we were always hard up at home. Our mule died. We had the mule dead in the house, and my brother died too, because he'd fallen in the mud in his new suit, a brand new suit, and he was so scared of our mother—he was afraid she'd beat him—he was so scared that he fell ill, it upset his blood. There was my brother dying in bed, and the dead beast being carried out of the house.

We'd bought the mule with some money my mother had managed to scrape together and put aside.

——What do you think a party is?

——Didn't we just say?

——What I asked just then was what a co-operative was. Would you say there was any difference between a co-operative and a party?

——Here in Sicily we say that the co-operative means a job; and the party is the Communists, Socialists, Monarchists—I don't know anything about those things.

——What d'you think the Monarchist party is?

——I'm not a politician—I don't know.

——Have you heard of the Christian Democrats?

——I've heard of them, but I don't know whether they're left or right . . . They're against the Communists.

——The Socialist party—have you heard of them?

——It's not my business to be mixed up in that sort of thing, because I can't read. But I would like to know a letter or two, and be able to read, and understand things. Someone who can read knows how to talk to people. If you can't read, you can't really talk properly to anyone.

A man who can't read doesn't have the experience. He thinks to himself: 'Now what can that bit of paper on the wall mean?' I stare at it: what can it say on that bit of paper? If people who do know how to read notice me staring, then sure as anything they'll make fun of me. I learnt to copy, but not to read. I can write one or two words out of my head, and I can read them because I know what I've written. But if you was to write them, I couldn't read them, because I wouldn't know what you were writing.

——Have you heard of the Communist party?

——I've heard it's on the side of the workers, to get them jobs and see they don't go hungry.

——What do you think the difference is between the *Camera del Lavoro* and the Communist party?

——Let's think . . . No, I've never noticed that there was any difference.

——D'you think it's possible for men to work together, to co-operate?

——Yes, of course they can co-operate, if they agree.

——And do you think they can agree?

——Sometimes yes, sometimes no.

——How would you say people ought to set about co-operating?

——They need to be united, and they need people there who are more intelligent, to explain how things are done.

I'm a creature who's never been united, partly because I was backward through not having any schooling, and partly because I've had to work all the time to keep my family from going hungry: I've got three children now.

But what I'd like . . .

I'll tell you something that happened to me once: I went out reaping—I was hired by a landowner, there were over twenty of us. Well, the boss gave us all a good looking over, and when he looked at me he said: 'Well now, you look to me like an intelligent fellow.' 'Why,' I says, 'what do you want of me?' 'Well,' he says, 'here are my mules: you can ride into town and get food for all of us.' Now one of his mules had only ever been ridden by him—it didn't know anyone else, he was the only master it knew; so he said: 'Salvatore, I warn you, don't touch that mule—not for anything in the world.' 'Why not?' I says. 'You know,' he says: 'that's a one-man mule.' 'I can ride it as well as you,' I told him, and I made him go away.

Now this mule was a biter—if anyone went near it, it would bite and kick. Well, I can't read and I can't write, but I'm crafty all the same: I got the mule on a long rope, and tied its back feet and its front feet together, and then I put the rope over its neck and pulled. The mule couldn't do anything because it was tied back and front. So I got the saddle and put it on its back. Then I let the rope run— I hadn't tied any knots, you see, just wound it round so it could slide—and I got the beast by the halter and pulled. I tied it to the foot of an olive tree and put four water bottles on its back, watching out all the while to see it didn't kick; it couldn't get at me with its teeth because it was tied. Then I stepped on a little hillock there and got on to its back—without saying a word. Well, the mule started off all right; and I kept quiet, you see, till we came to a steep place where it would have slipped and fallen if it had tried jumping about, and *then* I gave voice: and by that time the mule had already got used to me!

Well, just like I succeeded in dealing with that mule, watching to see it didn't kick, and trying to understand what sort of a mule it was—in the same way, I'd like to be able to read and write, and know how things and people work, like that mule, so I could deal with them too. I'd like to be able to manage cars and tractors, and people too, clever people, instead of having them make fun of me. I'd like to be able to deal with everything like I dealt with that mule.

A blind man goes tap-tapping along, feeling his way, not knowing what he's going to bump into. Being blind, he thinks to himself: 'How can I find the way?' It drives him frantic not being able to see his road, and he says, 'if only I wasn't blind I could *look* at the road.' He's nothing but a walking shadow, almost as if he wasn't in the world at all.

How is it that there's the sun that rises, how does it come up on this world and light the whole earth, and give light to us who are set on this earth? I don't know. And there's the moon, too, that turns towards us and gives light to the world at night, shines for all of us; and there are these stars that we say are in the sky: but is the sky really there? These mists that come up, too. And under the sun, under the moon, there's man and woman and everything else on this earth. I'm a dumb creature, but I would like to be able to understand all these things around us.

The world's full of things, but if I don't understand them I can't work them; the world's full of men, but if I don't understand them I can't work them, I can't deal with them; men are different from one another, and I'd like to be able to understand them, to know what they're saying and what they're not saying, and to know how to act towards them, for their good and my own: you need to study how to get on with other men, how to be together. Otherwise, it's as if a man was a millionaire, and he had an accident and got both his arms chopped off: what good are all his millions to him then?

I'm getting too worked up—it's because I've never really talked like this to anyone before. But there are plenty of questions I'd like to go into.

Sariddu Turdo, animator of the *Alleanza Contadina*

I think it's necessary for people to form groups. It can bring advantages if people are interested in the common good, in society. It can bring advantages both to economic and to agricultural development when people act not from selfish motives but in order to influence the management, those in power, to grant certain benefits and to allow the mass of workers their rights. It's a good thing to be able to unite and organize and claim our rights. For instance, suppose there's no convenient access to our land: our land could be productive if only there was a proper road, but if there's no road we can't grow, say, peaches, or if we do they'll be spoilt, wasted. But an organized group has some strength. Nothing comes without discussion and pressure: and a group gives strength, it can put pressure on the authorities to get things done.

——In what way, exactly, does a group give strength?

——If we're a group that discusses problems, and people see that these problems can be solved—that's how the organization gains strength, because other people will join too.

——Doesn't the group also gain strength because through thinking and discussing things together they find better solutions?

——Yes—for instance, at the moment it's just you and me talking together, but a third person might come up with things we hadn't thought of, he might find better solutions. And if there were five or six of us together instead of just two, one of us might think of something even better.

——In what other ways, for what other reasons, can the group gain strength, would you say?

——Yes, there are other reasons. If a group can get five hundred or a thousand members, then it can have a political function. If there's a really big group, it has more influence, and there's more chance of people getting improvements in their own town.

And also, if a man acts on his own he has to judge his own ideas himself, judge whether they're valid or not. But when there are ten men together, their judgement will be better. Besides, being part of

17

a group gives a person more responsibility; if he belongs to an organization he develops better himself, in my opinion. Do you suppose that at thirty I had even what feeble brains I have now? I did not. I'd never had anything to do with large numbers of people, you see, I wasn't used to it: but now I pick up a word here and a word there, and obviously my brains can develop.

——What do people in general think about the group?

——They'll all think my way, once it's made clear to them.

Lots of people still say it's best to keep yourself to yourself, because there's always been a tradition of mistrust. But once they come to trust us, then they can get organized.

Today there are few groups, if any; or if there are any they're not functioning properly.

——Why d'you think that is?

——It's very simple: they haven't had positive results, and so people lose faith in the organizations because they haven't functioned properly.—And why haven't they functioned properly?

——Either for internal reasons, because it's in the interests of certain individuals that they should not function; or else just out of incompetence.

Effective groups should consist of people who really have the common interest at heart, and who also have the capacity to guide a group and make it work. The group must know how to use its influence to claim its rights, and also it should meet often for discussions in order to find the most valid solutions.

——I've noticed that you're punctual. Why's that?

——I think that a punctual person is more correct. It's a notion I have. I don't want to be the sort of person that someone says: 'But why has Turdo let me down like this by not coming?' And it's also out of respect for the person I'm meeting: being unpunctual is treating them badly.

——Would you say people here were punctual, or not?

——Everyone answers for himself, according to how he sees things. If they're not punctual, it's not just because they have a notion to be unpunctual, but because things haven't been organized properly and so they're mistrustful. If a meeting is announced for a certain time, the ones who are most interested may even get there early (it depends whether people have had a good impression from the first meeting, whether they've been inspired by seeing good things done). Others who aren't so concerned won't be so punctual. But a lot of them are simple folk and don't think it's important to be punctual. And it also happens because a fellow gets up early in the morning and goes out to the fields without a clock. No one takes much notice of the clock. They do for school, though, and also for the works on the dam now.

At the moment there's only the one group functioning at all seriously here: the gang working on the dam.

The fanatical church-goers also function with a certain importance: since it's the priests who control the levers of power, many people turn to them, and offer to take part in processions and meetings—specially the women, who are more credulous. And when people are asked to take part in these demonstrations or meetings, they go. But as far as I know that's not an organization that undertakes any responsibility for people.

As for the trades unions and the parties, even there there aren't real effective groups. Each one has its own limited function; mostly it's just organizing propaganda for the elections, and afterwards things fall off again and come to a standstill.

To function properly a group needs to have a committee and secretary who can undertake responsibility and discuss things together. The secretary's job is to call committee meetings and organize discussions, and if necessary organize general meetings too. Then he has to see that the group's decisions are acted on; and it's also up to him to try and establish whether what each member says is right or wrong. But you're talking to an old man who's strictly speaking illiterate, from the legal point of view! What little I do know, even reading and writing, has been stolen—picked up here, there and everywhere in my dealings with other people.

——Why d'you think your group hasn't been functioning?

——I think it did at first, but then some of the founder members of the *Alleanza* gave it up, perhaps out of personal self-interest because they were a bit afraid: the *Alleanza* didn't give them much security, and so some of them became estranged and left. And there were other reasons too: some of the results of some of our undertakings were rather poor because we hadn't really been keen enough—and also partly because ERAS made difficulties.

Then on the first of January 1963, a provincial representative of
the *Alleanza* ordered it to be closed down and the lease given up and
the furniture taken away: he said they couldn't pay the rent any
more. Because the members were a bit mistrustful, it was difficult to
get them to pay their dues, part of which should have gone towards
the rent. We did manage to scrape up the money for a few months
more by going round begging shamelessly; but one day four months
ago we found the *Alleanza* shut—we hadn't heard anything about it
—and the secretary had removed the furniture to his house. Now
we want to start it up again.

——What do you mean to do?

——We've got some people who are willing to form a committee
and build up the *Alleanza* again. I'd like to invite them, and the
Alleanza from Palermo, and then hold a general meeting to see if
there are many who'd be willing to organize themselves (once the
definite advantages were pointed out to them), in order to make sure
the smallholder isn't left defenceless.

My proposal is that anyone who had a hand in the closure should
not have any positive rights any more. And the aim of the new
Alleanza should be to get improvements and benefits—I can't say
yet exactly what they should be because we'd have to all decide on
that together first. But to give you an example: at the moment the
State is widening the Alcamo road (is it the Regional Board or the
Minister of Public Works?)—without giving any explanations:
destroying people's olives and vineyards without even saying when
the compensation will be paid. And dozens of other things. For
instance, there's the problem of security in the countryside. In some
places the landowners have their own private guards, paid in money
and in kind: but in other places where robbery is much more likely,
such as on the outskirts of the town, they've got no guards at
all, because the guards just don't want to stay there now. So a
man won't sow oats and barley because he's afraid of having his
crop stolen; he won't plant potatoes, onions, garlic and so on,
because he's got no guarantee of being able to harvest them.
The *Alleanza* could create a body of country guards to act as a
security.

——Why are you doing all this, at the age of seventy-five, still so full
of strength and goodwill?

——Through the *Alleanza* a man can become educated, and can get things done.

I just have a notion that this is the right thing to do. I don't know if it's in my nature, my character or what—I don't know what it is that makes me feel this obligation towards society. But if I see a fruit skin on the pavement where it might cause an accident, I move it out of the way; if I see a stone on the road where a car could send it flying, then I move it, to prevent an accident. When I was young I didn't feel this duty—in those days I didn't understand things I can understand today.

I meet Sariddu Turdo again two months later and ask him if he and his friends have succeeded in reorganizing the local *Alleanza Contadina*.

——Hardly, yet: the *Alleanza* hasn't yet got a committee that can discuss the most urgent problems and the economic problems. People do come when there's a discussion meeting, but there aren't enough of them yet. They come, but not in the numbers they ought to. The *Alleanza* needs to achieve some new success so that the people will say: 'That's thanks to the *Alleanza*, we can have faith in it.'

We've got a little room, but it's such a small one it's humiliating—it's not worthy of the *Alleanza*. You can hardly fit thirty people in. But they've started coming back from the Palermo *Alleanza*, and we hope things are improving now. I'm pleased, yes: but you must always keep a critical eye on developments to be sure of doing what's best.

Four Fishermen

ORAZIO: The fishermen are organized at work: the owner of the boat acts as skipper, and the others do as he says. They can't manage on their own. It's nearly always the owner who's skipper.

When we go out fishing with the lamp, we're about ten to a boat. On the boats with drag-nets and on the sword-fishing boats they have about four or five men. On board we work always to the captain's orders, but the more trusted and more experienced men sometimes give a bit of advice too.

GIOVANNI: Here on Isole delle Femmine we haven't got a harbour —it's just a beach with a little platform. When a boat's coming in in bad weather, then we all collaborate in pulling her ashore, so's she doesn't get broken and so as the men on board don't get hurt. My turn today, your turn tomorrow.

MINICO: Sometimes a wind gets up suddenly and you can't go on fishing—you have to leave off fishing to save the boat. Out in the open sea the boat just goes up and down on the heavy swell, but close inshore where the big waves are breaking it gets thrown backwards and forwards and a sudden huge wave can fling it on the rocks.

It's heavy work pulling the boat ashore with the tackle when you've got the nets on board, and so we have to help each other— even the women may come and give a hand too: the government doesn't provide proper harbour facilities.

On the boat it's the skipper who tells the rest what to do on board—but back on shore it's every man for himself.

GIOVANNI: Sometimes at sea a quarrel blows up between one boat and another: my boat goes near the other one's nets, say, and the other one can't allow that. But there's no quarrelling on board the one boat. And if a boat's net gets fouled on rocks then another boat will at once come to help, to save the net: words are words, but nets are nets. That's always been the way here, ever since the days of our forefathers.

MINICO: Out at sea every boat drops its nets and tries not to foul the other boats; but each one goes wherever it fancies—there's no agreement beforehand. Sometimes it'll happen that two or three boats have the same idea and go and drop net in the same stretch of water, and that leads to a quarrel.

GIOVANNI: Before, there used to be a co-operative of almost all the fishermen: we used to hold meetings, we had a chairman. The sort of things the co-operative did was to go and tell the Port Authorities that our livelihood is being ruined because they're fishing with bombs, with dynamite that kills off the small fry as well as the grown fish, and destroys the sea . . .

MINICO: The bombs are illegal, they're absolutely forbidden, but everyone does it.

GIOVANNI: . . . And it was supposed to do things like getting money from the Sicilian Regional Government, or getting a slipway made. Or mediating between fishermen who'd had some disagreement at sea.

ORAZIO: But now it doesn't exist any more: we had to give it up— we couldn't get enough money to meet expenses. We had a dues collector, but the takings were only just enough to pay him and the rent and the light, there was none left over.

GIUSEPPE: Now we help one another in time of need, but there's no organization.

We have to pay a certain percentage of our catch to the Palermo fish market.

DANILO: What percentage?

GIUSEPPE: I don't know.

MINICO: We don't know.

ORAZIO: Maybe eight per cent. When the fish goes to market we have to pay the auction fee, and the porters who carry the fish boxes. Otherwise we can sell it here on the island. We have two representatives who sell the fish for us, and they tell us they take three per cent for themselves: but they pay us on the spot for the fish, out of their own capital, which means they buy it for, say, a thousand and may sell it for two thousand—and they don't have the expenses we have, either.

DANILO: Wouldn't it suit you better, then, to form a co-operative and sell to people directly?

GIOVANNI: We can't.

ORAZIO: We've got our own work to do: if we have to go out

fishing, then we have to delegate to someone else, even though it does mean paying another person.

MINICO: They[1] take advantage of our need; we're a bit stupid and they . . . they're in a strong position. That's all there is to it. You're intelligent . . . You know how things are.

Even a man who doesn't do any of the work still wants his share . . . Things have happened . . . they even cut one man's head off. The Prefect had a number of the middlemen arrested and put in confinement on the Island. We're not supposed to know anything . . . every now and again the police van comes along and picks up a pair of them . . . But it's always been done this way. We're not supposed to know anything.

There's always four or five of them there, sons and nephews, who've got the whole market in the palm of their hand . . . One of them can comfortably make as much as three hundred thousand lire in one day.

If we did get organized and tried to get someone else to sell our fish in Palermo, d'you suppose he could get a licence? D'you think their 'friends' would allow it? And anyway, d'you suppose we'd get a fair price for our fish? . . . You see what I mean . . .

DANILO: Have you at least got a union of some sort, and party organizations?

ORAZIO: No, nothing. We've got two parties, but that doesn't mean all the poor on one side and all the rich on the other: people join one or the other for personal reasons, or in exchange for favours. Political ideas just don't come into it: they're both parties for the rich.

Us fishermen get together on board, but ashore we're incapable of keeping our eyes open and getting together.

GIOVANNI: Even though there's over three hundred of us fishermen on Isola delle Femmine alone, we're still not a force. We're all friends, all good fellows, but we're not a unit. We've always been a bit stupid. Every election time they make their promises, and we give them our votes.

MINICO: We may sit together in the sun, or mending our nets, but still it's every man for himself. We only really get together when there's a storm, say, or when an old fisherman dies and every-

---

[1] i.e. the mafiosi who control the market (Tr. note).

one contributes to make him a wreath and they don't go to sea at all for a day: but that's only if he's old and much respected through having lots of relations and friends. Or perhaps if an accident happens to a young man. Otherwise, we never get together. There's never any consultation.

For christenings or weddings, too, but that's only guests and friends and relations: you can't expect the whole fleet to be invited!

Sometimes when there's bad weather or fog we light fires at certain points along the shore to guide the boats, and blow them warnings on big shells which you can blow like trumpets—the sound carries a long way if the sea and the wind are right.

GIOVANNI: We're all friends, but we seem to be incapable of getting together to look after our interests. We think of change as bad; it seems bad not to vote for whoever makes us promises—we know they won't keep them, we know they're deceiving us, but it's as if we pretended not to know.

GIUSEPPE: We're always waiting for some outsider to come along and do things for us—someone who'd know how to go about it, how to write certain letters, how to hold a meeting and argue a case in a discussion; and who'd know where and how to register complaints. Dear God—but that's what we're like around here! If we tried to put forward a local man, nobody would support him, because we just don't believe in one another.

A Provincial Mafioso

CALOGERO: The proverb says a man can't live in company even with his wife; but it is an advantage to the family to be united. If I go my way and my wife goes hers, it'll be difficult to make a place for the children.

It's best to be social in business as well—like when you have three partners leasing land and subletting: if they can collaborate, if they're united, then they'll get on. One man on his own can't manage so much land, if it's a big estate they've got the lease of, as is the custom round here; and so two or three get together and collaborate in working this extensive property. The leaseholder pays the landowner a fixed rent, whether things go well or badly, and then he'll hope for a good year, or trust in his own know-how.

To support my wife and children, one of the things I do is to buy up tomatoes and act as middleman. That's what I do in summer: I deal in tomatoes. I buy them from the peasants and supply a factory in Palermo. One can't manage this on one's own, one can't get anywhere, so I have my associates. It's a steady trade, the tomato business: I don't make all that much at a time, but it comes in steadily. It's the factory owner who sets the price—he pays it all: the tomatoes, my commission and the transport. 'Our rate today is so many lire,' he says—and of course the factory owners get together and fix things between them. It's all free enterprise, this: the government has nothing to do with it.

Another example: for the last three or four years I've been in partnership with two or three others, and together we protect the corn stooks for the landowners in summer. In exchange for guarding the grain we get two kilos per quintal. There are at least two or three hundred farmers who can leave their corn stooked up now with a quiet mind, knowing we're in charge. It could be stolen, otherwise, or set on fire. Anything could happen. Everybody prefers to pay a bit not to have to worry. It's the doggies who keep watch really—they bark at night.

It's the same sort of thing as I'm doing here: they need us for the same sort of reasons. When they took me on, the first thing they asked for was my penal record: mine was clean, and so they took me on as a confidential agent. It's my responsibility here to act as guard, though I'm not officially sworn in. The whole site is on our shoulders. It's the overseers' job to make the men work, and it's our duty to guard the whole site. That's what the firm pays us for.

——What relations do you have with the trade unions?

——As far as my job is concerned I'd have no reason to have any relations with the men at all. But I did join the union (not when I was single, of course, but when I married I had to) in order to get the insurance card and the family allowances. So I'm a member of the CISL. In the *Camera del Lavore* they have the poorest people, but in the CISL you find people of somewhat better means, and it's easier to get the cards through them because they've got power, they have strings they can pull, and so it's easier to get things.

——Do you have meetings?

——I've never been to any.

Another advantage of CISL is the assistance they can get from the Catholics in exchange for help in getting them votes at election time. A recommendation from a priest, an archbishop, a cardinal . . . nowadays these people have some say, they have authority. A post in a bank, or in an office. . . . These people can help if they wish. And if they have helped a person, then naturally he will follow them: after all, they've provided his children's daily bread. When someone's been given a post, if he can't return the favour any other way he'll naturally try and get votes for them: the debt must be paid back.

Another occasion for coming together is over the feast day celebrations, to celebrate the Madonna; we collect the money for the illuminations and the music and the fireworks in honour of Our Lady. We form a committee for collecting all the promises made by the people who owe a debt to Our Lady, who have made a vow of some offering in exchange for being cured.

Military life—I had a good impression of military life because I was nineteen when I went away; I was like an unbroken mule that doesn't know what danger is, not giving a thought to family ties because I'd no idea yet what separation meant. I had a good impression of military life because I saw things I'd never seen before

—I'd never been out of my home town; I met people I'd never met before; I soon learnt the ropes and began to find out what life was all about—I'd been so timid before I'd never mixed with other men. Military life sharpens a man's wits. And he becomes an expert with the women, too. I did three and a half years, and I enjoyed the discipline: there was order, and I like order. You have one man commanding, and the rest obey. I didn't enjoy the bombing, of course: in peacetime military life is amusing, but in time of war it's misery. That was a type of group I liked.

——How do you think a group should be? How do you see relations between people here?

——There ought to be one person in charge, to see that the right things get done, and that they don't get done badly; and the duty of the rest is to be disciplined. If any member isn't co-operative, he must be got rid of: anyone who is detrimental to the group must be turned out. Anyone who won't be kept in order must be got rid of.

Everyone will rally round a man who's in the money: he'll be favoured by everyone, the authorities and the people alike. If one has money one becomes a gentleman. If you're in with the Government party, you're well off; but if you're against them, things will go badly for you. If one has the good fortune to be employed on the estate of a rich landowner, one can support one's family, one can take them home their little bite of bread. A man with money finds all doors open, everyone makes way for him.

In one's own circle, if one knows how to keep order one can earn respect: like a father who comes home in the evening and the children come out to meet him and kiss him. As in the family, so in society. Each man tries to excel, everyone wants to be top; and even if a number of people do get together in order to win greater respect as a group, still each individual will try to excel over the others. The more a man gets ahead, the easier it becomes for him to make his way. If a man has a good name, a good reputation in the circles he moves in, then there's a chance that that man will not perish. A good reputation brings trust, power, money.

My father used to say to me: 'Some have one eye, some have two, and some have none at all'. The man with two always does better, he keeps a look out, he's aware of dangers, he knows the obstacles, he knows business—everything. The man with one eye only sees half; and the one with none at all is walking in the dark.

The big landowners, the barons and the marquises, are rather falling behind nowadays: it's the contractors and the business men who are making the giant strides. Take the landowner and myself, for example: sometimes I make more than he does. People who want to get ahead quickly are leaving the countryside and throwing in their lot with the contractors—it's them who are making the giant strides today. Or else they go into business and buy up land at a thousand lire the square metre and sell it again in a couple of years at ten thousand. That's how to get on. These are good times for us. A man who ten years ago might have been going round begging for dry figs to keep himself from starving may today own a lorry and housing estates, and be quite a gentleman.

But the priests have even more power; they're a superior force which keeps the people in check. Right at the summit there's the Cardinal, and below him there are the people with the money and those in the Government. The man who has his eyes shut, who doesn't know what's what, will perish—he's bound to go under.

A Group of Schoolchildren[1]

CIELO (*aged eleven*): At school when we're given a problem, I try to help my friend and explain the problem to him, but the teacher won't let me.

LIBERA (*aged twelve*): Our teacher won't let us help each other, either. She says: 'You must work it out by yourselves.' If my friend doesn't understand it, I try to explain it to her—I don't just get her to copy it, I try and explain. But the teacher won't let us.

CIELO: Our teacher won't let us do any of our exercises together—he says if we do we'll only copy. Suppose you're given a problem, and you think and think about it—well, you'll probably find the answer. Then if you're friendly with the others you'll want to help them find the answer too—but our teacher hardly ever lets us help each other at all.

CHIARA (*aged seven*): I always copy my teacher, and I sing with her when she sings, and I copy my teacher when we're doing gym.

CIELO: Me and my friends at school chat during break. On Mondays, for instance, we tell each other about the film, or whatever else we've seen or done on Sunday. It's only during break, when we're having our snack, that we can get together with our friends and talk.

LIBERA: When our teacher goes out of the room—when she goes to talk to another teacher, for instance—then we can talk to our friends, and get to know each other better. But when the teacher's there, we all have to sit still and keep ourselves to ourselves. We can only get together and do things together when the teacher's not there, or else during break when she's just sitting there doing her knitting or reading the papers.

AMICO (*aged nine*): I've got a friend I would like to work out sums with—we always want to help each other—and our teacher does sometimes let us, but usually not. And it's just the same in our class

[1] The ones whose names end with -o are boys: the girls' names end with -a. (Tr. note.)

as you others say—we can only get together with our friends when the teacher goes out.

RUGGERO (*aged nine*): Sometimes he pretends to go out of the classroom, but really he's hiding just outside the door. Then if we start to make a row he suddenly bursts into the room again, and he gets us all lined up against the wall, and makes us hold out our hands like this, and then he gets his great big stick and comes along the line hitting us all.

CIELO: The boys on the back benches say it doesn't hurt them so much. They're the poorest boys, you see, and they go out to work in the fields—breaking up wood, and loading it on carts, and hoeing, and so on—and so the skin of their hands gets all thick and tough.

AMICO: Yesterday just before we broke up for the holidays, our teacher gave Toia two strokes of the cane on his legs, and said: 'Happy Easter!' The other boys didn't know whether to be frightened or laugh!

CHIARA: When my teacher tells me to be quiet, I sit perfectly still, as if I was asleep, and so she gives me good marks.

DANILO: But do they teach any of you how to work together at all? Or how to play together, or how to set about finding things out together?

LIBERA: No, our school doesn't teach us how to get on with each other, or do anything together, or co-operate in any way. We get together at recreation time, but our teacher doesn't ever tell us what we ought to do to get on better with each other, or how each of us is supposed to organize herself so that it's possible to co-operate with the rest.

CIELO: They do *talk* about 'getting together', though, at school. When the priest comes, he preaches to us about what Jesus said—that we should all be brothers, that we should stick together, and love one another like brothers, and so on. But it's just words: they never try to teach us how we might get on better together.

LIBERA: Yes, it's just like Cielo says. And the priest also tells us that anyone who isn't a Catholic is damned!

CIELO: And he says that the Lord is our master, and that we must serve him, because we are the servants of God.

AMICO: The teacher's idea of what we should be like is just

the same as the priest's—he'd like us to be just a sort of well-drilled squad ready to carry out whatever order he cares to give us.

CHIARA: When my teacher says: 'Right, start your work now!'—when she says that, I do my copying in my copybook. I'm good at copying.

BRUNA (*aged fifteen*): Really I think it's true to say our school doesn't teach us to co-operate at all. What they want, rather, is for everyone to do their own work, and for everyone to think exactly the same—for instance, everyone ought to be Catholic. And everyone must do as the teacher says. You're not supposed to have your own opinions. Most of the teachers seem to want simply to drill us into neat, obedient squads.

It's only in the breaks that we really get together and make friends. We're not just sitting at a desk listening—we can discuss things then, and express our own opinions.

But in fact even us girls don't agree much among ourselves, because you get some from Catholic families, while others are Liberal, or Communist; and everyone prefers to make friends with other girls who share the same point of view. The class is really split up into a whole lot of little groups. And basically, of course, everybody's really only interested in their own things. We get this feeling of being united only in relation to the teacher—I mean, we're only a group in so far as we're opposed to the teacher. Out of about eight teachers, I can only think of two who would ever let us sit and work beside a friend—but none of them have ever taught us how to co-operate.

DANILO: Would you say that there's any sort of co-operation between you and your teachers?

CIELO: No, I'd say there was none.

BRUNA: Our teacher might perhaps co-operate occasionally with whoever was top of the class. She'll say: 'Here, help me with this . . .' but you can't really call that co-operation—the teacher's just getting whoever's best in the class to help her.

CIELO: Or our teacher might leave a boy in charge of the class: 'I've got to go out,' he says, 'you must write up on the blackboard the name of anyone who talks, or anyone who misbehaves.'

CHIARA: *We* do things together with *our* teacher. She says to us:

'You tell me the numbers and I'll write them up on the board.' Or else the teacher says: 'Throw that bit of paper in the waste paper basket,' and me and my friends all rush to throw it in the waste paper basket for her.

BRUNA: I'll tell you what it's like really: we mustn't do anything to harm one another, we must respect our elders and betters, and so on—but we can't have opinions. There's no question of me first having my say, and then you having your say, and then discussing the thing till we reach some conclusion that suits us all. We mustn't do anything to *harm* one another—but there's no question of me actually *helping* you, or you helping me.

It's just the same sort of thing with school games. The kind of games the teachers make us play are usually just boring drill—it's only amongst ourselves that we ever play games in groups. For instance, one of the schoolteacher's favourites is the silence game: the whole class sits as still as possible, and the teacher calls up whoever is sitting stillest and quietest, and he goes and stands by the blackboard and looks carefully round the class at the rest of them and sees who's quietest, and writes his name on the board: then *he* comes up to the board, and the first one goes and sits in the second one's place—and so on. But this so-called game isn't a game at all— it's just a trick to keep us all quiet when the teacher wants to read the paper. They play this game in all the elementary classes here—and the daft thing is, most of the kids like it!

AMICO: Well, I like it too. At least it means that instead of being stuck in my own seat all the time I might get the chance to go and sit in someone else's, if I'm called up.

CHIARA: And I like it too—it's nice to have a little walk.

BRUNA: Yes, even I used to like it—because it was about the only game they ever let us play.

CIELO and LIBERA: But those sort of games are stupid.

(A few days later)

DANILO: Well, I wonder if you've been having any more ideas about what we were discussing the other day. What would you say a group consisted of?

CIELO: A group is a collection of boys or girls or school friends who help each other, because they like each other, and so they form a group.

CHIARA: A group is when you get into fours, or twos, or when you all line up together.

BRUNA: What Chiara means is that in a group there should be some sort of order—but of course there's no need to be in twos or fours particularly. Cielo was saying that for it to be a proper group you must be in agreement: but it's more than just a matter of having some sort of order and saying: 'We all like each other'. You must also have some purpose—I mean, some sort of good aim—otherwise you're not going to get anywhere.

LIBERA: In a group, there has to be one person who says: 'Let's all do such and such,' and then they all have a meeting to decide how the work should be shared out among them. That way, they get the thing done quicker, and better.

BRUNA: Yes, I agree that the group should have a leader—but this leader mustn't just be someone who gives orders: his job should be to co-ordinate all the suggestions made by the rest of the group, and co-operate with them in planning and organizing things properly.

AMICO: You can't have a group if everyone is acting independently.

DANILO: Would you say the potatoes in a sack are a group?

CHIARA: Yes.

LIBERA: They're a sack of potatoes!

AMICO: They can't be a group because they're not really alive.

LIBERA: No, they're just a collection of potatoes, they're not a group.

BRUNA: Well, you can have a collection of children, or men, who aren't a group any more than a sack of potatoes is a group. It's not just being together that counts.

DANILO: Have any of you ever had an experience of being in charge of a group?

AMICO: Yes, I have.

CIELO: So've I. But I suppose really that was more like a team. But sometimes I have taken charge, too, when we've got into a group of our own accord.

AMICO: I've been left responsible sometimes, when the teacher went away.

LIBERA: In a team, you see, you have a captain, and the rest have to do whatever he says. But in a group it's different: instead of just obeying, or copying like so many parrots, each person has his own little job to do, his own particular contribution towards whatever it is that the group is working on.

RUGGERO: I've never been in charge—but how d'you mean exactly, being in charge . . . being responsible . . . I don't quite see.

AMICO: Well, being responsible means more or less the same as being in command.

BRUNA: No—it isn't the same as being in command. Being responsible means knowing what you're doing, really understanding what's going on.

LIBERA: For instance, suppose the mistress in a nursery school isn't looking after the children properly and one of them gets hurt—well, she's in charge, and she's responsible.

DANILO: Do you like having responsibility? D'you like taking charge in a group?

AMICO: Yes.

CHIARA: Yes.

LIBERA: It's nice being in charge when you're good at something.

BRUNA: I like being in a group, and I like being responsible, I don't know why.

RUGGERO: Yes—for instance, if there's someone quarrelling and I stop them quarrelling.

BRUNA: But a person shouldn't want to take charge just so as to get the admiration and respect of the others.

CIELO: The important thing is to have a sense of responsibility towards yourself and towards other people. The more responsibility you're allowed, the more ideas you'll have, and the better you'll get.

RUGGERO: Yes, that's just what I was trying to say.

DANILO: Which do you like best: being with people older than yourselves, or the same age, or younger?

CIELO: I think I prefer playing with younger boys, or else ones of my own age.

AMICO: I like being with younger ones.

RUGGERO: Yes, I agree—I think they're better to play with.

CHIARA: I like playing with children smaller than me too.

LIBERA: Yes, I like playing with really little children, under five

—I can pick them up and carry them. But I like girls of my own age as well, because we can talk and play together. And I like bigger ones, too—as long as they're nice!

BRUNA: I think it depends entirely on whether they're nice or not: it doesn't matter at all whether they're younger or older than me, as long as I like them.

LIBERA: When I play with little children I feel just like a mother!

RUGGERO: It's better playing with people younger than yourself.

AMICO: Yes: when you play with younger boys, you don't quarrel with them—they don't quarrel because they're too young. But if you play with the older ones, you always quarrel.

CIELO: Yes, and it's difficult when you play with older boys because they try and boss you around—they want the game to go their way. The big boys aren't very easy to get on with. But when I play with smaller boys, it's *me* who says how we'll play!

LIBERA: I like telling the little ones stories. They're sweet, they sit there listening with their eyes wide open . . .

DANILO: What sort of grown-ups do you like being with best?

CIELO: The ones we're most friendly with.

RUGGERO: I like being with my papa.

BRUNA: The ones who take us seriously—the ones who bother to talk to us, and discuss things with us. Not the sort of grown-ups who just say: 'Yes, yes, of course,' without even hearing what you've said, or who won't listen to you, or who just say 'no' without giving you any reason. We like the ones who understand.

AMICO: I like grown-ups who are amusing, and tell funny jokes and stories, and make us laugh all the time.

CIELO: I like grown-ups who give us nice things; and I like the ones I know really well, and also the ones who like me.

BRUNA: And I like being with grown-ups who I can learn things from.

DANILO: One more question: do you think this discussion we've been having here should be reported and written down for other people to read?

CIELO: No, I don't think so really, because if my teacher hears of it I'll get into trouble.

RUGGERO: Well, I think it should—I think it would be nice if other people could hear our arguments.

BRUNA: Yes, I think so too. If our teachers read it, perhaps they'll wake up a bit and try to improve! And after all, in discussing things together like this we're only trying to be more responsible.

LIBERA: I think what we've been saying should be made public, because we've been giving our own opinions quite sincerely, and everything we've said is true, and also I think most of it's interesting.

CIELO: Yes, on second thoughts, I agree too. It should be reported. Everyone else agrees, and I think they're right, so I've changed my mind.

LIBERA: Another time, maybe one of us could be chairman of the meeting? When can we have another little meeting? Tomorrow, perhaps?

Provincial Nobles

DANILO: On what occasions, and in what ways, do people come together?

DONNA ROSARIO: Do you mean for reasons of work, or living together?

DON ALFONSO (*her husband*): People come together only for work, otherwise they have no thought of meeting. There's no unity among them.

DONNA ROSARIO: For example, a landowner requires a certain number of workers, and they cannot help being together because they have to work together. But it's only while they're actually working. People prefer working as day-labourers to share-cropping, because it's more profitable.

DON ALFONSO: Certain smallholders are content to abandon their land to go and work as day-labourers in industry: they find it more profitable, and more secure: there they don't have to think about rain, wind—always some excuse or other for the harvest's being bad.

DANILO: Then are people working together now more than they used to?

DONNA ROSARIO: Someone leaving the country and going to work in industry will find himself working with others; he's less alone, he'll be one of a group. But it's not a question of deciding between solitude and company: he goes there because it's convenient.

DON ALFONSO: But after work each man goes back to his own house and thinks no more about it.

DANILO: With people working together, isn't it easier for trades unions to be formed?

DON ALFONSO: Yes, they join the unions. Then when a firm wants labour for some job it's starting, it goes to the *Camera del Lavoro* to get the list of names.

DANILO: Aren't you confusing the *Camera del Lavoro* with the Labour Exchange? What is the function of the trade union?

DONNA ROSARIO: If they don't give them the family allowances, they go on strike.

DON ALFONSO: But with the peasants who stay on working in the country, smallholders and labourers, it's every man for himself.

DANILO: Why is that?

DONNA ROSARIO: They're afraid of the unfamiliar, they have no initiative.

DON ALFONSO: Each man is afraid of being robbed by the next. Suppose one man would like to have a tractor, for example, but hasn't the means to buy one: well, the government will give some help—that's all very well, but where is the rest of the money to come from? If he clubs together with others, they'll only quarrel. One of them will want the tractor on a particular day—and as likely as not so will one of the others. And also, a man pays for petrol, oil, and then . . . 'What's this? All that petrol used up?' Each one feels he's been robbed—and that's why they prefer to be on their own. Joining together leads to too many quarrels.

DONNA ROSARIO: The tenant farmer, the share-cropper, isn't honest with the landowners, either. Before this land of ours was reafforested, we had more than ten share-croppers, some years even fifteen—they weren't always the same people—and we always had to be on the watch, especially at sowing and harvest time.

DON ALFONSO: When it's time for the sowing, they carry off seed corn to their houses, and so there's less to sow. Then in spring all that comes up is a blade here and a blade there: but if they don't sow it, what can they expect to reap? Then at harvest time, even when it's a poor crop, they bundle it up into good big sheaves in the day time for it to be counted; but at night they go and remove a bunch from each sheaf—so that the number will still be the same, you see—and load up the mule in the night, and so the corn disappears. During the threshing we have to stay up all night to keep a watch on them ourselves, because if I left an agent he'd take his share too.

DONNA ROSARIO: At the olive gathering we used to leave sacks so full that you couldn't tie the top. When they reached the house they'd be half empty.

DON ALFONSO: One morning when they were picking the olives a strong wind got up, and they couldn't go on with it. The men all went back to the village. Then at about ten o'clock I go out again: and what do I find but one of the tenants—one of the ones who'd gone home—back there picking olives again! Well, I took him along to his father—he wasn't a youngster, either, he was a married man: 'What terrible luck' he was saying, because he'd been caught.

DONNA ROSARIO (*laughing*): My husband was armed—the fellow was dying of fright!

DANILO: What sort of relations did there use to be between people, and what are they like now, in your world?

DON ALFONSO: The nobility was always isolated. On my mother's side they were marquises, on my father's they were gentlemen, big landowners, with plenty of livestock.

DONNA ROSALIA: The nobility were always isolated. In the small towns there aren't many of them, so who were they to have contact with? My grandmother used to have certain days when she received the most important people in town. She was a great friend of Vittorio Emanuele Orlando.[1] When my grandfather went about the countryside, he was always accompanied by his confidential agents,[2] to ensure proper respect: even the Marquis was always escorted. When the Police Superintendent needed anything, he just went round to call on the Marquis. At the time of the Sicilian Fasces there was a sort of revolution, and my grandfather kept the carriage entrance shut.

DON ALFONSO: But their way of life couldn't last—they were accustomed to having coachmen and carriages, servants, a cook, a seamstress, maids (they called them 'domestics'), a majordomo, stewards, factors, agents: and while they were spending the peasants were buying, and so the clerks and the peasants got ahead and the nobility fell behind.

DONNA ROSALIA: Nowadays one is no longer important. They were large families: some of the girls became nuns, some of the men sold up and today most of them are office workers in the city. Everything is changed now. There are not many tenant farmers left, they're abandoning the land, they're on the climb: nowadays they all like to

[1] A former Prime Minister of Italy who came from Partinico: notorious as a 'friend of friends'. (Tr. note.)

[2] *Gente di fiducia:* a traditional role of the old-fashioned mafia. (Tr. note.)

think of themselves as people of refinement—there's no distinction left between the civilized person and the peasant.

GIOACCHINO: I remember this house belonging to this family ever since I was a boy. There were Austrian prisoners in one bit of the house in the '15–'18 War; I remember them going along the street on their way out to work in the fields—they were shared out among the biggest landowners: they had wooden shoes, big wooden clogs, and I used to hear them walking past, all forty of them, clop-clop, clop-clop. That was the first we'd seen of the enemy, us children. They used to go through the streets clop-clopping with their clogs, escorted by Italian corporals. Sometimes they'd stop for water, and all the women who had relatives far away at the war were moved to pity and gave them bread and a drop of wine, and some of the prisoners had tears in their eyes. Some of the men used to give them a bit of stuff to smoke.

I'd never been inside this building, but I used to stand and watch the black carriages with two horses go by—they had quite a few of them. They used to go out for rides in the carriages—on Sundays they used to ride up and down the *Corso*. Sometimes the coachman used to wear his gala uniform, with a cocked hat like a gendarme's, and an overcoat split up the back and buttoned with huge great buttons.

From outside you couldn't see anything of what went on inside the house. All you could see was that it belonged to a rich gentleman who owned a lot of land and buildings and servants, who dressed very well, and had moustaches like a senior officer. Later they put up a monument to him. Every evening before the Ave Maria they used to light the crystal lantern over the carriage entrance, and that gave a bit of light to the whole of the little square.

I used to think about one family owning the whole of that house, with so many rooms and cellars and outhouses, but there was no question of envying them: the rich are rich, you see, and the poor are poor.

Every Friday the Marquis would hand out two cents to the poor who used to come and beg for alms. On Sundays the peasants gathered outside the door and waited till they were called in by the factor to get their wages.

The children of the house were all failures. They were never rich. I don't know if the father began to sell off land, or what—I'm not sure: but a number of nobles around here became poor through gambling and womanizing. And this particular family also got involved in an enormous feud with another family, over some land or something, which meant that they shot each other whenever they met.

They had a daughter, a beautiful girl, but she killed herself because they wouldn't let her marry a poor young man she was in love with.

Trades Unionists in Palermo Province

——How long have you been a trade unionist?

SALVATORE CALECA: For a year and a half, in CISL.

——What are your main difficulties?

——We're always having to press the government to increase family allowances, pensions, and all the benefits that can assist the working man.

We're all brothers, so what we ask for is a sufficient old age pension: that is the goal the CISL is seeking to achieve.

——Are you a Catholic?

——Yes.

——D'you take part in any group activity as a Catholic?

——No. Sunday is the day I have to go and get my pay from the boss . . . One is a Catholic but . . . well, no doubt some can afford to waste the time.

As for political parties, there's no making head or tail of them. If I ask a fellow what a trade union is, he won't know what to answer: he'll follow one person or another, but without understanding what the real purpose is.

——How long have you been a trade unionist?

CICCIO DA TRAPANI: Since 1947. In UIL.

——What are your main difficulties?

——Our only difficulties are financial, otherwise we have no difficulties.

——No difficulties of organization, of relations?

——No. Only financial.

——Are you a Social Democrat?

——Yes.

——What group activity do you take part in as a Social Democrat?

——I've always belonged to the Federation—I've always belonged to any Federation there has been. And I'm a Saragat supporter.

——What do you think are the obstacles to group life in the area?

——We haven't got the intellectuals: we have to do things that are

43

beyond our powers; I have to force myself to be what I'm not. The intellectuals leave the area and go where they can fill their pockets, they go where there's money to be made.

LORENZO GERACI: I've been a trade unionist for twenty-four years.
——Why are you in CISNAL?
——Why? Because I've been in this organization ten years now, and I'm doing all right. I might have joined any of them, it just happened to be CISNAL. First I was in *Siculterra*, a Sicilian organization set up by Cavaliere Santangelo who was in the Post. I just happened to hear about it, and there was another man who wasn't able to cope with things and so I took over from him. Then I was with ACLI for a year and a half. Then there was EAS, which was later absorbed by CISNAL. There are so many different names you get lost among them! But the people who join are my personal friends. They follow me because they trust me. If I go with the devil, they'll come too; if I go with the Communists they'll come with the Communists; if I go with the Christian Democrats they'll come with the Christian Democrats. When I got a hundred membership cards Comandante Gullo wrote my praises in the newspaper. Whichever way I go, the people follow me personally.
——What are your main difficulties?
——The difficulties are these: you work first for one man, then for another, for doubtful returns, with no security; and we only get a small percentage on the membership cards.
——Do you belong to any political party?
——I have to belong to the MSI because they're at the head of CISNAL.
——What active part do you play in your party?
——No active part: I'm an MSI Local Councillor.

ANTONIO FERRANTE: When I was still a boy I learnt from the confidences of my father what are the sort of difficulties one comes across.
——Why are you in the CGIL rather than any other union?
——It's the only organization, I think, that looks after the real interests of the workers: not just in getting benefits like the other organizations, but in aiming to transform society.

——What are your major difficulties?

——Emigration means that we lose the active people who would otherwise give us the strength to tackle problems.

We would like to have students working among us, too—people properly qualified through study. But if we wanted them to work for us, we wouldn't be able to pay them, so that often the help they give us isn't much more than moral support, help in words only.

There are so many difficulties. For example: we haven't got a car, so it's often difficult even to get about.

People very often aren't even aware of their rights—half our members don't realize they have rights: this is largely due to illiteracy. Believe me, fifty per cent of our members can't even sign their names.

Then the difficulties are doubled, of course, if we try to tackle new problems.

Most of the men who've stayed on down here are the older ones, the ones with less fresh minds.

So many men come back from abroad and call in at the *Camera del Lavoro* to see what the prospects are, what jobs are likely to be going: but then they just go away again. They need to eat at once, they can't wait. There would be proper jobs for them, but not at once—only after long and hard struggles. We're not able to provide immediate solutions.

There's another difficulty on the organizational field (but perhaps this is too personal): I myself live here with no family, and go without regular meals—I may have to have supper at nine o'clock, or eleven, and sometimes I haven't anything to eat at all. However, one carries on because one believes in it (and it's only possible in collaboration with others—one man alone couldn't manage it).

Another cause of difficulties is this: sometimes the meetings are unsuccessful. Often it's not easy to get people to understand important problems—they're not interested in them, it's the trivial problems that come to have more importance. It generally takes quite a bit of preparation before people can understand the important problems, there's much more interest in the simpler problems. One of our main difficulties is getting it clear which the more important problems are.

Sometimes our meetings are unsuccessful even when lots of

people attend. At certain meetings—on forming co-operatives, for example, when we know we've got to settle things finally in order to be able to get a certain job—even though people stay on at the meeting, all we do is to sit there looking at each other and saying: 'Well, what do we do now?' We lack the knowledge of what exactly to do. And that goes for me too, of course. A lot of the laws are difficult. There's a lack of leaders.

Vito Tornambé,
Provincial Chairman of the League of Co-operatives

There are three co-operative union organizations, corresponding to the three main national political organizations: the left-wing League of Co-operatives, the Christian Democrat and right-wing Confederation, and the Republican & Social Democrat Association, which has only recently been recognized. (To be recognized, these organizations have to have a minimum membership of a thousand officially registered co-operatives.)

In Sicily there are about two thousand co-operatives, of which four hundred belong to our League; about three hundred are Christian Democrat, and about eighty Republican-Social Democrat. All the rest are independent, they don't have any connection with the political movements. But how many of these two thousand do you suppose function properly?

We, the Provincial League, have about 106 co-operatives: 33 agricultural, 35 manufacturing, labour, etc., 29 housing, and 9 retail. A number of these co-operatives are organized in syndicates to take advantage of shared facilities.

——How many members do you have in the Province, and how many in Palermo itself?

——In the Province we have 4,300 members in agriculture: in wine co-operatives, in services, and in rented farm land; 885 construction workers, drivers, and artisans (basket-makers, coopers, etc.), 105 of them in Palermo; and 900 in house building, 390 of them in Palermo. That comes to about 7,535 members in all.

——What proportion of the co-operatives function regularly?

——Unfortunately many of them—most of them—don't function properly at all, or only to a very limited extent: only 30 per cent function properly.

——Why don't they function?

——There are various reasons, depending on the category: the difficulty of obtaining credit at low interest rates—or even indeed

47

at high rates; the difficulty of finding capable organizers; the difficulty of sustaining continuous action in an atmosphere of indif-
erence or even outright hostility.

——In the ones which do work, what proportion of the members
play an active part?

——About 80 per cent. But unfortunately even their participation
is limited to particular occasions, such as the annual passing of the
balance sheet, or the reappointment of the executive. What we
ought to have is members' participation also in the formulation and
control of development plans and projects. The problem of credit,
for example, can't be the sole responsibility of the administrative
council—it ought to involve every member.

I think it's best that I should speak frankly, because for a thorough
and accurate diagnosis one has to know the full facts.

——In general, what are your main difficulties?

——Inadequate government support for the development of co-
operatives; what few incentives the law does provide are all too often
exploited by the clientship system: the greater part of the national
or Regional funds for agricultural development is generally diverted
into the big capitalist concerns. And left-wing movements in general
have only very recently begun to take more interest in specific
co-operative action.

In the retail field, there's a growing invasion of the massive
capitalist organizations (for instance the big city chain stores like
STANDA, UPIM, and so on).

It's relatively easy to start up a co-operative: what's difficult is to
turn it into a properly structured organization with continuous
activity.

One must also bear in mind the opposition and the difficulties
met with by co-operatives in the past; and also the fact that alongside the *bona fide* co-operatives are other bodies masquerading as
co-operatives whose sole function is to qualify legally as co-operatives in order to enjoy the benefits and subsidies provided by the
Regional Government laws. For example, just in the last few days
there has been this great scandal over certain so-called co-operatives
which had succeeded in getting hold of thirty million lire in government subsidies by claiming for worn-out old vehicles they had
bought as if they had been brand new. This sort of thing of course

does damage in that it makes people suspicious of even the *bona fide* co-operatives.

——How does the average co-operative function, out of those that do function?

——Every co-operative is regulated by its own statute, according to Italian law; in an average one the administrative council would meet about once a month, with about seventy to eighty per cent attendance. The agenda and the minutes are regularly drawn up each time. These meetings usually begin half an hour to an hour late. The general meetings are held twice a year, though perhaps they may meet more often informally. They usually begin an hour late too.

When the discussions do arouse interest and controversy, particularly over administrative details, they easily become chaotic: everyone talks at once, most people talk rather than listen, they get off the point and start the whole discussion over again, ignoring the agenda and decisions already taken; there's difficulty in finding common ground for agreement, the meetings drag on interminably —and of course less and less fruitfully as people get more and more tired.

A Christian Democrat Mayor

——What are the main obstacles to associate life in the Belice valley?

LEONARDO DI SALVO (*Christian Democrat Mayor of Roccamena and Chairman of the Belice Valley Intercommunal Planning Committee*): The individual's mistrust of other people, and of organizations at whatever level, base or summit. This mistrust can only be overcome when honest people doing concrete, practical work can demonstrate that associate life is more fruitful than isolation.

Besides this difficulty, the people in general are more ready to discuss superficial problems than the fundamental ones: they'd rather discuss, say, a pavement than the most important problem in the zone. The pavement may be useful, of course, but the fundamental problems cannot be ignored or not treated with the seriousness they deserve.

What the people want to see is rapid change: their mistrust is due to the fact that changes are so often delayed—the results are too long in coming.

——I asked another Mayor in your valley to what extent the people participate in the life of the commune. Let me read you his answer: 'They participate to a certain extent through the parties and the trades unions, but only very few are aware of the decisions taken, for example, in the local Council. The people are content with following certain questions. They follow the election of the Mayor, for instance, and the election of the Council. The local administration is easily identified with the person of the Mayor himself. Other important decisions are followed by only a tiny handful of people. On average in our commune, out of 13,000 inhabitants, only about fifty attend Council meetings.

'The newspaper only reaches the reading élite; posters have a wider range: they may reach as much as fifty per cent of the population. Local government election meetings have more following than political ones: in the eyes of the people, the political meeting achieves nothing; the participants stick to their own opinions, it is a soliloquy that never gets through to the adversary, and nothing any-one says is generally taken seriously. Public meetings in the squares, by their very nature, do nothing but reaffirm the presence of a party. More useful are the smaller meetings indoors, at which dia-logue is possible. People will take an active interest if they feel they are participating themselves.

'The best thing would be to have large numbers of meetings and get people to participate directly, to discuss their problems and suggest possible solutions themselves. The problem is to ensure the active participation of every individual by making him feel he is really needed.

'In other words, it is also necessary for each party and each mass organization to revise its methods.'

——Yes, that's absolutely true. At times one feels one is working in a vacuum. But today the people are more aware of their needs, they're more mature, and it's not true to say that they're unwilling to play their part. In most cases it is those in authority, those with most responsibility, who are at fault—as is clearly the case with our Intercommunal scheme—because they have never succeeded in rous-ing the people's interest and stimulating them to action. The interest is there, underneath, but you have to know how to draw it out.

Even among the communes of the same valley it's sometimes impossible to find points of common interest, not so much because of the different political persuasions of the different Councils, or even because of rivalry, but mostly simply because of people's ignorance of the problems of neighbouring towns—and indeed even of their own town.

It is so easy for people to see things only from the most selfish point of view: their outlook is too narrow, they can't see things in a wide perspective. But fundamental problems such as that of work, for example, can only be tackled in the much wider context of the community as a whole. The greater the lack of culture (in the widest sense), the less clarity of thought there is, and the firmer the hold of the clientship system. And another thing we must remember is this: if we want to solve the problems of the zone, it is not enough just to study and to put forward concrete proposals. It's one thing to see the problems from one's arm chair—and quite another to experience them in the midst of the people.

Giuseppe Pintacuda,
Provincial Secretary of the *Alleanza Contadina*, describes Palermo Province

——How would you describe the socio-economic structure of the rural part of Palermo Province?

——From the socio-economic point of view, our Province can be divided into four zones:

1: The inland region, about forty per cent of the Province, consisting of big feudal estates now partly abandoned, a lot of tenant farmers, a few owner-farmers, and nowadays, as a result of emigration, only a very small number of real farm labourers: what you often find instead is the man who doesn't come into any single category since he works as labourer, as share-cropper, and as partner in a smallholding, in the attempt to make up his hundred working days a year. These feudal estates belong mostly to rich aristocrats or *nouveau-riche* mafiosi, especially around Caccamo and Corleone. A lot of the land in some areas is let on long leases—there are about eight thousand of these tenant holdings: four thousand of them at Caccamo alone, on noblemen's land administered by mafiosi; and at Montemaggiore a thousand all belonging to one nobleman. The Church owns about another twenty per cent. Some of the big landowners have transformed the farms into capitalist concerns by mechanization, eliminating the tenant farmers, but most have virtually abandoned their farms and continue to pocket the government subsidies for themselves, either to spend or to invest elsewhere, especially in new property in Palermo. About half the land is still in the hands of some forty families (many of them interconnected), in spite of the legislation to limit ownership. In between the big landowners and the peasants are the mafiosi: they carry on in the country for as long as it suits them, then when there's not much more to be got there they turn their attentions to the developing areas or to the city, and get in on land and building speculation.

The peasants in these inland areas have no real organization or unity: they may come together momentarily for particular purposes, but not with any continuity, and with no overall view of the problems. There is some movement towards change on the part of some of the grantees of the area, but they are not yet uniting in order to bring about changes.

Even when there is water in these areas, even if there are possibilities for development, in general they have not been utilized; often there aren't even any plans: thousands of millions of lire have been drawn from State funds, yet not only has the money failed to reach the land, but often the plans for transformation don't even exist.

It's only very recently that some of the long leases have lapsed, as a result of pressure by the peasants.

2: The second zone consists of arable land and olive groves of the plains and hills, differing from the interior zone in that it is capable of mechanization and more productive. In this area they are largely owner-farmers, and also to a lesser extent tenant farmers. Here too there are difficulties in organizing and forming co-operatives.

3: The third zone, about five per cent of the Province, consists of the vineyards, mainly concentrated in two areas. Here most of the farmers are share-croppers who have generally rented uncultivated land and transformed it by planting vines; a strong nucleus of owner-farmers; farm labourers of mixed category; and one or two big landowners who are installing considerable plant. This is a more modern zone, with a certain degree of continuous organization and unity that isn't just limited to particular momentary issues.

4: The fourth zone is the coastal strip of citrus groves, orchards, artichoke fields, and various soft fruit and vegetables: although these crops cover only two per cent of the Province, they produce fifty per cent of its agricultural wealth.

One or two big landowners, some of them aristocrats; quite a few share-croppers; but the commonest categories here are the owner-farmer, the smallholder, and the agricultural labourer. The owner-farmers are fairly well organized, but more for the sake of State benefits than from any commitment to solving problems of development. Here, unlike in the other zones, there is a certain degree of technical and agricultural development: but the ultimate aim should be the improvement of commercial organization, and democratic reform of the water distribution system which is still

3*

largely in the hands of the mafia. The recent worsening of the situation has in fact been a spur to some of the owner-farmers to form an association. The most advanced, the best organized, are the agricultural labourers.

——How many members do you have?

——Last year there were 3,400 altogether: enrolment for this year is still in progress.

——What proportion of them are engaged in continuous, methodical action?

——There are only four of us working full time, and there's also an active administration of about thirty people who follow and organize the *Alleanza*'s activities in their free time, and often sacrifice part of their working hours too.

——What are your main difficulties?

——From the financial point of view, we only have enough money for six months of the year; and in fact part of this money doesn't come from the peasants at all but from the Regional Government by way of subsidy for our welfare activities.

This is a vast province, divided into eighty communes, without any pilot centres; and there are so few of us that we risk getting lost in this huge area and amidst such a multiplicity of problems. We have to pick on particular problems and particular communes because we just can't deal with the whole lot. That's why our aim is to construct a few really sound centres in one or two key communes, right in the midst of some of the fundamental problems.

It's very difficult to find qualified and capable organizers.

Up till now people have always been educated (by the *Bonomiana*, in particular), to an attitude of dependence, to the idea of being assisted, to paternalism; and so they naturally find it more difficult to co-operate and to commit themselves to dealing with more general problems. Also it's difficult to organize workers of no definite category.

We also have to contend with the old-fashioned types of syndicates which are at odds with the new exigencies of today because they were created as organizations of farmers protected and financed by the Government. No organization can bring about new achievements in the countryside unless these old institutions are first abolished.

——What, briefly, are the Province's most serious problems today?

——Emigration and social disintegration in the countryside; the lack of organic or comprehensive development plans for homogeneous zones; the lack of a proper agricultural training college to prepare the cadres to carry out the new developments.

——In what ways do you think the mafia nowadays obstructs development in the countryside of Palermo Province?

——As far as the large feudal estates are concerned, enough has already been written about that, and in any case what is involved there is an organization more or less in decline.

In the developed zones, though, it does still have a positive bad influence: in the vine-growing areas, for instance, through the control of wine distribution, adulteration of wine, and in certain wine co-operatives; in the citrus-growing areas it controls trade, and also —what is indispensable for production—water.

We can see this more clearly, I think, if we take a particular concrete example such as that of the Bagheria zone, a very fragmented area where the peasants have had great difficulty in forming associations strong enough to stand up to the pressures and bullying of mafia organizations.

From 1926 on, the water resources of this zone (wells and diverted river water) were entirely controlled by mafia groups. In '26, with the construction of the Piana degli Albanesi dam, the authorities set up irrigation Syndicates on a Communal and in some cases (as at Bagheria) an inter-Communal basis. The main purpose of the Government authorities (and therefore of the Prefect) in obliging the peasants to form these Syndicates was to ensure additional profit to the Electricity Company through the distribution of water already being exploited for electrical energy production. This new development meant a slump for the old water pumping and diversion system: however, the mafia group which controlled this rapidly transferred itself to the heart of the Syndicate; and so, helped as much by the anti-democratic statutes as by their own sinister influence, they became absolute masters of the new system. The situation was in no way altered even by Mori's[1] campaign to suppress

[1] Prefect Cesare Mori, to whom Mussolini gave the task of eliminating the mafia in the 'twenties. (Tr. note.)

the mafia: even from banishment the mafiosi continued to run things. The first more or less democratic assembly of the Bagheria Syndicate wasn't till 1944, twenty years after its formation. That was the result of a powerful peasant protest movement.

How has the mafia managed to keep control? The main reason is a general political one: their influence and control over the masses. The Bagheria Syndicate has three thousand members, and whoever has power over the Syndicate has power over the lives of three thousand families: it depends on the Syndicate whether or not the smallholder's garden is watered at the right time, and therefore whether or not he can produce anything. The second reason is an economic one: the owners of the old water-pumping plants refused to abandon them in spite of their being uneconomical compared with the new possibilities (for example, a lot of the water has to be pumped up fifty metres from the bottom of the well itself, and then raised another hundred metres or so); and since the appreciable difference in cost would mean they could no longer sell their water to the peasants, particularly in times of normal supply, they forced the Syndicates to buy their water. And so the Syndicates, which would have been able to sell the water from the Piana reservoir quite cheaply, have been forced to sell at an average price between the two. And every attempt to extend the area irrigated, to get new dams and channels built, has always been sabotaged by every means. Also, the old mafia well water often has to be raised to a height of, say, two hundred metres in order to bring it into the channel, even though it may be going to run out again at a height of only fifty metres or so. And another thing: since this water is generally ground-water from near the sea, it is nearly always excessively salty and therefore particularly unsuitable for citrus cultivation. The only way it can be made usable is by mixing it with the good water— and this can only be done by the Syndicate hitherto dominated by mafia interests.

In 1952 when we first got onto the Bagheria local Council, we proposed taking a firm initiative for the utilization of water from the Scansano River. The Mayor at that time, who up till then had been Chairman of the Syndicate, replied that Bagheria was the Commune furthest from the Scansano and therefore should be the last to take any initiative. And from that day to this it has been impossible to make the Commune of Bagheria take any initiative whatever, either for the utilization of the Scansano or for the planned construction of the dam on the San Leonardo, which could provide a hundred million cubic metres of water a year.

Two years ago some charges of TNT were blown up on the Scansano work site: who do you suppose would have planted those bombs? The situation is complex, there are various interests opposed to the project. Do you suppose they've ever found out who it was?

In neighbouring areas, for example at Ficarazzi where the democratic movement was not so strong, many of the people who have attempted to oppose the mafia have been murdered.

A Lawyer

This group life—I see no sign of it here.

In the middle classes, apart from the game of *scopone* among acquaintances (people are very rarely friends), everyone is isolated.

Suspiciousness is innate in us. Any kind of grouping is only momentary.

The bar is the place where one goes for a coffee or a drink, and without spending much one can sit outside with some acquaintance or other and watch passers-by, and pass the time criticizing them. Discussions are usually nothing but gossip or chat about current political events which leaves everyone with exactly the same opinions as before.

Celebrations like weddings or christenings are other occasions for a momentary grouping: there the atmosphere isn't like that of the café, and it isn't intimate either; but it is cordial: it's a moment of friendliness and cordiality linked with the actual occasion.

There is something approaching a group among huntsmen: huntsmen are practically always found in company—if you see one you're certain to see another not far off. They talk about dogs, about the prowess of one dog or another; one huntsman will boast . . . We saw the rabbit but the dog didn't scent it in time and so it got away . . . and so on, always the same old rigmarole. Their passion for sport brings them together to talk about it. In fact they have a kind of club of their own. Generally they are small landowners, one or two office workers, *petits bourgeois*.

For over sixty years, up till three years ago, there used to be the *Circolo dei Civili Umberto*, membership of which was limited by statute to the local élite, to the very rich and to people of good family. They used to play cards, and watch passers-by in the street, and take the *Giornale di Sicilia* and the *Giornale d'Italia* and *L'Ora*. After the war a great number of extraneous elements found their way in, people who probably didn't even pay their monthly subscriptions; and in order to eliminate certain undesirable elements even among the paying members, and also owing to lack of funds, the Club closed down.

There had been a proposal to abolish the title of *Circolo dei Civili*, but in that case it would have been possible for anyone to join, and it would no longer have been able to preserve a certain tone.

One or two other clubs were started up, but nothing came of them, they didn't catch on: there was always the suspicion that they had some ulterior motive, some political aim or other.

Even sport here doesn't create groups, strictly speaking.

Billiards . . . as there's nowhere else to go, if there's someone you enjoy playing with you'll have a little game to while away half an hour or so.

In the evenings, and on Sundays and holidays, people walk up and down the *Corso* showing off a spurious material wellbeing that's based on hire purchase: the labourer's wife and the peasant's wife push their *de luxe* prams along and feel themselves more important. The students walk apart.

At Church it's just the same as on the *Corso*: people go there to show off their clothes, a girl goes to see her young man, they go out of habit, or to let other people see that they go to church—only a tiny minority really go there to pray.

The local feast day is an event for the common people rather than the middle class: it's the common people who insist on having their horse races and their fireworks. Office workers and professional people and *petits bourgeois*, if they have a car, prefer to get away from all the confusion whenever there's a feast day, and go out for a meal in the country with their families or neighbours. But they still only come together for the moment.

Among professional people, for instance among doctors or lawyers, there's competition: there's a show of friendliness, but really the aim is to try and get hold of each other's clients, to further their own interests. Of course this doesn't apply to the really well-established ones, who don't need to go treading on each other's heels because people come to them on their own account.

The countryside is dying. Only a very few are still tied to it by love of the land.

Among office workers, too, there's acquaintanceship rather than real friendship.

What the political parties stand for in the eyes of the masses is not ideas but immediate personal interest. A man is a Christian Democrat because it's to his advantage to be a Christian Democrat—he knows he can expect favours, he knows he can get things through belonging to the party. Ideology is only for a few, for a few idealists: ordinary people look for immediate rewards. That's why people are able to change so casually from one party to another.

The unions are mostly just branches, pawns of the parties.

The electoral canvasser gradually works his way up by means of his friends within the power groups, and they in their turn make use of him for procuring votes. To begin with, the canvasser doesn't work for himself, but gradually he comes to work more and more on his own account, as his credit increases in proportion to the following he gains.

The mass parties are better organized, but there are only a few there who have any influence on the masses, and the rest are generally just victims of demagogy.

——What groups do you belong to?

——I'm still a Liberal by persuasion, but I left the party when they imposed the civic list. We used to have occasional irregular meetings. Nowadays I'm no longer active in politics. I go to College—for six years now I've been Secretary to the Technical College at Piana degli Albanesi, which is fifty kilometres away. But I don't know anyone there apart from the vet, the magistrate, and very few others: I don't live at Piana.

I studied Law because of lack of funds: I wanted to do Chemistry but I couldn't afford to board in Palermo. So I put myself down for the course which would take up least time and cost least money. I remember before I put my name down I spun a coin: heads for Literature, tails for Law.

I gave up being a lawyer because I found I had to do things like distrainments and executions of judgement—I had to act in a way that often revolted me, inhumanly; and besides, the money was difficult and uncertain.

——Within the College, do you have at least an elementary group life?

——Each person does his own work.

——Do you feel a need for group work, group life?

——Yes.

——And what are you doing towards bringing this about?

——Unfortunately it's impossible to form groups. There's such prejudice. People come together to conquer the boredom—the anguish, almost—of being alone: but there's no desire for mutual understanding. Each person feels he's in an oppressed position, and is on the defensive. If you say to an acquaintance that such and such ought to be done, he'll say: 'But why should *you* want to make the move? Who says it should be you? D'you want to do the impossible? Things have always been that way. . . .'

Groups . . ., one might say the police are a group: but that's not a group created by the environment, it's created by the State, it's completely extraneous.

The mafia are the only ones who realize that unity makes for strength: their unity is the secret of their success. They know they can count on the strength of elements in other towns, too, and as a result their strength is really effective, since everyone else is isolated and therefore weak.

The few people who read the papers (though there are more of them than there used to be), and the ones who watch television (and there are a fair number of them now, too), watch what's happening with curiosity, but don't really care what happens as they're inclined to be fatalistic. Everything's happening somewhere else, and the individual feels it's impossible for him to have any influence.

We're stuck in a closed circle. To change the situation there would have to be discussions, the problems would have to be debated calmly and objectively. People would have to learn how to work together. But they never succeed in getting together, and so the circle remains closed. There's nothing to be done.

We're stuck in a closed circle, a blind alley.

A Parish Priest

(One of the most cultured and active in the region)

I have had occasion to encourage one or two groups of labourers to get together to form a co-operative; but there is always mutual mistrust, each man is afraid of being cheated by the others. The older men have memories of certain attempts at association that came to grief.

Another difficulty could be the lack, the relative lack, of people capable of devoting themselves to society: rather than lack I should perhaps say the dearth, or deficiency, of people capable of dedicating themselves to those around them.

Two factors that I think can contribute much towards an associate life are, first, the inculcation of the concepts underlined by the conciliar constitutions On the Church and On the Sacred Liturgy, which emphasize the Christian congregation as a community, with the small family of the parish as part of the larger family of the Diocese, and this in turn part of the family of the Church; and, second, naturally, making Christian people more sensible to Charity, in the widest sense, as they were in the first few centuries of Christianity.

The recent innovations in the liturgy, the introduction of the Italian language, the allotting to the people of their own part in the responses at Mass (I have already, for example, turned the altar round towards the people according to the latest instructions), the dialogue between priest and congregation—these will all contribute towards a growing sense of community.

The whole of my parish is baptized, with the exception of one child of six months. If by practising members we understand the united in spirit, then we may say that ninety per cent are practising: if, on the other hand, we mean those who attend services weekly, then the number drops (according to the time of year, among other things), to as low as thirty per cent.

Processions are very well attended, on Good Friday and Corpus

Christi. Christmas, Easter, Saint Lucy's day and Saint Joseph's day are recognized as important Feasts; the celebration of Easter, as a participation in the sacraments, is considered an important rite.

By way of groups, we have the four branches of Catholic Action: the boys', the girls', the men's, and the women's. The activities of each group are directed towards the moulding, the religious education, of the individual, whose duty it then is to communicate to others what he himself has received. For example, the women have recently been approaching those families furthest from the Church in order to pass on the education they themselves have acquired: this year, the concept of Grace, and participation in the sacraments. Next year the theme will be the liturgy; and subsequently, the parish as a community of faith, prayer, and charity. People collaborate to the best of their ability, and we make use of everyone; they distribute printed or cyclostyled matter, the young men go round with the loudspeaker on particular occasions to inculcate certain ideas in the form of slogans—this is a form of enterprise which I am endeavouring to inculcate into others: we must be able to take advantage of methods of publicity.

Closed meetings are held weekly from October to May, and open meetings at Christmas and Easter and on Whit Sunday. Each group has a Chairman, appointed by the Bishop on the recommendation of the priest. The function of the priest himself is that of directing religious education, of forming people's ideas. The Chairman is supposed to attend to the carrying out of the programme, and also to co-ordinate external activities, such as demonstrations, expeditions, and occasional sporting events and games. At each meeting there is a talk, generally given by the priest since the Chairman is not always qualified to do this himself, especially where dogmatic truths are concerned. Afterwards there are questions and answers.

Besides these four groups, there are also the ACLI organizations, but there has recently been a crisis among the staff here, with quarrels leading to the Chairman's being deposed. The Chairman is supposed to be elected by the assembly, and they are supposed to pursue charitable and welfare activities, much like a trade union, with monthly meetings. But at the moment these are not taking place.

Other groups are the Church Guilds, whose object is to keep

people close to religious observances and the sacraments; there are three of these here: the Guilds of Our Lady of Sorrows, one for men and the other for women, and the Guild of Christ Crucified, for men.

Every person ought to have the opportunity to work, if possible near his home, without having to emigrate. But as for a levelling of society—the integral Christian communities are a special case, but in general we cannot think of that: that is part of the Communist ideology. What is necessary is that there should be nothing to hinder the expression of the personality. The realization of a social and economic community is not our business: our concern is to inculcate principles. In the social doctrine of the Church there are certain principles binding under pain of mortal sin, such as damage to others' property, etcetera; whereas there are methods, suggestions, recommendations in which one has to distinguish what is essential from what is a matter of opinion, and which may be applied differently according to different cases and different times.

The parish priest is the spiritual father, his aim is to create unity among his people; he seeks to encourage a cultural and social process; I am seeking to encourage the students who, for particular reasons, are inactive here. The priest's wish is that all his people should see themselves as brothers and children of God; he inculcates principles in those around him, and also tries to reach people in their own homes, even those further away, for this purpose making use of the members of the associations.

There is a small group of evangelists here, and I have tried to knock them on the head: however, they do not constitute a danger—for the moment at least.

In this milieu the parish priest is recognized as the person who has the right, and indeed the duty, to concern himself with everything. He is influential, his presence is felt.

Electoral Complicity
between the gangster Frank Coppola and
Christian Democrat Senator Girolamo Messeri

*(pages from the diary of Franco Alasia, collaborator at
the Study and Action Centre[1])*

July 1962

In October 1960 ERAS, the public works department responsible for agrarian reform in Sicily, invited construction tenders for the Iato dam. There was no response. About a month later (again in Palermo) they called for tenders a second time: still no response. It was not until January 1961, when the *Cassa per il Mezzogiorno*[2] arrogated the matter to itself and repeated the process in Rome, that the contract was taken up. The firm of Vianini was engaged, and shortly afterwards sent a first group of technicians to Partinico.

At last it seemed that the years-old question was going to be resolved. Much had already been done since 1955—when from Partinico we had first begun to attract public attention and the attention of the relevant authorities to the possibility of building a dam on the River Iato which would be the starting point for a radical transformation of the zone (from Montelepre, the town of Giuliano and Pisciotta, to Castellammare, the town of Mattarella and Messeri), and which would also absorb unemployed labour in the area with consequent benefit to the local population: the plans had been prepared by ERAS and approved by the *Cassa per il Mazzogiorno*; the project had been declared of public utility; and now the last unaccountable obstacles blocking the whole operation in Palermo had apparently been overcome, and the contract was finally awarded.

But the spring of 1961 went by, summer came, and still nothing happened about the dam. The Vianini technicians had disappeared. 'Is it true they're going to build the dam?' people were asking.

[1] Some of this material was presented to the Parliamentary Commission of Enquiry into the Mafia, together with more not reproduced here.

[2] Government Fund for the South. (Tr. note.)

On 26th August 1961 a meeting to discuss the dam was held in Partinico, and it was attended by the Hon. Corallo, President of the Sicilian Regional Government. The dam, concluded the meeting, was to be made; the owners of the land to be expropriated were to be paid fair compensation. The presence of the President of the Regional Government seemed to confirm the supposition that this was the end of the road.

But the valuation surveys on the land to be expropriated, to determine the amount of compensation payable, had not been carried out. What concrete basis was there, then, for negotiations? Winter was approaching, and unless the necessary surveys (which involved over six hundred smallholders) were carried out, construction of the dam would not be able to start even in the spring of 1962. The amount of compensation payable by the State to the firm which had been prevented from beginning the work was meanwhile mounting all the time. The water continued to run to waste in the sea; and thousands of men from the towns around the Gulf of Castellammare which would benefit from the dam were emigrating to North Italy and abroad in search of work.

On 20th October 1961, the Minister Pastore gave an assurance that the *Cassa per il Mezzogiorno* had given and would continue to give all due assistance towards the immediate and satisfactory solution of the matter. But nothing happened. Then, in conversations with prominent officials in the *Cassa*, we were given renewed assurances: the problem of the dam, they said, was well on the way to being solved—whence our decision, at the end of November 1961, not to start our campaign of strong pressure from below. It seemed as though the difficulties could be resolved by normal methods.

But still the situation remains unchanged, in spite of those assurances, in spite of the promises. In fact, things have got worse: there is some doubt now as to whether the dam will be built at all. Someone has even put about a rumour that 'the people would throw bombs at the dam if it was begun'.

26th July 1962, 10 a.m.

We meet two high up officials from ERAS. One of them tells us: 'It's true that the *Cassa per il Mezzogiorno* has put pressure on us to start work on the dam and to open two Technical and Agricultural Assistance Centres, at Partinico and at Balestrate. But there has also been political interference to counter this. And as for the Technical Assistance Centres for ensuring proper use of the irrigation scheme—*what is the point of setting them up if it isn't even certain that the dam will be built?*

The same afternoon

From usually well-informed sources, we hear that the firm of Vianini are already owed nearly four hundred million lire in compensation for losses incurred through the delay. (Someone else says it's less: ten per cent of the agreed price, if the work is not carried out.)

A student architect who is a friend of ours went to ERAS to get information about the dam: 'The dam's not going to be built now,' he was told.

We have heard that the man who planned the scheme went to complain to a Regional Deputy: 'They intend not to build the dam now.'

9.15 p.m.

We go to the Partinico headquarters of the Syndicate of the Owners of the land to be expropriated, to meet Gaspare Centineo, their Chairman.

Up on the wall is a large poster inviting public solidarity with the farmers whose land is to be flooded: and attached to this manifesto is a letter from the Chairman of the *Cassa per il Mezzogiorno*, Doctor Pescatore, addressed to the Honourable Calogero Volpe,[1] in which he assures him (in itself the document is formally irreproachable) that the interests of the Syndicate will not be forgotten. Knowing which local forces support Volpe in election campaigns, we realize now which political forces this Syndicate is turning to.

In the course of our conversation with Centineo:

[1] See page 92, and Part III. (Tr. note.)

'We don't know anything more: it's months since we heard anything about negotiations.'

'What—you, who are directly concerned, don't know anything about it? You don't know if they've agreed on a price for the land that's to be flooded?'

'No, we don't.'

'But how much are you asking?'

'We don't know.'

'You don't know how much you want for your land?'

'We had a report drawn up; our claims were submitted; those prices were compared with the ERAS valuation, they were modified, corrected, in agreement with the other technician: but nothing has come of it since.'

'Could we see this report?'

'Well . . . no, we haven't got it here, we haven't got the keys.'

'Could we meet your technician? Where does he live?'

'I don't know . . .'

'But it's important to meet him, to get an agreement. You don't even know where your own technician lives?'

'No, I don't. But I tell you: *for us, this land is priceless.* We've always farmed this land, and our fathers and grandfathers and great-grandfathers before us, and this is the only living we know, we've never learnt any other trade. It's this land that gives us our daily bread, *and anyone who tries to get their hands on it had better watch out.*'

1st August 1962

A friend informs us: 'I was talking yesterday evening to a relative of Frank Coppola: he said the dam was definitely not going to be built. He looked as if he knew a lot. A few months ago, some owners of springs around Cannizzaro said to me: "We're not going to accept our water being worth nothing"—they were worried that their water would lose its value.'

And a high-up official in the Agricultural Inspectorate in Palermo adds: 'I think the solution is being held up now by a speculator who has bought up some of the land which is to be flooded'—alluding to Centineo.

The same afternoon

A peasant says to me: 'Who are the mafiosi? Why are they powerful?' '*Persone intese*',[1] they call themselves, and everybody should respect them.

That's how folk reason here. It's power that counts. And why these mafiosi are powerful is because whatever they decide on, they do. "You talk too much—I'll snuff you out. You refuse to hear sense, you go trotting about here and there where you've no business to be, instead of minding your own affairs: *astutamu sta cannila*— we'll snuff you out."

Of course the people don't really respect them, not a bit. Their respect is just submission. They are stronger. The mafia was here before the law. For them, it's their own law that counts. A real mafioso never moves alone. A real mafia crime is always decided by all of them: they meet, discuss, and decide.

Then you see them, these mafiosi, arm in arm with the cops, and with the priests; you find them in the *Bonomiana*, and among the Christian Democrats; you find them on the local Council, and in the Insurance; whenever you need anything you always come up against them. They're friends with the Honourables: wherever there's politics, there's mafia. And if you talk . . . you let slip any little remark, and they're sure to hear of it. You see how strong they are? That's why if somebody knows or sees something, he doesn't know anything, he hasn't seen anything. No one trusts anybody these days. The cops—trust them? Not even your own family!

And so? Best mind your own business. 'The man who plays alone never loses.' You must be on your best behaviour when you're with other people: speak well, speak clean; because, as the saying goes, '*una parola mal detta, ne viene una vendetta*'—a careless word, and a vendetta will follow. We have to be on our guard against our tongues. For me, blessed is the man who minds his own business. The man who doesn't is asking for trouble.

These parties—they're all the same. I don't believe in any of them. The *Camera del Lavoro* is a party, the *Bonomiana*'s a party, and

[1] Mafiosi often describe themselves as '*persone intese*': people respectfully listened to and obeyed by others. (Tr. note.)

the mafia's a party too; Communists, Christian Democrats, Monarchists, Fascists—they're all alike. All nice and friendly, of course,
when it comes to getting our votes. Most of the time as like as
not they'll ignore you completely—then at election time along
they come all ingratiating: "Do vote for me, won't you please
vote for me." Or else: "Do vote for my son: then when he
gets in, if you need some favour done—ah! you can count on
us!"

2nd August 1962

Salvatore D'Anna, officer in charge of Finances and of Water in
the Commune of Terrasini tells us:

In connection with the Piano del Re spring, I came into contact
with Gaspare Centineo. A dispute had arisen between the Commune
of Terrasini, represented by me, and a group of landowners with
interests in the water from the spring.

Because too many wells have been dug in the area, there was a
shortage of water. The Civil Engineers had the wells closed. The
owners of the place protested. Their spokesman was Centineo, who
maintained that in time of shortage the water should be divided
equally between the Commune of Terrasini and the landowners. I
maintained that priority should be given to the Commune's water
supply: we couldn't leave the people without water. I illustrated
my point to Centineo: 'You'd give drinking water to your child
first, naturally, and only afterwards to animals and plants.' To
which he replied: 'You're insulting us!' I said: 'Soon you'll have the
Iato dam water for your land,' and he replied: 'As Chairman of the
Syndicate of landowners to be expropriated, I am looking after
their interests, and I have no intention of the dam being made.' And
then, seeing I held firm on my position, he added: 'All right. What
will happen, will happen.'

We have realized now that without total commitment, the dam
will not be built: every single person, starting with ourselves,
must shoulder his own individual responsibility, if we want everyone else to shoulder theirs.

7th August 1962

We have decided to take action. Individuals, trades unions, and political groups are being asked: 'What are *you* doing about it? What do you think you can do?' And their attention is being drawn to the doubts that are now cast on the implementation of this scheme for a reservoir of 45 million cubic metres of water capable of irrigating about nine thousand hectares and of creating over three thousand new jobs in the area through the transformation from dry to irrigated cultivation; the construction work itself would employ as many as five hundred men for at least four years, and once it was completed production in the area would be tripled.

One by one the various trade union and political groups decide to join the pressure campaign; in the end even the Christian Democrats give way, afraid of being left out on a limb alongside Centineo in the eyes of public opinion.

23rd August, 3.0 p.m.

A local Councillor:
'Some Councillors—I know them only too well: they *say* they are in favour of the dam, but then there are strong pressures, opposing interests, and so they change their tune.'

We tell him: 'We'd like to invite the Mayors of the towns concerned to come to our meetings in preparation of concerted action on the dam.'

'Yes,' he replies, 'a Mayor will agree to come: then Centineo goes and has a word with him and tells him the dam must not be built, and so he retracts.'

10th September 1962

L'Ora reports: 'Yesterday was a day of great civic emotion in Partinico, as was proved not only by the planned demonstrations of popular protest against the delay in starting work on the Iato dam, but also (within the context of common agreement on aims) by an intense, lively, and sometimes agitated debate on certain topics of broader significance: Does the mafia exist? In what ways does it manifest its anti-social power? Why is Italian bureaucracy so clogged and sluggish? What must be done to promote the harmonious economic development of a zone destined to be radically transformed by a large government project? Throughout the day many eminent speakers were heard: two members of the Government, about a dozen members of the Regional and National Parliaments (all left wing), representatives of national culture (among them Bruno Zevi), Sicilian journalists of every political colour, and reporters from big daily and weekly papers of mainland Italy, Local Government officials and local representatives of parties, trades unions and other associations, the young intelligentsia, thousands of ordinary people . . . The day was not without its moments of tension . . .'

14th September 1962

The Minister Pastore has at last decided that the valuation surveys on the land to be expropriated will be carried out, and that by February '63 work on the dam will have started.

6th November 1962

The technicians commissioned to conduct the surveys have started work.

27th February 1963

Work on the dam has begun.

28th April 1963

Girolamo Messeri has been re-elected Senator in the electoral college of Partinico-Monreale.

November–December 1963

How can the construction of a dam be prevented like this? How on earth can a few provincial mafiosi have such power?

An illuminating answer to this question is found in the numerous documents we have been collecting in the area. Here are just a few extracts:

I

'Frank Coppola[1] has come to Partinico not only before every election, both national and region, but also whenever there has been a crisis in the local government. Even non-left-wing people agree that Frank Coppola is one of Messeri's election campaigners.

. . . As for the association between a number of Church men and well-known mafiosi: Padre La Rocca, priest of the Church of the Holy Sufferers in Partinico, together with prominent civic authorities, and a brass band, went to Partinico Station to welcome Frank Coppola. They then attended a banquet together in the *Casa del fanciullo* in Piazza Vittorio Emanuele, villa Margherita. The witness who told me this is willing to take an oath.

One afternoon shortly before the 1958 elections I saw the same Padre La Rocca handing out leaflets telling people to vote for Calogero Volpe, at that time unknown in Partinico. When all the leaflets were gone, he sent someone to fetch more from the Church.

. . . In '53, furthermore, Frank Coppola was made an honorary member of FUCI, the Catholic Students' Federation, in the presence of Padre La Franca; during the ceremony the white hat of the Philosophy Faculty was placed on his head (the hat belonged to Pino Cammarata, who was a student at the time): the members of FUCI then present can testify to this incident.'

II

'At every election Frank Coppola comes to Partinico. He has always supported the Christian Democrats: he was the chief campaigner for Santi Savarino, and subsequently for Messeri.

One of the most active groups canvassing for Messeri is that of the young FUCI members.

It is well known what excellent terms the FUCI are on with Frank Coppola. On the occasion of a collection in aid of the flooded lower

[1] Notorious Sicilian-American gangster and mafioso. (Tr. note.)

Po valley which Frank Coppola had helped to organize (this is a traditional activity of local mafiosi), he was fetêd in the local FUCI rooms and awarded honorary membership, with the title *Fucino ad honorem*. Also present were Padre La Franca, Assistant of FUCI, and thirty or so students. I remember that at the end of the ceremony Frank Coppola had the white medieval tricorne of the Faculty of Philosophy placed on his head. Then as a token of his gratitude he offered round spiced cakes.'

III

'. . . Whenever Coppola arrived in Partinico, he was welcomed as a guest of honour by the local notables.

One Sunday shortly before the 1958 elections there was a noticeable bustle of people and cars in Via Principe Umberto, near the office of the Bricklayers' Co-operative: my friends and I discovered that Frank Coppola was introducing Girolamo Messeri and recommending him with particular warmth as the new Christian Democrat for the Senate to replace Santi Savarino.

Since the Hon. Girolamao Li Causi had during the course of that same election campaign made a reference to the former head of the Partinico mafia Santo Fleres (murdered a few years before), on the Friday evening before the election Girolamo Messeri publicly denounced Li Causi, among other things "for having insulted the grave of the dead with blasphemous speech".

Frank Coppola came to Partinico for other elections.

On the 28th April 1963, towards midnight, I myself saw Frank Coppola coming out of the Christian Democrat rooms in Partinico, in the company of his relative Domenico Coppola (at present wanted by the police), and Pino Blanda, local secretary of the DC. The group stayed talking outside the DC rooms for about twenty minutes. We could easily identify them even though it was late at night because the street was well lit.

It is well known in Partinico that Frank Coppola also campaigns for Girolamo Messeri through his associates.'

IV

'A few days before the '58 elections I attended a meeting at the Bricklayers' Co-operative, in Via Principe Umberto. At that time I was on the Board of Directors of the Co-operative. About forty people were present at the meeting, almost all members of the Co-operative; and in their midst were Frank Coppola and Senator Messeri. We didn't know Messeri, and Frank Coppola explained to us that he was the new Christian Democrat candidate for whom we were to vote at the coming election.'

V

'Frank Coppola comes to Partinico several days before the elections. In 1958 Frank Coppola came up to me not far from our house and told me to vote for Messeri. "You will vote for Messeri?" he said, and he gave me a slip of paper where it said to vote for Messeri. "We must get this person in," he said, "and then we can get him to help us in return."

Frank Coppola also did propaganda for Messeri through his relatives Giacomo Coppola (who handed out facsimiles[1] saying "vote for Messeri"), and his sister. During the 1958 elections Frank Coppola's cronies were sent *pasta*, which was distributed among everybody who had got other people to vote for Messeri.

During the last elections, on the 28th April 1963, a nephew of Frank Coppola, Pino Coppola, was driving people to vote in his Fiat.'

VI

'A few days before the General Election in '63, I was invited to the house of the Christian Democrat ex-mayor Lo Grasso. There was a large crowd there surrounding Senator Messeri and Frank Coppola who sat beside him during the meeting. The purpose of the meeting was to get Senator Messeri elected. There were one or two requests for favours or assistance, to which Frank Coppola replied

[1] Facsimiles of the ballot papers with the party vote and the preference vote appropriately filled in—a common form of election propaganda. (Tr. note.)

authoritatively: "For the moment let's concentrate on giving him our votes, and we'll talk about that afterwards—he'll help us afterwards. When he's secured his place, then we can ask him."

The meeting started at 9 p.m., and ended at about 10.

I think that out of everyone at the meeting, including Messeri, the most respected figure was Frank Coppola.'

VII

'On Sunday November 17th in the vicinity of the Extra Bar we met Police Sergeant Zito: during a protracted and confidential conversation we commented on the posters recently put out by Messeri. Zito told us plainly: "Here in Partinico it's well known—we've all seen—that Frank Coppola has been campaigning for Messeri."

We also spoke of a closed meeting of DC members which Frank Coppola had attended: Sergeant Zito affirmed his knowledge of this.'

VIII

This, in essence, is what we were told by the Christian Democrat ex-Mayor of Partinico:

'The association between Frank Coppola and Messeri is common knowledge in and around Partinico . . . In fact this association was to a large extent quite open because it never occurred to anyone that a Parliamentary Commission of Enquiry into the Mafia would be set up, and it was assumed that things would just continue in the same way. In other words, that it would go on being possible to procure votes by bribes (apparently Messeri distributed large sums of money in order to become a Senator) and by ensuring protection for mafiosi supporters by way of an opportune telephone call through the Home Office or the Prefect of Police.'

Meanwhile we hear that Frank Coppola told a number of people: 'I've come from Rome to help Messeri, we're old friends from Chicago days.'

IX

. . . In the course of a conversation a policeman expressed his scepticism about the Antimafia Commission. He said: 'But do you really believe the Commission is in earnest?' As regards the part played by the police themselves in the battle against the mafia, he said (to quote his own words): 'We're too obstructed by political interference from above to be able to act.'

X

We go to the *carabinieri* offices to report to the Lieutenant of the *carabinieri* (presumably the only person in the area who, as representative of the State, proposes to document and to combat the phenomenon of the mafia) that on the 13th of last month we handed over documents, as we were asked, to the Parliamentary Commission of Enquiry into the Mafia. We asked for the Lieutenant. A young Lieutenant whom we have never seen before appears.

'Is Lieutenant Lancieri here?'

'He's been transferred, I'm here in his place.'

'How can he have been transferred? Barely a week ago he had no idea he was to be transferred.'

'I had no idea I was to come here, either: I was sent down suddenly two days ago to replace him.'

Later we are to find out that Lieutenant Lancieri (being a conscientious man, he has no doubt been exactly documenting the situation of particular local mafiosi) has been sent to Palermo, where he will remain off duty for a month; subsequently he will be appointed to command over the practically disused airport of Boccadifalco. Promoted to Captain, of course. But far removed from anything that smells of mafia.

Who is it who has had the Lieutenant removed so suddenly, after his name had been quoted with respect to the Commission? And why?

XI

'Don't you know that Gaspare Centineo (who has now replaced Santo Fleres, the old capomafia who was murdered) is a man not to

4

leave tracks behind him? He's Frank Coppola's man in the area: it's his house that Frank Coppola comes to when he arrives, the neighbours see that—and others not so near know it too. Both these two are linked with Messeri: Centineo, at Coppola's instigation, gets the *Bonomiana* to vote for Messeri. These men are capable of having someone shot in broad daylight, and no one would be able to bring anything against them because they've got the Government and the police on their side.'

XII

In Corso dei Mille in front of the mother church, Police Sergeant Zito:

'The police are under no obligation to ascertain and note the presence and the movements of Frank Coppola, who is free to move about like any ordinary citizen.'

XIII

From the report presented by Lieutenant Colonel Vittorio Montanari of the Customs and Excise at the Attorney's Office, Trapani, 1952:

'Coppola, Francesco Paolo, is undoubtedly the key figure in the drug traffic of which a part was uncovered at Alcamo. His full responsibility is amply proven by evidence collected at Anzio and Aprilia, from which it clearly emerged that the trunk containing the drugs had been in his house and in his custody, and that on his orders it was handed over by his son-in-law Corso, Giuseppe, to Manzini, Paolo, in order that the latter should have custody of it and subsequently effect its transfer into the custody of Mancuso, Serafino.

He appears, moreover, to be at the head of the whole drug traffic organization which during these last few years has been hoarding and smuggling out to America large quantities of narcotics, as related in this same report and in those drawn up on 8th June 1951 and 14th November 1951.

Further proof of his role as ringleader lies in the fact that all his accomplices refer to him for orders. He is the recipient of an abundant flow of the wherewithal to pay for the goods, this being delivered either by post, or in person by trusted agents appointed to collect the drugs. All the correspondence confiscated, whether from Coppola himself or from Carollo or Mancuso, fully demonstrates that no step was taken without Coppola himself having first issued the orders.'

XIV

Copy of a letter addressed to one of Girolamo Messeri's electoral propagandists.

ENEL
Sicilian Electricity Board
TIFEO, *Energy Production Co.*
Sicilian Thermoelectric Co.
Provisional Manager

Palermo, 12th September '63

Dear Sir,
    Senator Girolamo Messeri has made warm recommendations to me on your behalf, drawing my attention to the fact that on March 15th last he presented a request for your appointment to this Company.
    It is my fervent wish to be able to further your ambitions, particularly if this will afford some gratification to Senator Messeri.
    I can assure you, therefore, that I have taken note of your name and hope to be able to oblige at the earliest opportunity.
    Meanwhile I remain, Sir,
                    Yours sincerely,
                    Avv. Filippo Maniscalco

XV

'This year on the Feast of the Madonna of the Bridge, before the General Election, I was standing beside my car at the edge of the road, not far from the Sanctuary.

Just next to us, in front, was the Partinico Police van. Officer Esposito was telling me to move my car in order to leave the road clear, when along came another car containing Valenza[1] of Borgetto, Pino Blanda, branch secretary of the Partinico Christian Democrats, and Senator Girolamo Messeri. That it was Senator Messeri I am quite certain, becaus e Officer Esposito said out loud: "So it's come to that, now! Messeri going around with Valenza!"—because the police know quite well what sort of a mafioso Valenza is.

As soon as the road was cleared, Messeri's and Valenza's car continued on its way and stopped in front of the Sanctuary.'

9th December 1963

Senator Girolamo Messeri has been appointed Under-Secretary of State to the Ministry of Foreign Trade, the Minister being his fellow townsman Bernardo Mattarella. Among other things Messeri is Chairman of the Interministerial Committee for the Examination of Temporary Import and Export Licences, of the Committee for interest rebate grants to exporters of market garden produce and citrus fruits, and of the Foreign Trade Subsidies Fund.

7th July 1964

The first Moro Government fell on June 26th, and at the moment a new government is being formed. Copies of the documents on the Messeri–Coppola association have been sent confidentially to various Members of Parliament: Rumor, Moro, Tanassi, Saragat, Reale, Longo, De Martino and Nenni.

18th July 1964

We have received assurances from some of the party secretaries that they have 'carefully examined the documents received' and that in one way or another they will take due action.

24th July 1964

Senator Messeri is reconfirmed in his appointment as Under-

---

[1] See p. 84, under *March 1966*. (Tr.)

Secretary for Foreign Trade—the Minister being Bernardo Mattarella—in the second Moro Government.

3rd–4th October 1964

Rome. At the Study Conference on the mafia held under the auspices of the journals *Astrolabio, Espresso, Nuovi Argomenti, Ponte, Cronache Meridionali, Politica e Mezzogiorno,* the documents relating to the Messeri–Coppola association are made public.

October–November 1964

The Italian and foreign press devotes considerable attention to the report on the Messeri–Coppola association, giving long extracts: one or two journals publish all the above documents in full (*Nord e Sud, Questitalia, Cronache Meridionali*).

6th December 1964

Under-Secretary Giromalo Messeri, for reasons which are not made clear, tenders his resignation. Within the next few days this is accepted: if there is to be a scandal, better that it should be outside the Government—or better still if it could be avoided altogether.

For the next few days no one, not even the left-wing parties, mentions Messeri in public. If the phenomenon is not firmly exposed, another man no different from Santi Savarino and Messeri will be elected in their place next time. Even though there is no such thing in the area as a left-wing politician who is a mafioso or in definite electoral complicity with mafiosi, nevertheless it is plain that a number of them are still carrying on according to the rules of the old clientship game.

16th February 1965

Gaspare Centineo, Director of the Partinico *Bonomiana*, ex-Chairman of the syndicate of landowners to be expropriated for the Iato dam, has been arrested and charged with 'conspiring for criminal purposes and for carrying arms'.

In January of last year he had appeared before the criminal section of the special Court in Palermo and been sentenced to four years of special surveillance for having attempted to monopolize—obviously not by legitimate commercial means—the transport of earth for the Iato dam: having vainly opposed the construction of the dam, he was now trying to profit from it. Subsequently Centineo returned to the limelight on the occasion of the arrest of the multi-murderer Luciano Liggio, capomafia of Corleone, who, when arrested on 15th May '64, was found to be carrying identification papers in the name of Gaspare Centineo of Partinico. The investigating police 'with said identification papers traced Centineo in Partinico: he declared that he had lost them in a bus and had duly reported loss of same to the police . . .' In the course of the inquiry the police authorities ascertained that Luciano Liggio had been running the one-arm bandit and pin table racket in Palermo and Province; the profits, amounting to over a million lire a day, were divided among supervisors, promoters and friends.

A large number of the machines located in the area of Partinico, Borgetto, Trappeto, Cinisi, Carini, Montelepre and Torretta were controlled by the brothers Domenico and Giacomo Coppola, nephews of Frank Coppola. And Centineo himself controlled about thirty of them in Palermo, San Giuseppe Iato, Balestrate, Cinisi, Sferracavallo, Monreale: all towns within the same electoral college.

In the winter of '63, the mechanic in charge of maintenance was taken by Centineo to Florence to learn how to repair a new type of machine from the firm that made them. During his stay in Florence he received numerous telephone calls from Anzio: this was Frank Coppola calling in case he needed any help or advice.

2nd August 1965

Frank Coppola is arrested in the course of an anti-drug operation carried out by the Palermo police in collaboration with Interpol. Others arrested with him are Genco Russo[1] (the capomafia of Mussomeli who had been exiled to Lovere), Filippo Joe Imperiale

[1] Successor to Don Calo Vizzini as Head of the whole Sicilian mafia (cf. p. 311) (Tr. note).

of Palermo, Rosario Vitaliti of Giardini, Vincenzo Martinez of Marsala, Calogero Orlando of Terrasini (living in New York), and Frank Garofalo, Diego Plaja, Giuseppe Magaddino, Giuseppe Scandariato, all of Castellammare del Golfo. Four others cannot be traced.

All are accused of organizing or carrying on or financing illicit trade between Italy and the United States. The statement issued to the press by police headquarters in Palermo again confirms that Girolamo Messeri's chief election campaigner did not have an immaculate record:

'Coppola, Francesco Paolo (also known as Trigger-happy or Three-Finger Frank).

Previous convictions: murders, criminal association, clandestine drug-trafficking, extortion, armed robbery; deported as undesirable from the U.S.A. in 1948.'

All the papers report the news and give full particulars of the men accused (it is time now for even the *Giornale di Sicilia* to re-align itself—it is unwise and dangerous to go on backing losers): Frank Coppola, who entered the U.S. secretly in 1926, began by working with coin machines, earning himself the title of King of the coin machines of Kansas City. Expelled from the U.S. in 1948, he settled in Anzio: but apparently this did not prevent him from organizing international contraband trade and from attending, among other things, a meeting of Sicilian–American mafiosi held at the Grand Hotel delle Palme, preliminary to the big mafia gangland meeting at Apalachin in the U.S.

3rd August 1965

People in Partinico are puzzled by the news of Coppola's arrest.

An intelligent and well-informed person says to me: 'Clearly if they've given so much publicity to the news—it's even been talked about on T.V.—then they are taking it seriously. I hope so, I believe they will: but at the back of my mind there's still a doubt.'

Another, a poor young man with a prison record: 'No—he won't stay in prison, that one. Six months and he'll be out. He's got too much money. It's us who go to prison, not types like him. Six

months, and he's outside. There's a pipeline to him from America—
what d'you think! He'll be out soon. In any case, what's the charge?
Criminal association and trafficking in dust. And for that. . . ?'

Yesterday's *L'Ora* sold like hot cakes. Everyone who can read
is interested. But in general they don't talk. They easily change the
subject: 'Well, they've caught him . . .' 'So the papers say . . .'
'That's the end of the road, then . . .' 'But he's protected from
above . . .' 'We must just wait and see.'

One man says: 'They've put them inside for the time being, to
minimize the scandal: but before long—before the next elections—
they'll let them out again. The Christian Democrats are too compromised, and they need them. Even though people knew quite
well before who they were, they've always gone free.'[1]

21st December 1965

We learn from the papers that Frank Coppola, in his statement
before Magistrate Vigneri, has admitted to having supported
certain 'candidatures': among others, that of Girolamo Messeri.

March 1966

Over the last few months many people have at last begun to refer
openly to Valenza, Mayor of Borgetto, as a dangerous mafioso. On
the 19th March he is charged as instigator of four murders and four
attempted murders, but . . . he is not to be found: he has—comfortably, it's said—gone into hiding.

June–July–August 1966

Thousands, tens of thousands of people in the area are asking
themselves: years ago, the intimate association between DC Senator
Santi Savarino and Frank Coppola[2] had already been publicly

---

[1] In 1968, they were all acquitted.

[2] Notorious well beyond the bounds of this area is the letter from Santi
Savarino of Partinico to Frank Coppola ('Don Ciccio'), read out in the Senate
by Girolamo Li Causi on 14th October 1952:

denounced—but nothing was done. They said then that a Parliamentary Anti-mafia Commission ought to be set up, in which non-Sicilian Members of Parliament would also take part. Now this Commission exists: why does it not take a firm and explicit line on the Messeri case?

25th September 1966

According to the *Washington Post*, four days ago Girolamo Messeri had a private interview with MacNamara, lasting over an hour.

31st January 1967

Parliament learns to its great surprise and mortification, in the course of a fierce debate, that Messeri went to Washington 'for an exchange of ideas on the subject of NATO': in fact, unbeknown even to the Minister of Defence himself, the Hon. Tremelloni.

Giornale D'Italia
The Editor

My dear Don Ciccio,
   Though I must reproach you, I cannot but accept the kind thought that reveals your nature and bears witness to the warmth of your feeling for me. I am profoundly grateful. I can assure you that I reciprocate your valued friendship with equal warmth.
   We are both from Partinico, and understand one another perfectly. You can count on me. I have not yet received a reply from Athens, but as soon as it arrives I shall let you know. Come and see me whenever you like: it will always be a pleasure to see you.
   Thank you again for your splendid present.
                    Believe me,
                    Yours most affectionately,
                              Santi Savarino

Workers on the Iato Dam Site

A hundred and eighty-one workers are suddenly dismissed without notice from the Iato dam site, and construction work is suspended. Together with about a hundred workers we decide to resist on the site.

At the same time, we were supposed to have been having a discussion with twenty schoolteachers on the theme: 'What are the obstacles to group work, to group life, in our area?' We decide to hold a joint meeting of workers and teachers, on the dam site itself.

Here is the rough summary of points that emerged from the discussion:

——It is above all the moment of revolution that brings people into association; but revolutions happen when people are driven by need, and need here has never reached the point of explosion: it doesn't snow here in winter, and so for centuries even when people have had nothing they could always fall back on eating wild herbs.

——There's passivity, stagnation; there's no impetus towards change. We wait for other people to solve our problems.

——There's a lack of initiative, and of organizational sense.

——Fear of the bosses, of the ruling class.

——People talk and don't act; they make decisions but don't stick to them.

——Those in power won't help, in fact they try to hinder the formation and development of self-reliant groups.

——People's differences of character and differences of opinion.

——People are suspicious, they don't trust others.

——The difficulty of coming to an agreement within the group.

——A lack of trust in the leaders.

——A lack of courage and of self-confidence.

——There aren't meetings.

——We're not taught to live in groups, either at school or anywhere else.

——We don't encourage each other.

——The difficulty of expressing oneself.

——A lack of culture, of clearness.

——It's difficult to keep democracy moving forward all the time.

——We lack experience of group life even in the home.

——The false education we get; the superstitions and the inadequate traditions we're surrounded by.

On these last two points I have a conversation with three of the workmen: Giuseppe, aged fifty-five; Castrense, thirty-five; and Salvatore, thirty-eight.

SALVATORE: The unity of a family comes more from self-interest than for social reasons.

GIUSEPPE: The father represents a kind of dictator; he says a thing, and he enforces it, and the son must obey, otherwise people will say he's badly brought up. The father teaches them how to live in society; he says: mind who has good intentions towards you and who has bad intentions. That's what the father's duty consists of: if he isn't a kind of dictator, the sons'll start saying: 'My father's always telling us off, but he never actually does anything to stop us.'

A child grows up and sees that he has to obey his father, the family's the first group he comes across. It's logical, then, that people get the idea that to stay united a group needs to have one man who says: 'We must do this, we must do that' and the rest who are smaller must obey. This authority of the father used to be very powerful here, but now it's beginning to wane a bit as the children get educated, and the more they go to school the more knowing they get.

People say that the mother must be obedient to her husband. In Albania I saw women veiled—here in Sicily they're not veiled, but they're held on a tight rein just the same. A man wants to be master of his property: I'm jealous of my family like I'm jealous of the money in my pocket. But when a man sees that his woman is sensible, then he'll leave things to her. If she starts to go askew, though, he'll put the pressure on her. As long as the wife and children act according to his orders, then there's freedom, and he'll consult the family too before making decisions.

SALVATORE: I'll give you my humble opinion: the father is the main support of the family, and if the mother agrees with him then she's a support too. As for this dictatorship: this dictatorship Giuseppe was talking about may not be a good thing, but in certain cases it has to be asserted. Why? If in a family neither the father nor the mother imposes this strictness, then there can't be any discipline or any education.

GIUSEPPE: But the mother leaves things to the father, she says to the children: 'Just you wait till your father gets home, then we'll see . . .'

SALVATORE: Yes, but it's the mother who has most contact with the children.

CASTRENSE: It's not as if people's understanding of the world has only just dawned this minute—it's been going round for generations. I feel happier educating the old-fashioned ways to my child. Good tradition is handed down from father to son. A father ought to carry a certain awe in the house, there ought to be a certain superstition around him; even if it's not in his nature to be totalitarian, he should be able to make the children do as they ought.

GIUSEPPE: But men should live by their own experience, too: what my father taught me is all very well, but as well as that I ought to hand on to my son what I've learnt myself. For instance, my father used to order me: 'You've got to be in by such and such a time—full stop.' It didn't occur to him to give reasons. But now that I'm grown up, I see that was wrong of him. A man can learn to live by making steps on his own, too: if he lets himself be led by others the whole time, then there's no more progress.

SALVATORE: We've always lived off fear. For instance, it's always said that if you stay out late at night you may get shot, even if it's only by mistake. That's why the father has to give orders, because the son doesn't know about that sort of thing. He doesn't know—and so the father has to dictate.

CASTRENSE: That's why it's right that until the son grows up to be a man the father should feel responsible for teaching him the good things he's learnt himself.

GIUSEPPE: To the boy, the father gives orders and advice: to the girl, it's just orders—no advice. 'Don't stand at the door', 'don't catch cold'—which means don't stand there looking at the young men. But he doesn't give any reasons or explanations of the good and the bad that might come of it, because they think that would be too shocking. The sons are allowed to look after their own affairs, though, and when the father or mother notice something's going on, if she's a suitable match they keep quiet about it—but if she's unsuitable, they'll say: 'Aren't you ashamed of yourself carrying on like that?'

We're not mature yet. The idea a boy forms of a group is first of all the family as he's known it; then later when he goes out to play with other boys it's always the biggest one who says: 'You've got to do as I say or I'll knock your block off!' Then at school it's just discipline; and then in the world around him he sees co-operatives failing all over the place (though just now it's true there's a bit of progress in the Union). And so it's very hard for a fellow to learn these things.

What ought to be done is to give these grown men a certain importance so that they can have a chance to experience these things themselves. Because if they haven't tried living this way, working together, it'll always be impossible to create new ideas, we'll never succeed in changing things, in making everything different from what it is now.

Anyone who goes in for trade union activities gets denounced by the bosses as *infame*: that means someone who acts as an informer, someone who breaks the old rules we have here which say the boss should be boss and whoever is under stays under. And because people are afraid of this, progress is impossible.

For example—here's how you'll hear people talk about someone who's the son of a mafioso: 'His father owned seven pair of . . .' and so on. Because he'd no doubt done his little bit of robbery, and a spot of bullying, and perhaps a murder or two, the people have a certain respect and admiration—not just for the father, but even for the sons as well.

CASTRENSE: If some big fellow has decided something, and I who count for nothing in society come along and say to somebody: 'But d'you think that's right?' he'll only answer: 'Well, d'you want to go and have a word with him about it then?'—as much as to say, 'how could a silly ass like you be right!' and he'll just call me an ignorant fool, and my things just won't enter into his head.

GIUSEPPE: There was a man here who worked for a boss—Russo was his name; he'd worked for him all his life. And when he died, what little he had to leave—he left it to his boss, and not to his nephews. He was so subjugated by that man that he must have felt like a dog feels about its master. A good hunting dog catches a rabbit and takes it to its master.

The Honourable Grimaldi,
Head of Sicilian Regional Development

The Hon. Grimaldi, Officer in charge of Development, has the reputation of being a reasonable man, one of the best members of the Regional Government. I ring his secretary to arrange an appointment, which is readily agreed on. I dictate to the secretary the questions I intend to ask, so that the none too simple theme will be quite clear:

1: To what extent do you consider the difficulty of group work, of associative life, a hindrance to the development of Sicily?

2: What do you think are the main obstacles in Sicily to the realization of genuinely democratic planning: i.e. planning that involves maximum participation by the people and effective development for the whole population?

3: For what reasons have the various attempts at a Regional Plan so far failed to achieve any positive results?

I am particularly anxious to have this discussion with the man (we might call him, in effect, the minister for Sicilian development) who is now preparing to launch the new Regional Development Plan.

He is friendly when we meet. He reads and rereads the questions, but apparently he does not understand them: even when I try to clarify, his answers have nothing to do with the questions. In the end he makes a decision which is a relief to both of us: he will think it over and send me the answers in writing.

In spite of repeated solicitations on my part, and repeated assurances on his (the Hon. Member has now moved to another department), these answers have never arrived.

The Honourable Calogero Volpe

I meet the Honourable Calogero Volpe, repeatedly referred to in the national and foreign Press as the Deputy for the rural mafia; Under-Secretary of State to the Ministry of Health, ex-Under-Secretary to the Ministry of Transport, elected as a Christian Democrat in the electoral college of Western Sicily uninterruptedly since 1946. These are the questions I put to him:

——How would you describe the socio-political structure of the countryside around Palermo?

——What, in your opinion, are the greatest obstacles to associative life in Palermo Province?

——What are the forms of collaboration that function most actively in the Province?

——What do you think is the reason for the scarce participation in political and trade union activities?

——What are the forces that elect you, and what is your relationship with them?

——Which groups do you think ought to be developed and encouraged?

From the Under-Secretary's confused reply (studded with 'these are my own original ideas . . .' 'This is medical psychology which you non-doctors cannot grasp . . .') the following observations stand out: . . . As for the parties, ninety per cent join them because the Christian Democrats say: 'I promise you so and so', and the Communist Party says: 'I promise you such and such', and the other parties: 'I promise you this or that'. Then when the man joins one or the other, he has to wait and see before he's convinced; he suspends judgement until he gets what he's been promised. It's one thing to give formal allegiance, but quite another matter to give substantial support. If a man doesn't get what he wants, he changes sides, he swaps parties. If his wishes aren't immediately fulfilled, he immediately changes over to a different party or organization because he's in need. In what I call a hyperevolutionary milieu, there is freedom from need: not here.

. . . When Volpe is standing, even certain Communist sectors vote Volpe. They greet me with the closed fist salute, and I answer them the same way, as much as to say 'just leave things to me to settle as I think best!'

My electorate is made up of peasants, owner-farmers, a few masons, artisans; but above all swarms and swarms of peasants, 81,000 votes. And to this 81,000 one must add a further 80,000 who say they will vote for me and then don't: 'I'll vote for you, so you must remember me.'

There isn't a single party demonstration at which I don't speak; there isn't a single demonstration of the Owner-farmers' Association at which I don't speak. During the election campaign, in a month and a half I attend as many as a hundred and fifty meetings. They call me the electoral bomber! As many as three public meetings a day, quite apart from all the private ones. They call me the electoral bomber. In normal times I have at least one meeting a week. Today I've spoken here, tomorrow I'll be speaking in Palermo, the next day in Bari, and the day after that in Rome. . . .

I chanced upon this interesting statement, written and signed by the Honourable Member himself on paper headed *Chamber of Deputies*: "The Mafia, in the sense of development of the human personality, is an expression of the Sicilian mentality."

From the record of proceedings at the Colajanni trial (no. 1291/51 at the Court of Palermo) we learn that Calogero Volpe, who is related to well-known ringleaders of the American underworld, is godfather to the daughter of the notorious mafioso Calogero Castiglione of Mussumeli, known as 'Farfariello' (brother-in-law of capomafia Giuseppe Genco Russo); we also learn, among other things, that Volpe was doctor to the former head of the mafia, Calogero Vizzini, and on friendly terms with his circle. Volpe doesn't remember whether or not he is also godfather to the son of Genco Russo.

A Group of Children

Early one morning when it was still quite dark, Bruna, Libera, Cielo, Ruggero, Amico and I set off from Partinico to walk all the way over the mountains to Palermo.

After we had gone a few kilometres, Libera observed that if she looked down at her feet as she walked, the earth seemed to be rushing away beneath her, and yet in the distance it seemed to be standing still—it *seemed* to be. Then someone suggested that we should try making a poem together, and I agreed to join in too; and in the end not one but four poems were composed (at least, for us they were poems), before we came out at last on Bellolampo and looked down on Palermo, clear and beautiful in its wide bay.

I

When you look down at the earth beneath you
When you are walking
It whirls away giddily under your feet.
But if you look some way ahead
It comes more slowly towards you,
And the further you look, the stiller it seems.
Firm in the flow of the ages,
Blue under the wheeling stars.
The earth seems still.

II

Even smoke can be beautiful too,
Rising from burning weeds,
Or from the chalk pits
Or from some chimney in winter
As we saw at Borgetto,
Gently rising into the thinning mist,
Into the clean sky.

94

III

Up in the open above Montelepre
Eating our fresh-baked bread and cheese
Looking down over the wide bay,
Cielo flings sharp blue rockets into the valley.
Now we are walking through white fields scented with honey.
'What shall we call this walk today,
All the way to Palermo?' asks Libera.
'A walk,' says Danilo,
'A journey,' says Cielo.
'Then what would it be if I went to India?'
'A journey,' they say.
'Then what should we call our walk today?'
'An excursion,' says Libera.
'And in fifty years' time if you go to the moon?'
'A journey,' they say.
'And in fifty years' time if you go to India?'
'Just an excursion.'
'In a hundred years' time . . .'

IV

Walking, walking . . .
'What do you think poetry is?' asks Danilo.
Bruna: 'It's verses.'
'So if there aren't verses, then it's not poetry?'
'It's something that comes from your mind and your heart.'
Cielo says: 'Poetry's looking at mountains,
And the sea and the earth and trees and plants,
And getting to know the whole world,
And then writing it down,
And then starting again to try to learn something else.'
'It's something so subtle,' says Bruna,
'That there's no other way of expressing it.'
'Poetry's this,' says Cielo: 'when you really understand it,
Then everything seems better,
And it makes a person happier.'

As we round the curve of the mountain road
A placard comes into view.
'If I see on that placard the name "LEACRIL"
Is that a poem?'
Cielo: 'No, it's a poster.'
Libera: 'But you could make poetry even out of a poster.'
Cielo: 'But there's nothing beautiful in an advertisement, is
    there?'
Libera: 'You can make poetry out of any word, anything.'
Bruna: 'But it must be a thing that already has poetry in it.'
Cielo: 'Poetry's not just a matter of, say, ending the line with
    an "m".'
Amico: 'Poetry and music say things that can't be said with
    ordinary words.'
'But what *is* poetry?'
'I know what it is,' says Ruggero:
'You must think of something quite new,
Something that doesn't exist yet.'
'So poetry's like a journey, then, always going further and further.'
Cielo: 'Icarus was poetry at first—
The dream of being able to fly.
But now there are aeroplanes, so it's not a dream any more.'
Ruggero: 'Flying can still be a dream, for someone who's never
    done it.'
Cielo: 'So flying can still be poetry.'
Libera: 'And for a bird, too, flying is still poetry.'
Bruna: 'If the bird feels like we do this morning,
Going on its way, journeying, discovering new things.'
Danilo: 'So you think, then, that poetry's a journey, always going
    further and further—
And also a way of seeing better a thing that is near and
    familiar?'

Now Daniela (aged four) and Chiara (aged six) are also with us.

AMICO: White horses are always the fastest runners.
DANIELA: Yes, white horses are more beautiful, and they're
stronger too.

CIELO: Because they're lighter.

DANIELA: Yes, they're lighter.

CHIARA: Yes, of course the white ones are lighter.

DANILO: Why are the white ones lighter?

CIELO: Because they're happier.

AMICO: They're lighter because the white is paler, and so it's lighter. For instance, when I'm wearing white, I can run faster.

CHIARA: The white's lighter.

LIBERA: But there are some white horses that are not so strong, and some dark ones that are stronger. At last year's August races, I remember, there were three horses: one dark brown and two light brown—and it was the dark horse that won.

CIELO: Ah, but the two that lost weren't *white* horses, were they?

DANILO: Chiara and Amico, what do you say?

AMICO: Well, if we go by what Libera just told us, then it's the dark ones that are fastest.

CIELO: But if the two paler ones had been *white* horses, they could have won.

LIBERA: But what if the white horses were tired, and couldn't manage to overtake the dark one?

CIELO: Well, perhaps the dark one might be in better training than the white ones—or perhaps it might be the other way round.

Then I suppose that would mean that running faster and winning depends on training more than on the colour of the horse.

LIBERA: Yes, that's just what I was getting at.

AMICO: Now I come to think of it, I agree with Libera and Cielo —I think they must be right. If a horse is tired or weak, how can it run well?

CIELO: Perhaps the two pale horses ran less fast because their shoes hadn't been put on properly, and a nail had come loose, or something. Or maybe they were smaller, and took shorter strides.

RUGGERO: It depends on the jockeys, too.

DANILO: Well then, what does the greater speed of a horse depend on?

CHIARA: How d'you mean?

LIBERA: He means, what makes one horse run faster.

AMICO: I'm not a specialist in horses, so I couldn't say which sort are fastest. To find out for certain, I'd like to try out a whole lot, and make them run one by one, and see which was fastest.

CIELO: It depends on their training, it depends on their strength, and on the length of their legs. And on their age, too.

CHIARA: Yes, when a horse is old it's not quite so strong.

DANILO: And does it depend on the colour, too, if a horse is faster or slower?

DANIELA: White horses are faster—I like them best.

CHIARA: A white horse is faster when it's well trained, and when its legs are longer, and when it's stronger.

LIBERA: Could you repeat the question you asked just then?

DANILO: Does it depend on the colour as well, if a horse is faster or slower?

LIBERA: The thing is, we like white horses best, and so we *want* them to be stronger and faster than other horses. But in order to be certain that what we *want* to be true really *is* true, we'd have to test it out, like Amico said.

CIELO: Yes—for instance, we like to think that trees talk to each other—that even trees are alive too. We like to think that all sorts of things do really talk to each other; even though we can't hear them, we like to think they do talk all the same. But we would have to test it out to see if it was really true.

LIBERA: And also we'd like it if the stars talked to each other: but we'd have to try to test if it was true. It must be true in a way, though, because we know they attract each other, and so there must be some sort of communication between them.

BRUNA: And another example. People say that all men are brothers, because they'd *like* that to be true: but we only have to look around to see how the mafia oppresses the peasants, and how no one does anything to find work for all the unemployed, and how people won't get together and co-operate but go round shooting each other instead, and making war. For men to be brothers really, they'd have to unite and co-operate—whereas now it's still 'every man for himself'.

CIELO: You know when we went on the Peace March the other day? You remember the policemen marching along on our left, every ten metres or so? Well, why didn't the one beside us answer when I asked him what his name was? And then when Amico said, 'Perhaps he's dumb'—I still don't see why he gave us such a nasty look.

Vincenzo Tusa,
an archaeologist, outlines Palermo's history

It is impossible, I think, to understand the present situation of Palermo without knowing the city's history; and we cannot trace even the bare outline of the city's history unless we see it as part of the history of Sicily as a whole. So I will try to give you a summary of some of the basic facts, as well as I can off the cuff like this.

In very ancient times, I mean at least two thousand years B.C., Sicily may have been inhabited by a single people, possibly autochthonous, possibly come from elsewhere, though no one can say where. However, there is no real evidence for this, either historical or archaeological: it is only a hypothesis. The earliest reliable evidence is provided by Greek writers of the fifth century B.C., writing about prehistoric times: they refer to two different peoples, of different origins, one lot inhabiting Western and the other Eastern Sicily. The first were the Sicani (later apparently united with the Elimi), and the second the Siculi. We cannot draw an exact boundary between them, even for historic times, but it is certain that there was this distinction between the two peoples. Both the Siculi and the Sicani were basically farmers, and we can assume that each town (among both Sicani and Siculi) would have had its chief, who would be a kind of little king. In prehistoric times, all over the countryside around Palermo—and in Palermo itself in the Bronze Age and the Iron Age—there were little clusters of dwellings, little groups of a few dozen people each, making their living out of rudimentary agriculture. The nucleus of the group would be the hut of the father of the family, or the village chief.

Coming to historic times, we find the Phoenicians at Palermo; they were seafaring traders, and it is very unlikely that they developed any advanced form of community life. About the twelfth century B.C. the Phoenicians first put out from the coast of what is now Lebanon and Israel, and sailed across the Mediterranean to Gibraltar; at the end of the twelfth century, according to reliable historical and archaeological evidence, they founded Cadiz. In the region of what is now Palermo they came upon these little farming settlements, and tried to sell them their merchandise. Then sooner or later they decided to stay themselves, at Palermo, and Mozia, and Solunto—as we learn also from written tradition, from Thucydides, Diodorus Siculus and others.

In the light of both historical and archaeological evidence we can say that the Greek presence never penetrated westwards of an imaginary line between Imera in the north and Selinunte in the south: there was never a Greek political presence in this area. In the eighth century, when the Greeks began to establish their colonies in Sicily and in Magna Graeca, and after the Phoenicians had founded Carthage (814 B.C.), these two peoples more or less reached a *modus vivendi* with regard to Sicily: the Phoenicians (who after the founding of Carthage were known as Poeni, Punics,) confined themselves to Western Sicily, while the Greeks occupied Central and Eastern Sicily.

The Punic townships have never been excavated, so we do not know how the people lived—we have no archaeological data to tell us what sort of life they led: the settlement at Mozia, for example, has never been excavated. One reason for this is that it is only quite recently that the specific aim of the archaeologist has become that of studying the origins and the nature of the people who preceded us, studying every aspect of their lives: previously their chief interest was the romantic search for the beautiful object.

The Romans who united Sicily by force in the second half of the third century B.C. certainly did not arrive there with benevolent intentions: under them, conditions for the Sicilians (who under the Greeks had at least enjoyed a certain freedom) grew worse. It was then that the *latifundium* became a serious evil in the agrarian economy of the Island; there was less free labour, the land was entrusted mainly to slaves from the Orient, and arable farming gave way to pastoral farming. That was the period of the great slave revolts, forcibly suppressed by the Romans who devastated both towns and countryside of their 'granary', as Sicily used to be called.

Early Christianity scarcely touched Western Sicily; it was stronger in the East, particularly at Syracuse: we know this from the vast number of relics found there, while in Western Sicily there are very few.

When Carthage under the Vandals rose again to dominate the Mediterranean, Sicily underwent another period of Carthaginian occupation.

During the Byzantine period, the capital of the Empire was moved for a short time to Syracuse, and so all Sicily came under Byzantine rule, in spite of the resistance of Palermo: and so Greek influence—predominant in Eastern Sicily—was renewed again, though this time with a Byzantine flavour.

The Byzantine rule was succeeded by Arab rule, which lasted for three centuries: this was a period of growth for Palermo in particular. But in spite of a certain prosperity, in spite of Palermo's glittering mosques—four hundred of them—and the refined culture of the Court, it cannot be said that the Sicilians enjoyed much freedom under the Arabs. The Arabs applied in Sicily the usual Muslim laws applied in lands conquered from the Infidel, and the bulk of the population lived in extreme poverty.

When the Normans reached Sicily at the end of the eleventh century, this did not mean the arrival of a population: it was an army that came, with its leaders, to rule over a native population of mixed Sicanian, Phoenician, Carthaginian and Arab origin. Whereas under Greece, despite the existence of slavery, there had been (within the limits of the different classes) a certain respect for the individual, and a certain weight given to each person's opinion, there is no record of anything of the sort under the Normans.

After the Norman and Swabian monarchy came the Angevins (with the episode of the Sicilian Vespers in 1282); and then, after the brief reign of the House of Aragon, the Spaniards: real obscurantism. Just think—to underline still more the difference between Western and Eastern Sicily: whereas in 1434 Alfonso of Aragon had founded the University in Catania, in Palermo his successor Ferdinand the Catholic set up in 1487 the Tribunal of the Holy Office, the Inquisition. And in this city, while the Viceroy's vast Court was full of favourites and protégés who earned their keep by singing the Viceroy's praises, the large plebeian population went hungry.

When has there ever been a real community here?

When has there ever been a proper community life?

After 1712, through the wars of the Spanish Succession, Sicily again changed hands, passing from the Spaniards to the Savoyards, then to the Austrians, and then to the Bourbon kings of Naples—just like any bit of property to be inherited or bought. The Bourbons ruled Sicily until 1860, and it certainly cannot be said that democracy made much progress during that period. It is well known, for instance, that the Bourbons hired out responsibility for Public Security on contract: and since the contractor's chief concern was to save money, to try and make something out of it for himself, the feudal landowners, seeing that the State was neglecting to safeguard their interests, took to hiring their own strong-arm men, the mafiosi, to protect them. So what else could the small peasant do but shrink into his shell?

The results of the union of Sicily with Italy we already know. And we know even better what a burden the feudal land system has been (in Western Sicily it was not until the last century that it even began to split up), and how the direct consequence of this system was the mafia. Over the last few hundred years Palermo has functioned as a centre for consumption of agricultural produce, its administration and its social life being dominated by the power of the feudal estates. The population of Palermo increased under the shadow of the great palaces, the poor lived off alms from the great landowners who stifled and smothered every revolution: the history of Palermo is one long story of abortive revolutions. When a Palermitan talks, you can hear in his voice the centuries of failure, humiliation, and defeat.

Since there has never been a central power for the protection of the individual, the individual—whether intellectual or starving poor—has always had to try and solve his problems by direct recourse to those in power: this is the origin of the political tradition of the exercise of power through personal relationships.

And so we see that the history of Sicily as a whole, and of Palermo in particular, is one long story of occupation, oppression, favouritism, patronage and clientship. I don't claim to know the whole history of this region in detail, but I believe I can truthfully say that there has never been any government in Sicily that was genuinely concerned with the good of the citizens: they have always been regarded as a more or less amorphous mass to be exploited in the interests of the various rulers who at various times have controlled the destiny of the Island. In this situation it is only natural, really, that the citizen, despairing of getting any help from his fellow men, should always have acted on his own behalf, trying to work on his own, and defending himself from injustice: and this is still the fundamental reason today for the lack of any effective forms of association, and of collective work.

The setting up of the autonomous Regional Government has given Sicily the first chance she has had in all her history to transform the situation. We must now make use of this opportunity: we must study carefully every aspect of the Island's situation, and then act accordingly.

A Street Cleaner

Beautiful, yes, very beautiful—but filthy. Filthy on the outskirts—but also in the centre, in certain places. In Via Maqueda, it's kept clean; in Via Roma and Via Liberta, it's kept clean. But Via Carini, now—that's filthy, and just about all the rest of the city is filthy.

Except for the workers, this is a city that wakes up late. At four o'clock, five o'clock, there's still nothing stirring. About six you begin to get one or two itinerant tradesmen going round the outlying districts, selling brooms, say, or vegetables, and here and there a basket is let down on string from a balcony. The cowmen go round with their cows selling milk, gradually the buses fill up; by about seven o'clock the building workers are on their way to work, some walking, some on bicycles, some on scooters. The bulk of us start work at half past six.

If my beat is here, but I have to go a long way off to tip the rubbish, it'll be an hour before I'm back. And by the time I get back, there's already as much rubbish again as what there was before I started. I mean to say, I sweep all this bit—this is my stretch—but by the time I've finished my stretch they've chucked out a whole lot more rubbish behind me. I can go back again and pick up a second lot in Via Maqueda, and the central bits where the gentry are, but in the less important places like Piazza Capo and Piazza Garraffello, where the filth would make your skin crawl, I'm not allowed to go back, I just have to push straight on.

Sometimes when the lorry doesn't come round we have to leave all the rubbish in the street to be collected next day, piled up in a little back alley—we're supposed to always dump it in the poorest bit, always at the feet and under the noses of the poorest people.

That alley between Piazza Bandiera and Via Napoli, in the centre —that's often completely blocked: the posh shops in the streets round there chuck all their rubbish into the alley, and then people come and pick through it for cardboard and other bits and pieces that might come in handy. Quite a few of the poor streets in the centre are used as rubbish dumps like that.

It's the firm of Vaselli who have the contract from the Council; but because they want to save money and make as much profit as possible, they don't have the proper equipment, so they don't do the job properly. You can take it from me—I know that's why. When the lorry comes round to pick up the refuse at the various collection points—we start work at half past six in the morning, so by quarter past or half past seven our bins are already full, but we have to wait till the lorry comes round before we can unload, and the lorry doesn't come till about quarter past or half past eight. Well, when the lorry does come, we tip in our first load, and then while it stands and waits we go back and fill our bins again. If there's room on the lorry then, you tip in your second load, but if there isn't room you have to hang about there waiting for an hour or an hour and a half, because the lorry has to go a long way off to tip the rubbish. It may be two hours, even, before it's back, but we just have to sit there waiting. And it's not as if our bins were just brim full and hermetically sealed—we pile baskets and stuff on top of the rubbish, too, we pile it up just out of love, every one of us, for the sake of keeping our own particular bit clean.

There's another thing, now: it's my day off today, and they're supposed to send another man along to take my place. However, rather than employ someone else, the superintendent will come along to you and say: 'Here, dustman, you'll have to do a bit extra today to cover the next stretch too.' And he'll say the same to the other fellow on the other side; and so the money stays in the pockets of Vaselli and Co., while the dustmen have to toil away even harder.

Lots of people loathe us. The streets are always dirty, no matter how hard we try. There are lots of beautiful houses here, palaces, old ones and new, and all this filth spoils the look of the place. But it's all so difficult. Sometimes you're sent to do a place in the early morning but the rubbish isn't thrown out till later on, after the people have got up, about eight or nine, and so it has to lie there in the street all day.

The Palermo the street cleaners know isn't the same Palermo you'd see by driving round in a posh car—we see it always through dust.

One swish of the broom, and up comes the dust, all over the legs of passers-by too—I ask you! But our own noses are so full of it we hardly notice it any more. When you first start, you feel it all going up your nose, and it stinks, and you get it in your eyes; when there's a wind it blows in your eyes and stings, and when you sweep the dust gets in your mouth, and in your ears, and everywhere. One sweep of the broom in an unpaved street will send dust right up to the first floor. People are annoyed, they get cross with us: 'Get along!' they say, 'Is this the time of day to be doing that?'

But it all depends whereabouts you're working. Some people understand all right, but there are others who don't understand at all: 'What are you doing here?' they say. 'Why don't you be off!'—or worse. Of course it's always the best-dressed people who object most when they get dust on them.

Some people do understand what a sacrifice our work is, but others—they really make my blood boil. What I say to them is this: 'All right,' I say; 'if you think I'm not doing anything, or if you think it would be better if I wasn't here at all, just you take the broom and have a go at sweeping yourself!' But on the other hand there are people who pity us—'Poor devils!' they say, when they see us toiling away in the dust. People come past sometimes while we're sitting waiting at one of the collection points—we're not sitting there just because we fancy it: we have to wait for the lorry—and they say, 'those lazy beggars won't do a hand's turn!' Where I work there's a fellow who's so poor I could buy him for a slave, and he comes by and he says to me: 'You just don't want to do this work!'

The dust gets in our socks, in our shoes, in our trousers; our clothes go quite stiff with all the dust and sweat, they turn into cardboard. You sweep and sweep, and thoughts keep coming into your head; you sweep away and think about home, each one of us as he sweeps is thinking about his own private affairs, thinking his own particular thoughts.

At half past eight or nine, the shops open. Office workers are supposed to start work then too, but . . . Say I'm the head of the office: I go in, ring the bell, and the porter appears: 'Listen, if anyone comes, say I'm in the bar, or tell them I've gone out for a moment.' Some of them just sign the register and go home again.

But at the end of the month, they get their pay all right.[1] There are lots of them like that—not all, of course, but there are lots like that in the Regional Government offices, in the Provincial Administration, the Town Hall, the Labour Exchange—all the various Council offices. The Health Insurance place is almost like a brothel at certain moments! Even at eleven o'clock in some offices there's still no one to be seen; and then by one o'clock or half past, they've all disappeared again. We're rotten with that sort of thing. Rotten. That's how Sicily was born, and that's how she's dying.

Giuliano had the whole of Sicily intimidated: *he* could have put everything right. He should have been King of Sicily and put everything in order. But they killed him: here anyone who wants to do something for the poor gets killed.

Our brooms stir up the dust, dust is stirred up by the lorries, dust is stirred up by the wind. Most passers-by just go about their own business, they carry on walking and keep themselves to themselves, they don't want anything to do with us. Every now and again there may be one who'll talk to us, but usually they don't. I might get one who'd talk to me today, say, and then maybe another the day after tomorrow: you go whole days alone among the dust.

Everybody goes about their own affairs, you don't often get a person sticking his nose into other people's business. But that's another thing I like about Palermo: it's beautiful, even though it is dirty—and it's a city where people mind their own business. Not everybody, but most people mind their own business. The rich man is rich, the poor man is poor, and they all mind their own business. Of course I'd like to be well-off too. But what am I supposed to do about it? Go out stealing? '*Lavoro e Chiesa,*' the saying is: work and Church, which means *Lavoro e Casa*, work and home. I'm just a humble working man.

This eye can't see the other eye. I work as a street cleaner, now, and let's suppose another fellow comes along to work as a street cleaner too: well, I've got my bit of bread, and it's only natural I

---

[1] It is by no means rare for civil servants to go into the office only on the 27th of the month: the Regional, Provincial, and Local Administration and the various Government agencies (such as ERAS, etc.) are grossly overstaffed with all the 'supernumeraries', etc., who have been given posts in exchange for services at elections.

should be jealous and not want somebody else to take it from me—
there are plenty who would. But on the whole people keep themselves to themselves.

We're in two groups, us cleaners: Group A, employed by the
Council—there's about 230 of them; and Group B, we're about
1,200 or 1,300, I'm not sure exactly how many, and we're employed
by the firm of Vaselli. It's always Vaselli who get the contract.
About fifty to fifty-three cleaners work at the Palace of Justice.
Then there are the watchmen: in my stretch alone there are eight
of them, and about forty or fifty altogether—and I tell you, they do
nothing. That's the watchman's job—to do nothing. Then there
are about forty supervisors, and they do practically nothing. That's
Palermo for you: if you have friends to pull strings, you can make
your living doing nothing at all. If not, you stay down in the
dust.

In some families the women go out shopping, but often it's the
men who go. Men here are strict about keeping their wives and
daughters indoors. From one o'clock till two is the busiest time of
day, for people and cars. That's when most office workers go for
lunch. But building workers mostly eat on the spot, sitting on the
pavements. In the poorer quarters they just have bread or chick-pea
cakes with a bit of cheese or something.

Then the office workers go home for a sleep—and that's the end
of their working day: the offices are closed till ten next morning,
even if it's a matter of life and death. In the evening, people from
upper-class Palermo stroll down towards the centre, and in summer
they go down to the sea at Mondello. The poor folk stand in their
doorways in the evening, or sit on their balconies; or those who can
afford it go down to the harbour and eat oysters and squids. In the
poorer suburbs it gets quiet very early because they have to go to
work early in the morning. But in the centre, at the Politeama, in
Piazza Massimo, in all the posh places, there are crowds of office
workers strolling about till one o'clock or even two in the morning.

We knock off at four-thirty, us street cleaners. You feel all chewed
up, you're full of dust, filthy, you still stink of all the stuff you've
been handling. You can get poisoning sometimes; your eyes sting,
and often your skin prickles and itches. If it's cold weather and you
get wet, that'll probably bring on the rheumatism. *We* can't go

5

strolling about amusing ourselves till midnight or two o'clock in the morning: by eight o'clock I'm already in bed.

When we go on strike the city becomes a real cess-pit. In two days you can't even walk—paper, rubbish, flies, babies and children all among the filth: but we really have to strike sometimes for our rights, even though we hate to see the city in that state. If I live in this quarter, I like it to be clean; I even have a flower garden at home, I grow jasmine and passion flowers. They say, 'Don't do to others what you wouldn't like them to do to you': I'd like to see the whole city clean—it's my native city, and I'm fond of it.

There are thousands of other people after our job, thousands of applications, thousands of people who'd like to take our place. To get taken on, though . . . every saint has his own band of faithful. You go and recommend yourself to your own particular little bene-factor, and the next man goes to his, and so on. There are thousands who envy us our job! To be sure of getting in, you have to be able to procure a certain number of votes for some friend on the Council when elections come round. Because of the lack of industry here, one of the dreams of the people of the poor quarters of Palermo is to be a street cleaner, so as to have a steady job all the year round, and to get the family allowances.

Some Artisans and their Families

VINCENZO: I don't belong to anything.

——Why not?

——In my trade we don't belong to anything; we're free, us *sarcitori*.

——What does *sarcitori* mean?

——When a shoe is broken, I stitch it, I put the patch in it.

——What's the difference between you and a cobbler?

——The cobbler mends soles and heels: the *sarcitore* only patches the uppers.

——Isn't there some association for cobblers?

——There's a trade union for the ones that work together, but I work on my own. Today I may take a thousand lire, tomorrow two thousand, so I'm not interested in the union.

——Do you belong to any other sort of group?

——No, nothing, nothing at all.

——Have you got a family?

——Family is family.

——You've never belonged to a co-operative?

——No, nothing. I signed on in the Fascist party once when I got a job as a cinema attendant, otherwise they'd have turned me down, so it was only natural.

——Why don't you belong to any party?

——Why on earth should *I* care who's in and who's out? It doesn't do *me* any good, whoever gets in: I just mind my own business.

——Which do people generally think is best: being on their own, or together?

——I know what I think, but I can't answer for anyone else. Why should I want to get mixed up in other people's affairs? That's their business. All I'm interested in is my earnings and my home.

——How are the people organized in Palermo?

——I only know about my own home. Is that fair, or not? Each man can answer for his own home.

——But isn't Palermo your home too?

——But what on earth has it to do with *me* how it's organized? I'm nothing, so why should it concern me?

CONCETTA: Looking after the children, looking after my husband, making the *pasta* when he comes home from work . . . then when he brings home the money we quarrel because there's so little, and he gets angry and goes off, and I send someone out after him to try and get him to come home and make it up!

I see a lot of my mother and my sisters, we live close together. My husband's gone away to Germany now.

I go out to work in the mornings as a domestic help.

——And apart from your family and your work?

——Nobody.

——Haven't you any girl friends?

——No, no.

Not one friend?

——There are the girls who live round us, but I haven't any close friends.

——Are you religious?

——I go to Church on Sunday, I take Communion, but I don't meet anyone there—we're all strangers.

——Why d'you go to Church?

——It's our duty to go once a week, on Sundays; and it's become a habit.

And in any case, if they see me in Church they'll take my children at the Day Nursery: if I don't go, they won't. They don't accept the children of women who don't go to Church.

——Are you active at all in any political party?

——No.

——Why not?

——When there are elections on I go and vote, and that's all.

——What do you think the Monarchist party stands for?

——I don't know.

——And the Fascists?

——I've heard people say, but I've forgotten.

——The Christian Democrats?

——That's the Americans' party. The Americans have got a hold on Sicily, and it's them who run it, through Moro.

——The Socialist Party?

——I don't know.

——And the Communists?

——They're for the workers: if wages are low they fight for a rise, they back up the people.

——Is it better working alone, or together with other people?

——Better on my own.

——What sort of a world would you wish for?

——I'd like to have my home all nice, and have my husband here, along with the children, and him bringing in the money. It's best when it's just the family at home, no one else. Just the family, all on our own and happy in our home. Best not having anything to do with anyone else—just us on our own.

Best not having anything to do with other people.

——Why?

——Because that way you see nothing and hear nothing.

——Don't you and the neighbours help each other?

——Yes, we do. We help each other fetch water—we haven't got water in the houses. Someone'll say 'give us a hand?' and I'll help her carry the water. And sometimes the baby starts crying while I'm doing the housework inside, and then a neighbour will pick him up for me.

——Do you ever meet the neighbours any other way?

——On Sunday afternoons we play at Tombola, just the women, when the men go off to play at the tavern or when they go to a match.

Sometimes in summer we go out into the country.

——Who d'you think runs Palermo?

Isn't it Moro at the head of the government? It's him who has houses built, and gets things done at the Town Hall, pensions and so on, and he allots the council houses and says when the roads are to be mended.

Up San Salvatore there's the Council of Cardinals, music and stuff, and one day Cardinal Ruffini arrived. My husband was in the tavern, he didn't have a single lira; and as soon as the Cardinal got out my husband went and kissed his ring, kissed his hand, and spoke to him about a job; and he told my husband to come to the Papal Offices, and he gave him a letter for a firm. But there was no job going there, and so when my husband went back the Cardinal gave him 500 lire.

——Do you think the world's all right as it is?

STEFANIA (*Concetta's elder sister*): It's just a world of troubles.

——What d'you think you can do to change it?

——Have a fortune fall at my feet. I do the Lottery every week.

In the copper-smiths' street

——Are you organized in any way?

——No, we're in competition. We tear each other's eyes out. He tries to pinch my custom off me and I try to pinch his off him. When you sell, there's always somebody trying to undercut you.

Whoever's better off tries to eliminate the smaller men so as to have the trade to himself. 'How much d'you pay for that?' a man'll ask someone who's passing by. 'Two hundred lire.' 'I could've let you have it for one-fifty'—so the customer goes back to the first place and either wants to leave the stuff or get fifty lire back.

Or someone'll say to a customer: 'That man's a shoddy worker' or 'he's a cheat', and so they'll steer clear of him.

——Wouldn't it be better to collaborate, to try and get together?

——A proper man minds his own business and keeps himself to himself, right? He's a better man if he stands on his own feet and doesn't bother with other people.

It's better to stand alone.

It's difficult—it's impossible to change things.

——How long have you been doing this work?

——I must have been about seven when I started. My father took me by the hand and I went off with him to work with the copper and aluminium, forty-five years ago.

——How many of you are there in this street doing this work?

——About fifty shops.

——Is there really no sort of collaboration at all among you, in the whole street?

——None at all.

——Did you have any education?

——I've been in three wars.

——Have you ever wondered if some sort of collaboration might be possible?

——No.

——Why do you all stay in the same street?

——It's an old street, and the people from the villages and from the rest of the city all know about it. People come here specially, when they need anything.

——Nowadays the turners are scattered all over Palermo, but they used to be all together in Turners' street. Then they built the *Banco di Sicilia* there, and the street was abolished.

——Is there any sort of organization among you?

——No, it's every man for himself. There was once, though: fifty years ago we used to have our banner, with the lathe embroidered on it, and it was known as the Society.

You can't have a Society: that Society's all disbanded now because everyone went their own way, they all had their own ideas. It's impossible to get people to stick together.

Say I get a customer, and I charge him a thousand lire; the next man goes and offers him the same thing for 500 or 800 lire, so as to get the customer himself. If he wasn't a right bastard, he'd never think of doing the work for so little.

I've never worked with anyone. I've always followed my own ideas, and never had anything to do with anyone else. My mother, God rest her, taught me that you should be deaf and dumb and blind; and so I'm allowed in everywhere because I never interfere with anybody, and don't bother with anybody else's ideas. That way everything's all right, and I never get on the wrong side of anybody: that's the truth. Practice makes perfect.

——I stuff chairs with straw—I'm the girl: I work for someone else.

——Who?

——Someone who goes round the houses.

——Do any of you work together ever?

——No, on our own.

——Is it better working together or on your own?

——Better on your own.

——Why better on your own?

——I work on my own, they give me the broken chairs and I do the work.

——How many people in this street do this same work?

——There's over a hundred doing the straw chairs by hand, but everyone in this part does chairs.

——All competing with each other?

——I don't understand. It's my boss who brings me the work.

——Is there any kind of co-operation among you?

——No (*answers an old man for her*). Once, fifty years ago, the sawyers had their banner, with a picture of a saw on it. They had their banner—but even in those days each of them worked on his own, and it was only the prices they decided on together. Then with the coming of machines the trade wasn't what it used to be, and it all broke up.

In the Fringe-makers' street

——Once there were about twelve or fifteen of us in the trade, it used to pass from father to son. Now there's hardly anyone left.

——Has there ever been any sort of co-operation?

——No, we each work on our own. We keep ourselves to ourselves. It's always been that way.

You can't trust anybody. There's always rivalry, jealousy. Best to keep yourself to yourself.

In the Wax-workers' street

——We make wax offerings, *ex-votos*: hands, arms, legs, heads—everything you can think of, every part of the body: wax stomachs, wax breasts.

We're called *bambineddara* because when someone was expecting a baby they always used to make an offering of a little wax baby. That's still done a bit nowadays, but not so much. The babies are made either in a mould or freehand.

People make vows to the Saints—to Saint Rita, the Heart of Jesus, Saint Anthony—and if they recover they take them their offerings.

Once upon a time every single person in the street was a wax

worker, but a lot of them are dead now, and a lot have given up work. Trade is dwindling nowadays because the priests would rather people brought money instead, or images in silver and gold. That's what they tell their parishioners to do now, anyway, but people still go and leave the wax offerings in the church.
——Did you use to work together?
——No, each one of us on our own.

We also make mechanical baby dolls in wax, which open their eyes or lift up their heads; they're in a little glass box, and they have musical chimes.

We do a lot of work for the Sisters of Saint Paul: wax baby dolls, they export them. These wax babies are even prettier than real ones: after all, when you see a beautiful smooth baby, don't you say as a compliment, 'Ah, doesn't she look just like a little wax doll'? Then there are the beautiful pictures, all different colours, they're so lovely you can't believe your eyes.

In the chest-makers' street

——We used to make chests, in the old days we used to make green chests for the dowry linen; but nowadays we don't make so many chests. We make wash-tubs, and beech-wood poles for ovens.

My husband used to do the work, but now my son's taken over.

There used to be about thirty of us, but today there are scarcely ten.

We've always worked each of us on our own. It's always been like that. Any other way is impossible, it would be impossible together. It's always been impossible and it always will be.

It's a trade that's full of rivalry, even within the same family.

We're officially registered as artisans—we have to be, it's compulsory.

Once upon a time the whole street was chest-makers, right the way down to Piazza Garraffello where the live crocodile came out of the fountain. Chest-makers right the way up to the Cortile Vecchio where they had death, where they had the guillotine thing for chopping off people's heads.

Bastiano: Church Guilds

Here there's even a street called Via Congregazione, after the Church Guilds or Brotherhoods.

We each of us join whichever one we like best. The Guild I belong to is the *Congregazione di Maria Santissima del Rosario di Pompei*. On the 17th, now, there's the procession for the Festival of Corpus Christi: we're invited along, and we meet at the Cathedral at five in the evening, and then from there we go right the way down to the sea. We have a nice frock—red, with pale blue ribbons, and the badge with the Madonna of Pompei on; in our hand we carry the rod with the star on top, to make sure the people walk straight. Behind all us Guild Brothers (there's about twenty of us) come the Right-hand Brother and the Left-hand Brother—they come behind because that's where they belong.

It was back in 1914 that I first took a liking for this Guild, because my wife's father was a member, and when we got engaged he made me join.

We have a long, long procession to escort whichever Saint it may be. There's over fifty Guilds: the *Madonna del Rosario*, Saint Joseph's, Saint Anthony's, the *Madonna della Cintura*, the *Madonna della Merce*, the *Madonna del Carmine*, the Immaculate Virgin—there's heaps of them, fifty, I don't know them all. Each Guild has its own clothes and its own colour: coffee-colour, or pale blue, or black. The Brothers of the Holy Father have a dark coffee-coloured hood; and then there's the ones that have their faces covered, the *Babbuini*; and some of the Brothers carry candles, too.

To become Superior, or Right-hand or Left-hand Brother, we have elections. We all vote, twenty or thirty of us, inside the Church, it's an ancient custom: each man writes a name on a slip of paper and then they're all collected up and the priest reads them. And whoever has the biggest majority is Superior, and next comes the Right-hand Brother (it's him who takes the place of the Superior when he's not there), and then the Left-hand Brother. If they do well in office, elections aren't held for another three years: if not, we

118

make them stand down after one year. It's them who are responsible for the festivals, you see, and paying for the music, and the
lights, and the flowers. If they're good at collecting the money then
we let them be, but if not someone else will take their place. The
priest can't appoint them himself, it's us who have to elect them.
After your three years you can't be re-elected.

The first and last Wednesday of every month we have a meeting
and discuss how to make the money go round, and if there are debts
we each fork out a bit ourselves. If I die, we have this fund which will
give 30,000 lire to my family, and so we get our funeral.

There's one President in charge of all fifty Guilds, and that's the
Cardinal himself; but as well as that each Guild has its own Superior.
When there's something to discuss at our meeting, it's him who gets
us to speak one at a time—you can't listen to two people at once—
and we decide everything together. If we can't agree, we call the
Council: there's nine of us on the Council, and we meet together
with the priest and discuss the matter, and decide amongst ourselves.

If we didn't go on the Corpus Christi procession, the Cardinal
would cancel our festival—we all have to go. But in fact we go
willingly because we're fond of our Madonna. It warms your heart
to see the festival of the Madonna, it's like Paradise: you ought to
see the statue, it's as if it filled the whole Church, the Madonna
seems to speak, she seems to laugh, lots of people are crying outright, and the Baby Jesus is all rosy pink, and then there's all the
stars . . .

In the Capo district there's the Madonna of the Miners; and then
there's Saint Joseph's, a big Guild for the carpenters; the shoemakers have Saint Crispin. I've heard tell that even the *Camera del
Lavoro* started through some of these Church Guilds.

The business of these Guilds is to organize the festivals and processions. There are young people in them too, men and women. The
whole of Palermo comes out for the festival, you can't move for the
crowds. If it wasn't for the festivals, the Christian Democrat party
wouldn't exist: everybody would be Communist. Take my wife,
now: she votes DC for the sake of the festivals. What she doesn't
realize, though, is that if the Communists were in power they'd have
even better festivals. There'd be more fireworks, more games, and
competitions, and sack races, and so on. They only think the

Christian Democrats have better games because they don't know any better. I think we ought to give the Communists a try—I'm sure they'd have more games.

Every quarter has its own Church Guild, and almost as many people attend now as in the old days.

Some of the Guilds sing the Church stuff, and then behind the canopy there's the music. You have to walk slowly, slowly, and look straight ahead all the time, and the monks look at the ground so as not to look at the people, they go along with their heads down. The Cardinal walks along all substantial, dressed in silk and velvet; gold ring, gold necklace, gold crucifix. The police keep order. Right at the front are the Municipal Guards on their bicycles, and then come all the bands of children: the Little Pages, the Little Brothers of Saint Aloysius, the Young Crusaders, the Little Heralds, the Cordeliers, then the Orphan children, the *Boccone del Povero*, the Egyptian Missionary Sisters, the Handmaidens of the Sacred Heart, the *Ritiri di Perseveranza*, the *Adoratrici delle Ancelle*; and then all of us Guilds and sodalities. Behind the Cardinal comes the Regional President and the Members of Parliament—but of course I don't see them because I'm there with the other Brothers. People start waiting four hours beforehand so as to make sure of getting the best places. There's always a few who faint, out there in the full heat of the sun, specially for Santa Rosalia, who has the biggest festival because she's a good little Saint. Five days of celebrations—everybody enjoys that. The fireworks are what people like best. The women look forward to the festivals because then they're allowed out.

What I'd like would be for the Church Guilds to be good at running the festivals, and the *Camera del Lavoro* and the Communists to be good at providing work.

——Within each Guild, is there any form of co-operation between you, apart from organizing the festivals, and the occasional funeral?
——No.
——Apart from the Guild, do you take part in any other group?
——At the tavern sometimes, and at the *Camera del Lavoro*. I also help with the *Unità* fête, to help *Unità*. I can't read the paper any more myself, but I want to go on helping it till the day I die because it's the paper that takes our side—it fights to get work for our children; and with any luck it might help me, too, by fighting for

bigger pensions: I get 15,000 lire a month, and that's supposed to pay the rent as well as feed three of us—I've got an unmarried daughter too.

Every week I go to the *Camera del Lavoro* to hear the Chairman speak. I like listening to him, because he speaks for us. In the Guilds there's no mention of work, no mention of how we're to eat. But the Guild is better organized, so more people go there. And the Guild Meetings are better, too—there are more of us, more people go.

——Do neighbours in this street help each other?

——Every man for himself.

——Who is it that runs Palermo, do you think?

——The Chief of Police has the most power, with the Police. After him, the Regional President. Under him, the Cardinal: the Cardinal is powerful too.

Under the Cardinal, the priests. The Mayor doesn't count for much. For instance, to get money for Saint Rosalia's festival it's the Cardinal you go to, not the Mayor.

The nobility's nothing these days.

There's practically no industry in Palermo.

Right at the bottom, you eat if you can get work. The political parties don't count for much. The Communists would be good, but at the moment they're not worth anything because it's the priests and the monks and the Christian Democrats who are in power.

——Which are there most of in Palermo, poor people or rich?

——More poor.

——If the poor united, couldn't they get control themselves?

——The Christian Democrats hand out money and *pasta* at election time, they go round from door to door with Assistance Board money and San Vincenzo Charity money, and so the poor people vote for the rich. They can't refuse the stuff because they need it, but at the same time they don't want to be dishonest, so if they take the *pasta* they feel obliged to vote for whoever gave them the *pasta*.

In any case, it wouldn't be possible for everyone to unite. How could they unite? Can people ever co-operate? You can't even get one street to co-operate, let alone a whole city!

If only we could get a change of government, then it would be possible to co-operate. Then there won't be rich and poor any more, we'd all meet each other face to face. People must understand, they must realize that the Communists can have even bigger and better festivals. We wouldn't even need to bother with scraping up the money—they'd take care of that, and they'd put on a much better show.

It's a pity the *Camera del Lavoro* isn't organized like the Guilds are. There's a Guild in every quarter, but not a *Camera del Lavoro*.

Gino Orlando, a barber[1]

The main change in Palermo over the last ten years has been this: a lot of the sub-proletariat who used to live in slums like the Pozzo della Morte have been moved out. They're no longer a distinct group in themselves—they've been scattered and absorbed in other parts of town, for example in some of the rehousing areas. And the same goes for various other slums of the four old central districts. Whole streets of people—the Cortile Scalilla, for example—have been rehoused elsewhere. It's not a mass phenomenon yet, but it's quite noticeable. The old houses are either demolished or boarded up so that no one can live in them any more.

So you see, something has been achieved as a result of our pressure on the authorities to get these people rehoused in more human conditions—but not in the way that was intended: because the new houses were built on land that had fallen into the hands of speculators—in fact a lot of it actually belonged to big mafiosi—and so what ought to have been social improvement turned out to be a boom for speculators. Two years ago an official Commission published a report which showed that over the previous four years the Council had awarded 80 per cent of the contracts (i.e. 3,200 out of 4,000) to five obscure figures whose names were used as a cover, and who didn't even have the necessary qualifications. But nothing was done about it. When you hear that part of the city of Agrigento is collapsing in a landslide under the impossible weight of huge blocks put up by spec builders who are 'friends of friends', you could only be surprised at that if you were quite ignorant of Sicilian ways.

And that's not the only trouble: a lot of these people who've moved out of the old slums without having a proper steady job fixed up are regretting their old homes now, because living on the outskirts they've got the problem of travel; and also they're often

---

[1] For the remarkable story of Gino's life, and the vivid picture he gives of the Palermo underworld, see Dolci's *Poverty in Sicily*. (Tr. note.)

without facilities such as drains, roads, nursery schools, postal services, doctors and first aid.

In the old days each neighbourhood—Cortile Cascino, for instance, or the ex-Pozzo della Morte, and all the others—each had a life of its own, a feeling of community, however primitive and rough it may have seemed: but now the families are mostly isolated, cut off from one another. Supposing someone in one of the old quarters was broke—he could go out into the street knowing he could touch some acquaintance or other for a thousand lire, or get a coffee off a friend here, comfort from a friend there; or help in case of sudden misfortune, or someone to look after his children: I mean, there was a certain solidarity. But in these new estates they suffer a kind of miserable bourgeoisification, they're atomized, isolated. You might think that the families in big blocks on the same estate were living together, but in fact they're often quite cut off from each other. And the lot of them are like prisoners out there, cut off like that on the outskirts off the city; whereas before at least they had their own old community life.

The men who did have a trade of some sort—bricklayers, blacksmiths, carpenters, shoemakers and so on, people who had proper jobs—they went up to North Italy. Vast numbers of men left, leaving their families behind, wives and children and old parents. That was another disruptive influence; and what the usual consequences are of this breaking up of families is well known, or can easily be imagined.

After a while, a lot of the men came back disillusioned, having failed to improve their lot, and were more or less reabsorbed into the old environment. At the time of the so-called boom when emigration was at its highest, unemployment here went down; then when economic conditions in the North took a turn for the worse, the consequences were felt in the South too, and we're still feeling them now. Men come back south hoping to take up their old jobs again, even if they are less profitable, but often they find they can't even get them back.

When there was more work going in Italy, all the men who used to do things like selling raffle tickets or cows' feet or roasted seeds, or running lotteries with dice and spinning-tops—all those sort of people tried to adapt themselves to doing labouring jobs. But once the boom was over they just had to go back to whatever it was they'd been doing before, and manage as best they could.

Then there's another thing: in this last couple of years, during the election campaign, a number of them have been given posts as a reward for their 'services' to the Government party—though of course they're classified (more or less legally) as 'supernumeraries'. Then as well as all the old 'trades' resorted to by the unemployed (you can't really call them jobs) there are some new ones: you see even quite little children going up to someone who's getting into a car, giving the windscreen a wipe with a rag and opening the door and holding out their hand. They're popping up all over the place—in front of the Station, the Government offices, everywhere.

I don't know if there can be said to have been any awakening of political consciousness in the last few years in this sub-working-class environment. It's my impression there hasn't been any at all, that we're still in the grip of the various forms of electoral corruption. (Which is also the reason why the clean Left-wing parties are doing so badly in Palermo.) What I understand by a group is some form of associate life, of collaboration. But they're still just as politically disunited as they ever were: during the election campaign, for about forty days there is a kind of momentary concentration in, say, the Christian Democrat headquarters; but they haven't any particular end in view, and it never results in them doing any work in common.

As for religion, the national festivals like Christmas, Easter and Corpus Christi are as big as ever. But with local ones like Saint Rosalia, and all the other minor festivals of each quarter, the processions and the traditions and all the apparatus of religious propaganda are losing ground. Sometimes you'll see hardly anyone following the Madonna—just the musicians (two pairs of cobblers and two pairs of barbers out to make a little bit of pocket money) and perhaps a Municipal Guard or two in full uniform.

In the old quarters of the city centre, the most intimate community feeling comes in times of death or calamity. One of the best known neighbours in the street or in the immediate vicinity takes the initiative for collecting money for a wreath and for the 'consolation' for the dead person's family. This is what happens: the poor family who have the body there in the house don't do any cooking that day, and the 'consolation' consists of the neighbours going and paying their respects to the dead and consoling the family and bringing them food, generally soup and a bite of something. And then they accompany them to the Cemetery.

There are other occasions, too, when there is some sort of community feeling, though not so much: weddings, for instance, and baptisms and so on. In moments of suffering and at festivals the people get together, but only to return to their own homes afterwards, each family to itself. It's only a momentary bond.

There's no such thing as a permanent organization of people co-operating in order to avoid calamities—they only come together after the thing's actually happened. A person doesn't belong to the community through some form of continuous co-operation, but only momentarily, spontaneously, at times of death or dire need.

One important thing is that in the face of death all quarrels are cancelled out: relatives who haven't spoken for years will meet and make things up, often even without the intervention of a third party. On a smaller scale, it's the same as used to happen during the air raids, when everybody found themselves in the shelter together.

The proverb says: '*Cu havi, mancia; cu nun havi, talia*': the man who has, eats; the man who has not, stands and stares. It's taken for granted that it's every man for himself, and it never occurs to anyone that it could be entirely different. The thing that counts is the family—at least for as long as they're all living under the one roof: but often with this splitting up of families even these family ties are lost.

Old people are respected, and often an old man living alone will be lovingly looked after by his neighbours. There used to be a little old man living near here who went round the streets scratching about among the rubbish for something to eat, but when people saw him going home they'd stop him and take away the stuff he'd picked up, and tick him off affectionately, and feed him themselves: one of them might give him a bit of bread, another a bowl of soup, somebody else would do his washing, and somebody else would wash the old bloke himself—he was eighty-four.

One place where there is some form of temporary community life is the local drinking shops. Generally on a Sunday they'll be full of bricklayers, shoemakers, artisans and small shopkeepers; on weekdays it's the regulars, unemployed and pensioners. Some of them go there for the company, or to hear of any job that might be going, or some to play at *passatella*: that's a kind of lottery with wine which is very common in the working-class areas here. Some of them play it just for amusement, to while away an hour or so, whereas others play it seriously for the sake of possibly winning and being able to drink their fill; in that case quarrels sometimes break out, if one of them drinks the whole lot and leaves the others dry. They may even come to blows.

Apart from the family, for many men this is the only form of associate life, the only form of social activity or collaboration they know. To the bourgeoisie, it may seem a worthless kind of social activity, but for a lonely person who has neither the capacity nor any other opportunities for an associate life which would allow the unfolding of his own personality, this is at least an elementary way of meeting other people, of taking part in some common activity, such as others in more fortunate economic and cultural circumstances can afford to find elsewhere.

The people I know in this quarter generally want just a home and a job, and nothing more. I don't think there's anyone here who'd ever discuss the prospect of a new society or the forms it might take, apart from my comrades in the Party. People aspire to a better life, but they never give any thought to the problems of organization, of how groups should be formed, or how the city should be run, or the State, or anything else. In my experience, people don't have any clear idea of what ought to be done, or how to set about doing it, or of the sort of association that's necessary in order to get things moving.

At a local level, people manage to associate for an hour or so at the barber's, or in a café or drinking shop, and they may even get as far as discussing certain problems that interest them. People look around, and what do they see? A landlord who collects the rents as by right. It never occurs to the tenants that there might be any possibility of him not being the landlord, that the house might be run communally, or as a co-operative, or in some other way. The landlord takes it for granted that the houses are his by divine right, because he's either inherited them or bought them, and so he chucks out anyone who doesn't pay the rent, even if it's because the bloke can't get work. The landlord has even less notion than the others that anything could be changed. The most they ever aspire to is haggling over the rent.

When people go out shopping, too, they look around, and what they see is shopkeepers and shop assistants who depend on the boss who pays them their weekly or monthly wages in exchange for their work. But each one feels forced to work harder than normal—simply out of fear of being sacked, not out of any desire to co-operate for the good of the shop, or out of any interest in the work itself, except in rare cases. They realize they have to work hard to protect their own interests: if the shop does well, it means a secure job; it means that at least they'll be in a stronger position to claim the proper terms and conditions of work (which are often disregarded)—like insurance, stamps, holidays and so on. But it never even enters their heads that the set-up could be any different—except perhaps people on the Left, even here: people who in one way or another are beginning to see the light and becoming aware of themselves as individual personalities, and realizing the value of their own work. What I'm getting at is this: wherever people look, they see bosses and dependents as the natural pattern of things.

I'm talking about the majority, of course: in fact we mustn't forget that there are always one or two here and there who, even though they don't have a true political conscience, are at least aware of being exploited. They realize the need to belong to some sort of organized force to protect their interest over work, and so they join the *Camera del Lavoro*, or the CISL, or the UIL. The group is seen as a power to counteract the power of the bosses. But don't forget that at the local level, though the Monarchists and the Catholics and the Christian Democrats have their social clubs, there are no local trade union branches. There was an attempt to set one up once, but it failed.

The matter is getting serious here. Why? I'll tell you what I think: it seems to me that apart from the Communist Party none of the parties are active enough at a local level to give people any prospect of a new life, or to give anyone a sense of personal responsibility or awareness of their own social function. We used to have street groups, in theory at any rate, and they were supposed to constitute the basic cells: and in some streets the cell did work, its function being to study the problems of that street and find solutions. But now they only exist on paper, they're not functioning any more. There's no one capable of organizing, it's impossible to find the sort of people who could make them work, people capable of realizing exactly what the problems are and inspiring the rest to solve them, mobilizing the other comrades in the street to join the battle front. This applies at street level and also at a local level, in the various sectors of the city. It's true that it's the commitment and the struggle that creates the cadres, but extremist protest and vague good intentions are not enough: what's needed is a definite, practical preparation.

There are many more Party cards than there are people really effectively committed to the work. When it comes down to it, our role seems to be mainly one of propaganda and conversion. Out of an organization of two hundred and fifty in this quarter, only four or five of us are really dedicated; and it's not constant work but, rather, a matter of improvisation. And with the whole load of the work weighing on just a few of us, it becomes impossible ever to complete anything: problems and needs pile up, and we can never see anything through properly to the end.

A comrade won't go on coming to the Branch if all he does there is to listen: he needs to feel he's being useful. Let's take an example: suppose I win over someone to the Party, and he takes out a card, and comes to the Branch. Now in order to make a bloke really want to take part, the most important thing is that he should find himself in a completely different atmosphere—he must feel he's really being treated differently. He must be made to feel he's not just a number but a thinking man, working things out with other men. He's not there just to listen to other people's ideas—he's got to feel he's taking an active part himself in changing the situation. Of course he does find things different in the Party—it's not like what he's used to in the shop, with the boss at the top and all the workers depending on him: but all the same, the chances are that he'll find his only function there is to be counted, to swell the ranks for the good of some cause which otherwise he has nothing to do with.

Everybody wants to be somebody. The other day there was a little group collecting for the hospital in Vietnam. The comrade in charge came along—and afterwards an argument broke out about whether he'd greeted them or not! 'He comes along,' one of them said, 'and he doesn't even say hello!' This may seem trivial and petty, but it does show how much people need respect and recognition. I think a lot of the dissatisfaction is not so much political as personal. At some of the meetings, you can see how one intellectual will go and sit beside another intellectual, one labourer beside another from the same builder's yard, or someone from a certain block by someone else from the same block. And they each feel detached, isolated from the rest.

To achieve real democracy, a structure and a form of organization has got to be found in which each individual can have his say, and play his part in working things out, making decisions and then putting them into practice. The propaganda function of the old-fashioned type of political meeting can be fulfilled now by radio and television. At that sort of meeting all you can do is listen. But the people at the bottom (even though they don't consciously formulate this) are becoming less and less willing to accept the old priest—congregation pattern of things, with the priest, the authority, preaching while the others just listen and pray, never having any sort of co-operation except perhaps in running the local festival and that sort of thing. And people are also less and less willing to have things run along the sort of lines the police force still works on, with the Superintendent alone consulting the code (which is all too often still the Fascist code) and giving the orders, and the rest obeying.

Salvatore Vilardo, sports organizer

At the Stadium you may get as many as 35,000 people watching a match together; for two hours all sections of the population are absorbed by the working class, it's as if they formed one single body, with epidemic outbreaks of paroxysms of love for their own team. An Army General blows his top just like a navvy if a player misses; a Chief Justice is a boy again yelling 'bastard!' at the referee, and the Bank Manager may have to be calmed down by individuals a good deal less distinguished socially. They're united in a single mass—for two hours all distinctions disappear: the Chief Justice, with tears in his eyes, hugs the workman beside him when a goal's scored. I remember one high-up official once—a man who'd probably have yelled the place out if anyone at the office had slammed the door: one day he came three hours early, with a little parcel. We thought it was stuff he'd brought along to eat while he waited, but the minute the ref gave the starting signal he ripped open the packet and scattered the contents—it was salt he'd brought to ward off bad luck!

For two hours, all social distinctions disappear, everyone forgets who he is, what he is, they become just one common mass, everybody welded together in one, forgetting their own personalities, forgetting themselves. Police forget they're police, Customs and Excise officers applaud the team's victory, or protest if things go badly. We have to change the police on duty every Sunday, otherwise they get bitten themselves and forget their job!

If things go badly, the ref gets showered with abuse from all sides, pelted with oranges and lemons and bottles. After matches we've picked up assorted shoes, cigarette lighters, umbrellas, bundles of coins tied up in handkerchiefs. Up till 1930 they were practically all men, but now the percentage of women has gone up—maybe as much as 25 per cent now—and they're often the most fanatical; there are some, though, who aren't really supporters at all: they come to the Stadium just to be seen, to show themselves off.

The pitch unites them all: but as soon as they go out, they divide off again into their private lives, each one goes back to his own home

—they're strangers again, there's no longer any contact between them. The minute they get outside, the civil servant and the navvy who were behaving like brothers before just don't know each other any more. Any attempt to translate sport into concrete forms of association, to unite the different strata of society and different people outside the Stadium, has always failed here in Palermo.

During a match, the social strata disappear, and for two hours there's this kind of socialization: but once the match is over and tension starts to return to normal voltage, then each man takes up his individual personality again, and things gradually get back to normal. In the higher social strata the match is forgotten at once, but in the lower classes it's more gradual—they'll go on talking about the match for a couple of days afterwards, still with eagerness and excitement, infecting each other, converting new supporters who get bitten just by listening to the others and so become fans themselves.

On Saturday they're plugged in and switched on, on Sunday it's high tension again.

Undoubtedly sport is an occasion for sociability in Palermo, in so far as it's a meeting of the masses. But in the Capo and in Ballarò, in the poor areas, its influence is really strongly felt: the mass of the working class are really fascinated by it, they're intensely keen. You might even say that a kind of social relationship springs from their differences of opinion. In the more wealthy areas, on the other hand, sport is only appreciated up to a certain point; and it's often exploited for other ends which I will not hesitate to call false, opportunistic, exhibitionist. Often people's spontaneous feeling for sport is blatantly exploited for political purposes, as we've seen all too clearly over these last few years. In these cases, as soon as the political objective no longer exists, or as soon as they realize they've failed, then they vanish from the scene themselves.

The most popular sport here is football, the only officially subsidized sport in Sicily.

Then there's also a very high degree of horse awareness: the Favorita racecourse is one of the oldest in Italy. This passion derives from the close relationship many people, both in the country and in town, have with their horses, which often sleep in the house along with the people. From time immemorial there have been horse races here, even in the villages, before the racecourse ever existed. In some Communes they've got a register of all the winners going back eighty years. Nowadays the snob element in horse racing, the nobility, goes in for steeple-chasing. For centuries there hasn't been a single festival without a race. It's the horses that make a festival.

Next after horse racing comes cycling. Whereas football and horse racing are sustained by State-authorized betting through the *Toto-calcio* and SISAL, cycling is poor: it's never had any boost from the State and so, although initially it did rouse the masses, now it's gradually losing ground.

Other sports don't have much weight. Tennis is confined to smart circles—among ordinary people it's quite unknown.

Within the football team there are disparities: there's friction and resentment caused by differences of mentality and of background (we have carters playing alongside university graduates); everyone's struggling to secure his own place in the team, competing against rivals. And the trainer's job is to get them all united, to educate them, to iron out the differences, to boost their morale by making them feel they're champions even if they're not, making them feel they're superior to anyone else. Nowadays the most powerful spur to the professionals is winning the match prize: they don't play for medals and diplomas any more.

Apart from looking after the technical training of each member of the team, the trainer's job is to weld them into a unit. The more united a team is, the stronger it'll be. The trainer has to try and stamp out individualism and personal ambition, because that's harmful to the team. He tries to create a single organism skilled in strategy: football is a team game.

The spectators fall into two categories: we have eighty per cent fans, and twenty per cent real sportsmen—connoisseurs whose passion is a good game, and who'll applaud even the opposing side for a display of first-rate team technique. What the fans go for, on the other hand, is the prowess of individual players, even when it's harmful to the team. But the percentage is gradually going up, the fans are becoming more knowledgeable.

In taverns and cafés and at various strategic points of the city, for instance in the market places, you get little gatherings of people discussing the game, so many little social centres. It even has a bearing on people's private moral and cultural life. On the field, when the leading supporters notice any disaffection among the other fans they try to get everyone to shout in unison if there's a goal or something, so as to restore the team spirit. 'Come on! Come on!' they shout, trying to revive the passionate feeling of unity and boost the team. And I don't believe this sense of strength in unity is left behind in the Stadium at the end of the match—I think it carries over into their private lives, too.

It's the Society that picks the teams and acts as a club where enthusiasts can meet, and gives notice of meetings, and organizes trips for supporters to away matches, and keeps the passion for the favourite team burning.

There's no other event in the city that can unite and interest so many people. Even the festival of Saint Rosalia has little support in comparison. People go and buy an ice, and hear the *Te Deum*, and they go to the fireworks: there's something worth going to perhaps once or twice a year. Maybe ten or fifteen thousand people will take part in the procession: but it leaves no trace, it's just an isolated manifestation, just folklore. It doesn't form any constructive aware- ness, it doesn't give classified results; once the festival's over, that's that. There's no comparison. At the Stadium, there's an organized unity—you've only to look at all the stalls and the attendants and the car parks: our Sunday's more than just a matter of sixteen degrees wine. In life, you have some particular end in view, some final aim to struggle for. Well, the crowd that goes to the Stadium has this final aim: it has the immediate aim of winning the day, and the final aim of classification, which can lead to promotion; and this is the end purpose of all this crowd, all this enthusiasm.

What effect does Saint Rosalia leave, though? A city dirtier than before, littered with snail shells and pumpkin seeds—that's all. There's absolutely no comparison. Our objectives are up-to-date: theirs are old, and need modernizing.

Quite apart from the thirty-five thousand who are there to see the match with their own eyes, in a city like Palermo there'll be another two hundred thousand interested followers betting on the *Totocalcio* or reading the sporting papers and arguing and quarrelling over them. There are little old men of seventy who go and put money on without even knowing what football is. Even the old men who would otherwise have been lost to football—we've caught them too through the Pools. And our numbers are swelling. The Stadium's already been modernized twice and it's still clearly inadequate, and there's talk now of increasing the seats to eighty thousand.

The crowd goes there to relax, to forget about their worries— they forget all about the H.P. instalment to pay next day. We all need to let ourselves go from time to time. There are some who'll go without food rather than miss the match. Once the spectator has caught the bug he can identify with the team, he can get real spiritual pleasure from a player's ability; the players really become part of him. It's like being in love with a woman: you may find her beautiful and you may like her, but if you love her you feel really passionate.

When the Palermo side is unlucky enough to lose, people are sometimes so upset they can't eat—and if the wife insists the bloke'll throw the *pasta* out of the window. Last Sunday there was even one bloke died of a heart attack. But if they score a goal, jackets and hats go flying up in the air, and there's clapping and hugging. It really gets you, once you know it. It's a perpetual struggle, perpetual tension. You must have some final aim in life: the matches form a series and the results are classified—it's not just a momentary affair like Saint Rosalia. A match lost today has incalculable consequences for the rest of the year. It's not over and done with in a single day— there's a long-term aim, it's not an end in itself. It's a perpetual striving for victory, against the danger of relegation. It's a never-ending battle.

The Governor of the Ucciardone Prison

Once the initial period of solitary confinement is over, they want company, they don't want to be alone any more, except in order to study. But whether they get on with each other or not is quite another matter.

This isn't a penal establishment—we're dealing with prisoners awaiting trial, and we don't have any therapy. Any special attempt to train them for collaboration, for social life, is beyond our scope. There are too many of them. Certainly some training would be a good thing; but sometimes we can't even allow them to mix with each other, when they come from six or seven different criminal associations. We cannot allow accomplices to be together, either. Nine hundred, a thousand people—just imagine.

The maximum time they can spend here is two years. The situation here is more difficult than in a penal establishment because there's this feeling of transitoriness.

There are technical training courses, but they're scarcely attended; the men don't come, perhaps because they think they'll earn more in their old trade.

We have classes for illiterates, which are compulsory up to the age of forty: many of them are illiterate. A lot of letters leave the prison starting: 'The first letter which I have ever written I am writing to you, with my own hand.'

We have a five thousand-volume library. The men in solitary confinement are allowed up to three books a week because they are on their own all day.

The prison ought to be different: every fifty men at least ought to have someone with them. But I don't think that will ever happen.

We do try to do something with the young men. But what can one do with someone of forty? It's difficult. The Assistant Governor and the Commandant and the Chaplain all have orientation talks with the young men of eighteen to twenty-five, and find out about family conditions. But there are too many of them, too, so what can one do? No one here has any inclination.

They are allowed to buy magazines and newspapers, but they find them boring, and besides they cost too much.

We have two Chaplains who try to link up with the families and help them with ECA and charity money; they preach, too, and their main task is to comfort people: they break any bad news tactfully— if a man's mother dies, they know how to break it to him. That is their main function.

When it's a mafia affair, there is little one can do: there's no getting anything out of them, not a word, and there's nothing one can do about it.

They haven't the courage to say who it was that did something. Someone makes a rude noise behind a warden's back: 'Who was that?' but no one speaks. So they are all punished. What else can I do?

It's difficult to understand people when you only see them here inside: they're quite different in here from what they are outside. But even outside there's the same fecklessness, the same isolation; they may seem willing enough, but only when there's some immediate advantage to themselves.

I'm strict, yes, but I'm fair. When I first came here, it was the big gang leaders who ran the whole thing: authority was completely undermined. We found thousands of bottles, and goodness knows what else besides: it's not like that today.

In town, in the Vucceria district and in the Capo, I've had some very odd things happen. One man introduced me to a friend of his: 'This is the prison Governor. He punished me, but he was right.' At the cinema, people give up their seats for me. And I'm by no means gentle. There's no question of gentleness in running the Ucciardone. However, as far as the mafia is concerned I mind my own business, I don't interfere with their affairs; and in fact they are the best prisoners, polite and well-behaved: they give so little trouble you don't even notice them. I don't want to meddle in their affairs: we're in charge here, and that's enough.

I've got a Fiat 600, and one day in the Vucceria I met a man selling cigarettes who'd only recently been let out of prison. 'What are you doing selling cigarettes, then?' I asked him: 'Weren't you stealing cars?' 'Don't you worry, sir,' he said, and he pulled a piece of paper out of his pocket and showed me he'd got a note of my car number!

They suck fear with their mother's milk.

One day when I was walking along Via Maqueda—it was full of people—I saw a lout trying to steal a girl's handbag: he pushed her down on the ground to get it from her—but no one moved, no one said a thing. I was running up from quite a distance, and everyone else scuttled away. No one must see anything. It's fear. One can't blame them, though—they're born afraid.

If a man's dying, then he'll talk. But if he recovers, he withdraws everything at once. That's what they call being manly.

There's never been proper justice here—no one's ever bothered to make it work. So of course each man says to himself, 'I'll be my own justice.' Blood washes clean, they say, blood washes clean, blood washes clean.

Reveille here is at 6.45.

At 7.30 the coffee is taken to the cells.

From 8.0 till 11.0, out in the yards for exercise, thirty or forty men to each courtyard of 25 metres by 20. I can't allow them to play with a ball, or bowls, because they can hurt each other and start fighting.

At 11.0 they get their food in their cells.

At midday, silence, and they rest on their bunks till 2.0. Then another meal in the cells, and inspection.

We even pay them to attend the training courses, but they don't want to come. At the beginning of the month, perhaps twenty will turn up, then they gradually fall off till there are none left. Next month there'll be another twenty, but after a bit they won't want to come any more either.

We're on duty here on Sundays, too, till 1 p.m.

In this job one is a prisoner oneself. Once we're in it, we're trapped—we're all prisoners. When someone tells me he's done twenty years in prison, I reply that I've done thirty-three myself. And of course I don't get overtime on Sundays! They're people in here, not just names on paper: we can't just lock up and go off. In the Army, you can give everyone leave and so be free to go off yourself. But here Christmas and Easter are the worst days of all; at the big holidays we have to make sure they see us around, we try and keep their spirits up. We're under no obligation, but we're sorry for the poor devils—they don't see anyone else: those are the

times they suffer most. I feel the least I can do is stay with them—
there may be an attempted suicide, or a riot. I'm a prisoner myself.

It's thirty years since I spent Christmas or Easter at home. I eat
with my heart in my mouth. People think of us as tyrants—they
don't realize that we're all prisoners alike. If we do something kind,
nobody knows, it's never reported, never mentioned. But let one
little thing go wrong and they're down on us at once, down on the
tyrants.

What we need is a new type of society, a different kind of organization, new possibilities open to people; we need different staff here,
different buildings; new rules, new laws. We're not mature enough
for democracy, we're not ready for it: with our immaturity, what
we need is dictatorship, a dictatorship of the right or of the left.

Giuseppe Gulí, industrialist

Our industry was born through the great enterprise of our grandfather, who was an artisan, a silk weaver. A large number of the tapestries and damasks in Palazzo Mazzarino were woven by him. Countess Mazzarino had him brought up to the Palace, and when the work was finished she was so pleased that she not only paid him but presented him with the loom: and that was the basis of the industry. With that loom, my grandfather was able to set up on his own; then he began to hire out piecework to other weavers, men and women; and before long the little workshop in Via Sopra Le Mura di Porta Carini was thriving.

When the first Palermo International Fair was held in 1891, my grandfather saw one of the early mechanical looms, and at once ordered one himself—the first in Palermo. From then on the business grew and grew, from one loom to two, then four, and so on.

Every business here seems to be a self-contained unit, separate and closed and mistrustful of everyone else: I think this is one of the major impediments to development in our part of the world. Professional jealousy is much more pronounced here: instead of growing and gaining strength by uniting with others, each little industry withdraws into its own narrow shell and gets stifled and bound in by the limits imposed by its own smallness. A group should have the force to expand, to grow, to co-operate and compete with others in a wider field. Many businesses here would have been able to grow much more and much faster given another environment. (Whenever difficulties cropped up my grandfather used to try and encourage us to go up North, but we were attached to this part of the world, and so we stayed.) Given a different environment, many businesses could have become proper associations. Here, very few joint-stock companies exist, just because of this lack of any spirit of co-operation, or any experience of association.

Nowadays it's no longer possible to start up an industry in the way my grandfather did. In this age of big monopolies and big industrial syndicates you need to have very broadly based industries.

The small family group with its small capital can't compete with the more mature industries which have a vast capital at their disposal: one has to resort to bank credit, which of course puts up costs.

In these closed circles, it's difficult to create a new industry. In the North, the birth of one new industry immediately brings to life about nine other smaller satellite industries integrating with the parent one. But this doesn't happen here. In general people here don't have any faith in another person's enterprise, and this works both ways, so that neither side will risk taking the initiative. People here prefer to work for pay, even by the day, rather than commit themselves to any enterprise. Up till now, that is: in fact, in the city at least, things are just beginning to stir a bit even here.

Since this isn't an industrial environment, it's very much more difficult to operate in any branch than it would be in a more advanced industrial society: anyone operating here finds himself dependent on other areas from which he has to get raw materials and equipment. If we were in Milan, for instance, we wouldn't be obliged to keep huge stocks of things like hundreds of bobbins, because we could always get anything we needed at once simply by making a telephone call. The result is higher costs, due to transport and greater capital outlay.

Since there are so few openings in industry, workers are unable or unwilling to undertake a specific training on their own account, to qualify for a specific job, and so each firm has to provide its own apprenticeship and training schemes. We lack technical training colleges, and this generates difficulties also for outside industrialists who might otherwise wish to come to Sicily: obviously they wouldn't want to come to a place where there was no training.

Suppliers around here are not prepared to trust any but the very few businesses they know to be solvent, since they're afraid of not being paid for the goods they supply: and this of course makes the creation and development of new businesses still more difficult. As for dealings with clients—we have to be very careful, too, in selecting our customers. Nowadays paying by instalment is a very common practice, but in our case it is limited by the fact that the consumer can rarely give sufficient material and moral security. I believe that in places like Milan and elsewhere insolvency is less frequent than here because the sources of income are greater. Also, unfortunately, there is a certain mentality still prevalent among a large section of the population here which considers it clever to get something for nothing, to get away with stuff without having to pay. What we have here is a vast mass of sub-proletariat: under-employed, unemployed, destitute. The businessman who doesn't have a network of information on people risks being seriously taken in—which of course means further costs.

Industrialists and the business class in general have a complete mistrust of the ruling class, the Regional Government politicians. Unfortunately, there's a conviction—which I think is perfectly justified—that most politicians are only concerned with their own personal interests and not those of the community. In Sicily more than in other places politics is a personal business, and bureaucratic organization here is so clumsy and muddled and corrupt that it is extremely difficult to get anything done officially. Sometimes one simply doesn't bother with certain grants and facilities provided for by law because dealing with officials and politicians is so difficult and so slow: one would rather get credit from the bank even if it does mean paying more, because less time is wasted.

But this running sore in our society is spreading still further. What we have now is a clientship system that involves a large part of the population and the men who are supposed to be governing. And often even decent people can't escape this corruption, they get dragged in too. What frequently happens is that things which are officially supposed to be rights become favours to be conceded by politicians in exchange for votes, and often for something more substantial which—at best—will go towards election campaign funds. Often an official grant is more profitable to the politician who concedes it than to the man whose legal right it is supposed to be.

The Member of Parliament or the local Councillor is so intent on securing his own seat, so intent on getting into politics and on ways and means of catching and keeping votes, that he doesn't see any further. And so these politicians end up intriguing even with the mafia, which in many areas of Western Sicily is the electoral organization *par excellence*.

Good planning produces better structures; better technical and social structures lead to better planning: in my opinion this is a direct and continuous relationship.

But democratic planning is impossible as long as there are still serfs and subjects. You can't have programmes until you have free men, with a sense of duty: the spearhead of economic planning must be the education of the people: technical and moral education —we have to prepare workers and citizens. Until the poor labourer can throw off his sense of being a slave to the mafioso or to his boss or to the big politician, new structures won't come. It's absurd to think of planning when we lack the men who are the essential part of any plan. Schools are what we must have. I put schools above anything else, because we've already wasted precious time; if only we'd thought of preparing men over these last twenty years, we could be reaping the benefits and making use of them today.

I'm pessimistic about adults, because in mature men it's impossible to eliminate the most ingrained environmental influences. But I don't want to seem completely pessimistic. I do dream of a better Sicily, and I do think about how this could be achieved. There are forces for good, despite the bad things: there are values worth preserving and qualities worth exploiting. We have men who are potentially first-rate; but unfortunately people still pursue chimeras, and are often incapable of making even elementary plans. To give you an example—in the Provincial Commission for Economic Planning, after months and months they still haven't even decided on the methodology for initiating the provincial plan.

This is another of the basic difficulties: the egocentric self-absorption, the endless long, ill-conceived and irrelevant discussions in which everyone is only intent on asserting his own opinion, and which often end in quarrels; they argue on, constantly interrupting one another: there's no discipline, either in discussions or in working together.

Putting plans into operation is a formative experience, morally and culturally too: but only if they're proper democratic plans, and not when they're just vague chimeras or pursued merely out of self-interest.

Beppe Fazio, intellectual

This is how I would sum up the situation in Palermo: within the sub-proletariat (a relatively recent phenomenon) there is a dense network of local solidarity and protectionism, often headed still by the local capomafia. The proletariat has neither the force to destroy nor the capacity to co-ordinate. Next comes the lower middle class, which is fairly mobile; then above that a rigid middle class. At the top is the upper middle class and the aristocracy, a class apart.

At the apex of the social pyramid in the old days was the Palermo Senate, consisting of the aristocratic families, big feudal landowners who often secured for themselves the important public contracts like the Postal Service. This senatorial régime survived, though with some modifications, until a few years ago. The nobility and the big legal names, linked by ties of family and mutual deference, together ruled the city. But now they no longer have supreme power. They're still at the top of the social ladder, but in a sense they're suspended; as a power they're disintegrating. One of the reasons for this is that their economic basis, agriculture, is failing: with the crisis in agriculture, they no longer have the profits and the power they once enjoyed. Y.Z., a typical political servant of the big landowners, originally a Monarchist, who used to command more than twenty thousand votes in the city for the landowning nobility, has now transferred his allegiance to the new group, because he realizes that that's where the power lies now. And other leading Monarchist supporters have done the same, for considerable rewards.

The power has passed from the upper middle class and the aristocracy to another group of a somewhat unscrupulous type, whose main supporters are certain categories formerly kept in a state of subjection, certain categories of businessmen and people connected with commerce who would not have been accepted in Palermo society by the ruling class a few years ago.

As for the intellectuals, if anyone does stay in Palermo it's probably because he has a calling for a solitary life. Sicilians of any ability tend to leave the place, to go and live in a society that's less provincial, more in touch with the industrial, scientific and literary world. The very fact that a person stays in Sicily, in Palermo, may well be due to a conviction that it's better to live more or less in isolation than to become part of a society that can be as backward in the big Italian cities as in Sicily itself. This may be a sign of lack of faith in a certain type of progress, and lack of faith in one's own ability to change things.

Gaetano Alfano and others: industrial relations

Immediately after the war, in '45, I was working as a baker. My father, a stoker, had died on the job. I decided to be a baker because I thought that way I could get bread to eat myself and some to take home.

Nowadays, though, a baker is paid daily instead of weekly—he's counted as a day-labourer: the boss can just say to him: 'I don't need you tomorrow.' And the hours are longer. They're not a united branch of workers; one man's working here, another there, another somewhere else, so it's difficult for them to meet like the workers in a factory can, to get together and discuss their problems.

In '49 I joined the Navy, not having done my service yet, but in '51 I quit and got a job in the shipyard as an unskilled labourer. I was very struck at first by the huge size of a ship in dry dock: how on earth did it get in there? I wondered—and how did they empty all the water out? Then I saw the pumps, and the workmen explained. There were eighteen hundred workmen. When I was little I'd had an uncle who was an electrician in the shipyard, and he used to be perpetually worrying that he wouldn't finish his piece-work and they'd give him the sack: he often used to work after hours to get the job done. Before the war the workers were just treated as unskilled labour, and they hardly even dared ask to be allowed to go to the lavatory. My uncle told me how one day there were some steam cranes lifting sheet iron, and one of the sheets got caught in a sudden gust of wind and broke some glass; and the Director, who was looking out of the window, had the men fined five lire and suspended for three days. The workers protested, saying that it was the fault of the wind, but the Director himself appeared then and said: 'Evidently three days is too little: we'll make it five'—and all because they'd had the courage to protest.

During the war, a number of these workers were transferred to various places in the North, and there many of them got recognition as skilled workers: some of them stayed on after the war, but some of them came back and began to spread knowledge of what working

145

conditions were like in other shipyards. And so a movement began within the shipyard, and a lot of riots. Immediately after the war, you could only get a job through the mafia, and also there were still one or two chiefs left over from Fascist days: well, the workers rioted to get rid of the most hated Fascist dictator, and one or two things were tried against the mafia too—they tried to keep them out of the business, not to let them have any hand in it; but they had to give way on practically everything because our union leaders were beaten up and threatened and blackmailed. We had to give way on a lot of things. They even went as far as shooting: one day, to give the workers a scare, they started firing at them, and several were wounded.

When I first joined, at the mass meetings they held there the workers were very enthusiastic about the speeches of their representatives, they had complete faith in whatever they said. But if you were to ask them, 'What did he say?' they'd only be able to tell you: 'He said good things'. 'He spoke out against the Management'. 'How brave he is, he spoke out against the Director—he's defending our interests all right!': they were content just with hearing the Management criticized—they weren't ready to consider themselves an integral part of the transformation that had to come about, and they found it difficult to see just what the problems were. Meanwhile the Management watched, noted, and then—with the aid of the mafia—tried to corrupt. Men who put themselves forward as members of the works council very often weren't equipped to face the problems: as soon as they saw an opportunity for personal advancement, they'd become docile employees and leave the others in the lurch. That was the Management's policy: to sap the strength of the workers and make them lose hope and become mistrustful. The ones who were better qualified, ideologically and politically, they sacked.

In '52, at a time when the workers were seeing themselves let down by some of the people they'd trusted, and seeing a lot of the activists sacked, they received letters from the Management saying that if things went on like this the whole yard would be closed down. And about that time, too, the CISL was trying to work its way in there, trying to persuade the men that by organizing with them they'd make their jobs more secure.

By '53 the number of men employed at the shipyard was up to six thousand. A lot of petrol tankers used to come here for repairs, as prices were lower because of the very low wages. However, not all the six thousand men were actually working: sometimes they might have twenty or thirty ships in dry dock, but often they'd only have ten or so. And what happened? Whenever the men actually working wanted to strike for some claim, the Management would be quite happy because there was always a big reserve of labour, and so the shipyard need never close down. To prevent any union action, they kept this permanent big reserve force of men recommended to them either by Government politicians or the Cardinal's Curia, or by the mafia.

And in the shipyard what was happening? In the old days, a foreman would be assigned a job of work to do with his gang, and they'd work freely under him, getting their card stamped when they arrived and when they knocked off. But then they started this new system: as well as having the card stamped at the beginning and end of the day, every single workman had to have a special 'economy stamp' for when he began and ended each job: in that way they could compare the time taken by each man on a particular job. And this meant the foreman had to become a kind of slave-driver—'We can't have you taking longer on this than that other chap'—and if a man was slower he was called off. The workers found themselves under heavy pressure; work which was already hard before became a real torture, there was greater risk of injury—the accident rate went up— and every man worked under constant worry.

The CISL didn't get a great many members, but it was a nuisance, it was enough to destroy unity. During my last few years there, '53, '54 and '55, the situation was getting worse and worse. The postwar years had convinced the men of the need to press forward and win all their claims, and some were even convinced of the possibility of achieving a more democratic form of administration, with labour having its proper weight; but instead, what happened was a kind of demoralization among the workers, with the shortage of work and the crowds of men always hanging about outside the gates waiting for jobs. A number of workers—the best men—who'd been dreaming of a new society and hoping to change conditions and life around them, emigrated to the North or abroad in search of better prospects, not just economic. The ones that stayed behind were becoming inured to their conditions, their impulse to get things moving had begun to wane. The firm became more and more paternalistic towards the tame workers, and more and more hostile to the few who still had hopes of changing things. As soon as a worker was promoted, he'd begin to drift away from his old friends and workmates and become another class—often he'd even stop greeting them.

It was because of these same conditions that I left the shipyard: I felt a need to meet other men, see other ways of life; I wanted to understand how society could be changed, I wanted to see different social customs, I wanted to see how they lived in other parts of the world, and I wanted to earn more in order to set up house. In '57 I decided to go to sea.

I travelled about the world till 1960 as a ship's mechanic: on the first trip I went to Conakry in French Guinea, Newcastle in Scotland, and Liverpool; then to Yokohama in Japan, and a whole year in the Far East between Java, Sumatra, and Indonesia. In America I only went to Newfoundland in Canada. Also to Holland, where I met many old mates from the shipyard. And so I was able to get some idea of our level of civilization compared with other countries.

On the ship, of course, what goes is God's law and the Captain's; the sailor on board has to submit to the Captain's rule because he's the boss of the whole crew. The commander has special food, the other officers different food, something different again for the warrant officers, and different again for the crew. This created perpetual resentment at the bottom, and at the top a sense of remoteness and detachment that almost seemed to justify the difference.

In '57, before going to sea, I'd got married. Now after three years I had two children, and I was feeling the separation more and more: so I decided to come home for good. I got myself a stoker's licence and found a job at the Barbera dairy, where we lived in the hope of being taken over by the Council, like in other big cities, and so having a secure job and being paid at least trade union rates. As we were such a small group it was run rather like a family business. Then, as I was only doing night work, I decided to change, and got a job in a new laundry. There we were well and truly exploited. There were about sixty of us: boys and girls of fourteen or fifteen getting—in 1961 this was—only 250 or 300 lire a day, and a grown

man 1,200. It was difficult to get any union activity going because
they were nearly all young girls and women, and they were frightened—it didn't seem right to them. 'We need the money . . . We
must be satisfied with what we've got because if we do anything
they'll sack us and we won't be able to get another job.' They had
no experience.

I knew one of the chiefs in Maintenance at SELIT, the electronics
firm, and I did a psychological and aptitude test with the head of
the department, and was taken on at once. The factory had started
in '57, and when I went there were about three hundred people
working there. There was quite a difference between this place and
the shipyard: whereas down there they'd been getting more and
more hardened and apathetic, here at the factory, oddly enough, as
soon as they arrived—ex-tailors, fruit-sellers, cobblers, and above
all peasants—these workers began to get together and have meetings
and discussions and to form a surprisingly powerful progressive
force.

In the early days, the workers had begun by accepting extremely
low pay, and they could only get jobs through the Archbishop's
Curia or through the mafioso Paolino Bontade: it was enough for
him to mention a man's name and he was sure to be taken on. There
was one boy called Puleo, an intelligent lad, who wanted to get certain things done, but he was at once told off by the mafia and forced
to leave. However, the workers were feeling the pressure of the ex-
hausting work and low pay, and they were frightened by this man
Bontade who was always getting in their way at the factory. (There
was also a certain Don Tricomi who went about trying to soothe
troubled spirits, acting as go-between for workers and management;
he doesn't come there much these days because the people have
woken up now and got organized in the union.) Anyway, immediately after the Ciacculli massacre when that car full of explosives
blew up and killed seven policemen, Paolino Bontade retired from
the scene to go into hiding. So when a hundred and fifty men were
threatened with dismissal one day, the workers suddenly found
themselves united to a man, and the ones from ELSI too—that's the
other half of the firm. Thanks to the fear of dismissal, and thanks to
Bontade's absence, we were all united. The economic situation was
bad at the time, and we knew there were plenty of unskilled workers
6*

pressing at the doors for jobs. So we decided to call a total strike, and the whole factory was shut down—to the great surprise of the Management. They went from door to door trying to talk the workers round, but with no result. After three days, the notices were withdrawn; and we also succeeded in getting a ten per cent rise in basic pay, and a bonus of twenty-five thousand lire for every employee, including the clerical staff.

Before, each man used to think only about his own particular problem, believing that he could find his way out best on his own: now suddenly they realized that everybody had the same problem, and that the way to solve it was by all getting together.

From then on, every worker made his voice heard—it was like waking up from a nightmare. They began to insist on claiming all their rights, even down to things like ventilation. 'I've been doing this job for years and it's time I got promotion . . .' 'On this type of work I'm entitled to milk . . .' What mattered wasn't so much the particular things they were claiming—the important thing was that they were demanding respect for the individual, and respect for the works council.

Immediately after the strike we held elections for a proper works council, and the CGIL got three members on, and the CISL one. People had thrown off their fear, they'd begun to say; 'Well, so I'm in the CGIL—what's wrong with that?' You'd even get a man saying to the chief: 'Do you know I'm in the CGIL?' And as soon as it began to be known in Palermo that something was being done against the mafia,[1] then factory workers and office workers and trade union activists alike felt braver, less anxious: they felt the law was on their side, they had more faith in the law. And when it came to claiming their legal rights in the factory, they couldn't but remember that the Management had been in direct contact with the mafia and had accepted this liaison more or less willingly, and so they felt even more justified in their actions. New hopes were growing.

The firm has continued to expand: counting both parts, over 1,200 employees now, and according to forecasts this should be more than doubled by '69. From a technical point of view, it's a modern factory, and the outlook is good; from the industrial rela-

[1] The Parliamentary Commission of Enquiry into the Mafia, set up in 1963. (Tr. note.)

tions point of view, whereas in the shipyard you come up against a front of 'That's how things are, full stop'—here the front is much more elastic. But they're more devious—they let discussions drag on and on in order to gain time, and in a way they still treat the worker like a child. It is a democratic system in so far as things can be discussed, and in so far as the personal conditions of each worker are considered; also there's a certain concern with leisure activities, recreation and so on, and there's even talk of setting up a factory shop to make the workers' pay go further: but all the same, the boss is the boss, and it's him who makes the ultimate decisions. There are discussions, maybe, but the last word is his.

When the men saw the union representatives taking such an interest in workers' claims all over the country (we wanted to start our own factory newspaper, but we couldn't get a permit because there wasn't a journalist among us), and seeing the close contact they had with individual workers in discussing their problems, more and more of them joined the union—'Look, I haven't had my card yet'— 'When are you bringing my card?'—'Let me pay my dues now all at once'; the worker feels more at ease. The thing is, though, it's still too much the responsibility of individual members of the works council, both as regards internal affairs (we still haven't got a committee) and in external relations with trade union centres. In one year we may have four or five assemblies. In my view, if we could get a committee going and get lots more workers to share the responsibility, we could widen our scope and get better communications all round, and then we'd be able to study long-term prospects as well, instead of just concentrating on fighting for higher wages: we could work towards real workers' ownership of the factory. At the moment, the worker tends to think that the members of the works council can solve every problem: it's either the boss's decision, or the decision of the works council. When there's a summit meeting between Management and works council to weigh up a problem and seek a compromise, if certain demands are not met then (when people aren't mature) all the discontent falls on the union.

Why aren't people mature yet? As far as the union is concerned, no one has yet succeeded in making the workers understand that the union has got to be made up of the workers themselves. When I was elected onto the works council I had men come up to me and say:

'I voted for you—now how about standing me a coffee?' 'I voted for you—I'm your friend.' They hadn't understood that it was a responsibility I was undertaking.

My ambition is to make some contribution towards changing society. I belong to the citizens' committee of the PSIUP—I've always been a socialist, but I felt I couldn't go on following Nenni as he got further and further away from Socialism as I'd always understood it. Sometimes my wife says something to me and I just don't notice—I'm thinking about something else, and I just don't hear her, and she has to tell me again later. I don't like living life just as it comes: I want my life to have some definite aim, some method; I don't want to be led, I don't want to just stand and wait for things to happen. I want to make my own contribution, and I want the people around me to make theirs too—no matter how small they are individually, together they'll add up to something important to society. Man isn't made just for money—it's not money that makes a man important: it's what he can contribute to society.

Sometimes I seem to see things, see myself, from far off, from a great height: a man seems a tiny little thing crawling about, yet if you look closer you find he gets bigger. A man may seem to be a separate being, but in fact he needs other people, he can't live on his own. People try to cut themselves off, but the fact is they can't live alone.

AN ANONYMOUS WORKER IN THE SAME FIRM

I'd rather you didn't take my name.

I've been working in this factory for five years now.

In these five years, I've learnt how very different factory life is from what you expect when you first arrive. I used to think the relationship with work-mates would be one of harmony and sincerity, and instead I've found it's a life full of hypocrisy: lying gossip and telling false tales. As for our superiors, I haven't yet made out the best way to deal with them, whether you ought to do what they say, whether you ought to be hypocritical: I still can't tell whether it's true co-operation they want or mere servility.

I'd got the impression before, from my reading and from conversations, that the atmosphere among the workers would be one of harmony and sincerity. I've been enormously disappointed.

I've withdrawn into myself, so as not to appear in a bad light by rebelling, and also so as to avoid having to be servile. Lots of the factory's problems I won't even discuss with my mates, in case they should go and give some twisted report of what I say to get themselves into the good books of the Management.

There was a time when I began to take part in a union group: I had thought their aims were genuine, but in fact they seldom achieved what they were supposed to be after. Our interests which they were meant to be working for would be either forgotten or set aside, and it would turn out to be something quite different they were concerned with; we would discover afterwards, or sometimes even in the midst of our agitating, that the reasons for provoking action were merely political and nothing to do with the interests of individual workers. I felt I was being used. If I join up with a trade union group in order to protect my interests, it seems only fair they should explain clearly each time exactly what the real motives for the agitation are.

I am discontented. I haven't got the sort of job I want: nobody's interested in what I might be able to do, my potentialities are going to waste. I don't earn enough to keep my family. I see my hopes fading away as the years go by. I feel my life is being wasted.

I would like to have some more human sort of work. The air you breathe here is a mixture of dust, smoke, acid fumes. The seasons go by outside and we're not even aware of them. The firm should be properly organized, with everybody's ideas clear. We ought to be properly prepared for the work that needs doing, so that we could all take an active part in it. There are a lot of us who feel like this, all the more sensitive and thoughtful people.

Should we hold meetings? Should we put up more posters? We don't know what to do, or how to do it. But as long as these conditions continue, we won't join in. It's not within my powers to do anything to alter the situation. I'm just a minute pawn in the establishment. What can I do?

THE DIRECTOR OF RAYTHEON-ELSI

——What are the chief obstacles to associate life in your factory?

INGEGNERE PROFUMO: The chief obstacle here is the missing link in the communications chain: it is extremely difficult to create fore-men. The training of workers in general isn't an insoluble problem —it just costs a lot. We're not even too bad at forming technicians, from skilled workers to highly skilled engineers: again it's a prob-lem of time and costs—the raw material is there, and it responds. But between these two groups there has got to be a link, the fore-man: and he is extremely difficult to create, because he has to com-bine specialized technical skill with the ability to deal with people, to mediate between the planner and the men who have to put the plan into practice. It is very difficult to train them here: all we can do is to select them from among the best workers; but unfortunately, as soon as they are selected, this step up in the hierarchy gives them the feeling of being in a different class altogether. They nearly always end up in opposition to both management and workers, unable to mediate. In the North, the old firms have inherited the tradition of having collaborators among the older employees, who manage more or less instinctively to speak both languages at the same time and so can mediate successfully.

A difficulty of another kind and at a different level concerns mainly the technicians. Technical specialization inevitably means that in the solution of a given problem the contribution of the indi-vidual is only partial: a problem can only be solved by a synthesis of various scientific aspects and techniques, a combination of studies in depth by individual specialists in the various fields. Today, no matter how well qualified and intelligent a man may be, his general knowledge and even his specific technical knowledge can only be partial, and so he inevitably needs to combine his brains with other partially specialized brains to form an integrated whole.

Out of this necessity two difficulties arise: first, that everyone is obliged to play a more humble part, when what each one wants is to solve the problem himself, with the result that he either does the work badly or tries to score off the others. The second difficulty is the lack of men capable of carrying out the necessary synthesis. As far as I can see, it is partly the Italian mentality, and partly the type of education that fosters that mentality, which make it impossible to find people who can co-ordinate the various partial specializa-tions: this lack is more serious in the South than in the North, I think mainly from want of experience here.

Out of our sixty-four graduates, fifty-four are local; and I think our findings are revealing. They are intelligent, well educated—but they are not as productive as they ought to be, because of their instinctive competitiveness. We have one or two extremely high-powered technicians who still have these primitive defects. And of course it's the same at every level: even the ordinary worker is convinced his own work is more substantial than that of his neighbours.

Six months later I meet Gaetano Alfano again:

——I've heard that large numbers of workers have been dismissed from ELSI recently.

——Only a few minutes ago I was arguing with someone who was accusing me of being an extremist and trying to do too much.

Quite unexpectedly, at the end of August '65 (when the factory was shut down for the holiday), in spite of the fact that it is shortly to be expanded for the production of colour television the Management announced the dismissal of three hundred and eighteen employees—no more sign of the so-called 'good relations': the boss was boss.

The holiday was turned upside-down. We held meetings: the workers saw clearly that without a united struggle there would be disastrous consequences. But in the meantime the unions came to an agreement with the Management, and accepted the dismissal of forty-one clerical workers and seventy-five other workers, as well as the suspension of a hundred and nine workers on redundancy pay. They thought it was realistic to give way and accept a compromise at once. They ought to have stood firm: either all in, or all out. Now the workers, whether those dismissed or those still at work, are gravely dissatisfied because they feel they've been overridden and largely abandoned by the trade unions. They don't feel so strong any more. A lot have lost faith. We'll have to start all over again.

One day in July '66 I again meet Gaetano who has in the meantime been denounced for defamation after handing out leaflets severely criticizing the firm's policies.

——It's not that they've lost faith in the union as such—it's the individuals who represent union action that they mistrust: and I don't think it's just our union that's like this, I think it's the same with most of them down here.

Since the sackings last August the workers have been obliged to think about the security of their own jobs, and haven't been able to consider campaigning within the firm. They live in constant worry that the same thing will happen every August. The manœuvre is obvious: at the beginning, the main pressure within the factory was from the mafia; then, as their influence gradually diminished and the workers began to show their worth, the Management tried to interfere in union organization—and unfortunately they've succeeded. It's been a blow to the workers to see the union representatives not speaking for them but agreeing with the bosses.

Some of us who were dismissed (there was political discrimination in a lot of the dismissals) have organized ourselves into a co-operative which aims to treat the individual more humanely (which is also economic sense); and we'll also have a compensation fund which will enable us to make up the pay of anyone who's out of work at certain times. There are about fifty of us pioneering this new electro-mechanical co-operative.

Besides this development, there's been a certain maturing recently among the workers at the shipyard. At the Sicilian Dry Docks they've at last woken up to the need for action. In May they occupied the docks, and all the shipyard workers supported them; and although the police were tough and made dozens of arrests—thirty-one workers were handcuffed and chained like a gang of criminals—their requests were met.

Angela Alfano, Gaetano's wife

When I first met my husband I was fifteen. I used to live with my granny—my mother died when I was four. I'd always lived in that house at Arenella with my granny and my aunt. I never went out of the house, and never knew anyone. Good folk, but jealous: I mustn't stand at the door . . . I was the second youngest of seven children. Honest folk: too honest: I wasn't allowed to meet anyone. My granny had a grocery shop, and when young men came in—we sold cigarettes too—if I was there she signalled to me to go away. She was over cautious because I had no mother and she felt too responsible. I only went out once a week, to Mass, and afterwards I came straight home. I didn't have any close girl friends, but I was fond of children, and I got on well with the mothers too. The girls I knew were mostly the same as me.

Then one day I was looking out of the door and I heard a motor bike, and this young man came past. I took a liking to him, but I also found fault with the way he went past, the way he twitched at his jacket made him seem nervous. I just saw him that once, and then a whole month went by without me seeing him again. Then a cousin of mine went to the cinema, and next morning she came to see me, because I was ill, and she said: 'Listen, there was a young man there staring at our family.' 'Could it be that young man who went by on the motor bike?' I said—I'd told her about that, you see. Well, the days passed; and then I saw there was this new bakery at Arenella, and one day when I was on my way to buy a kilo of spaghetti I saw this young man inside the bakery. And he looked at me, and I looked at him. From that day on, he kept coming to the bakery, because the owner was a friend of his, and he used to stand in front of the bakery, and I went out to buy packets of biscuits and things, and when I went past him I felt all ashamed, because I could feel him looking at me, and the things would slip out of my hand and I'd feel even more ashamed.

Then one day one of my brothers says to me: 'This can't go on, this young man standing there in front of the bakery like that. It's a dishonour, it's not the sort of treatment we're accustomed to.' And after that my brother wouldn't allow me to go between the house and the shop any more—it made him jealous, so he kept me indoors.

Then my husband came and explained to my family he was thinking of marriage: we'd never spoken—he'd made a sign from time to time but I couldn't answer because it wasn't proper to answer. And then he'd sent me a little note through the baker's wife, saying, 'If you love me say yes, if you don't love me say no.' So I wrote: 'Yes yes yes yes,' four times. My brother had warned me: 'You mind out now, there's someone after you who's ten years older than you: he's too old for you.' I was fifteen, yet they were still treating me like a child! But I was already grown up—I looked about seventeen or eighteen.

And so the marriage was agreed, and we got engaged. And we were so fond of each other, we used to talk all the time whenever we were together—we were together too much, my granny used to say, they were all ashamed of us. But we loved each other so much that their nagging seemed silly. We went on like that for two years. He was a mechanic at the shipyard. Every now and again we'd quarrel, but we'd make it up again at once.

My granny was always telling me: 'There are thorns as well as roses in married life: marriage isn't easy, there's a lot of suffering in it as well.' But I loved him, and it seemed ridiculous to think of unhappiness, and I thought: 'Whatever happens, good or bad, I should welcome it with open arms.' I suppose they thought I was more of a child than I really was.

Sometimes he and my aunt used to quarrel, because he was a Socialist and she was a very devout Catholic, a Christian Democrat. He wanted everyone to see things his way, but my aunt was worried that if Socialism won they'd kill the priests and shut down the churches and that would be the end of religion. I didn't want to displease him, but in my heart of hearts I felt my aunt was right. And it terrified me that they could quarrel.

Well, we got married, and for a while he went on working at the shipyard. Then one evening he said to me: 'Listen, I'm going to sea.' 'Why?' I said. I was in an interesting condition then, and I cried—I didn't want my husband to go away, I didn't want to be left alone. But he wasn't earning much at the shipyard, and he thought that since children were coming we'd need a home of our own. 'We must think ahead,' he said. But I said: 'You're bringing in enough, these rooms will do—don't go.' But he wouldn't listen, he was already dedicated to go, he really wanted to.

'And what about me—are you leaving me here? At least leave me with my granny!' So he left me with my granny, and I rented rooms nearby, and bit by bit I bought the furniture with the money he sent. I had a baby girl, and he came back ten months later from the Persian Gulf. I hadn't lit the gas all that time—my husband wasn't there and I didn't feel like cooking, I just used to eat whatever my granny sent round: cooking a meal would have felt like celebrating without my husband.

When he came back, he stayed two months. I kept on telling him: 'Leave it at that, don't go to sea again.' I'd already managed to pay off the last instalment on the furniture. 'Find a job here,' I kept saying. While he was waiting for his orders to embark again, he wasn't idle—he'd already found a job as a mechanic. And for a treat he took me to Turin, where a brother of his was living, and I saw Northern Italy for the first time—I'd never left home before. It was like a honeymoon, I felt. Their place was in the suburbs, out near the open fields, the flowers. He took me out on trips, and it was lovely seeing so much green even in summer.

After we came back, he was away again for two years. Every twenty-six days he'd either telephone me or send me a parcel. And sometimes I used to go to Naples when his ship was stopping there for a day before leaving again for the Persian Gulf.

Then he came home. I was so happy when he came home. But still it seemed to me he spent too much time out and not enough at home: he always had trade union business, Party business. I didn't take any interest because I thought I was an ignorant person, and I didn't understand anything. And he used to say to me: 'You don't know anything about life outside, you only know about things in the home.' And I used to tell him: 'Keep yourself to yourself—don't bother with other people's affairs. Are you the only one? D'you have to do everything yourself? People don't appreciate the good things you do for them.' And he would answer: 'The day's got to come when they will understand. If we all minded our own business, nothing would ever get done.'

By this time I'd become a little more resigned. I'd had other children. When he came home in the evenings he'd be so tired he'd go straight to bed. He had so much on his mind. Sometimes I'd talk to him and he wouldn't hear, and then I'd get angry: 'What's got into your head now, that you come home and don't say a word to me?' Sometimes he'd try and explain things, but I found it difficult, and boring, and I'd start thinking of all the housework to be done. Sometimes he didn't even seem affectionate any more, he was so dedicated. Sometimes it used to make me cry. I thought: 'Nothing but work, trade union, Party—what's the point of living then?' I'd have liked to have him always at home, at least when he wasn't at work.

And this sort of life still goes on the same as ever. Only yesterday evening there was a telephone call and he had to go off to the trade union, and I don't know when I can get to talk to him.

I'm glad I married him, and he's right to do trade union stuff— but he's wearing himself out, because he puts too much into it, he doesn't think of himself at all. I can't believe it's a good thing if he comes home with his head aching. Often and often I think: 'What on earth makes you do it when you could stay comfortably at home?' Often I say to him: 'I know I don't know anything about it, but the other people aren't like you, they only think of themselves—and so why should you bother to think of other people?' He's killing himself for the workers. And it seems to me they'll only think the worse of him, for not minding his own business. And I'm always worrying that from one moment to the next he might get the sack. Though to tell the truth I'm not really anxious, because I have faith in my husband. But it often occurs to me that they could hurt him, that someone could hurt him out of spite.

This is what worries me: if he's worried, he won't eat—his worries upset him so that he can't eat. It's all very well to think of other people, but there are ways and ways . . . I wish he could be calmer, more peaceful. It's true I'm very proud of him, though to tell the truth I've never told him so.

This is my dream: for my husband to get me a house of my own, with its own garden all round, on the outskirts of town—perhaps even in the hills. And we could grow flowers, and have quiet. The sort of life I had as a girl, I wasn't happy, but I had to put up with

Above: Senator Girolamo Messeri and the American-Italian gangster, Frank Coppola. *Below:* Calogero Volpe with two mafiosi in the 1958 election campaign.

Above: Calogero Volpe, in office. *Left:* Bernardo Matterella and Cardinal Ruffini.

it: but even now that I'm married my life isn't any different, except that I am a bit more free. Occasionally I may take the children out for a treat, we go and pick flowers at La Favorita, and I buy them an ice. In Palermo us women all keep ourselves to ourselves: we greet each other, and lend each other whatever we need, but each one stays in her own house. Things aren't as I'd like them to be. I'd like to see more of the old-fashioned propriety, and parents being gentle with their children. I don't like to see casual behaviour, and confidences too easily given. One good new thing, though, is television: it means a lot for mothers and children, it makes life better.

It oughtn't to be so easy for a person to waste himself. I'd like men to be brothers, and I'd like there to be good health and work for all. But everyone should have their quiet, too, and feel themselves live—the body needs that too. I'd like everyone to be friends and brothers, yes, but I'd like to have my husband at home more.

Three 'Supernumeraries'

A telephone call from Palermo: someone wants to see me urgently, together with some of his colleagues, about a serious situation. We make an appointment. We meet. The three tell me their story but, fearing reprisals, ask me to keep their names secret.

FIRST: The story began in 1961. In November 1960, the administrative set-up of the Sicilian Provinces was changed, and they instituted elected administrative Councils to replace the commissarial administration. And as is now the custom—in fact practically the law—the Chief Officers of the various departments summoned to the administrative offices certain young men who were seeking secure and permanent jobs.

SECOND: Let's not mince words: each official came in with his own band of hangers-on, election campaigners who'd been deluded into thinking they'd find an easy living this way. We all had some particular connection of friendship or family either with the head of department or with the Council chairman. Our confidence about getting a post was due either to promises received or to knowledge of situations vacant in the offices.

THIRD: Seeing that other personnel in the Administration in the same position as ourselves were being selected for permanent posts we naturally thought the same was likely to happen to us, since in most of the public bodies they no longer have open competition, or if they do it's a formality and limited to personnel already employed as supernumeraries.

SECOND: And now not one of us (there are 148 of us in all)—not one of us has received any remuneration whatsoever over the last eighteen months. A number of us are fathers with families to support; and rather than abandon hope of being taken on by the Administration, many of us have got to the point of having to sell off our furniture, and being evicted from our homes, or having our electricity and gas and water cut off, while we go on counting on the jobs promised as certain from one day to the next.

But now we just can't wait any longer.

FIRST: Don't forget that up till December '63 us invoice clerks were paid . . .

SECOND: When you hear 'invoice clerks' or 'piece-workers' or 'supernumeraries' or 'diurnals' or 'ancillaries'—it's always us they mean: people still don't know quite what to call us.

FIRST: . . . Up till '63 we were paid a lump sum, from some fund or other—no one knew quite where it came from.

THIRD: I've heard that one Council paid by putting their employees down in the books as *lamps and pictures purchased*, because the term 'invoice clerks' doesn't exist in the books. And some get paid through the Mental Health Centre.

FIRST: So, as I was saying, up till the end of '63 we were getting this lump sum of sixty or seventy thousand lire a month.

THIRD: And then came this crisis on the Council, though in fact it was already four months since we'd last been paid. The Council which succeeded continued to withhold the pay which—though minimal—we still counted on: we were signing I.O.U.s which we could not repay. The new Council was faced with the problem of how to find the funds in a regular way, but it failed, and then had to draw the attention of the proper authorities to the situation. However, we did receive on two or three occasions a partial payment of thirty thousand lire.

FIRST: The main point is this: it's now widely known that the failure so far to set up a proper selection process is due to the trial of strength that's going on between the Head of the Regional department of local bodies, Carollo, a *Doroteo*, and the Hon. Gioia, a Fanfani supporter. Carollo has stipulated that a stock of his protégés should be included among the candidates for selection, before he approves the selection process; and for his part Gioia does not intend to let Carollo have his way because he doesn't want him to strengthen his electoral position in Palermo. We are now the victims of these political ambitions.

DANILO: Wait a moment—I'm not quite clear about all this.

SECOND: Well, let's suppose he's Gioia, I'm Lima, and you're Carollo. You, Carollo, say: 'To approve this selection, I want thirty posts.' Gioia answers: 'I can't give you thirty posts, because if I give you thirty posts you'll give them to thirty sons or relatives or friends of Secretaries of Christian Democrat branches that support you, and then I'll be in a minority. If you want thirty, you'll have to give me eighty.' And Lima, Provincial Secretary of the Christian Democrats, will say: 'If you're taking eighty, then I'm taking eighty too.' Well, eighty and eighty make a hundred and sixty, and thirty is a hundred and ninety—so what are they to give all the other politicians if they've already gobbled up all the posts themselves? D'you suppose a Mattarella won't want his share? that a Restivo won't want his?

DANILO: Could you tell me exactly what happened: one day, each of you went to the office, right? and you were given a desk, and a chair, or at least some work to do. Were you really classed officially as voluntary workers?

THIRD: The first day, I was shown how to compile forms, etcetera, and I began on it myself. Some sort of working relationship was set up, even though equivocal.

FIRST: A step backwards: last January some 'piece-workers' formed a union affiliated to the CGIL, and asked the Administration to suspend all further appointments pending the regularization of personnel already in service, payment of their salaries to date, and the appointment of a commission of enquiry to ascertain the personnel in service: because the Administration doesn't know who we are, or even how many we are.

THIRD: Our presence is only vaguely recognized: they've no idea of our numbers or of our names. The General Secretary, in charge of all personnel, ought to know who is working in his offices, who the people are sitting regularly behind the desks, at the telephones, at the typewriters, with the Administration's documents in their hands, official papers, official secrets.

When this union was formed, they only collected sixty supporters!

FIRST: Our uncertain position also includes a fear of reprisals by our protectors: the minute we were to take up a firm position in defence of our interests, they would at once become our enemies, after having done us the favour of getting us in in the first place. Everyone's afraid. We've been two years already not daring to hold a meeting. Nearly all of us are young men, with no trade-union experience.

SECOND: Each man thinks he's in a stronger position than the next: 'I'm all right—you do as you like.' But once their protector is no longer in office, then they feel themselves weaker and try to unite. As long as their protector is in office they keep themselves to themselves, confident that the recommendation they had is still powerful enough. Apparently at Catania a fortnight ago they regularized a similar situation involving three hundred people through a proper selection process organized by the Provincial Administration.

THIRD: The ones whose benefactors are in office won't come forward. They're even warned: 'You keep out of it, otherwise your situation will be made more difficult—you don't want to make yourselves unpopular.' But now we are thinking of forming a group. Seeing that the way of individual recommendations has failed us, we're convinced that it's only by uniting that we can succeed in getting things moving again.

SECOND: We all feel drained of our own personality in this situation, this kind of limbo: we feel we're failures. Outsiders who aren't aware of this nasty life inside the Provincial Administration can't understand, they think of us as useless good-for-nothings. A man gets home and tells the family: 'I had a word with the Head today—he said he'd be sure to see me fixed up shortly, he promised.' So the family say: 'All right, we'll manage to get by somehow for one more month . . .' thinking that next month all will be well. But next month comes—and you're back to square one. Sometimes even your parents or your wife or your fiancée will say: 'You're useless! How can we go on like this?' Eighteen months. Eighteen months! Some men have even got to the point of considering murder or suicide.

Lots of people just haven't the strength of mind to give up and go, because they keep thinking: 'Maybe the minute I'm gone they'll settle it after all.'

There are grown-up men, fathers in despair, who are driven to tears. Give it up and go—but go where?

Over a year passes. In July '66 this statement appears in the local papers: 'It is now thirty-one months since the supernumeraries in the Provincial Administration received any pay . . . The internal competitions will not be held for at least a year. . . .'

24th September '66. The landslide in Agrigento[1] (19th July 1966) has helped to uncover whole chains of corruption, client-patron deals, calculated muddle: everybody talks about it, from the man in the street to Parliament.

Quite undaunted, Vincenzo Carollo, head of the Regional Department of local bodies, writes to a high-up official of Palermo Province the following letter concerning three of *his* 'supernumeraries':

'I gather that Naselli, Napoli, and Rusotto are no longer going to the Institute of Mental Health, after scarcely a month in service. I must remind you that the pledges given, and confirmed recently by telephone, were quite otherwise. Since I am obviously not in the habit of letting down those who trust me, would you kindly see to the matter as you, and Riggio and Lima, know how. I should be grateful if you would let me have an assurance on this matter. Your sincerely, Carollo.

P.S. Please let Riggio read this letter, so that he can give the necessary orders.'

[1] See page 123. (Tr.)

Sonia Alliata, Duchess of Salaparuta

In my view, the aristocracy live an isolated life, cut off from one another, each within his own narrow family circle.

No one of the aristocracy still lives in the country today: only one or two, perhaps, such as myself and the Princess Paternò here at Bagheria, twelve kilometres from Palermo.

Even in the old days, though, each family lived its own independent life, except that then the families were very rich and could give large parties, and so they kept more in touch with one another.

They had money, but I do not think there was any collaboration at all among the nobility, except within the narrow family circle, children and grandchildren: it didn't even extend to cousins. Each thought only of the glory of his own house, and that cannot but be founded on the poverty of others. That is how it always was, I am quite sure of it.

One goes to the few parties (there are only a few nowadays because it costs so much to give a party), and to the Massimo Theatre; people enjoy showing off their jewels, seeing others envy them: they enjoy trying to outshine everyone else. I enjoy it too, to tell you the truth: as long as I am alive, I hope it may always be said that the house of Villafranca Salaparuta conducted itself worthily, and that I made my contribution to its lustre and to its dignity in modern times.

The nobility is dying: it is the twilight of the gods. Once upon a time we were indeed gods, and all the great geniuses, from Michelangelo to Leonardo, were our subjects, for we are a chosen people. Now we are like museums, good for little more than for people to go and stare at. There is not much life left in us. Even our children are no longer princes and princesses, neither financially nor morally. But I am attached to the old ways: I am old, and I cannot change.

There is one link which, though invisible, binds us all, and that is our pride in belonging to the nobility. A race-horse is not the same

as a cart-horse. Some scientist—or perhaps he was a philosopher—
once said that it takes many generations for a cart-horse to lose its
long hair. Centuries and centuries of refinement.

Nowadays it is all materialism—the spirit no longer has any
expression today.

Although it doesn't take any organized form, there is a feeling—
a feeling for the defence of certain values, but . . . it is the twilight
of the gods. We no longer have the will to fight back, since ours is a
debased coinage. What holds us together still is our resistance to
vulgarization.

There is naturally a difference between the great families and the
lesser ones, counts and barons. But there are some barons who are
worth as much as princes: it is all a question of money. Even within
our aristocratic circle, whoever has more money is considered more
important, and whoever has none left is considered a nobody. Once
upon a time all the peasants used to vote for their master: every
nobleman had his own province, so to speak. The house of Villafranca had forty estates. So of course they had their own Senators,
whose living depended on them. Everyone votes according to
where his daily bread comes from.

Nowadays the lower orders are better off than we are. There is no
poverty: if a man is poor it is because he chooses to do nothing. I
know Generals' wives, Duchesses—even Princesses, who can no
longer afford to keep women-servants because they cost too much,
their pretensions are too high. These families only have one or two
servants left, it is the end of the relationship between aristocracy
and common people: they no longer have their peasants, they no
longer have their valets. In the old days, there was a beautiful relationship: our dependents served us willingly for generations (our
gardener had been with us for five generations, father to son,
father to son). And even today disengaged servants choose rather
to go into service with the nobility, even for lower wages, than with
the middle classes, because they are humiliated less: 'If I am to
serve, I will serve a gentlemen'—not an ordinary person like themselves: they recognize the superiority. The middle classes treat
them badly, whereas we treat them in a gentlemanly way, and take
them into our confidence.

I find it distressing to see the lower orders getting ahead, because naturally others' gain is my loss. But of course I do recognize, with my head at least, that it has to be that way: I only wish they could do it rather more slowly. *Natura aborret saltum*—sudden changes are painful.

There used to be a paternal relationship, paternalism: '*Voscieza mi benedica*'—'Your Excellency's blessing on us!' they used to say (and many still do); and the expression shows how they felt themselves to be in this position, in the position of being protected, like a child by its father. Once upon a time it was very very common, but now it is becoming a thing of the past, it is disappearing. The nobility (not the middle classes) were kind to them, though of course always keeping them in their place, you understand—I don't want to make myself out to be better than I am!—always keeping them at a certain distance. I adore dogs, I take them to the vet, feed them, cry when they die—but a dog is a dog. No, it never occurred to them that people's position could change: the peasants were to be peasants for ever—which I personally think is wrong, but I believe there are very few of us who think so. The world is changing, and change brings sorrow to whoever has to pass away: you must be understanding, and try to forgive us.

They ought to be ruthless with breakers of the law. And they ought to abolish the secrecy of the vote. Every man, or woman, ought to have the courage of his convictions and show his loyalty to the person he has chosen to represent him, since there is so much talk of ideals. And voters ought to have the necessary qualifications to vote: that is, they ought to undergo some small examination to prove their mental education, to show they have at least a minimal understanding of social problems, and common sense.

The grandees of the old days used to bring geniuses to their courts and feed them gratis. This is what makes me weep: today, whichever way one turns, one sees idiocies: beatniks—and think of what has happened to music, and painting. Look at these flowers now, these roses: why shouldn't they be a delight? People should think of spiritual joys, of the love of beauty.

We still have one thing to bring us together every day: canasta. There are twenty-four of us who meet to play daily—not for the money, but because it is an intelligent game and there is a spirit of competition amongst us. One day at the Marchioness of X's, another day at Countess Y's: an innocent occupation, very superficial, and of very little value. I play every day—what else would you have me do? I lead a useless life.

A Protestant, a Jesuit, a Cardinal

PIETRO PANASCIA, *Pastor of the Waldensian Church of Palermo*: For us, the meeting point is not any human ideology, but Christian faith, the religion of a love which does not divide men but makes them brothers, unites them. Wherever we have preached the Gospel over these last few years, in La Noce, for example, and Sferracavallo, people and families who before were complete strangers to one another have come together and established ties of friendship and affection.

Obviously Christianity, a common faith in the same Lord, represents *par excellence* the meeting point for men of different social categories and of different cultural backgrounds, because the love of Christ moves us to discover in our neighbour, who before was a stranger to us, a brother whom we can no longer ignore. Ever since the earliest days of Christianity, people of the same Faith have naturally formed a community, feeling the need to know one another, to be together.

——How many Waldensians are there in Palermo?

——It is difficult to get exact statistics. There are not many of us: including other denominations of Evangelists, I don't think there can be more than two thousand, and about half of them are Waldensians. The mileu in which we operate is that of the mass of Catholics by birth who are no longer practising but live completely outside Catholicism, either because they see in Catholicism the ally of the rich, of those in power, and therefore attribute to it responsibility for a social order manifestly contrary to any sense of justice; or because Catholicism has failed to help them to solve their own problems; or because they have not found within their church that love which ought to distinguish the Christian community. Some of these find in the small Evangelical communities a warmth and a human sympathy and a new vision of life such as they had never experienced before.

——How many of these attend the Church services?

——Virtually everyone of the Evangelical faith attends the services: it is well known that minorities are more active. The same frequency of attendance is not found in countries where Protestants are in the majority.

——How many of them are actively trying, and in what ways, to transform the world around them?

——It is a principle that everyone of the Evangelical faith ought to seek to transform the world around him by word and deed; in practice, many are hindered by their own work and by family responsibilities. However, there are frequent cases of people periodically dedicating part of their time to a particular social service in our area, in the most disinterested way. In recent years we have had collaborators from abroad who, abandoning their normal work, devote their services to our cause, sometimes for as much as a year, without receiving any payment.

Here in Palermo we have recently set up, side by side with the Church, two local groups, one at La Noce and the other at Sferracavallo. The group at La Noce grew out of activities begun in 1959 in aid of children belonging to particularly needy families. It began very modestly, for we had no financial means at our disposal—only plenty of faith and goodwill, and the desire to serve the Lord in the person of our humblest brethren, above all through the children. Nevertheless the work has been expanded and consolidated year by year. It was originally inspired by an Italian-American lady who offered us the use of her villa.

——What kind of role does the Pastor play?

——The Pastor is not the head of the Church, nor does he even represent church 'authority'. His role is to co-ordinate activities, to conduct worship, to expound the Gospel, to attend to spiritual needs. The life of our community is run on what, in political terms, one might call absolutely democratic lines: it is a self-governing community, and all decisions regarding group life, from the timetable for services to the appointment of members to positions of responsibility, of delegates to meetings or to the regional Synods— all these decisions are taken by the community. The Pastor's authority lies only in the moral example he sets, in his spirit of service, in his theological training and preparation.

——What are the particular difficulties within your groups?

——One of our most saddening experiences is that of frequently coming across people who find their way into our Church not as a result of genuine conversion but merely in order to get material benefits or aid, or a post, or some work.

Our communities are well run: the first thing that strikes an outsider is the orderliness. The timetable is always respected: our meetings always begin at the appointed time, never late, and are never postponed. This is part of a discipline that has always distinguished our movement. We consider punctuality an essential quality of the Christian character: it's almost our motto, we see it as a sign of consideration for others.

Another thing we find is that some people, for no apparent reason, become less and less regular in attendance at services, and eventually lapse altogether. In the last few years we have had a loss of about ten per cent, while on the other hand we have been increasing by something like twenty per cent. One must also take into consideration the fact that we have fairly strict criteria for recruitment: new members are only admitted to the Church after a trial period lasting from two to four years. Notwithstanding the notable relaxation of the climate of opinion over recent years with regard to religious minorities, it must be admitted that not everyone is capable of sustaining for very long the struggle that profession of the Evangelical faith in Italy entails.

Padre Noto

I ask Padre Noto (whom I do not know), director of the Casaprofessa Social Centre, for an appointment: 'I'll tell you what,' answers the Jesuit politely, 'would it suit you if we met at the house of the director of the United States Information Service, rather than at Casaprofessa?' Since I cannot imagine being compromised myself by any place in the world, naturally this suits me as well as anywhere. We meet at the house of our host, who for the occasion has also invited the American Consul. Out of the long conversation —frank and cordial, as they say of diplomatic meetings—emerge these key points in Padre Noto's thought:

7

A world of the American order, cultural, judicial, and structural, is basically the sort of world to be developed: and there is nothing political about American financial investment;

The Casaprofessa Centre, 'in conformity with the Jesuit vocation, is concerned with the formation of cadres at the apex of the social pyramid'.

At the end of our conversation I leave him a few questions I have noted down; he will consider them, he says, and send me his answers: which he duly does.

——What do you think are the major obstacles to associate life in the area?

——In the economic and commercial field: mutual mistrust among the citizens; uncertainty due to ignorance and to the absence of proper channels of communication; the citizen's lack of faith in the protective organs of the State, whose effective presence ought to diminish the risks involved in investing private capital.

In the cultural, social and political field: lack of leadership, of disinterested, capable and dedicated organizers able to make the objectives of the association desirable to actual or potential members; the inadequacy of the organizational formula: organizational structures corresponding to the real needs of individuals are too seldom effectively put into practice; lack of true culture at the base: true cultural values are not adequately appreciated, whether from ignorance or under the influence of certain practices now common in a society accustomed to graft, string-pulling, and the system of patronage and clientship.

——How far does your activity as religious people succeed in overcoming these difficulties?

——The organizations pursuing religious ends are sensitive to these deficiencies at a local level. Nevertheless we are directing our efforts towards the formation of leaders who will be (a) dedicated, keen, responsible; (b) capable in the organizational field and in the field of direction.

There are organizations pursuing cultural ends which are directed by religious people not in their capacity as men of religion but as men of culture.

Cardinal Ruffini[1]

It would be useful to have an interview with Cardinal Ernesto
Ruffini (whose motto is *'firmiter stat'*), the most authoritative representative of the Church in Sicily: among other things Doctor of
Philosophy, Professor of Holy Scripture, appointed Consultor of
the Holy Office and Assistant Censor of Books in '24, Domestic
Prelate in '25, Secretary of the Sacred Congregation of Seminaries
in '28, Archbishop of Palermo in '45, raised to the rank of Cardinal
with the title of Santa Sabina in '46, *Cavaliere di Gran Croce* from
'63, made an honorary citizen by the Council of Palermo in '64; a
notorious admirer of Franco's Spain. His coat of arms shows two
lions rampant on either side of a crown, protected by a double
Cross and by a wide Cardinal's hat.

I ask to speak to the Cardinal's secretary on the telephone.
They hand me over to him. I ask if he could arrange an appointment for me with the Cardinal, explaining that I would like to find
out what he thinks about group life, and about obstacles to group
life in Palermo Province. He laughs in reply, though in a not un-
friendly way, then: 'Danilo Dolci himself? One hears so many
rumours about you . . . that are somewhat disturbing. I will
speak to the Cardinal. Ring again at about eleven. I am Monsignor
Luigi Longhi—ask for Don Luigi.'

At eleven the appointment is fixed for five p.m.

The Cardinal receives me kindly, even cordially, and talks for
about an hour, almost in soliloquy, about various matters which I
am not authorized to repeat.

I had jotted down a few preliminary questions, some of which I
proposed to go into in more detail according to what turn the conversation might take: How do you see group life in Palermo? What
do you think are the difficulties of group life here? How would you
like Palermo to be? What do you think is most urgent for the development of the city and the surrounding region? What is your
exact function in Palermo today? Do you have meetings with the

---

[1] Cardinal Ruffini died in June 1967. The appointment of Cardinal Carpino
as his successor indicates that Cardinal Ruffini's policies and attitudes were not
after all personal and fortuitous but are shared by the Catholic hierarchy, in
Sicily and in Rome.

parish priests? What form do they take? In the Seminary, do you have meetings between seminarists and teachers? What are these meetings like?

During the course of the conversation, His Eminence only glanced at the sheet of paper I had handed him, and in the end smilingly warded off the questions ('Between you and me there is a gulf') essentially because of his position, which he indicated thus:

——I have responsibilities; Pulcinella once said there were only two free men in the kingdom—himself, a nobody, and the King: the rest in between have to watch how they go.

——I think conscientious objection is stupid: the individual ought to take it that the authorities know more than he does; and moreover it would be a good thing to have a single national party.

——Non-violence? Certainly I am against war, but even the Ancients taught us: '*Si vis pacem para bellum*'.[1]

Though direct answers to my questions are not to be found, revealing light (and official, so to speak,) is thrown by the Pastoral Letters sent out between 1947 and 1965 from the Archbishop's Palace 'to the holy flock', if we read them with the attention they deserve.

Here are just a few brief extracts relevant to our theme:

'Authority comes from God.'

'It is clear that the Church by its very nature is an unequal society, and perfectly organized from its earliest beginnings . . . Its hierarchy does not rise from below, as in modern democracies: it descends from on high.

'. . . clear distinction, therefore, between ecclesiastical and lay authority: it is for the first to teach and to govern, the second is disciple and subject.'

'Our Divine Saviour seeks the aid of the members of His mystic Body, not because He has any need thereof, but out of His infinite mercy and condescension.'

'. . . "He who doeth works unbeknown to the Bishop," says Saint Ignatius of Antioch, "serveth the devil".'

'How often on our pastoral rounds, as we linger to ask one or two simple questions on the Catechism, do we find among the faithful (and this among the most regular churchgoers) not one who is able

[1] 'If you want peace, prepare for war.' (Tr.)

to reply! They cannot distinguish between perfect contrition for sin and imperfect contrition . . . And it happens also that even the parish priests often lose heart, and feel themselves almost constrained to omit the explanation of the Catechism because they find the Church deserted.'

'The French Revolution of evil fame . . .'

'Conscious of the terrible responsibility that weighs upon us in the sight of Christ our High Priest who is soon to be our Judge, we again urge the reverend parish priests to devote particular care and attention (both by means of their own labours and through the intermediary of other priests) to the twenty lessons that the Government programme has introduced into the IIIrd, IVth and Vth classes of elementary schools, to complement the religious instruction imparted by the teachers. We have so much difficulty in getting children for the Christian Doctrine, why not make use of the elementary schools, which gather together in a disciplined atmosphere practically all children? In agreement with the schoolmasters and schoolmistresses, the great majority of whom are a shining example of the Christian life, we could put this opportunity to the best advantage also for the preparation for the Sacraments of Confession, Communion and Confirmation.'

'There is as great a difference (teaches St Pius X) between the priest and the ordinary man of goodwill, as between heaven and earth.'

'Democracy, which properly understood is just and fitting and Christian, sometimes ends up by provoking in certain circles the strange idea that the Church herself ought to become more democratic.'

'Some people claim in relation to the Church complete independence in the social and political field, thus insinuating a distinction between the sacred and the profane . . . It has not escaped our notice, moreover, that some of our own people have repeatedly attempted to associate themselves with certain enemies of the Church and of Religion, in view of possible social reforms.'

'To work in effective collaboration with the Hierarchy, the laity must be docile, sincere, and devout towards their pastors.'

'When Jesus said: "Render unto Caesar the things which are Caesar's, and unto God the things that are God's", he was affirming the distinction between the two orders of things: but in inculcating the superiority of spiritual values over material values, and of eternal life over this earthly life, he established the predominance of the one and the consequent subordination of the other.'

'The Church founded by Jesus Christ is one alone. The Holy Fathers saw it foreshadowed in Noah's Ark, the sole means to salvation amidst the universal flood.

. . . The doctrine of Christ is one alone, and is revealed by the Apostles and their successors: he who believes it is saved, he who accepts it not is damned; we become Christians through baptism, and there is but one baptism; the members are many, but are united socially by one single authority, the sacred Hierarchy with Peter at its head, whom all must obey.'

'During the last few years there have emerged here and there attempts to promote the union of the Churches—held to be sisters—: Anglican, Greek Orthodox, and Roman, by means of a species of compromise which is incompatible with certain dogmas and with the supreme jurisdiction of the Pope; however, that can never happen, since it is impossible to divide up piecemeal our Faith which as one indivisible block constitutes the foundation of our holy religion. To achieve this desirable union, there is only one possible way: the way of reconciliation to the Holy See, which was consecrated by the blood of the chief of the Apostles, Peter and Paul, and submission to its authority and to its rule.

. . . The weakening of nationalism, which had raised high barriers to divide men, and the ever-growing need for a guide to direct, a power to sustain, will make it easier for these our dear brethren to take the way that leads to Rome.'

'The priest, though a man, must yet be one apart from other men, to be, with Christ, their Mediator and Advocate with the Most High.'

'A Christian people, without a doubt, values its priest, and when it finds itself without one will allow itself no rest until it has obtained one. Immediately after the last world war—for us Italians the most disastrous ever recorded in history—in towns where all had been destroyed, if among the smoking ruins a man of the government appeared, the desolate families would issue forth from their improvised shelters and in plaintive tones beg before all else for the reconstruction of the Church, and with the Church the priest . . .'

'. . . The pupils of the Secondary Schools, lower and upper, and at their head the Principals and staff, make a spectacle of eminent piety as they throng round the confessionals and the altars; the directors and teachers of the Primary Schools collaborate with enthusiasm in the preparation of children for the First Communion.'

'The rite of baptism, through which we become part of the flock of Jesus Christ, is singularly instructive. As the baby, desiring that his original sin be wiped out, enters into the Temple, the priest meets him at the door and straightway, with great solemnity, asks of him: "What do you ask of the Church of God?" "Faith!" reply the godparents on behalf of the infant. And the holy minister, as though amazed by so wise an answer, asks for an explanation: "Why do you seek faith? What does faith offer you?" "Life everlasting!" This, then, is the fervent desire of the new-born babe: he has but recently entered into this earthly life, yet already his soul transcends the heavens to secure unto itself life everlasting. "If, then, you desire to enter into life (everlasting)", continues the priest, "keep the Commandments."'

'Some are Christians only on occasion, when a religious feast procures for all a holiday from work, and entertainment; but when their presence outside might be needed to bear witness to Jesus Christ, they shut themselves away indoors. Such behaviour is ingratitude . . . it is betrayal. How is it possible to forget the undertaking made at Baptism, and the solemn promises of the First Communion?'

' "The preservation of property," admonishes the Supreme Pontiff, "is the corner-stone of social order." It is, in fact, normally the natural foundation of a life lived according to the requirements of human dignity; it is the prop and stay of family stability; it gives nobility to work, and increases productivity.'

'It is not riches that make man happy: they are, rather, the cause of habitual worries and frequent anguish to the man who possesses them; often their hollowness is most bitterly felt by the dying man who finds himself constrained to leave his vast properties to heirs who will probably squander his wealth.'

'Some Christians appear to have an inferiority complex; they consider Religion good enough for private life, but not sufficiently valid for social life: for which reason they seem to behave as though, for example, Catholic social doctrine in order to be adequate for our day and age needed to be supplemented or perfected by other doctrines or other systems.'

The University

A student, Piero Calcara

I don't in fact take part in any real group life, any organic group with a stable structure that holds meetings and takes decisions and acts on them: what I have is a series of contacts with people or groups of people on various occasions, and there's not necessarily any continuity, even though there is generally a basic logical unity in this type of contact.

Fundamentally, I should say that here in Palermo where organic groups don't exist, most individuals are in the same position as me: in fact, I'd even say that my social life was more active than the average.

I don't think many people here reflect on the necessity for group life. It seems to me that among the most active people there's a certain feeling of distrust towards group life, and an exaltation of individual life; the less active ones seek occasions for meeting other people not in order to get new things done but simply for the sake of being with other people.

As regards my educational experience, I'd always wanted a group life, and tried to create groups. The difficulties I met with weren't so much in the students themselves as in the actual structure of the establishment, from secondary school onwards: whether it was a matter of trying to form a students' association, for example, or trying to produce an Institute magazine. The support from the students was there all right, but we were held back by the obstacles put in our way: once, our editorial staff even got an official warning from the Principal to stop producing the magazine. We should concentrate on our work, he said, and stop bothering ourselves with problems too big for us.

My first three years at University, I had no group life at all, largely because not having an incentive to attend courses I preferred to devote most of my time to political activity.

However, I came back to University again when they started a course on philosophers which I was very keen on: I was interested

7*

both in the course itself and in the way the professor handled it. Before, working for exams, I'd had to study books and listen to lectures and learn things up for an interrogation that was just a kind of memory test; but in this course, throughout the year we were able to have a dialogue with the professor and the other students. The Professor's attitude was: 'I am studying with you, I am trying to learn with you, and anything I learn I'll share with you.' And he was willing to listen to any observation or contribution a student might make. He was even capable of putting his own thesis to discussion.

In general, though, I've only come across very few attempts at active education.

One thing to bear in mind concerning our faculty is that well over half the students registered don't in fact attend. There isn't even room for the ones who do want to attend. And well under a third of the students who do attend participate in the various associations: the biggest is the Catholic Association.

Being in touch with an organized political force was the first structural formative occasion that allowed me to live a group life and to understand its importance. There were certain things I'd always intuitively believed, even as a child, and I found them in the political organization. Ever since I was a little boy, there'd been two things I'd always thought were useless: the State, and money. When I first became politically active, Stalin had been dead two years. I can say now—though probably at the time my motives for joining weren't consciously these—that one important element that drove me into more and more active political commitment was the fact that group life enriched my personality, made me feel more responsible: I felt I was being an active agent, and not merely passive. There were the meetings of the Party Youth Club, and the committee on which every member had his own particular responsibilities. To start with I was in charge of the library, then after a year I became Secretary of the Youth Club. We organized assemblies—at one time we had six hundred members in that quarter of Palermo alone—and we organized conferences and discussions on particular themes.

Sometimes I would listen with interest while others spoke, other times I would speak myself, about the library, and about what we thought we might do. What inspired me most was the wish to work together with other people towards the realization of some meaningful aim, something that I was thinking and discovering for myself too. Also, the workers expected more of me, and that was an added spur, and in particular an incentive to clarity. I used to go into other quarters of Palermo, and to other towns in the Province, and my responsibilities even put me in touch with Rome: bit by bit I was discovering new worlds. I tried to share with others whatever I thought I'd understood, and to learn from others whatever they could teach me. In my relations with other people my aims were not specifically educational—it was just an instinctive liking for communication and for finding the best in other people.

——Thinking of the various political groups you've belonged to, could you describe how they worked as groups?

——Procedure varied according to the level of the various groups. In any case, rather than working groups they were organs for direction: group life is limited in that the members of a political organization meet only intermittently, on specific occasions, and the rest of the time they go on with their normal activities. The supporters participate in each campaign more or less as a separate thing in itself, not as part of a continuous process.

Plans are fairly precise and detailed, but generally there is difficulty in carrying them out—for one reason or another, the individuals responsible often don't manage to put them into practice.

In general, concern for the development of the individual and of group life isn't a primary intention, isn't a specific aim in itself. It comes about, to a greater or lesser degree, as a by-product of the main aim, which is to get certain things done.

——What would you say is happening among university students today, as regards our theme?

——Students today feel they want more collective life, and they're refusing to go on being crammed and spoon-fed. They've been putting suggestions before the professors: so far, they haven't achieved anything, but at least now they are getting together to press for changes. People are aware of the need for group life—but the necessary channels and the structures that would make group life feasible just don't exist. Various suggestions have been made in various departments, but it's only in the architecture faculty that they've got as far as asking specifically for seminars, and a different system of lectures and exams, and a different relationship between students and professors. However, the reaction to this was that the students who had been most actively concerned in it were subjected to an official investigation.

A research assistant

I am engaged in scientific research. There's one director here who's in charge of the whole Institute, and another who hasn't got an institute of his own and who's here as assistant director: this means in practice there are two directors of equal grade, but one has complete control. Everyone here works on his own. For instance, I'm doing my own research: if I have an idea, I work on it myself. And it's the same with all the others, each on his own. I do try to collaborate. But since the director has carried out practically every piece of research single-handed for more than twenty years, each of us is going the same way. Rather than risk seeing someone else go off with your work, you shut yourself up, you don't communicate with the others, not even for advice—you go into isolation. If there are several names to a paper, it's the first who'll get the credit for the idea and for most of the work. None of us want our own ideas attributed to other people. We don't ask each other things—we get information from books in the library whenever possible. The ones who've been here longest lock the doors when they're doing an experiment, and they feel it's their right to make use of other people. All this means that months and months are wasted in finding out something that's quite likely known already. And it results in all sorts of personal feuds and jealousies and childish rivalries—a real psychological warfare, with half-words, half-sentences, and people ending up refusing even to speak to each other.
——Do all of you ever meet together?
——I did think of suggesting this to the director, but I don't see how we can break out of this climate: with everyone so frightened of giving away something important, there's a negative attitude in this respect.
——As far as you know, does the same thing go on in many other institutes?

——In our Institute I think the friction is mitigated to a certain extent by the fact that the people are fairly intelligent. In other institutes, I've known open hostility break out—they'll sometimes get as far as real serious intrigue. In many university institutes and in many clinics this sort of thing is largely mitigated by people's relatively greater caution, greater cunning, greater subtlety in deception. Outside, on the other hand, dishonesty is much more open—in the world of politics and business and so on. But it's the clever swindler who seems to be the type people admire most: he knows what's what, he knows how to get on in the world.

In our university institutes, the director often has absolute power: nobody who wants to go in for a university career can get in unless he's in the good graces of the director. In some people this causes servility, in others a hyper-reaction—they kill themselves with overwork in the effort to show they're worth something themselves. Between the various directors there are naturally exchanges of favours to friends and relations.

This situation derives largely from the structure of the university and the rules at present in force; and also partly from the fact that the Machiavellian schemer is the type who's commonly admired.

Ugo Palma, *Professor of Physics*

——Has there been any evolution, do you think, among university students in relation to group work and group life?
——The answer could be 'yes', or 'no', or 'I don't know', depending on the group or faculty or institute. Here, I think there has been. I was here as a student, too: my first year I was the only one attending the degree course, and my second year too; the third year there was one other, and the fourth year I was on my own again. I used to have to go to lectures with students in other faculties. So it's difficult to compare with today.

Today there are many more students in this Institute, and they are also much better, more awake: nowadays they feel it's necessary, and also a pleasure, to live their own group life. And there are other factors which stimulate them to group activity: the existence of a genuinely impartial selection on grounds of merit, with recommendations not counting at all, helps to bring together the ones who 'make it'. Even more important as an incentive, I think, is our own example: they see us working as a group, united by strong ties of friendship; they see us taking the most important decisions as a group, and they see how group life expands our own individual interests.

Rather than just attending the Institute, the students more or less live here, and there is a powerful interaction between them and us teachers. They have a double incentive: their own new awareness, and this interaction with us—it would be quite difficult to draw the boundary between our group and theirs. Suggestions, wishes, requests, criticisms: there's a constant two-way exchange.

All this springs up around what is the central interest of us all: our research. The young people are drawn here by this central interest, and then they see that they can work most effectively through the group. The research itself gives the initial stimulus to group activity. And on the other hand, the existence of the group serves to broaden and stimulate a range of interests that goes far beyond the original starting point. This makes the work more enjoyable, and extends its implications. Besides, why should someone whose interests are limited solely to physics research choose to work here in Palermo, of all places, where one has to work much harder to achieve the same results?

To sum up, then, I should think it approximately true to say briefly, that whereas in those days I was isolated, today the students do have a group life.

——How far does this go against the general trend?

——Well, it does, and it doesn't: it doesn't, in that no one actually tells us not to do this. On the other hand, to see to what extent it does go against the trend, you have only to take a look at the world around us, and at the University world in particular.

What goes against the trend perhaps more than anything else is the mentality necessary for an honest and disinterested group life. People new to the idea find it very difficult to understand. It would take a foreign friend or acquaintance only a few minutes to understand our situation. A few people here understand and help too: for example, Alberto Monroj, the well-known biologist—he has an excellent Institute; and there are one or two others. But most people wouldn't understand in ten years. When they see a closely-knit group like this, they assume there's a dictator at the head of it—and they're astonished to see (if indeed they manage to see at all) that what binds us together is in fact the complete absence of inhibitions, the sharing of decisions, the quantity and the cordiality of our reciprocal criticism, our genuine friendship, and sincerity.

We are convinced that, in a world like ours, it is at least as important to demonstrate that it is possible, and indeed enjoyable, to have compact groups working openly and honestly together, as it is to turn out technically and scientifically well-qualified young men.

——Have you suffered from interference and pressures?

——Yes. Especially at the beginning, pressures for passing people in exams have been put on us in every way you could possibly think of: someone comes to see you, to have a word with you, and you're left just with a person's name and so many things understood—this is the form of pressure that bothers us most. Or else some acquaintance will come along and try and insist that you let him have a look at the written paper beforehand. There are the requests for private tuition ('not from yourself, of course, but from someone you recommend')—and then the various hard-luck stories. The whole range, from the subtle pressure exercised by the powerful, down to the desperate pleading of the hopeless poor.

Giovanni Sprini, a social psychologist

I believe that in the University Institutes of Palermo, except in one or two exceptional cases, not only does group work not exist— it is not even thought of. This is a common characteristic of Italian universities, but I think in Sicily it has a particular flavour of its own because of people's excessive fear of being tricked, of laying themselves open to betrayal. In general, this is concealed, but it can become a real paranoia.

Interdisciplinary activities don't exist: to get something of this sort going at an academic level is really an undertaking beyond normal capacities. When attempts fail, the most diverse reasons are called to account: in reality it is the people themselves who are incapable of speaking and of listening.

In any case, the University committees aren't keen on team work, on papers with several names to them—perhaps not so much from fear of not being able to judge the individual contribution, as just out of a sort of cultural stagnation.

The lecturer-examiners themselves have generally worked on their own private research—which may even have been quite intricate, though often not very significant: and given a choice between normally unexceptionable research whose only value is as methodological exercise, and research based on everyday reality, research with a precise human and social application, they are undoubtedly in favour of the first.

I don't know how far we are capable even of seeing what interests we have in common with our neighbour. None of us, whether from inability or unwillingness, ever seems to be able to humble himself enough to listen to other people. The result is a dialogue of the deaf. And this attitude isn't confined to education—it's the same in politics and administration. The 'dialogue' becomes simply an exercise in rhetoric—no one is willing to listen to the others properly, and any sort of acceptance of one's adversary's position is considered a surrender of one's own position of power.

In recent years I have witnessed, and also from time to time participated in, a series of enterprises initiated with great enthusiasm but regularly ending in failure. In trying to make a diagnosis, one has to bear in mind the lack of documentation, and the difficulty of precisely defining the problems: all too often things are a matter of improvisation, without any preliminary study.

Even business enterprises are undertaken for the most part without a serious preliminary examination of anything further than what the product is to be: no consideration of why the factory should be built in one place rather than another, or the exact amount of capital required, or any of the other essential factors. Often people aren't even aware of the laws and regulations, or what grants and subsidies they are entitled to.

Since there is no group work, what remain in every sector are still the clans formed to defend certain ideological positions or positions of personal power.

Political Parties

I put the following questions to the Provincial Secretaries of the main political parties:

1: How would you define the social and political structure of Palermo?

2: What are your main difficulties?

3: What, briefly, are the most serious problems of Palermo and the Province today?

4: What do you think is the reason for the small participation in party activities?

5: In what ways is the mafia at present an obstacle to the development of Palermo?

The diagram below shows the results of recent elections:

	Regional 1959	National 1963	Regional 1963	Local 1964
DC	216,375	225,036	227,485	193,079
PCI	91,405	104,372	103,452	56,460
PSI	50,125	58,560	44,062	31,351
PSDI	13,143	24,994	31,051	23,201
PRI	5,672	12,431	17,498	15,945
PLI	27,629	58,899	51,166	37,754
PDIUM	36,075	28,047	12,846	10,353
MSI	39,604	42,568	38,049	28,079
USCS	77,743	—	5,533	—
PCI—PSIUP	—	—	—	10,613
PSIUP	—	—	—	12,466
Others	1,914	13,222	9,136	—

Girolamo Leto, Provincial Secretary of the PLI

1: In the city, people are better informed: in the Province the social structure is more backward because of illiteracy, and there

189

people don't choose a political party according to ideas but simply follow one local personality or another. If one examines the voting figures for each town, one sees what leaps and bounds there are in all parties from one election to the next: they may drop from a thousand to a hundred according to who is standing. In Palermo, there is a distinction to be made between the urban centre and the outer districts: in the centre, the vote is somewhat more consistent, whereas further out it fluctuates more according to particular personalities. The less education or preparation people have, the more likely they are to fall under the spell of individual personalities, of those who can intercede for them at the seat of power. The better qualified person is more able to justify the line he follows, whereas the ignorant person easily falls under the spell of the mafioso, the politician, the *carabinieri* Inspector.

2: Not everyone can understand the ideology of the PLI. It's no use going and talking about the defence of liberty to a man who's in need of a job, who's in need of everything, when his problem is how to fill the pot that day. A party like ours therefore has difficulty in penetrating to large sections of society.

Unfortunately, in Sicily as in Southern Italy, people behave with too much Spanish-style contempt for others; everyone complains, but it doesn't change. For instance, it can happen that someone agrees to an appointment just to get rid of a person, and then doesn't turn up; or someone commits himself to too many engagements and then just abandons the ones he thinks less important; or perhaps at the last minute he'll take on something quite new and drop everything else. People also generally dislike being punctual, because they don't want to be the first to arrive; they feel that diminishes prestige: the more important person arrives later. At work, too, people only begin when the authorities arrive, and the authorities make sure they don't arrive till the last possible minute.

In Palermo, our meetings consist of report, discussion, comments, proposed resolutions, then voting. In the smaller towns, it's all much simpler because there are only a few people; they can meet informally, perhaps even in a bar.

3: The most serious problems: I will mention only one, and that is the need for elementary schools and trade schools. Really good trade schools. Today we no longer need the manual labourer. The

man who goes around not knowing what to do or how to do it just
gets crushed.

Tourism? That's all very well. But we can't have hotels and
restaurants with waiters who don't know how to wait—and so on.

4: The endless scandals over the post-war years have made
people distrust politicians—they have confirmed the notion that
politics is something dirty. And so people vote because they have to,
but they try not to get involved except when it's to their immediate
advantage.

People also feel it's useless to commit themselves and discuss
things when in the end decisions are made solely by those in charge,
whether at a provincial, or regional or national level. In general
there is no real fabric of democracy through which people can feel
they have a say. If a man knows he counts for something, then he'll
participate, but if he knows he counts for nothing anyway, then he
won't.

5: The mafia, like the clergy, sides with power.

I too could say like Orlando:[1] 'if the mafia is an element of order,
then we are mafiosi.' On the other hand, we obviously cannot
accept mafia-gangsterism.

In my opinion the mafia is an obstacle at present in that it blocks
certain branches of the city and the Province: it still has control of
certain markets. But, again, I would call this gangsterism rather
than mafia.

It's an embarrassing question.

Today the real trouble in industry isn't so much the mafiosi as
the politicians who put pressure on to get jobs for their own clients;
this is what's known as 'white mafia': the 'black mafia' shoots, the
other kills without shooting. Certain politicians use the mafia as a
tool to get power. The business of 'recommendations' didn't start
in industry, which didn't exist: it started with the public bodies, the
Local Councils, the Provincial Administration, the Regional
Government, ERAS, and so on. Unfortunately, the parties accepted
the string-pulling game: to be quite frank, they've all accepted it to
a certain extent—but naturally it's the parties in power that have
most opportunities, and those in opposition least.

The mafia and the clergy don't join in inter-party contest: their

[1] See note p. 40. (Tr.)

game is with the preference votes,[1] supporting the people closest
to them. Both clergy and mafiosi do put a certain amount of
direct pressure on people—often they come in person—but when
they aren't powerful enough to do this themselves they turn
to their particular politician. And so there is only a relatively
small amount of direct recommendation and pressure by mafiosi,
the determining force being pressure by Deputy So-and-so (who,
along with his clientèle, belongs to whichever party is most
advantageous to him). The politician steps in on behalf of the
people who serve his ends, allowing it to be understood, or even
saying explicitly, that in exchange for their services he is disposed
to make himself . . . useful, by means of the instruments of power
in his hands.

DANILO (*on the telephone*): Excuse me, is that the Provincial Secre-
tary of the Social Democrat Party? Who is your present Provincial
Secretary?
　VOICE: Nobody.
　DANILO: How do you mean, nobody?!
　VOICE: There's a deputy.
　DANILO: What's he called?
　VOICE: Nicolazzi.
　DANILO: How can I meet him?
　VOICE: He's in Rome most of the time.
　DANILO: Thank you. And what's his other name?
　Long pause: evidently the person is consulting with others.
　VOICE: Franco.

Lino Motta, Provincial Secretary of the PSIUP

　1: How on earth can Palermo still give the Christian Democrats
a hundred and twenty thousand votes after all those scandals, and in
spite of their obvious inability to solve the fundamental problems?
　The most significant characteristics of the social structure of
Palermo as compared with other cities are I think these:

[1] See note p. 213 (Tr.)

Above: A non-violent 'pressure' meeting in Petrolo, 1966. *Right:* the first witness, Vito Ferrante of Castellammare.

The trial in
Rome.

the superabundance of the middle class of civil servants and bureaucrats who, together with the commercial middle class, and the bourgeoisie (made up of speculators rather than neo-capitalists, of cunning people rather than intelligent), constitute the social kernel of the city, with all their opportunism and political indifference, occupying the administrative centres of the city and manipulating the sub-proletariat;

the almost non-existence of an industrial capitalist bourgeoisie;

the big sub-proletariat class—large sub-proletariat areas in the city centre, in old Palermo;

the working-class forces (concentrated in a few factories—shipyards, ELSI, SIMENS, *Aeronautica Sicula*, the SOFIS works) are very active in the unions, but they are an *avant-garde*, and don't succeed in making any political impression in the city;

the peasant class (relegated in Palermo to the outskirts of the city) and the rural proletariat, particularly labourers, are fairly active, but only united at moments of conflict, and otherwise easily dispersed: there's a lack of initiative due to the deficiencies of the parties and the mass organizations, which have failed to understand the problems of today;

the upper class which lives off private income rather than profits.

2: Our main difficulties are of a political nature. We are a young party and we find it difficult—though in fact less and less so, with the continual decline of the PSI—to get people to appreciate the responsibility we have undertaken in forming the new socialist party.

Difficulties of a practical nature: those encountered by a young party whose structure and organization are still unsteady, in a disjointed environment like Palermo.

3: The most serious problems for Palermo: the absence or insufficiency of industry; the urban jungle—from the old city districts, to speculation in building land, and disorderly growth with no regard for a regulating plan; problems of transport, and the Docks; educational problems that are quite horrifying. For the Province, the fundamental problem is the development of agriculture and all that that entails, and the eventual development of industries.

4: We are confronting a disintegrated society, in which the

element of government corruption is spreading: faced with this, the opposition is weak. In a situation where corruption prevails, where the individual's relation to power is one of clientship through intermediaries, we cannot provide a complete answer to the needs of the citizens; our activity is too sporadic and occasional: and so we don't succeed in getting the population sufficiently interested, we don't succeed in linking the peasants with other workers, or in bringing political maturity to the sub-proletariat. Of course it's no use expecting to achieve this unity just by calling for it: obviously it can only be done by having precise objectives and by creating the necessary tools.

5: The mafia still exerts a decisive influence on the centres of power, both local and Provincial—not as directly as in previous years, when one might have thought one was in the Chicago of 1929, but under cover of the parties which have been in control of our city's administration; it has a direct influence in certain key economic centres such as markets, and in building and land speculation and water supplies on the outskirts of the city; it makes its weight felt in the most diverse sections of society, from university faculties to the Magistrature, and the various Regional public works bodies— though it is notably different today from the traditional mafia.

The mafioso needs a certain new type of alliance, he needs to insinuate himself in a particular way, in order to cope with new situations: he certainly doesn't wear the peaked cap any more. Nowadays he wears a dinner jacket and goes to parties, and maybe owns a villa—he's become urbanized.

What is the city's response to all this? The great majority, wittingly or unwittingly, blackmailed or not, have up to now all been involved in this mafia game. How can one possibly think seriously here of a dialogue between Socialist forces and the more advanced Catholics when the other side—forces such as the *Fanfaniani* with whom on a national level it is possible to start an interchange of ideas that is not mere tactics but a matter of bold long-term politics —when these forces are represented here by people like Lima[1] and Giancimino? Characters who, thanks to their own power, have allowed mafia groups to get control of the greater part of the city,

[1] Lima—(see p. 199–202) ex-Mayor of Palermo and Provincial Secretary of the Christian Democrat Party. (Tr. note.)

and to determine development in a direction that serves the private interests of the mafiosi speculators!

Michelangelo Russo, Provincial Secretary of the PCI

1: The chief characteristic is the small weight of the industrial working class.

The most important category is that of building workers, who are the largest group—about twenty thousand of them, out of whom six or seven thousand are at present employed; this category, together with the shipyard and the mechanical industries of the SOFIS group, represents the mass basis of the working class. An important part is also played now by the workers in the public services such as tramways, gas, water, etc.

Another fundamental element is the existence of the vast mass of the sub-proletariat, swelled by an influx from the Province at the time of the boom, particularly in building, these people being the first to be left stranded. (Many of the new generation of sub-proletariat have moved into the working class, particularly into building, which is in a sense the link between them.) Quite apart from social considerations, this phenomenon has important political consequences in that this class tends to fluctuate from one position to another, from one extreme to the other.

The lower middle class also has more weight than usual: in all the poorer districts of Palermo, every five yards or so you'll pass a little shop that's run on credit; often the small men are in difficulties with creditors, but they keep themselves distinct from the others both in the social and in the political field. Next come the higher commercial and business classes, already integrated with the centres of power.

Then there's the vast sea of bureaucracy. Altogether, it's estimated that there are thirty thousand civil servants in Palermo,[1] what with the Regional government and the State, the Provincial administration, the Municipal offices, and Regional organizations like ERAS, IRFIS, SOFIS, etcetera. From the numerical point of view, this category is the most powerful. Since everyone knows that a job is not to be had through open competition or on merit but only by means of string-pulling, they turn to the politicians in power in

[1] Out of a population of 550,000. (Tr. note.)

order to get the necessary recommendation. Once a man is fixed up
in a job, he may sometimes feel a little more free to get organized,
and perhaps he'll join a union—but it's unlikely that he'll join any
left-wing party: obviously he's conditioned by how he got the job
in the first place. This system of taking on white-collar workers,
promoting them, transferring them, and all the rest of it, creates an
atmosphere of intrigue which affects everyone to a certain extent, in
that it cannot but influence people's characters; it makes for cynicism and political apathy at all levels, it weaves a thick unwhole-
some web which penetrates the whole city.

At the top, there are the owners of building land who now hold
the biggest amounts of capital; one or two opportunist builders of
the Vassallo type; one or two big notaries who have made a fortune
from the flood of bills under protest; well-to-do businessmen;
Ferruzza who has up to now had complete control of public transport; and certain high-up officials in local or Regional government,
in the various public works organizations, and in Banks, who have
power to divert money in whatever direction they choose.

In the belt round Palermo that isn't yet built up, there are farm
labourers, smallholders, and big market-garden owners.

2: Our chief difficulty in Palermo Province is that we have not
succeeded in creating a mass party. It's not just a matter of membership numbers: there's the problem of party activity. In a complex
situation like this, we don't want to limit ourselves to mere propaganda for the ideals of socialism: we must act today. At the moment,
however, our party in Palermo is weak, both as regards political
initiative and also in its lack of representation in the different strata
of society.

Another obstacle is the fact that our members are not sufficiently
well educated to read widely or to assimilate and discuss printed
matter, or to read our own publications.

3: The most serious problems are all basically due to the lack of
any development plan.

4: Immediately after the war there was a greater revolutionary
impetus: the parties at that time were better channels of information
than they are now—for example, the public meeting had a function
it no longer has today. It is most difficult in the city: sometimes it's
as much as we can do to get even fifteen people together in a Branch.

After the war people were confident of being able to change things quickly, or relatively quickly. But today the work is more difficult, more complicated, more detailed, and the prospects seem if anything even further off.

Often people think that once a man has voted he's done all he needs do. But there's also a deterioration in the democratic life of the parties themselves: when questions concerning the life of the party are decided at central party offices without any genuine participation by members, this is bound to do some damage to the conscience of the individual.

5: The mafia, working through its political connections, has monopolized wide areas of building land and so has succeeded here in carrying the phenomenon of speculation, which also exists in other cities, to its very extreme. Apart from points one could make about the mafia's criminal activities, the important thing to be stressed here is the connection it has succeeded in establishing with the public administration in order to further its own ends; throughout recent years there has been close interpenetration between groups of mafiosi and the Council. The present governing class has taken less interest in the problems of the Port, of the new mechanical industry, and of the iron and steel centre; they have been more interested in property speculation than in problems concerning the real development of the city. And the city has expanded considerably in a short time without any corresponding development in industrial structures. The key man in this whole situation has been the Mayor, Lima.

The consequences of all this become clear now that, with the building boom over, the problems of the real development of the city are all coming to the fore again. And one has the impression that yet again the important issues are being shirked, and that it will be the same old story of speculation only under other guises.

Naturally, the mafia being a parasitic force, it affects all the ganglia of urban life, from the soft-fruit market to the certificate of good character, from the recommendation of a son to get him through his exams to the recommendation for a job; permits for installing petrol pumps, the opening of new shops, location of industries, pressures in employment and in the field of trade union freedom—and so on.

Gaspare Saladino, Provincial Secretary of the PSI

1 : The social and political structure of Palermo reflects its level of economic development. Palermo is a city of the South and is therefore characterized by economic structures that are backward compared with other cities in the North, which have attained a very high level of development.

None of the attempts made so far, from the Florios on, to set up industries on any scale have ever succeeded—nor was it possible that they could have succeeded.

To appreciate the reason for this one must remember the whole story of the 'question of the South'—(to go into the position of the Socialist movement on this would be superfluous here). The liberal state first of all, then Fascism, and now the succession of centralized governments we have had since the war, have all blocked the development of the South. That is why one of its largest cities can still find itself beset by the same old problems even today—problems which even Sicilian autonomy has not helped to solve, in so far as it has been conditioned by forces subordinated to those of the big monopolies.

2 : Our difficulties arise out of backward social structures characterized by uncertainty, scepticism, closed-mindedness, susceptibility to the old system of favouritism and continued obedience to its rules.

3 : The most serious problems for Palermo are its industrialization and the clearance and redevelopment of the four old slum quarters. For the countryside, reform of agricultural structures, and the modification of existing social and economic relationships.

4 : In my opinion, people take little part in party activities because, on the one hand, the structure of the parties is outdated in the context of the new problems that are constantly arising, and so fail to stimulate more direct participation; and, on the other hand, because they accept a role of subordination to the traditional bourgeois governing class and passively follow the line it lays down.

The serious and committed forces that do exist are often out of tune with the parties today, finding them too slow in formulating problems, and the leaders too inclined to be closed-minded.

5: The mafia has always defended established interests, by integrating and identifying itself with them: guardian of the feudal estate against the peasants, guardian of building land in the city, of public works, of the markets, and of industrial firms—always against the workers, always against the healthy economic forces, always against the citizen consumers; this is why the mafia has always opposed the socialists and the democratic peasant movement, whose leaders, from Carnevale to Rizzotto, it has always shot without mercy.

Today, however, the works of this system are jammed: now the Antimafia Commission has started operating; the forces of democracy are on the advance and the mafia is retreating, and the old system of personal interests is cracking up: all this is undoubtedly the fruit of the long struggle by peasant and working-class forces, for which the socialists were able to provide a positive political outlet.

Of Palermo's governing group of Christian Democrats I had met only Avv. Gioia, on one occasion, years ago, when he was Provincial Secretary and I went to report to him on the wretched plight of Trappeto, administered at that time by the Christian Democrats. At one point during this interview Gioia, with incredible . . . self-possession, telephoned instructions for the Local Assistance Board at Torretta to hand out half a million lire at once—because, he explained, he was due to go there himself in two days' time to hold an election meeting.

For three weeks now I have been trying in vain to get an appointment with Mayor Lima, friend of Gioia and his successor to the provincial secretaryship of the Christian Democrats. Since I have been ringing up on average twice every day, except Sundays, I think I must have tried about forty times: but up till ten-thirty or eleven a.m. there is generally nobody at the office, according to the switchboard operator; and by one o'clock, and often earlier, they have all gone again. Between ten-thirty and one, if I am lucky, I get either a certain Doctor Gorgone, or Doctor Grafagnini, or Doctor Bellanca: each time they promise to give me an answer, but for one reason or another this answer never arrives.

Today at eleven o'clock Doctor Bellanca says: 'Ring again at twelve.' At twelve, when I ask for Doctor Bellanca, another secretary tells me: 'He's not here just at the moment, he's in the Mayor's office: ring again in twenty minutes.'

At twenty past twelve, the same secretary again tells me: 'Doctor Bellanca is still with the Mayor: ring again in twenty minutes.'

At twelve-forty exactly, I ring again. As has happened so many times before, again the operator tells me: 'There's nobody there, *dottore.*'

'Isn't Doctor Bellanca there still? None of the secretaries? We had arranged that I would ring now, at exactly this time, and they would speak to me.'

'I'll try again,' says the operator. But, after a pause: 'No, there's nobody there.'

'It's only twelve forty-five—how can there be nobody left in the offices?'

'*Dottore*, I'm only a switchboard operator—what can I say?'

I had already given up the idea of trying to arrange a meeting. But yesterday evening a friend of mine on the Palermo Council, who had heard about my difficulty in getting an interview with the Christian Democrat Mayor-cum-Provincial Secretary, rang him up to try and persuade him.

Lima replied: 'Tomorrow at eleven I shall be available, at the Town Hall.'

This morning at a quarter past eleven I ring: the Mayor has not arrived yet.

I ring again at twelve: it is impossible for me to speak to him, the Mayor is busy.

I re-read the conclusions of the—polished and cautious—report on Palermo which was presented to Parliament by the Parliamentary Commission of Enquiry into the mafia:

'. . . From the outset of its activity the Commission devoted particular attention to the events which have afflicted the city of Palermo (whole series of murders, attempted murders, acts of intimidation, etc.) and which have so roused national public opinion. These events, defined for the first time unanimously as manifestations of mafia activity of unprecedented intensity, are considered by those representatives of the public authorities questioned by the Commission to be due to rivalry between opposing factions of mafiosi in fierce competition for positions of supremacy, particularly in the spheres of building land, markets, and contracts and licences: spheres of activity closely linked with the public administration, in particular the City Council, to whose responsibility and control the proper observance of the laws is supposed to be entrusted.'

'. . . The sub-Commission appointed for the purpose has examined those aspects of the public administration chiefly concerned with building land, building licences and contracts, taking as its starting point the results of the administrative enquiry, and going into further detail on certain points by means of direct investigation; integrating the information thus obtained with evidence previously and subsequently obtained by means of questioning, from reports, and from information furnished by the Magistrature and Police.

The enquiry thus conducted has further ascertained:

1: that in particular the building business and the acquisition of building land has provided, with the determinative concurrence of the administrative irregularities observed in the town planning sector, extremely fertile ground for the prospering of illicit activities, for the flourishing of unlawful power exercised by pressure groups in the form of parasitic intermediation, and for conspicuous and frequent exchanges of favours;

2: that in the development of the building business there have emerged, within a short space of years, certain elements of obscure origin who have made rapid fortunes by the most suspect means;

3: that not a few of the irregular practices, particularly in the field of building licences, have been to the benefit of elements indicated as mafiosi by Police reports or by subsequent criminal activities;

4: that a number of the protagonists of the most notorious criminal incidents in the Palermo area figure in the changes of ownership of building land, and are indicated, in certain reports, as elements capable of exercising considerable influence on the organs of the city's administration.

While allowing the research hitherto effected the value of a sample analysis, it has nevertheless confirmed the hypothesis, formulated at the time of the initial broad survey, that the public administration, with its lacunae and its irregularities, has proved a permeable ground for the development of parasitic and unlawful activities which constitute the most profitable forms of transplantation of the phenomenon of the mafia from the country to the city. Such conclusions indicate above all the necessity of deepening the enquiry, with particular reference to the whole treatment of the Town Plan, to the sector of the markets, and to that of licences, contracts and Council concessions in general, reserving for the Commission the right to formulate concrete proposals for cleaning up the administrative situation, including the modification, where necessary, of the instruments of the public administration.

The months pass. In March 1966, Giovanni Gioia becomes an Under-Secretary in the new Government. On 3rd May, the newspapers announce that Lima is resigning as Mayor 'in order to devote himself to the Party, expressing his intention of standing as candidate for the Senate in '68'. It is expected as certain that in the next few months he will be promoted to the Chairmanship of IRFIS or SOFIS.

. . . He was—of SOFIS.

1968: in the General Election, Lima gets a massive vote and becomes a Deputy in the Italian Parliament.

Documentation on Bernardo Mattarella

But after all—after meeting peasants, fishermen, labourers, church-
men, nobles, mafiosi, industrialists, children, schoolteachers, clerks,
trades unionists, politicians and many many others—why 'the man
who plays alone never loses'?

One of the more illuminating answers, perhaps in many cases the
most illuminating, is to be found in the meaning attached locally to
the word 'association': it is very very often used in the sense of
'criminal association'.[1] This means that people who are anxious to
avoid taking risks are certainly not very willing to 'associate'.

At this point in our enquiry, in order to make it quite plain how
the type of association we are concerned with (i.e. the relationship
between mafia and politics) has prospered since the war, we had to
choose between two possible ways. We could have written a fictional
account of a fictional collusion, using invented names, deliberately
seeking to interest and perhaps even entertain, thus causing little
discomfort to anyone and avoiding physical risk to people in the
South and pecuniary risk to people in the North (the prudent eye
to the purse in many circles in the North when it is a question of
touching the powerful—we see this clearly in certain newspapers—is,
I think, quite as influential a factor as the fear of many poor wretches
in the South for their very lives), and with no danger of interrupting
the carefully veiled allusions of political gossip in the well-informed
corridors of the Metropolis, where intrigues are often brewed
almost as in Fascist times: instead, we chose to confront the phenomenon squarely and openly, face to face, trusting in the practical
and cultural value, to everyone, of the truth.

The person in the most official and public position in the area is
undoubtedly the Minister Bernardo Mattarella, foremost among the
government politicians from West Sicily, and by now a normative
model for many. In order to get to know this man more closely, I
went one day to listen to one of his speeches: he succeeded in talking

[1] *Associazione a delinquere*—conspiring for criminal purposes. (Tr. note.)

203

for three quarters of an hour—cleverly, but without saying a single really intelligent sentence: or at least so it seemed to me.

Skimming through an anthology of his official writings—leaving aside technical ministerial documents—one hears him thus 'take wing':

'. . . the secret virtue of this our Italian race of the many lives—which does not wish to perish and which shall not perish!—. . .'

'. . . The cultivation of universal and eternal values is the essence of our civilization.'

'. . . to prepare ourselves for tomorrow through delight in the Stage . . .'

'Tranquillity is one of the fundamental elements of peace . . .'

In the 'titanic struggle for liberation . . . the heroism and the spirit of self-sacrifice of student youth shines resplendent . . .' 'Students—launch out, full of impetuosity and youthful vigour . . .'

In the valleys of Assisi 'dominated by the gentle olive', Saint Francis 'could express as none other has done the joyful and pensive spirit of the Italic people': '. . . with the passing of the ages, the figure of the Poor Man of Assisi, far from fading, rises ever higher and higher, like a mountain to the eyes of the traveller as he leaves the plain.'

But the *Rerum Novarum*[1], too, 'rises as an imperishable monument . . . to dominate and overtop the lofty spheres of most elevated thought . . .'

He is not lacking in optimism: '. . . A democracy, we may boast with legitimate pride, as permeated with the Christian spirit as is ours . . .'; 'Not only on the moral plane it is to the highest credit of democracy that it has been capable of conceiving as possible and necessary, indeed as an indispensable condition for national rebirth, the rebirth of the South . . .'; 'The impressive work of reclamation pursued with tenacity and vigour throughout the South is even more evident in Sicily than elsewhere . . .'

His optimism is veined by a sharp flavour of originality: 'Rome . . . beacon of immense Christian light, which illuminates the most fruitful part of the spiritual life of men and of peoples, and by means of which we are able to maintain, deep and unalterable, our faith in

---

[1] Leo XIII's progressive encyclical of 1891. (Tr. note.)

the destiny of mankind . . .'; '. . . the greatness of her immortal destinies . . .'

But undoubtedly more interesting than his prose, or than a brief account of a possible meeting, is a study of the means by which His Excellency succeeded in becoming Under-Secretary and, repeatedly, Minister.

On 22nd September 1965, we presented to the Parliamentary Commission of Enquiry into the mafia, and also to the public in a special Press conference,[1] the first part of our documentation, fifty testimonies (other more serious material not concerning public matters being presented only to the Chairman of the Commission), with the following introduction:

'Being engaged in work for social and economic development in a part of Western Sicily, we could not fail to notice certain fundamental hindrances to democratic development in the area; we could not close our eyes and ears to what was happening there. We were also concerned to find out the exact truth, to distinguish gossip and unverifiable rumour from definite, demonstrable fact.

'Following your authoritative invitation of 13th November 1963 to furnish precise documentation on facts and events concerning the area in which our Study Centre operates, it seemed to us necessary to give full details of a phenomenon that has been, and still is, a powerful negative influence on development in this area: namely, the connection between the most authoritative government politician of the area and the mafia.

'We were particularly concerned with ascertaining whether, in the election of Bernardo Mattarella, the contribution of the mafia was marginal, occasional, unknown to himself—or whether, on the contrary, it was substantial and important and well known to him. For

---

[1] While the Parliamentary Antimafia Commission was initiating proceedings with regard to Bernardo Mattarella and (apparently) Calogero Volpe, these two (together with Ganci Antonino, Guido Anca Martinez, Giuseppe and Liborio Munna, Giambrone Carmelo, Michele Russo, Vito Messina, Vincenzo Messina, Geraci Luigi, Guagenti Francesco, Valenza Pietro) brought a suit against Danilo Dolci, Franco Alasia, and several editors of newspapers that gave full reports of the Press conference. (An account of the trial in Rome is given in Part Three.)

The Antimafia Commission sent the Court of Rome an authentic copy of the first dossier, together with a letter, on 6 May 1966: since the material thereby became officially public, we are now able to quote from it.

this reason the fifty documents herewith enclosed (which in no way claim to represent a complete picture of the Minister) have been collected in various places, and with a view to furnishing information covering different periods.

'The material has been collected with the greatest care, proportional to the seriousness of the facts, and our concern has been to focus attention on those *plain and evident public facts which are already common knowledge in the area*: which are, therefore, more readily verifiable, and which are already, one might say, part of the area's history.

'Each of the documents collected—and they are only a few out of the many possible testimonies—is signed either by an eye-witness of the actual events, or by witnesses to the declaration itself. Every source will of course (given the necessary security) be at the disposal of the Parliamentary Commission whenever they should wish.

'. . . Throughout this enquiry Franco Alasia of the Study Centre has been a scrupulous, shrewd, and tireless collaborator, working with me from the beginning, first on the collection and then on the sorting of the testimonies. We all owe a special debt of gratitude to the Sicilians who with clear courage have been willing to make their contribution towards crushing the old system of clientship and string-pulling and the old mafia groups, putting their faith instead in the growth of new democratic groups: knowing that, contrary to the general belief in this area that it is infamous to have any dealings with the representatives of public opinion and of the State, it would be infamous not to seek and openly declare the truth.'

The document goes on to say that clearly Mattarella's methods of getting votes have varied from place to place and from one period to another: 'In places where the critical faculties of the people are sharper, and political organization is cleaner, the mafiosi have little weight; this is generally in communes where the left-wing parties have an effective weight, as in Caltavuturo, Petralia, Santa Ninfa, Piana degli Albanesi, and occasionally also where the DC leaders are committed in a new way, as in Partanna and Roccamena. In some towns, the votes of the mafiosi are contributory but not decisive: in Altavilla, for instance, the old capimafia can only procure the votes of their own dependents. At the other extreme, in some towns, for example Caccamo, the Minister would have practically no votes at all without the backing of the mafia. In others, such as Vita, the mafia organization is so closely interwoven with the population that it is difficult to find out exactly what happens.' Over the years, too, Mattarella's own attitude has changed: immediately after the war his association with the mafia was quite open and unabashed; but since then, out of regard for a changing public opinion, he has behaved with increasing caution—though still only where this was necessary. Finally, I point out that it is obvious that many people have voted for him in perfect good faith, seeing him simply as an increasingly influential political representative of the Catholic tradition.

Extracts from the documentation

1, 2, 3

In the post-war period the whole town of Castellammare del Golfo used to see Bernardo Mattarella sitting about (even in public places such as the Café Navetta, the Café Russo, the Bar opposite the public gardens) with all the mafiosi of the area: the Rimis, the Plajas, the Magaddinos, the Buccellatos, and all the rest of them. Subsequently, every time he was elected Minister, when he came back to the town he was cordially welcomed by these men, with handshakes and embraces. All the mafia were present when Mattarella laid the corner stone for the pier at Castellammare, and likewise on other occasions.

There can be no doubt that Mattarella's votes came chiefly through the mafia and the local clergy, in that these were the most influential people in the town and in a certain sense in the whole area. Nowadays Mattarella is established and well known, having been several times Under-Secretary and Minister, but if in the early days immediately after the war he had not been launched and supported by the mafia, he could not have become a Deputy.

Many of Mattarella's election propagandists were fixed up with jobs in banks, or in key positions of the Regional Administration, in the Post Office, the State Railways, ERAS, and so on. His young supporters, instead of studying and preparing for entry by competition, cherished the hope that they would be fixed up with jobs through Mattarella, and so helped him at elections.

This was the order of events.

Bernardo Mattarella was born in Castellammare del Golfo on 15th September 1905. His father (who came from a fishing family) was in the service of the Foderàs, a big landowning family with mafia connections who also owned the tunny fisheries at Magazzinazzi; he was employed by them as a warden. Gaspare Magaddino —one of the fourteen mafiosi implicated in the drug traffic business who were recently caught by the police—was superintendent on the Foderà estates.

This was the milieu in which the present Minister Mattarella grew up. He was supported in his studies by the Foderàs themselves; then, qualified as a lawyer, and active in Catholic Action and in the *Partito Popolare*, he got the backing first of Cardinal Lavitrano and later of Cardinal Ruffini.

Chief Officer of Public Welfare and Charity in the first special administration of the Palermo Council; Deputy on the Constituent Assembly and elected Deputy in the first Republican legislature for the electoral college of Palermo-Trapani-Agrigento-Caltanissetta; Under-Secretary to the Ministry of Transport in the fourth, fifth, and sixth Cabinets of De Gasperi; Minister for the Merchant Navy in De Gasperi's eighth Cabinet; Minister of Transport in Pella's, Fanfani's and Scelba's Cabinets; Minister of Foreign Trade in the first Segni Cabinet; Post Office Minister in Zoli's Cabinet; again Minister of Transport under Fanfani, Minister of Agriculture under Leone, and Minister of Foreign Trade in the first Moro Cabinet; at present Minister of Foreign Trade in the second Moro Government.

How was Mattarella elected in Castellammare? Who are the men who have influenced his political career, from his native town, from the very beginning?

One thing to bear in mind is that in the Fascist period the weaker part of the mafia became Fascist, while the stronger local group stayed in the shade in opposition.

In Castellammare, the man whom the town had thought most likely to be official candidate was Avv. Giuseppe Foderà, nephew of the old owner of the tunny fishery. He had a reputation as a learned man—he was nicknamed 'The Philosopher'—but he was in fact rather timid and lacking in initiative. He did not succeed. In his place, the local notables preferred the more able and enterprising Mattarella. At a public rally, Ignazio Foderà, Giuseppe's nephew (a man with Fascist leanings but who was opposing the local mafia because he could not tolerate their abuses), referred to Bernardo Mattarella as the 'Monreale spy', i.e. anti-Fascist in league with the Americans. Foderà was later found dead in the countryside, killed by a burst of *lupara*[1] shot.

At the beginning, the whole of the Castellammare mafia was in league with Mattarella. His chief local supporters are all notorious mafiosi or linked with the mafia (only later did some of them, for reasons of rivalry, detach themselves, and we shall see how they ended up): men recognized as mafiosi not only by the local people but by the police too; a number of them are, or have been, in prison; one is now a Social Democrat Deputy in the Regional Government, having chopped and changed from party to party; among themselves—as often happens among mafiosi—they are connected by family and business ties; one or two have died violent deaths; one has emigrated to the United States; a number of them are involved in the latest arrests of mafia ringleaders suspected of drug trafficking; as owners of land, cows, and sheep, they have had power over peasants, cowmen and shepherds; all of them *'persone intese'*,[2] notables of the town, and linked with the mafia all over Sicily.

The best known among them are:

I. *Gaspare Magaddino*, implicated in the recent arrests for drug smuggling; related to Diego Plaja; formerly superintendent on the Foderà estates; a much feared man, at present in hiding.

II. *Giuseppe Magaddino*, son of Gaspare, son-in-law of Plaja, put under special surveillance, charged with criminal association, he has recently been arrested, with Plaja, under suspicion of drug trafficking.

III. *Diego Plaja*, reference point in the livestock stealing business, charged with criminal association, banished[3] once, linked by

---

[1] The *lupara* (literally 'wolf-gun'), a sawn-off shot-gun, is the usual weapon of the mafia. (Tr. note.)

[2] See note, page 69. (Tr.)

[3] *Al confino:* banished and confined to a certain place for a certain period as a punishment. (Tr. note.)

business ties with the capomafia of Alcamo, Vincenzo Rimi; he has recently been arrested.

IV. *Liborio Munna*, now deceased: big wine merchant and notorious racketeer, he was also implicated in a corn smuggling affair; a wealthy landowner, influential, also contributed financially to Mattarella's election campaigns; he was related to Diego Plaja.

V. *Giuseppe Munna*, son of Liborio, related to Plaja, a member (with Giuseppe Magaddino) of the Molitoria Co-operative mill, which was involved in a scandal concerning a forty-two million lire subsidy in 1960; he is at present Christian Democrat Mayor, in grave financial difficulties which he is trying to patch up through the banks with the help of Mattarella.

VI. *Nino Barone*, first a Christian Democrat, then in D'Antoni's party, then *Milazziano*, then a follower of Baron Majorana Della Nicchiara, then became a Liberal, and now gone over to the regional group of the PSDI.

VII. *Nino Buccellato*, a mafioso feared both for his own sake and on account of his father-in-law Vincenzo Rimi; at present in banishment after having made a fortune as a building contractor.

VIII. *Cola Buccellato*, at present in banishment; greatly feared as a violent man; after the war he assumed the role of peacemaker because of the great reputation he enjoyed in his own circles; respected by Vincenzo Rimi; got in on building contracts with Giuseppe Magaddino.

IX. *Salvatore Vitale*, of an old family of mafiosi, at present in banishment.

X. *Giuseppe Minori*, related to other mafiosi of Trapani, once arrested for cigarette smuggling.

XI. *Bernardo Stabile*, brother-in-law of Gaspare Magaddino, a dangerous character; after an attempt on his life he emigrated to the United States.

XII. *Nino, son of Giovanni, Belnome*, executive mafioso in the services of Nino Barone; at present employed at a fixed salary on Barone's property.

XIII. *Mario Ferro*, another mafioso indicated as executive agent in the services of Nino Barone; probable murderer of Ignazio Foderà, and himself killed ten years ago.

XIV. *Francesco Marchese*, building contractor linked with Magaddino; rather than an actual mafioso, he is indicated as an individual on good terms with mafiosi, living off favours from the mafia and being in turn exploited by them; at the beginning of this year he suffered two dynamiting attempts and had olives and vines destroyed.

XV. *Andrea Mancino*, lived for a long time in Tunisia, from where he was apparently expelled; indicated as a contraband cigarette and tobacco dealer on good terms with the mafia; a Fascist activist, he recruited volunteers for the Spanish campaign; owner of property at Scopello on which a Customs and Excise officer was found killed.

XVI. *Vincenzo Rimi*, charged with various serious crimes (cattle-stealing, murders, criminal association), a former labourer and cowman who made a rapid fortune; capomafia of Alcamo, now under arrest.

XVII. *The Lentini family*, shepherds and cowmen, well known as second-grade mafiosi; a very large family.

XVIII. *Gaspare Bonventre*, mafioso landowner, from a mafia family involved in serious blood feuds with other families; has shuttled to and fro between Castellammare and America.

XIX. *Vito Messina*, a retired schoolmaster with a foot in both camps: mafia and police.

XX. *Di Maggio and Fiordilino families*, second-grade mafiosi, but dangerous as executive mafia agents.

XXI. *Martino Di Benedetto*, wine merchant, high-powered mafioso with a criminal past.

In the 1950 Castellammare Council elections, Nino Barone had the Christian Democrat majority. However, another man was elected Mayor instead—a local competitor less ambitious and less dangerous than Nino Barone.

This is unacceptable to Barone and his followers. Chairs fly in the Christian Democrat headquarters. Nino Barone resigns, transfers his allegiance and becomes a D'Antoni supporter, and in subsequent elections stands on the non-party civil list in opposition to the Christian Democrats.

A reconciliation is attempted.

. . . This is opposed, however, by Doctor Camillo Colombo (who has succeeded Pennolino as Secretary of the Castellammare Christian Democrats). This rejection of Nino Barone's re-entry to the party results in a set-back for Mattarella: the section of the mafia that had backed Barone (thinking he would be more convenient on a local level and that he might well go further and become stronger) takes it as an affront, and causes Mattarella to lose two thousand votes in Castellammare alone, as well as further losses throughout the area. The reaction of the Christian Democrats is to expel Plaja from the party, with the notice of their decision publicly displayed on the notice board . . .

Dictated, re-read, and signed.

Testimony signed by three people

4

After every rally of Mattarella's (especially at the end of an election campaign)—the rallies were generally held in Corso Garibaldi, about at the level of Via Vasile—there used to be a procession back to the DC headquarters in Via Umberto Primo, and at the head of the procession would be Mattarella himself surrounded by all the mafia of the town (Salvatore and Leonardo Vitale, Gaspare and Giuseppe Magaddino—this last is only thirty but he has been active since he was a boy—the Bonventres, the Buccellatos, and Diego and Vincenzo Plaja, among the main local representatives); and often the Rimis of Alcamo, Minore from Trapani, and others, were seen as well. This was from the '46 elections for the Constituent Assembly up to the final break between Barone and Mattarella's men.

Both during these processions after the rallies, and on other occasions in cafés or in the actual Christian Democrat headquarters, (where these people were of course quite at home,) Mattarella was always extremely friendly with them—handshakes in front of everyone, drinking coffee together at the Navetta café; outside the café these mafiosi would gather round Mattarella, and every now and again one or other of them would draw him aside (perhaps putting in a word for some protégé), and often they would be seen arm in arm. Outside the Christian Democrat headquarters, too, they used to stand around together in friendly conversation.

The real, permanent link between these mafiosi who were Mattarella's big election supporters and Mattarella himself (who did not stay in Castellammare but only came down now and again) was maintained by Liborio Munna, who could be defined as a white-collar mafioso, an urban mafioso as opposed to the other country ones: Liborio Munna's son is the present Mayor, and is a godson of Mattarella.

In every election campaign these mafiosi would go from house to house distributing facsimiles of the voting slips for the Christian Democrats, with the preference vote[1] for Mattarella. These things are well known by the whole town: and the police certainly weren't blind, they saw all this going on perfectly clearly.

The relationship between Mattarella and his big mafiosi election supporters has hardly changed even over the last few years. The break between Mattarella and Barone involved a split in the mafia itself, but only in the field of local elections.

In the early days, Mattarella was extremely poor; a crafty petty lawyer, he is less than mediocre from a cultural and political point of view; but he is cunning, exceedingly ambitious, and quite un-principled. He seeks votes everywhere: at Montelepre, when no politician was allowed to speak without Salvatore Giuliano's per-mission, Mattarella was able to speak not only undisturbed but to a large crowd, and he got the preference votes.

Signed testimony

6. *Declaration by a group of people*

Before the First World War, the mafia of Castellammare and that of Monreale were probably the most powerful in Western Sicily, and were rooted chiefly in the big feudal estates. So many Castellam-marese emigrated to the United States that they practically con-stituted another Castellammare over there, specially at Brooklyn, and some of the mafiosi saw in and around New York how much more could be made by using more modern methods; the American branch of the mafia certainly had an influence on the mafiosi of Castellammare, and of Sicily in general. Not only did mafiosi from

[1] As well as voting for one party the voter may choose a particular candidate from the party list. (Tr. note.)

8*

Castellammare go to, and often stay in, the United States, but often mafiosi from the United States came over here.

A few years ago one such mafioso arrived here, for all to see: Joe Bonanno, known as Joe Banana, (his parents were from Castellammare,) said by some to have become head of Cosa Nostra after the murder of Anastasia—in other words, one of the really big shots of gangsterdom. (He has disappeared in the last year.) On the occasion of his arrival he was met at the ACI Motel with the greatest respect and deference by all the local mafiosi, among them his cousin Gaspare Magaddino with his son, Vincenzo Rimi, Diego Plaja, Joe Garofalo (another Castellammarese), Cola Buccellato, the Vitales, Vito Messina; in other words, in full view of anyone who had eyes to see, by all the chief mafiosi who had given substantial support to Mattarella at the start of his political career.

Signed by two witnesses

7

Mattarella succeeded in getting elected in Castellammare with the help of the priests, who to begin with were all for him, and with the support of the mafia. The people in closest contact with him, the most outstanding ones among his friends and his big election supporters, were the mafiosi Gaspare Magaddino and Diego Plaja, who were on the most intimate terms with him; the Buccellatos; and, to begin with, Barone. When Mattarella arrived in town, and before and after public meetings, he used to meet these people; they would go and eat together at what was then the Catalano restaurant, and every single person in Castellammare would have seen them together in the Navetta Café. Whenever Mattarella arrived in Castellammare, they used to go and meet him, and they would embrace each other—they made quite a thing of this embracing. Around them there would be the lesser mafiosi like the Vitales, Messina, Mancino, and the others.

Mattarella knew perfectly well who these men were, because he'd always known them, he knew just how they carried on, he was quite aware of their mafia influence, because their outrages first in country areas and then in the town itself were well known to everybody— and he made use of them: it was through them that he got all his votes. Immediately after the war the mafia of Castellammare was more feared than any other in the region, even more powerful than the Alcamo mafia: and what's more the chief mafioso there was Vincenzo Rimi, who was often seen in public with Mattarella.

It isn't quite clear why a rift later developed between part of the local mafia and Mattarella (and the priests got divided too, in just the same way as the mafiosi); some think it was due to conflicting interests, some think it was a power struggle between the two factions, the one headed by the Buccellatos and the other by Magaddino (who was the most influential also because of his American connections—he was Joe Bonanno's cousin); others think that perhaps in later years it was Mattarella himself who wanted to shuffle off the mafia connections that were likely to be the most compromising to him. In any case, there was an attempt at a reconciliation which they all took part in, with Mattarella acting as go-between and peace-maker; and in '54, immediately after the defeat of the Christian Democrats by the civil list, in a meeting at the Motel with all the bigwigs, Mattarella in a furious rage reproached Plaja and the others: 'You've all betrayed me!'—right there in the dining room, not bothering at all about who might hear him.

In order to make sure of lots of votes, the Mattarella campaigners at first made use of the Assistance Board, which handed out food parcels (two kilos of *pasta* and tinned food, sometimes tinned peas); but when the difficulties started between Mattarella and Barone and their respective factions, because Barone's side had set up a store of *pasta* in every quarter (certain families were even given as much as fifty kilos of *pasta*), Mattarella's men started to hand out cash, and money that came via the *Banco di Sicilia* (cheques for 5,000 lire each), or coupons to exchange for *pasta* in the shops. But of course much more effective than this cash or the coupons in raking in the votes were the favours Mattarella was able to do people, getting whole batches of them jobs, without competition, in various organizations, State or otherwise (mainly in the Post Office, the Railways, Regional Government bodies, and Banks).

The Police, up till a year and a half ago, always turned a blind eye to Mattarella's friends; sometimes the Superintendent and the Inspector of the *carabinieri*, and others too, would say confidentially

that these were people you couldn't touch, complaining about it in
private—but in public even going round arm in arm with some of
them. And the ones who weren't on Mattarella's side were gradually liquidated. The more observant people think that Mattarella
played his game here—he made use of the mafiosi in a quite unscrupulous way, and the mafia made use of him for as long as they
could; he took advantage of these people in order to get to the top,
and in turn each of them tried to take advantage of his position.

Signed testimony

8

Whenever Mattarella came to Alcamo for a rally in the post-war
years, he used to be accompanied by Castellammare mafiosi (such as
the Plajas, the Magaddinos, Antonio Buccellato, Liborio Munna,
Salvatore Vitale, Andrea Mancino, Gaspare Bonventre, Vito
Messina—a wealthy property-owning mafioso who made it his
business to 'arrange' things: he was known as '*Il Questore*', the Chief
of Police, because of his authority over local persons including the
police and *carabinieri*; he was the most active in procuring gun
licences and all kinds of other favours from the Town Hall, and
from the police and *carabinieri*); also mafiosi from Camporeale
(Vanni Sacco and others), from Partinico (Santo Fleres and others),
and from Palermo (Peppino Cottone, originally from Alcamo, the
most influential of the active mafiosi of the area). Vincenzo Rimi and
his brother Carlo, and the Gallo brothers and Stefano Leale, who belonged to Alcamo itself, were also part of the group, along with
Giovanni Stellino, the oldest of the local mafiosi but by now the
most cautious, intending from now on to enjoy his position in
peace: today he has become a man of order. They were all together
with Mattarella, either in the Christian Democrat headquarters
which were then in Via Don Rizzo, or in the Bar opposite the
mother church, in Piazzetta 4 Novembre. The whole town could
see they were having friendly conversations, paying each other
compliments; it was obvious that they knew each other well and
enjoyed meeting and being together. This was in the early days,
because subsequently Mattarella, while not actually breaking off
this liaison, began to behave more prudently. Mattarella's aim was

to get votes, and in exchange he promised or got people jobs: mostly in the Railways, in the Post Office, and in Banks.

The police authorities, though they knew these big mafia electors perfectly well, behaved subserviently towards them in public, and showed themselves very ready to attend to any recommendations they might make. The Rimis, for instance, owned a lot of cattle which were in the care of guards, and they frequently used to damage people's crops. Often the owners were afraid to report this: however, if someone did decide to report it, then Rimi or Gallo would intervene. To settle bigger things, though, it was Mattarella they turned to, as on the occasion when the post was held up: Giuliano[1] had given orders that the post would not go off unless a large sum of money was paid; so the mafia intervened, and there was a meeting. This time, Mattarella came down specially for that purpose, not just to hold rallies in his usual way. He was seen with them in public, and he settled the matter: this is common knowledge. And next morning, in fact, the post left.

In Alcamo everybody knows that the mafiosi used to hand out voting slip facsimiles for Mattarella.

Signed testimony

9

Immediately after the war Mattarella came to Alcamo to see Leonardo Renda, representative of Catholic Action, and Giovanni Stellino, then recognized capomafia of the Alcamo area. Together they founded the local branch of the DC party: the first group of leaders included (among others undoubtedly in good faith) Carlo Rimi, Vincenzo's brother, and Giovanni Stellino himself.

One thing to bear in mind is that in the early days, up till '45, a number of the local mafiosi had been on the side of the Separatists. From '45 onwards, though, they made themselves at home in the DC headquarters: Giovanni Stellino, Carlo and Vincenzo Rimi, Tatà Gallo (known to have a criminal past) and Serafino Mancuso— the man to whom Frank Coppola sent that crate of heroin in 1952.

People saw that the mafia was the product of democracy: with the

---

[1] The bandit Salvadore Giuliano. (Tr. note.)

return to democracy, the mafia had come back too—in a way the
mafia was the State. 'Now there's a Republic' meant 'now there's
disorder, chaos, the mafia's back again.' The mafia made their
weight felt particularly in elections, both Parliamentary and internal
party elections. Relations between Mattarella and the mafiosi were
always very friendly indeed; Giovanni Stellino was always on the
balcony beside Mattarella at rallies. Mattarella knew Stellino very
well because he had been to the High School in Alcamo and they
had been close friends; and he knew very well he was an old-style
mafioso. I remember seeing Mattarella and Stellino together on the
balcony in Piazza Ciullo at five or six rallies at least.

At the meetings held in the DC headquarters (and often it was
through Stellino that the news of Mattarella's arrival came), Stellino
was always there.

That time the post was unable to leave for Palermo for several
days because of the heavy toll demanded, creating a local scandal,
(it still isn't clear who had demanded this levy, whether it was
Giuliano or the Alcamo mafia themselves,) it's still widely remembered how Mattarella had a special meeting with Vincenzi Rimi,
Cottone, Gallo and Stellino. Next day the post left: the matter had
been settled. (The exact sum involved in the settlement has never
been known—there was talk of some ten millions, but one would
have to check on that.)

The Alcamo Police were at the service of Mattarella and the
mafia: the mafiosi had gun licences and permits and went about as
they pleased.

In July 1949, Leonardo Renda was murdered; he was found
stabbed in the back and hit by several rounds of *lupara* shot, and
with his identity card on his chest: this was to signify he had betrayed. The most likely hypothesis, also according to the trial proceedings, is that the bandits of Giuliano's band (the actual murderer
was identified), seeing that the promises of liberty and re-entry into
society that had been made to them in exchange for votes procured
for the Christian Democrats and for Mattarella were not being kept,
took their revenge. The Police Superintendent Doctor Carbonetto
who had begun enquiries along these lines was transferred to Sardinia.

Wherever Mattarella goes he tends to eliminate anyone who

might overshadow him. It makes an interesting study to see what has happened to each of his political rivals, within the DC party itself: some have disappeared from the political scene, some have been murdered, some have narrowly escaped murder, and others have been obliged to give way to him.

He has a keen nose for power: he first of all hitched himself firmly to the clergy (and in fact he still has some authority in the transferring of bishops, so that he can count certain bishops in the area among his friends); and next he chose the true, old-style mafia.

As for the Partinico area, I remember how one day I happened to be introduced to Frank Coppola: he asked me what side I was on and I told him. When I asked him what side he was on, he answered: 'In Partinico there's Messeri, a friend.'

Signed testimony

12. *Declaration by one person*

For the election campaign of '46, Bernardo Mattarella arrived in Salemi in the morning with five or six car-loads of people, most of whom looked like mafiosi. He got out in Piazza Libertà, and was at once met by some other men who had been waiting for him: a group was formed which included Mattarella himself; Santo Robino, capomafia of Salemi; Ignazio Salvo (son of Alberto Salvo), a notorious criminal; Vincenzo Mangogna, a very dangerous and violent mafioso, who had served a sentence for murder; Luigi Salvo (son of Alberto), returned from America; Foreddu Robino, who was later killed in America, involved in drug trafficking; Alberto Agueci, another mafioso later murdered in America, burnt, also involved in drugs; Mariano Licari, a big mafioso from Marsala, now in prison for kidnapping. Further off from Mattarella stood mafiosi of lower calibre, and onlookers and canvassers.

After greeting each other warmly, Mattarella and the rest of them stayed there talking for a while, for the whole town to see, and then set off for the DC headquarters, where these mafiosi were all at home, being members; after a bit Mattarella came out onto the balcony of Professor Favara's house to address the rally. With him on the balcony were Ignazio Salvo, one or two other mafiosi, and the current Branch Secretary of the Christian Democrats.

In the years that followed, too, the group of Mattarella's big election supporters was still substantially the same, along with the Church, up till 1952. Then there was a quarrel among the mafiosi, and the ones who stayed on Mattarella's side were Foreddu Robino and Mangogna, until their death. At present the person who gets votes for Mattarella is the Christian Democrat Secretary Palumbo, as well as Salvo's sons, and a number of priests who hand out facsimiles for Mattarella.

In every election campaign Mattarella, or the DC party, has left money to buy votes.

Signed by two witnesses

13

In the last local government election campaign, in '64, Mattarella stopped in Salemi and publicly met Ingraldi and the Salvo brothers, before going on to Marsala. One of Mattarella's chief election campaigners in recent times has been this Ingraldi, former Mayor of Salemi, who is connected with local mafiosi and with those of Vita, among them Zizzo who is at the moment in prison for criminal association and on a series of charges of murder, kidnapping, drug trafficking; and Zizzo himself campaigned for Mattarella, also handing out facsimiles.

In Marsala on various occasions at election rallies the whole town could see Mattarella in the company of: Anca Martinez, considered by many people to be the brain of the Marsala mafia; Giuseppe Bua, mafioso of the big feudal estates, chairman of the *Bonomiana*, now in prison for criminal association, and whose son is a godson of Mattarella's; and Giuseppe Lo Presti, mafioso of an old mafia family.

Signed testimony

14. *Declaration by one person*

When the time of the election campaign comes round, Salvatore Mancino comes up from Castellammare much more often, and calls on certain people or certain families indicated by the Christian Democrat leaders. Mancino and his brother go about things in a very different way from them: once people have given Mancino an undertaking, then they'll vote as he wants—because people are afraid of him, they're afraid of having their animals stolen, afraid of having their vines cut, of having their pensions taken away. Or on the other hand he can promise or provide money or jobs. Mancino sometimes calls by day, but often by night too, in certain cases, to avoid being seen; and of course if a man hears a knocking on his door at night, and sees Mancino there . . . well, who can tell what these people mightn't do?

At the Parliamentary elections, Mancino makes people vote for Mattarella, he even hands out facsimiles for him; he's particularly successful at intimidating people who own animals. At the local elections a few years ago, here at San Vita we saw Mattarella arrive in the company of Mancino and a number of others from Castellammare; they walked together along Via Vittorio Emanuele, and went into the DC Branch together. With them, on friendly terms, were Vincenzo Messina the DC secretary, a 'friend of friends'[1]; Pietro Venza, the local capomafia who stood as a Christian Democrat candidate in the '63 local elections, a close friend of Mancino's; Monaco Vito, a much-feared country mafioso, at present concessionaire and speculator in quarries here and at Custonaci, who makes a million lire a month without lifting a finger (and this sum has been carefully worked out and doesn't include his business earnings); Vincenzo La Sala, who was charged with criminal association but succeeded in getting off scot-free, a great friend of Mancino's.

However, out of the fifteen or so people who went into the DC Branch on that occasion, about ten were honest men.

Signed by two witnesses

15

I remember that for one of the first elections Mattarella came to Montelepre for a rally. Closest to him were old Peppino Filangeri, considered the most influential of the local mafiosi, and his son Giuseppe; old Maniaci and his sons, an old mafia family; old Gaglio; Salvatore Candela; Angelo and Giovanni Genovese who was later sentenced to penal servitude for life (these two were originally

---

[1] A common euphemism for people who have a relationship of reciprocal exploitation with the mafia. (Tr. note.)

mafiosi but had been with the bandits). Among others who came from outside with Mattarella was Don Turiddu Troia from San Giuseppe Iato, a powerful mafioso.

When they arrived by car from Partinico (there were four cars), they got out in Piazza Ventimiglia, and went to meet the archpriest Natale Ferrara in the church. They stayed in there chatting for half an hour, and had some refreshments in the sacristy: a little party with liqueurs and sweets. Then they came out again and hurried off on foot, chatting among themselves, to the café which was then called the Giacopelli. Mattarella was walking arm in arm with old Filangeri. There were also one or two with them who were not mafiosi, but the majority of them were.

Mattarella spoke from the balcony of Giuseppe Biondo, who used to hire it out for DC rallies: with Mattarella on the balcony was old Filangeri, as if to guarantee him to anyone who didn't know him.

It was evening. I remember Mattarella saying, among other things, that if people voted for the Christian Democrats and for him, the bandits would all be pardoned.

A few days before Mattarella's rally, someone had come from Alcamo (I don't know what his name was) with two trucks full of *pasta* which were unloaded in Angelo Genovese's warehouse: the *pasta* was then distributed by Genovese, who also handed out facsimiles with the vote for Mattarella—his was the only name put forward.

Signed testimony

20. *One person*

I remember at one election (I don't remember exactly whether it was '48 or another year) I saw Mattarella in Corleone in the Bentivegna Bar, in Via Bentivegna: he was in a group which included, among others, the three Mancuso-Marcello brothers, commonly known to be of an old mafia family, and Bernardo Raia, who had already been to prison, and who has since disappeared and is believed dead. (At that time these men were putting pressure on people to make them vote Christian Democrat, and handing out the facsimiles.) They were having a friendly conversation. Also with them was Doctor Monteleone, then DC Secretary, who had dealings with the mafia group. They went into the mother church, where they were received by the parish priest Girolamo Liggio, Luciano Liggio's cousin.

I don't remember seeing Mattarella in Corleone apart from that occasion. Calogero Volpe, on the other hand, has been seen a number of times—three times, at least—generally in the company of (among others) Doctor Navarra, who used to be a powerful capo-mafia of the area, and Collura Vincenzo, capomafia second in command to Navarra. When Calogero Volpe arrived, he and Navarra used to embrace and kiss each other in front of everybody. Navarra was always one of the most active in distributing facsimiles for the Christian Democrats, and specially for Calogero Volpe.

Liggio's followers made people vote for Mattarella, and Navarra's for Volpe.

Signed by three witnesses

21. *Extracts from the verbatim report of the trial in Viterbo of the bandits of Giuliano's band charged with the massacre of Portella della Ginestra:*[1]

Antonino Terranova, 10th May 1951: 'Giuliano said to me: "We must compel those gentlemen to keep their word; go to Castellammare del Golfo and kidnap Bernardino Mattarella and his family." But I told Giuliano that he ought to do the kidnapping himself, because it had always been him and him alone who had been in touch with certain persons.'

Gaspare Pisciotta, 14th May 1951: 'The ones who made us these promises were: Bernardo Mattarella . . .

It was Marchesano, the Prince of Alliata, and Bernardo Mattarella who ordered the massacre of Portella della Ginestra. Before the massacre they had a meeting with Giuliano.'

---

[1] On 1 May 1947, in the beautiful Portella della Ginestra pass on the edge of the mountains, the bandits suddenly started firing from the surrounding crags on to the festive crowd of men, women and children from the nearby towns who had gathered there for the traditional May Day celebration, particularly gay that year as they were also celebrating the local victory for the Popular Front (land reform movement) in April's Regional Government elections. Twelve people were killed and about fifty wounded. (Tr. note.)

Antonino Terranova, 17th May 1951: 'It was him, Giuliano, who'd been in touch with Mattarella.'

Mattarella, denounced as the instigator of the massacre, was acquitted in the preliminary investigation at the Palermo Court of Appeal.

22, 23. *Declaration by two people*

The man who backs Mattarella in Ficuzza is Vincenzo Catanzaro, a big capomafia who has actually been charged with murder, and who has often been sent to prison but has always been let out again at once: he is considered a dangerous man, and was a close friend of Doctor Navarra, who was Medical Officer of Health here too, and of Lorello: they used to kiss each other whenever they met.

Vincenzo Catanzaro was once very poor, and a fugitive from the law: now he has land, and big flocks and herds, and a new house where he has meetings with nasty-looking types from all over the place.

Zu Vincenzo has facsimiles distributed—he hands them out himself, too—getting people to vote Mattarella, Calogero Volpe and Barbaccia for Parliament; and for the Senate he backs Pecoraro.

People vote as Zu Vincenzo tells them, nearly everybody, because they're afraid of him; they could be landed without a job, he's a dangerous and violent man who's capable of taking up his pistol for the least trifle.

Barbaccia and Pecoraro have been here to have meetings with Catanzaro: I don't know if the others have been.

The Police Sergeant who used to be here was in league with him; but the present one is trying to enforce respect for the law, and Zu Vincenzo has been placed under special surveillance.

Signed by three witnesses

24. From *Cronache Sociali* of 1st September 1949, under the heading 'Mafia and Banditry in Sicily':

The interests that foster '*omertà*'[1] are more readily explained if one considers that the fundamental conservatism of the mafia is

[1] The ancient tradition of preserving 'manliness' by refusing to reveal anything, no matter what one has seen. (Tr. note.)

fully shared by the governing class of Sicily and therefore, in-directly or by extension, by that of Italy. Now undoubtedly this class is willing to extirpate banditry: but is it equally willing to extirpate the mafia?

. . . Into legitimate party politics intrudes the boundless cynicism of certain Sicilian politicians: in particular of those who, not kept in check by any serious party discipline, lacking any personal tech-nico-political prestige, and not having any national basis, had to try to neutralize any competition in their own wards and win almost unanimous support under pressure from the mafia and the outlaws. To these candidates goes the credit for having succeeded in securing the support not only of the mafia, which was logically predictable, but of the bandits as well. The local mafia factions came into a state of ferment again; the candidates already on the Constituent Assembly prided themselves on being able to give assurances, in strictly secret talks, of notable amnesties to be granted to the outlaws and their faithful emissaries; this form of electioneering went on, laborious but consistent, from Castellam-mare to Montelepre, from Balestrate to San Giuseppe Iato. On this basis, it is easy to explain not only the physical elimination of a number of small Sicilian trades unionists, presumably the work of local mafiosi, but also Portella della Ginestra and the outrages of the 22nd June following that.[1]

. . . The problem facing the governing class is how to crush banditry without destroying the mafia; in other words, how to free themselves of one awkward travelling companion while doing as little harm as possible to the other—since the other, already so use-ful in getting certain 'friends' into Parliament, might well be of service again next time. But the fact is, these conditions of crime have to be crushed completely, otherwise they will inexorably rise again like the hydra of Lerna. Consequently, under these sinister entanglements, Government action in Sicily is extremely hesitant and inhibited.

25. *Letter from Giuliano, 24th November 1948*

This letter which comes to you from the so-called outlaws is not

[1] Various left-wing party headquarters were bombed or set on fire. See p. 272. (Tr.)

the usual petition. Today we have quite a different matter to speak about to the Honourable Deputies.

After the unhappy events of the 3rd of September,[1] unhappy also for us who were forced into this by the need to save our own lives, the resulting situation requires clarifying, more for your own sakes than for ours.

The police forces of your chief and friend, the Christian Democrat Scelba, have invaded our part of the world, and are exercising there every abuse and every form of violence. Our womenfolk, our families, are the favourite target for this splendid campaign. What have they done to deserve it? You do not know, the police do not know, and neither do they know themselves, for in fact they are blameless.

We are not asking you to refrain from pursuing your campaign against us, the victims of these miserable post-war years, even though we would have a perfect right to do so: but leave our women and children alone.

Honourable Sirs: remember that these women who are now being ill-treated in prison voted for you because they put their faith in your sense of justice and, above all, in your promises. In our part of the world people voted only for you: we kept our promises. Now you keep yours.

Salvatore Giuliano

28

For the election on 18th April 1948, Mattarella came to Sciacca, with a number of cars, to hold a rally. I do not know who they were in the cars with him because they were outsiders.

When he got to Piazza del Popolo—late in the afternoon, about half past six—a group formed around Mattarella consisting of: (closest of all to him) Francesco Segreto, the capomafia who used to maintain—and still does—the link with Palermo; Carmelo Di Stefano, capomafia of Sciacca, implicated in the murder of the trade unionist Accurso Miraglia;[2] Soldano Antonino, local mafioso;

---

[1] On 3 September 1948, in an ambush by the gates of Partinico, Giuliano's band had killed a *carabinieri* captain, a Public Security officer and an N.C.O.

[2] See Dolci's *Waste*, part I, Chapter III. (Tr. note).

Luigi Fazio, a middle-rank mafioso; Michele Bono, a country mafioso who had already served nineteen years in prison for cattle-stealing and criminal association; Di Nino, known as 'Mpinna, a mafioso who had left the countryside to go in for sub-contracting for Di Stefano; Pellegrino Marciante and Curreri Calogero, the two suspected of actually murdering Miraglia; a man called Cavaliere, also I believe a mafioso, from Prizzi; Avv. Russo, a mafioso from an old mafia family who has been in trouble with the law; Don Aldino Luvaro, an old mafioso who has now retired; Venezia Salvatore, since sentenced to penal servitude for life. We here know the local ones, and these were the only ones I was able to recognize definitely.

After they had shaken hands in a friendly way with this crowd, including Marcianti and Curreri, they all went into the private room of what was then the Porello Café, now the Milleluci, and took some refreshments together; the ones with most authority were on the most friendly terms with Mattarella, the others less. They stayed inside the café for about twenty minutes. When they came out again, they went on strolling round Piazza del Popolo for another ten minutes or so, in full view of everybody. Walking with them, though at a distance of at least ten yards, was Police Superintendent Zincone, with an Inspector and a Sergeant, all in civilian clothes.

Then they went up to the platform and Mattarella addressed the rally. Also on the platform was the Mayor at that time, Molinari, who arrived just the moment before the meeting began, and one or two others.

The group named above had been campaigning for Mattarella (and they also campaigned for him at subsequent elections), putting pressure on people to vote for him, and handing out facsimiles for him; a lot of Mattarella's votes came to him through the Church, too, especially through the present archpriest Agostino Bono.

Signed testimony

36

During one of the post-war election campaigns in Villafrati I distinctly remember, in 1953, seeing Mattarella several times, on the occasion of various meetings or rallies, with mafiosi of Villafrati itself (such as Antonio and Pietro Santomauro—who was later killed; his son Salvatore, field-watcher on the Stallone estate; Salvatore Spitaliere—later killed; Salvatore Badami, died in banishment; the Chiruseddis); with mafiosi from Baucina (such as Salvatore Pinelli, now doing penal servitude for life); and mafiosi of Godrano (such as Salvatore Lorello, known as Zu Turiddu, the real capomafia of the area; and the Barbaccias).

I saw them walking about together, talking to each other, on very friendly—even affectionate—terms. I also saw with them the arch-priest Padre Terrana; I remember on one occasion seeing Padre Terrana embrace not only Mattarella but also Salvatore Pinelli, of an old mafia family; and the two of them stayed on together to listen to the whole of Mattarella's speech.

Many of these mafiosi, and in particular the Badami family, used to boast—even to the *carabinieri*—about being on intimate terms with Mattarella: it was no use arresting them, they said, because they would immediately be freed. Which did in fact happen from time to time. 'You're just wasting your time,' they would say to the *carabinieri*.

Mattarella and the Christian Democrat authorities in the area *must* have known these mafiosi for what they were: it's impossible that they didn't know—even the little children knew. A lot of them had shot at each other in the Piazza in broad daylight, and it was common knowledge that they were the most dangerous mafiosi in the area. In these particular elections, and in other elections since, Mattarella has always come out either top or among the first, in other words with the biggest preference vote. The facsimiles for Mattarella and Barbaccia were handed out in the street by these mafiosi, or taken round from house to house, whichever they thought best. I saw them repeatedly with my own eyes. (The archpriest, for his part, handed out facsimiles for Mattarella to the women in the sacristy.) It's not as if the mafiosi tried to hide it—on the contrary, they boasted about it; and for his part Mattarella was quite open about being seen with them.

Signed testimony

38, 39

After the last war, mafia power in Lercara was concentrated in Gioacchino Ferrara, who had the greatest economic—and not only economic—power in the place; this was also partly through his brothers Arturo (who is now the politician of the family) and Mario (who, like Gioacchino, always had a revolver in his pocket, and was the most violent, being quite capable of beating up the miners), and three or four gangers. In their time the Ferraras had been denounced and sentenced for cruelty and ill-treatment of juveniles employed in their mines: on medical and radiological examination some of the boys were found to have been deformed by the work.

Mattarella, who had also previously had the support of the Ferraras, came down twice in '63: once for a rally in Piazza Duomo, and the other time to promise action to get the waterworks functioning effectively (but nothing has been seen of that yet).

On each of these occasions, Mattarella went to the Ferraras' house, being a close friend of theirs. At that time they particularly needed political help to prevent their mining licence from being declared expired after the serious deficiencies found in the mine.

Testimony signed by two people

40. *A miner declares*

It's obvious to us on the spot here that the rise in Mattarella's votes in the '63 elections was due to the special backing of the Ferraras: Gioacchino Ferrara and his followers tried to tame, to subjugate the workers, and their wives and dependents, and the tradesmen who depended on the Ferraras, to make them all vote for Mattarella. In the same way as he spoke to me, Ferrara spoke one by one to all the miners, threatening us with the sack if we didn't vote as he said—because he told us he would count up the votes afterwards, section by section.

In '63 every worker received a Christian Democrat membership card free from Ferrara even if they hadn't wanted one.

Signed by four witnesses

Alia is a mafia centre. The votes for Mattarella here went up—
they almost exactly doubled, going from 203 to 403—when capomafia Ditta Vincenzo (a close friend of Genco Russo[1]) and Matteo
Vallone (another old mafioso very active in cattle-stealing and on the
big estates, with more than fifteen years of prison and banishment to
his name) became his chief election campaigners, which was a short
while before the 1958 elections. Whereas in the post-war years these
mafiosi and their group had been backing Liberals and Monarchists,
for '58 they had facsimiles distributed—and they took them round
themselves, too, from house to house—with Mattarella's name and
number on. They told people: 'I got you your land.' 'I got you that
loan from the Bank and now you've got to do me the favour of
voting for Mattarella.' 'If you'll do me this favour I'll get you some
land (or I'll get you a job) from the Prince.' And lots of people said
yes, and lots of them were afraid and in the end voted as they said.
They went round to people's houses by night, to frighten them
more.

In the weeks leading up to that election, Calogero Volpe came
here to Alia, not to hold a public rally but to meet in private with a
group of people said to have included Matteo Vallone son, Matteo
Vallone father, Ditta Vincenzo, Matassa Giuseppe, accused of
cattle-stealing and an executive mafia agent; and Don Botindari.
But there were also others who weren't mafiosi.

On 11th April 1955 the Honourable Mattarella came to inaugu-
rate the new village near the Station of Roccapalumba: also present
on that occasion were all the chief mafiosi of Alia (to be exact: Ditta
Vincenzo, Vallone Matteo, Castellana Francesco Paolo, and Rocco
Zummo, as well as others), and of Roccapalumba and Lercara
Friddi.

Even Santo Sciacca and Salvatore Martino, violent mafiosi
executive agents, were among those who got people to vote for
Mattarella.

The part played by the mafia was so crucial in determining
Mattarella's gains in '58 that after Matteo Vallone died, about '61,

[1] See p. 82. (Tr.)

and his son went away, Mattarella's votes in '63 fell to less than half: the fear gone, the votes dropped.

Signed testimony

46, 47. *Declaration by two people*

Gangi used to be famous for its old feudal mafia and for its banditry. After the war, the mafia split, and one half supported the Liberals and the other half certain Christian Democrats.

After the death of the old mafioso Cataldo Naselli, in prison, and of his priest brother, more famous as a mafioso than as a priest (he was co-owner with his brother of a big estate, and used to go round armed with a gun), their heirs, in a now rather changed world, were the sons Salvatore and Sante. The latter—a party official in Fascist days, an M.O.H. famous in the area as a gambler, and commonly rumoured to be responsible for the death in mysterious circumstances (the mystery still remains) of a person he had been having difficulties with—is Mattarella's big election supporter, and hands out voting-slip facsimiles for him even in the Municipal Clinic.

About '58, on the occasion of the laying of the foundation stone of the Post Office here in Gangi, Mattarella was cordially welcomed by this Sante Naselli, at that time Christian Democrat secretary: they were old friends.

Naselli, in his capacity as Chairman of the Saint Vincent Charity, has even supported election campaigns out of Charity funds. Another who helped get votes for Mattarella at the last elections was Pietro Restivo: after the elections he got 'the word' for an important post in Palermo. Without the massive intervention of Naselli and Pietro Restivo, Mattarella would never have been able to get all those preference votes in a place where he was unknown.

Signed by three witnesses

48, 49. *Declaration by two people*

In Caccamo Mattarella gets a lot of preference votes: practically all the Christian Democrat preference votes in 1958, in spite of

Aldisio being head of the list. When he arrived (we remember him coming at least three times) he met up with a group of people, on two occasions outside the gates at the entrance to the town, near the statue under the castle. The group immediately surrounding him consisted of Doctor Salvatore Cordone, Mayor for twenty years, a friend of friends; Francesco Guagenti, friend of friends, an intimate associate of Panzeca and of Cordone, and who had made a rapid fortune through profiteering; Peppino Panzeca, notorious capomafia of the whole zone, charged with murder and criminal association, and who went into hiding after the Ciacculli massacre;[1] Giorgio Ponte, Panzeca's wife's brother, a 'friend of friends'; Leonardo Panzeca, Peppino's cousin, a dangerous mafioso of many years' standing; Moriella Giovanni, a backer of the mafiosi; Giovanni Guzzino, another backer, now under surveillance; Mascia Nicasio, also mafiosi though not openly so. As well as these, we have sometimes seen the archpriest (though usually he's in a car): he's the brother of the capomafia, in every respect. And of course as well as these there are onlookers, and people who've come in the hope of obtaining favours, and canvassers.

All in a bunch, and very friendly with each other, (while around them the crowd grows to about a hundred or a hundred and fifty,) they go off together to the place where the rally is to be held: once it took place in Piazza del Duomo, another time in Piazza San Domenico, another time in Piazza Pusateri. On the balcony with Mattarella we remember seeing Ponte, Moriella, Cordone, and Guagenti: at the end of the rally they all shook hands and embraced each other. After the rally they usually all go off together to the bar owned by capomafia Panzeca, in Corso Umberto: refreshments are stood by Panzeca himself, though whether out of his own money or out of Council funds we don't know.

Just as we have seen them with our own eyes, so everyone else in town, including the *carabinieri*, can see for themselves the Panzecas and other mafiosi or friends of friends handing out facsimiles for Mattarella: the majority of the people don't know Mattarella, but they do know the men handing out the facsimiles, along with packets of *pasta*, perhaps, and a thousand lire here and there, or else with threats. If Panzeca and the other mafiosi were to decide to get

[1] See p. 236. (Tr.)

votes for someone else, Mattarella would hardly have a single vote in Caccamo.

Signed by two witnesses

50

. . . Bernardo Mattarella has from the beginning procured votes in Palermo city mainly through: (a) the Church; (b) political action and the control of certain key positions in public institutions and banks; (c) a group of fellow-Castellammarese supporters operating in the petty bourgeois and working-class strata; and (d) the circuit of 'friends' in the outer districts.

The following is a condensed version, though still using the actual words, of the declarations made by the most observant and most experienced people in the respective fields. Perhaps it will be opportune to dwell a little longer on channel (d), the least well known.

a: 'The success of Mattarella can only be understood if we bear in mind that he had already become to a certain extent a *"persona spiccata"*[1] as representative of Sicily for Catholic Youth before the fall of Fascism; because hardly anybody was then active in that direction, he frequently had occasion to go to Rome, and furthered certain causes in the ecclesiastical sphere; and so he was started off in his career immediately after the war mainly by the group around Ruffini.'[2]

b: 'From his base in Castellammare, Mattarella first makes his way into political life in Palermo (where he has practised as a lawyer, remaining in close contact with Catholic Action) above all as supporter of the younger ranks of the Christian Democrats who, in opposition to Restivo—the big man of the Palermo bourgeoisie—then succeed in getting hold of the party machine, with Gioia at their head. When the crisis comes in De Gasperi's government, Mattarella finds himself in *Iniziativa Democratica*,[3] opposing

---

[1] *Persona spiccata:* outstanding person; like *persona intesa*, an expression often used by mafiosi to describe themselves. (Tr. note).

[2] The late Cardinal of Palermo—see p. 175. (Tr. note.)

[3] A militant Christian group within the DC Party. (Tr. note.)

Restivo, and makes his way into the Christian Democrat divisions by means of his own activity and through his right-hand men.

The gradual but increasing disintegration of support for Restivo means at first undisputed leadership for Mattarella among the young Christian Democrats. At this stage, a very important factor in his successful entry is his connection with Lauro Chiazzese, Rector of the University, a key figure in the history of the Palermo of these years: having started out as a professor of the highest order and then become a financier, his ability and his position—in particular that of Chairman of the Savings Bank—have brought him into the struggle between the two rival factions of the Christian Democrats, more or less as adviser to the anti-Restivo younger ranks; and besides this, he is one of those Sicilian intellectuals who are not averse to having dealings with mafia circles. Through this Chiazzese, Mattarella—already in touch with certain traditional mafia elements by way of his Castellammare base—succeeds in fostering or in creating new client-patron relationships, while the clientship system centring on Restivo is gradually being dismantled.

Meanwhile on a Municipal level an alliance is formed between Mattarella and Ciancimino, a typical intriguer very active in Council business, unscrupulously making a fortune for himself. Other strong points for Mattarella are Scaglione, the Public Prosecutor; the Prefects; his own men in IRFIS, in the Port Authority, in ENEL, in the *Banco di Sicilia*, and on certain Credit committees and Boards of Directors. And on a national level Mattarella reinforces his personal power by putting his electoral strength at the disposal of the central government. With the break in *Iniziativa Democratica* comes the break here with Gioia and the candidates supporting Fanfani: while the young Christian Democrats (older by now) are sharpening political rivalry in the struggle for key positions, Mattarella on a national level joins the winning side: he joins the *Moro-Doroteo* faction.

His votes in Palermo in the various elections have been as follows: 6,292 in '46; 19,005 in '48; 19,735 in '53; 26,062 in '58; 22,849 in '63.'

c: 'In Palermo, among the group of Castellammarese introduced by Mattarella who procure votes for him, some of the most prominent have been: Doctor Camillo Caiozzo, regional manager, now retired, Secretary General to the Chamber of Commerce; Doctor Giralamo Buccellato, regional manager of the Department of Agriculture and Forestry, who introduced large numbers of Castellammarese into ERAS; Professor Scozia who, through the Emigration Authority, procured huge quantities of votes; Borruso, nicknamed *Terremoto*—"Earthquake"—, a businessman. Many votes were also procured by secondary characters, often whole families who had been fixed up with jobs, and who went round canvassing from door to door.'

'Nicolino Mattarella, Bernardo's brother, who used to run a bakery in Castellammare and got into trouble with the Rev. Caiozzo when the latter was Mayor because his bread didn't comply with regulations, was fixed up in Palermo in the Savings Bank, and was later given the title of *Commendatore*, and made Chairman of the Football Association; together with his brother-in-law Vito Buccellato, a bank clerk who had once been a very active dealer in eggs, oil, and bottled wine, he acted as intermediary with the electoral apparatus in Palermo.

The other brother, Santino Mattarella, was a good guitarist and a good barber; to avoid certain consequences, because he was also concerned with shipping people off to America illegally, he was fixed up at the Port warehouses, and naturally he too collects votes for his brother, mainly through the people in the Port.

d: 'After the war Liborio Munna, in collaboration with Stellino of Alcamo, entered into very close relations with Palermo. In the beginning Mattarella, a provincial lawyer with an occasional small case to defend, made his way into Palermo (besides through the Church) through business circles, as a 'friend of friends', boosted also by the mafia of Castellammare and Alcamo. To understand what happens in election campaigns in Palermo, one has to remember that the rural mafia has more of a sense of honour and of prestige than the city mafia has, specially at the middle and lower levels, among the rabble, who are more concerned with immediate profit. The rural mafiosi, while traditionally remaining open to possible winners on any side, also know very well that without the support of their politician, without his continued protection, they will go to prison.

Another thing to remember is that in the city Mattarella acted with far greater caution than he did in the country.'

'In the Borgo, as in all the suburbs of Palermo, the mafia plays a very big role in getting votes for candidates who apply to them: they receive the money and naturally they work to get the votes in return—they have to have something to show for it. Some of the mafiosi do it for friendship's sake, some do it to show themselves in a good light to the person they're getting votes for in order to obtain favours in exchange, and some do it for the money: for instance, they take a million lire ("the boys must have their bread"), spend two or three hundred thousand, and keep the rest for themselves. Among the mafiosi offering their services in this quarter (most of them used to get votes for the Liberals at first, and then for the Christian Democrats) were Leopoldo Cancelliere and Don Peppino Fiore, now in prison for the report on the 54.[1] Peppino Ingrassia, a man with a criminal record, used to go in for this business every season; Piazza il Magnaccia usually campaigned for Gioia and for Lima; when they arrested Pietro il Ladro, his wife said: "Just let Mattarella wait and see if we'll get votes for him again!" Also working for Mattarella in '58 were Beneditta la Niura's brothers, who used to be vagabonds but are now fixed up: they have a gambling den which they hire out at election time to the highest bidder; and they'll even lend their services to more than one party at a time (in '58, for instance, they had a Liberal and a Monarchist, in '63 a Liberal and a Christian Democrat, and so on).'

'In Palermo there are people who make a profession out of getting money in every election campaign, either from the candidates themselves or from their representatives, in exchange for electioneering. Such and such a person comes along to them and says: "I need to pick up a hundred votes here or a hundred and fifty," and asks how much he'll have to spend in order to get them. They ask their price, naturally. They come to an agreement, and get part of the money straight away and the rest immediately after the election, provided the votes come out all right.

This is common knowledge in this quarter, because we've known them come to blows with each other sometimes and start complaining out loud about the money not being shared out fairly, or

---

[1] The police report on the fifty-four people accused of blowing up the Alfa-Romeo *Giulietta* in Ciacculli, killing seven policemen and army engineers. (Tr. note.)

grumbling because the candidate hasn't given them as much as he'd promised.

They see this as a job. If somebody criticizes them for hanging around a couple of hundred yards away from the polling booth, they say: "Leave us alone, we've got to earn our bread"—"Let me get what I can out of these beggars." They're quite open about who they're working for: one time for one, another time for someone else, just depending on who pays most.

In Torrelunga and Settecannoli at election time the ones on this job are Vincenzo il Partinicoto; Muratore Francesco, a cousin of the mafioso Angelo Baiamonte: these are the fingers, so to speak. The arms are the Tenerellos, the Vitales—a large family, much feared— and the Zancas. Behind them, less conspicuous, are the types like Pietro and Vincenzo Chiaracane, an old and dangerous mafia family who have bushels of facsimiles in their house at election time, and tons of *pasta*; Francesco la Mantia—old-style mafia, with at least ten years' prison to his name for assocation—uncle of Liggio's doctor.

In '63, when Francesco la Mantia was talking about Mattarella's manifestoes, he referred to them as "our manifestoes": he didn't want "his" manifestoes, i.e. Mattarella's, to be touched by anyone else—he got quite angry with the others.'

'There are quite a few people who sell their voter's certificates. At Falsomiele there's a family called Settesoru who are so numerous they're like flies, and they sell their voter's certificates for five or ten thousand lire each: people are wise to all the tricks nowadays. As well as that, if they're paid, they'll go round collecting votes for whoever pays most, they offer their services quite openly. People are in awe of them because there are so many of them and they're such bullies.'

'The methods are always the same, though the people vary from one quarter to another. In the Albergheria quarter, or the Capo, for instance—I mean not in the suburbs but in the poor central quarters—the candidates apply to petty mafiosi of the lowest category through some experienced middleman who bargains with them to do the work for a certain fee. In the Albergheria district the best-known vote-catchers are the Cane brothers, pick-locks and pick-pockets, and Zu Giacomino Terrasone, a dangerous ex-convict.

9

It's like a seasonal job: they drop their usual trade to go round getting votes for the highest bidder. There's a ruffian in the Albergheria whose usual trade is in coffins—he's in prison now, but this is what he used to do in other campaigns: he would "work" for three different candidates, a Monarchist, a Christian Democrat and a Republican. In the same way others will work simultaneously for Liberals and Christian Democrats, in exchange for promises of jobs as street cleaners or doorkeepers, or other favours. It's a large-scale swindling market which many innocents fall into. In the working-class quarters, thirty to fifty per cent of a candidate's votes are obtained this way.

In an election campaign, this kind of bartering will cost a candidate of the Lima or Gioia or Mattarella type—in addition to what he spends on ordinary propaganda—at least ten million lire in cash (over the last few days of the campaign the price of a vote ranges from two to ten thousand lire), and about four million lire's worth of *pasta* which is handed round at the beginning.

Whereas the country mafiosi give more or less consistent support to their candidates, and the most influential and therefore most dangerous of the city mafiosi pick their candidates carefully on the basis of long-term calculations and even in special meetings held for the purpose—the lowest-grade mafiosi, especially in the old slum quarters, make themselves available turn and turn about to the highest bidder.'

'People are afraid and it's difficult to know. In the Pallavicino district at election time the confusion is fantastic. For the '63 and '64 elections they handed out *pasta*, cash and petrol coupons, lots and lots of petrol coupons, besides promises of jobs. The chief vote-catcher for the Christian Democrats here is Restante Marco Maiorana, a "friend of friends", of an old mafia family, and the brother of Ciccio who's now in hiding after being charged with murder and association; more influential than him, though keeping more in the shade, was Nicoletti, who has just been arrested for the report on the 54; and as well as these, Giuseppe Messina and his brother (who've so far managed to keep a clean record) also make their weight felt. These men were one and all mobilized for the Christian Democrats. One of the men who gets most support in that district is Mattarella—he doesn't even have to hold public meetings,

the votes just quietly roll in. They backed his son here, too, in the
'64 local elections.'

'At Cruillas and La Conceria, Mattarella gets a lot of votes, he's
the candidate who gets most. Most of his votes have been procured (as anyone can see with their own eyes) by a dozen or so
canvassers who hand out *pasta* and flour at every election to voters
they can really count on (five or six of these canvassers were taken
on about three years ago at the central Post Office, and one or two
others at SAIA); and also by the presence and the "advice" of Matteo
Citarda and his followers (he comes of an old mafia family) and De
Maria, now in prison for the report on the 54—both of them implicated in the building speculation of the district. These men would
plant themselves right outside the polling stations to put the wind
up people, and the people would be too terrified to disobey them or
refuse to do whatever they said.'

'At Brancaccio, besides the civic committee, the ones who get
votes for Mattarella—openly handing out facsimiles outside the
polling stations or from door to door, or going round the houses
picking people up in their cars—are Gioacchino Caccamo, Filippo
and Pietro Conte, Giovanni Alfano (through his son Giuseppe): all
from old mafia families, all charged with association; and Francesco
La Mantia, now the capomafia, who keeps more in the shade. Other
low-grade mafiosi are also used, such as Chiaracane, and the Chiazzese brothers—one of them's dead now, the one who'd made a
career for himself in the Banks.

These men have always collaborated with Mattarella, from the
very beginning right up to the present day. Mattarella is said to have
been to this district often, though usually only at night since the
Antimafia Commission was set up.

In '63 I myself was asked by Angelo Genova, the owner of the
petrol station in via Tasca Lanza, who comes of an old mafia family
and has influential contacts in various towns, to vote for Mattarella:
"Mattarella is a friend—we must help him, and then when we need
something he'll do us any favour in return".'

'A newspaper writes: "The accusations consist of a series of
statements asserting that Avv. Bernardo Mattarella, Deputy in the
National Parliament, has on many occasions smiled—as he passed
through the streets of the city of his electoral ward—at people 'well

known to be mafiosi': but who, we would point out, do not wear round their necks placards announcing, 'I am a mafioso—do not look at me'." With regard to this, I would like to make the following statement: Villabate is a suburb of Palermo, in fact it is virtually still part of Palermo. Bernardo Mattarella would have got only a tiny handful of votes here, practically none, if it hadn't been for the support of the local mafia. Do any of the ordinary people here know him at all? But the mafiosi know him as well as he knows them: they don't meet just by chance, nor just in passing. And the Minister also knows how to make use of the Police.

For the elections of either '48 or '53 I saw Mattarella here in the company of Antonino Cottone, capomafia of Villabate, father-in-law of Salvatore Greco who was arrested recently; Giuseppe Cottone, Antonino's brother, now in banishment; Giovanni di Peri, a crony of Cottone's at present in prison for the blowing up of the *Giulietta* in Villabate; Salvatore Di Peri, now under special restrictions; Antonio Vitale, known as the *Commendatore* (and in fact he was actually made a *Commendatore*), now considered the capomafia since Antonino Cottone was killed; and other touts and canvassers, low-ranking mafia with little authority. All these years these men have been Mattarella's big election campaigners: they have openly distributed, or got other people to distribute, facsimiles for him, saying: "You vote for this man—it's all the same to you—and then when you need something we'll help you, we'll have a word with him because we're friends of his." In fact, apparently Mattarella has even been entertained as a guest in their homes.'

'So often, people just don't know which way to vote. In Resuttana, Bernardo Mattarella gets lots of votes through his touts who hand out, publicly and in full view of everybody, *pasta* and cash; their chief leader is Gaetano Matranga—who has also been Superior of the Church Guild for religious feasts and processions—he comes of a mafia family: he is a brother of Nino Matranga, who has been in hiding since being charged with association.'

'In Roccella, Mattarella's big supporter is Giuseppe Inzerillo, a mafioso of the fruit and vegetable market; the executive agents are Francesco Tenerello, who is greatly respected; Giacomo Vitale; and Giuseppe Baimonti, a dangerous mafioso who, to be exact, collected votes for Mattarella in via Messina Marina and at Lo Sperone.'

'In Falsomiele, while Giovanni Acqua tried to buy votes with *pasta*, cash, and shoes for the children, one of the friends of friends who backed Mattarella was Michele Mondino, Manager of the Prince's estate and a crony of the capomafia Paolino Bontade: together with his son and his brother-in-law Massaro Francesco, Mondino called up the people and handed round facsimiles, saying: "You take my advice and vote for Mattarella—he's our affair."

Another man who gets votes for Mattarella in Falsomiele is Salvatore Sedita, son of Pietro Sedita, a notorious mafioso and crony of Stefano Bontà. His advice was the same: "Vote for Mattarella"—he'd say—"*E cosa nostra:* he's our affair." '

'Here in Palermo we use the normal system for electing certain Deputies: when the election comes round, they send for the old boss and together they'll come to some agreement. The more important they are, the more secretly they go about it. The old boss has certain friends among the young men, and it's us lads who procure the votes: it's the old fellows who tell us youngsters who we're to back in the election.

In one of the central districts the boss may ask for two million lire, and then he'll take care of the lads himself; and the candidates also have to provide him with twenty quintals of *pasta*, and sometimes they'll find a job for one or two of the lads. Us lads get ten thousand lire to start off with, for putting ourselves at their disposal; then after a fortnight another five or ten thousand; and at the end of the campaign we each hope we'll get a job—but in fact they hardly ever give them to anyone. At the last elections, each of us procured between fifty and two hundred votes that way, and in our quarter there were about ten of us lads on the job.

The ones who employ us most now are Lima and Gioia. Mattarella doesn't have much backing here—he has more supporters over in l'Uditore, and Passo di Rigano, and other suburban districts. But one of the old fellows told me that Mattarella—the one who's in Rome—is a man of honour: he's not the sort to turn against the mafia, he said. He's a man we can trust—he's not the type who'd turn round and side with the Antimafia Commission and start trying to oust the mafia from Palermo.'

Signed by two witnesses

On 23rd February 1966, Bernardo Mattarella is left out of the third Moro Government.

On the 24th and 25th February, the papers publish extracts from a letter and a telegram sent by Moro to Mattarella, in which he declares that he has 'always considered him one of his most able colleagues'. ('It is with a sense of deep regret that, owing to superior exigencies of internal equilibrium, I now have to forego your invaluable, loyal and dedicated services . . .') He expresses the wish that he 'may one day again assume a position of governmental responsibility . . .' 'It is for me an occasion for the deepest regret that I have had to forego your collaboration, of which I shall always retain the most vivid and agreeable memory.'

Part Two

From a Meeting in Palermo, 6 October 1965

DANILO: . . . from your own and other people's information, as you will also have noted in reading the documentation I have so far collected, I think certain observations emerge clearly:

1: The present situation has been partly built up out of layer upon layer of interdependent historical factors: among these was the insufficient pressure of need in previous centuries, and an insufficient awareness of need; continual domination by alien powers; the particular condition and culture of these dominators and exploiters; the non-development of any authentic Christian tradition; the part played by the big feudal estates in repressing individual and collective development; the non-development of a popular and democratic state, one that would represent and protect its citizens; the absence of any autonomous development of work and of local culture.

2: In particular, on the negative role of the feudal estates—still not overcome in the area—here is what an economic historian has to say: 'Justice in the modern sense does not exist in the feudal system, the feudal lord does as he pleases. The lack of any sense of justice is due to a situation in which the old feudal type of justice is transformed into a type of social relationship which is still based on the abuse of power but which no longer has (on the national level) the sort of judicial recognition it would have had in the feudal system. The absence of technical and economic development in the area conditions people's behaviour and general attitude.'

3: The system of clientship and string-pulling, developed out of the individual's bid for survival, has become a phenomenon of reciprocal parasitism, an unhealthy symbiosis—and reciprocal exploitation, reciprocal parasitism, is the very antithesis of development in common—and it has never managed to evolve into the positive symbiosis of the creative democratic group.

The generous hospitality of the people, and their habit of fraternizing on a geographical basis (by streets or quarters or villages), and on particular occasions, do not yet amount to an effective

245

capacity for association: in most cases this coming together is either self-defence or an unconscious attempt to find an emotional escape from personal unhappiness.

4: If one of the essential characteristics of the clientship system is that the 'politician' makes use of his 'clients' in order to obtain influence and votes even among people whose real interests may well be the very opposite to his, one of the essential characteristics of the mafia-clientship type of association (which is a cross between the secret violence of the mafia and the system of clientship which tries to disguise itself under the cloak of representative democracy) is the particular violence, the particular terror, the particular secrecy with which pressure is put on individuals and peoples.

As long as the normal form of collaboration is the mafia-clientship type (and it is significant that for many people the word 'association' stands for 'criminal association': 'he was charged with association'), and as long as people lack any sound and positive experience of other forms, it is quite understandable that the group should generally seem to them risky and impossible, and that they should keep repeating, 'The man who plays alone never loses.'

5: Until the clientship system—whether it appears under the diplomatic guise of political power, or the elegantly unscrupulous guise of the industrialist and businessman; or in the form of secret mafia violence, or in the form of *coronelismo*,[1] or in the paternalism of the boss and the false priest, or whatever other form it may take— until this is resolutely and clearly unmasked, it is difficult for people to recognize even where their own real interests lie, what they ought to oppose, or what should be fought for: even conflicting class interests have not been clearly distinguished yet. Whereas in more advanced societies the need to overcome class differences is recognized and acted upon, here the continuation of the clientship system has prevented even any clear distinction between opposing interests.

6: The present inadequate democratic associative structures (co-operatives, trades unions, political parties and so on are inadequate both in quality and in numbers) are not capable of stimulating any appreciable forward impetus.

In so far as active centres for directing and supporting projects are lacking, the circle tends to remain closed.

[1] A mafia-like system of political patronage in Brazil. (Tr. note.)

In general, even among those most concerned, people don't have a sufficiently clear view of the situation, and not enough care and attention is given to the preparation of the new tools that are needed: this results in a great waste of time and energy. Because problems are not identified clearly, action tends to be vague and ill-defined, and so objectives are only partially realized, if at all. For clear examples of this, we need only look at the lack of preparation with which the political parties approach the socially and econo-mically complex business of planning; or at the general imprecision of even the Left in denouncing mafia phenomena. (One detail: until the Press in general, and 'clean' Sicilian correspondents in particu-lar, are prepared to report publicly and in detail at election time, from every commune in Sicily, exactly which mafiosi are being employed to back those candidates usually supported by mafia organization, and until the mafiosi are obliged to hide from the eyes of public opinion, little progress can be achieved.)

This lack of precision inevitably militates also against people's commitment to associative life: their keenness will naturally be proportionate to the clarity and the obvious validity of the aims, and to the likelihood of their being achieved.

The big mass gatherings generally function on a sentimental or emotional level (for instance, the football match or the religious procession), and do not touch on the essential problems.

7: Even a meeting organized for the purpose of launching a particular project can easily become merely an emotional outlet for the speaker, an occasion for parading his own ideas, instead of an occasion for functional communication and co-operative planning.

The existing associative mechanisms give people no encourage-ment at all to find points and fields of common interest. The dis-contented are isolated and distracted, and there is not sufficient in-ducement for them to meet and organize themselves into a unit.

8: The present administrators for the most part have more of a talent for intrigue and self-aggrandisement than any effective practical ability for promoting development.

9: The 'normal' practice of personal recommendations and the clientship system impedes the development of a state of law, it in-fects and corrupts an already inadequate social organization, and by stifling hopes it precludes new commitment. The young men of this area, for example, find that it is not possible to get a job through personal ability or by right. Often even the best men among the *carabinieri* and Police are humiliated by politicians more concerned about their own electoral fortunes than with the law or the common good.

This infection tends to spread, and it is sustained and as it were justified by the infection that flourishes elsewhere. Certain evils are not purely local—often they are just local variations of a situation common throughout Italy. And when even national scandals fail to find a just solution, the pus is bound to spread, and the citizens will be confirmed in their feeling that any healthy development that might be initiated is most unlikely to succeed.

10: Religious organizations here, apart from some rare exceptions, tend towards closedness and conservatism ('inculcating') rather than openness and innovation: in many cases mafiosi and politicians are regarded by 'men of religion' simply as open-minded crusaders effectively opposing change.

Scholastic and religious education tends to emphasize individual achievement rather than the need to develop and mature the personality through integration in a sound community life.

11: If even among peoples with advanced experience of group work and group life it is easy to succumb to the rapid ebb and flow of majorities and minorities, or to fail because of an inadequately prepared basis of unity (through a failure to understand how necessary it is that the individual should act as a conscientious objector within the group so that each group can count on the conviction of every single member), here, where there is scarcely any experience of the kind of group that realizes its members' potential to the full, a person of merit will very likely have little confidence (and to a great extent justifiably) in the kind of group where his position of conscience doesn't count.

12: Emigration abroad (which, besides destroying the family unit, undermines any pressure for change that might exist in the already scarcely connected urban groupings) can only give new understanding and experience of associative life to people who, having already attained a certain cultural minimum, are open to new experience: otherwise, it only makes a person even more closed.

13: Since those in authority at present use their power more as an instrument for domination than as the means for promoting action, spreading responsibility, and expanding the forces for progress, the weak remain systematically excluded from the possibility of comprehensive development, apart from the rare cases of exceptionally gifted individuals: one thing to notice particularly in this connection is the way women, especially in the country, are still almost untouched by social progress.

14: On the other hand, certain enterprises—whether among the peasants, or the urban working class, or in the intellectual or the cultural field—give the clearest proof that even here, amid so many and such serious difficulties, given commitment and enthusiasm, really impressive achievements are possible.

The rejection of the old barriers, of economic and social stratification, the rejection of structural and traditional impediments, the need for communication, for effective participation—one finds these in the people almost as a desperate need.

Among the young, among the most aware, there is increasingly urgent recognition of the need for groups that will accurately and boldly identify particular problems and set about finding the solutions, urgently and yet with patience; groups that will promote new enterprises and special courses for training new cadres in the techniques of active education, group work, and new socio-economic development, and in the techniques of the kind of planning that works methodically on various levels and increasingly involves every single person in the comprehensive solution of the problems.

15: It is obvious that in order to transform the present situation the people must become aware, as rapidly and as fully as possible, of their own need for association; but it's also more and more obvious that it is only through new work in which each individual can become involved with increasing responsibility that we can achieve a society different from that of today.

Present conditions being what they are, stratified over thousands of years, it is of course essential that the greatest possible encouragement should be given to the development of local forces: but at the same time this must also be accompanied by opportune and effective intervention by the national conscience—which means, in the first place, action by the State authorities. (. . .)

Meeting in Castellammare, 12 January 1966

The documentation on the relationship between the mafia and certain Government politicians increases in volume and in precision; the Parliamentary Antimafia Commission and local, national, and international public opinion become increasingly aware of the exact nature of this relationship: yet nothing happens.

Our Study Centre, after consultations with the more advanced section of the population, decides on a week of non-violent pressure based in Castellammare, from 10th to 16th January 1966: 'to help this movement for personal and collective liberation; to help to bring truth out into the open and let it flow freely through the houses, the streets, the squares; and to try and get the Government to make responsible choices, with the civil and moral sensibility that is required of them, since by continuing to support the mafia's politicians they can only create worse tangles of complicity in the eyes of Italy and the rest of the world.'

The leaflet announcing the pressure campaign also says, among other things: 'Government politicians—not all, of course, and certainly not the better ones—although quite aware of the situation, behave as if they were made of rubber, entrusting the responsibilities of Minister and Under-Secretary to men of the mafia, maintaining them in office even after the Antimafia Commission has initiated serious proceedings against them: the mafia flourishes—the time has come to state this quite plainly—not only in Parliament but actually in the Italian Government.

A new, democratic life cannot exist as long as so great a part of the life of the State is based on lies, on fear, on submission to the abuse of power: it was on foundations like this that, not so very long ago, Fascism was able to grow . . .'

The Police of Castellammare and Palermo then denounced us for 'public defamation of the constitutional institutions' . . . 'for damaging the prestige of the Government and of Parliament'. Bernardo Mattarella and Calogero Volpe also brought actions against us over the leaflet: these too were referred to Section IV of the Court of Rome.

Every day throughout the week two to three hundred people crowded into the meetings, which took place in a house in Petrolo, a quarter renowned for very important mafia meetings. Readings of documents alternated with discussions, the essential part of which (having first asked everyone's permission to make tape recordings) we reproduce here.

(. . .)

DANILO: One at a time—this gentleman first. Your name, please?

GENTLEMAN: I'm not giving my name.

DANILO: But at a meeting everybody introduces himself.

GENTLEMAN: I've no objection: Palazzolo, Salvatore. I would like to ask this: are these declarations yours, signed by you?

DANILO: No, they're not my declarations; I've collected them with the idea of trying to get people to undertake responsibility themselves.

PALAZZOLO: Then I would say that in collecting them you have shown a certain lack of responsibility, because you make accusations that are simply fantasies. Your political purpose is the lynching of one man—and you know very well who that man is—and that is your sole aim. Because you yourself were in the service of the DC until a few years ago and nevertheless got your corns trodden on at a certain historic point in your life, as a result you are now claiming that the DC is hand in glove with the supposed (I put what you say in inverted commas)—with supposed 'mafiosi', as you call them. I would like to point out that you are conducting a one-sided campaign in the exclusive services of a single party. May I say that this party, the Communist Party, has collaborated with all these men you are now defining as mafiosi: you can see the Civic List of '58 and '61, when all these men you now call 'mafiosi' came into the election campaign on the side of the Communist Party. I can tell you more: in '58 when I was Administrative Secretary of the DC, this Magaddino you name, in the presence of people to whom I can refer you as witnesses, brought me a bill of exchange bearing the signature of the Secretary of the Castellammare Communist Party, and asked me if I could pay it for him; at the time I did not have the financial means, for business reasons, and so Magaddino—or, in other words, the so-called 'mafiosi' you speak of—paid it himself. He paid this sum to the Communist Party. Whether it was through a bank or in cash I don't know: it's not my business to know the details of the transaction. But I can tell you that he brought me this bill in the presence of three people; I do not know how authentic the bill was— I don't know the signature of the then Secretary of the Communist Party—but what I do know is that in the name of the Communist Party he got Magaddino to pay him this 300,000 lire.[1] So this shows you that beyond a certain level the alleged support of these gentlemen for the DC is not unilateral, but that these gentlemen have collaborated at every period of time both with the DC—because you say so—and with the Communist Party, because we have evidence of this, both on the Council and in everyday life. The then secretary of the Communist Party was Deputy Mayor, if I am not mistaken, and Councillor in charge of Public Works, and he was hand in glove with the men you now describe as mafiosi. Tell me now: why have you not raised your voice to crucify the Communist Party as well at this period of time? I will tell you: unless you're not a Judas, instead of crucifying one Christ for thirty pieces of silver you crucify thirty Christs for one piece of silver. That is all I have to say.

DANILO: You say my aim has been the lynching of one man. I can assure you that the aim of the study which I began a year ago was just this: to understand exactly what the obstacles to associative life in Western Sicily are. And when I began this study, I knew that these obstacles aren't confined to Sicily but exist also throughout the whole of Italy, throughout the world, everywhere——

PALAZZOLO: There are depressed areas in the North too—why don't you go and do your fast there?

DANILO: Do you want me to answer you or not? At a democratic meeting people take it in turns to talk.

PALAZZOLO: It was just a remark.

DANILO: Difficulties aren't exclusive to here: there are countries with incredible difficulties—we have only to remember that Denmark and Sweden have the highest suicide rate in the world. Different countries have different problems: and every country needs to study its own.

[1] For the Secretary's explanation at the Trial, see p. 350. (Tr.)

PALAZZOLO: I thought it was the United States that had the highest suicide rate.

DANILO: I repeat: if you'd rather speak yourself, you may.

PALAZZOLO: No—it was just to get statistics right.

DANILO: When we've finished then we can check on statistics.

What I was saying was that if certain evils exist in particular countries, then their committed research workers, their universities, and their citizens, should not be ashamed to study those problems.

In the course of this study I mentioned, we came across an old Sicilian proverb: *'cu ioca sulu 'un perdi mai'*—'the man who plays alone never loses'. I and my colleagues at the Centre—very many of whom are Sicilians, and very many actually from this area—wondered: why 'the man who plays alone never loses'? Why, in the old city and in the country, do they say so often 'the man who plays alone never loses'?

In the course of this enquiry we also became aware of another interesting fact—namely, that the word 'association' often stands for 'criminal association'. This seemed to us important: the word 'association', we realized, is often used—particularly in the old city and among the peasants—in this negative sense. In other words, they don't recognize the positive value of association. And so we began to examine more closely and systematically just what was understood by 'association'; we wanted to find out, also because of certain serious negative experiences in the Partinico and Belice areas, just how this association came to be so strong. And that was how it came about—*not* from any personal knowledge of the man, or any personal rancour against him—that we decided to check and study the background of the foremost Western Sicilian politician elected to Government, of whom we so often heard it said that he had connections with the mafia. And this work of ours wasn't an academic affair, a matter of sitting at a desk, an enquiry *à la* Perry Mason: as I said, our aim was, and is, to do it in a way that will get everybody (including ourselves) as far as possible to act according to their consciences and to shoulder their responsibilities.

I must also correct you on your second point: I have never served in either the Communist Party or the DC. When I first came here I had Christian Democrat friends, and I still have. Indeed I can say—

and I would emphasize this—that there are many Christian Democrats in Italy, in Sicily, and in Castellammare itself, who have
nothing whatever to do with the mafia. That, to my mind, goes
without saying.

PALAZZOLO: You've put yourself in the position . . .

DANILO: To finish: it isn't a question of crucifying or not crucifying. And if you want to present the Antimafia Commission with any
documentation about mafiosi acting on behalf of any party whatsoever, that is excellent. I'm quite sure most of the people of Castellammare want the mafia eliminated——

PALAZZOLO: In Castellammare we're all respectable people.

DANILO: If you say there is unfavourable evidence relating to the
Communists, you will do very well to report it to the Antimafia
Commission, if your aim is the elimination of the mafia.

Now I believe another Christian Democrat gentleman would
like to speak.

MARIO BARBARA: I am very proud to be a Christian Democrat.

DANILO: I don't doubt that one can be.

BARBARA: I could perhaps appreciate what you are doing, if it was
what you call conscientious objection: but it is an ideological flaw,
and as I see it this flaw consists in the aim you have set yourself:
namely, to demolish Mattarella, and by so doing render a service to
the Communists—there's no other explanation for it. Because it's
well known that you're nothing but—if you'll pardon the expression—a foolish slave of the Communist Party.

I'm convinced that you are probably doing this just as a pose.
You don't know what the mafia is, because if you knew what the
mafia was you wouldn't behave like this—you wouldn't come here
to provoke fire, to mortify the self-respect of Sicilians; you wouldn't
come here to put forward arguments that merely turn the knife in
the wound. That's not the way to fight the mafia; you're going about
it the wrong way—perhaps on purpose, because you want to humi-
liate us, you want to provoke us and mortify us. You think the
Sicilians are an ignorant people—you don't know them, you'll never
know the Sicilian people because you aren't Sicilian. To know the
Sicilian people a man must be fruit of this earth: you won't know
them even if you stay twenty years in Sicily. We are the expression
of the children of toil, and we know the meaning of the Sicilian

people. And the wound of the mafia—we have lived it, my distinguished friend: but you can never understand it, because the mafia must be fought, yes, but it must be fought with understanding, with education: that's how the mafia must be fought. Above all, with education, penetrating into the conscience of the people, of men—not with provocation. With your provocations you will continue to hurt us, because ever since you came to Sicily you've done nothing but act like the man who goes up to the poor stinking beggar and tells him: 'You stink. That's what you do'.

PALAZZOLO: 'Speak of rope in the house of the hanged.'

BARBARA: You constantly—you must excuse me if some of my expressions perhaps offend you—you have the courage of the jackal, who comes down into the trenches after the fighting is over to pick up the dead, or else to get amusement from the misery of those who were in fact fighting in the trenches against the mafia. Why didn't you come and fight the mafia twenty years ago, in the days when a man could pay with his life for daring to speak up, or even just look up? It was then that you should have had the courage to come to our part of the world—not now after we have already conquered the mafia through action, example, and education of the young.

I have read the whole of your memorandum, and I can tell you that I am one of the instigators of a counter-memorandum presented to Senator Pafundi;[1] I am proud of this because if I knew, or had any suspicion, that any Christian Democrat politician had been in collusion with the mafia, I would be the first to cast a stone, I would be the first, because it is unjust that others should grow rich or speculate on our sacrifices.

Speaking of this counter-memorandum, I was saying that I am one of those best qualified: there were many inconsistencies in yours, many inaccuracies, and I shall be glad if I have the fortune to be heard, to be picked from among those who presented this memorial, to expound my views and my attitude before the competent authorities. I have served in the DC party since 1950, and have occupied positions of responsibility.

DANILO: Could you tell me what these inaccuracies are?

BARBARA: I just dropped in here casually, I'm not prepared—I

[1] Chairman of the Antimafia Commission. (Tr. note.)

was on my way to the Bank, and I'm taking at least three-quarters of an hour off work . . . There are a number of inaccuracies. As I was saying, I have been active in the DC party since 1950, and have really followed the course of the DC, at a local and also at a Provincial level.

VOICE: He used to be in the MSI.

BARBARA: In '46, the first national elections, we organized the DC's first battle, and that was the first time the DC stood alone in the electoral contest. On the opposing side was the Civic List, on which there were quite a number of those men you indicate as mafiosi.

Mafiosi—*I* don't know about that: there is a proper body for dealing with that sort of question, and if the Magistrature should say that about certain people—having proof—then they will be quite right to condemn them; and we too will say 'the Magistrature did well to condemn them', because it is right to eliminate this gangrenous sore that exists in our society.

Immediately after that there was the Constituent Assembly, and Mattarella was elected for the first time, after only a few months. I remember how even though the DC was beaten in that contest against the Civic List, we celebrated that defeat like a victory because we interpreted it as a victory for pure ideals; and we had a dinner—without mafiosi—in a restaurant run by Arcangelo Catalano, and perhaps he will be able to remember that I was present, and who else attended that dinner. I maintain that there cannot have been any collusion then, only a month after our fighting such a fierce battle against those groups of people—there couldn't have been any collusion with the mafia within a matter of months. That, in my view, is the first inaccuracy.

In 1950, Barone was a member of the DC and he came out first in the election, I remember it well: however, since we had never regarded him favourably, especially the younger ones among us—not because he was a mafioso (I don't know about that. If the Magistrature ascertains that Signor Barone is a mafioso, they will condemn him, but if the Magistrature does not have sufficient proof to point him out to society as a mafioso, then he is an honest man and will have all due respect from society)—but because he was a type whose sole concern was to get power; an ambitious little man who wanted to get somewhere. And so Barone was not elected Mayor.

If I am not mistaken, you refer to a certain meeting that took place at the Motel. Seeing I myself was also present at that meeting, I will tell you what happened. In the '58 general election, we had reached the highest peak of success. In fact, if I remember rightly, we got almost 6,600 votes, and Mattarella got about 5,200 preference votes. Within a matter of months, in November, the local government elections came round: the DC entered the lists alone, while Barone, the Communist Party, and many of those names you cite as mafiosi, formed a coalition and therefore got the absolute majority (at that time the majority system was still in force), and so took over the administration. We waited for the results at the Motel, it's true, but at the Motel there were no mafiosi with Mattarella.

VOICE: That time, perhaps.

BARBARA: It is true that on that occasion Mattarella was in, one might say, a bitter frame of mind; he did have something to say, but he did not say: 'You have betrayed me.' What he said was: 'After all I have done for my home town, I didn't deserve to be treated like this. After such ingratitude I ought to go round by the ring road.' Those were his very words. Because for us, for Castellammare, Mattarella did indeed represent something superior, because he was a product of our own soil, and we were as proud of him as a father who sees a new star rising in his offspring and watches it soaring to the heights.

VOICES: But the ring road didn't even exist then!

BARBARA: Obviously we have almost always looked to Mattarella not only as a great example, but as our master and teacher. That is why we have always regarded him with respect, why we have held him up as an example, and why we are proud to have been his pupils. And this is another of the inaccuracies with regard to the '58 elections and the meeting at the Motel. I took a few notes, let's see now —because in my emotion I might . . . '48, '50 . . . the last election in '60 . . .

However, I should like instead to add something about you, and so I return to my first theme. I don't understand you. Because I cannot find the explanation of how you manage to put on all these theatrical exhibitions. Who pays for your fasts? How do you keep going? I don't believe in your fast. Certain problems can be approached in different ways: through a study conference, perhaps or a public debate—those are better ways. But approaching the people in this way, trying to shock public opinion—I don't think this will achieve anything at all. However, if you weren't acting in bad faith, it's possible that something useful and in the common interest could come of it—but you must prove you're not in bad faith. Provided you weren't in bad faith, you might well succeed in approaching the new classes who are coming to the fore—but not by acts of provocation. That's all I have to say.

DANILO: Thank you. In your speech there were matters deserving attention, and I promise you I'll study what you said carefully. I will answer as briefly as possible so as to leave time for all the others who want to speak too.

I agree with your calling this an act of provocation: but it is non-violent. Things have reached such a point that I think there is a real need for a shock, as well as for reflection and for open and probing discussion. If you can prove any of this evidence false, and if you can make any corrections, I'll be pleased.

You say you don't understand me. Maybe not. I would be very happy if we could understand each other properly. But people who aren't criminals, such as Russell, Sartre, Huxley, Carlo Levi, Don Zeno, Aldo Capitini, are my friends, and so are hundreds and hundreds, in fact thousands, of peasants and fishermen and workers with whom I get on equally well. I'm sorry you and I are unable to see eye to eye at once, but I'm not surprised, because understanding one another isn't easy.

To return to the main point: do you positively deny that Mattarella made use of the mafia and the bandits in order to obtain votes?

BARBARA: I deny it.

VOICE: Barbara was only a young boy after the war.

VOICE: How did he get his job in the Bank?

DANILO: For instance, you absolutely deny that Mattarella used the Rimis to get votes in Alcamo?

BARBARA: I deny it.

DANILO: Thank you.

Someone else wanted to speak.

SAVERIO MAZZARA: Unfortunately I missed the earlier speeches. I have been told one thing, though, and that is that a representative of the Communist Party is alleged to have had a bill of exchange for three hundred thousand lire cashed for his party by a mafioso. I would like you to name the Communist who went and got the bill cashed.

PALAZZOLO: The bill was signed by you, personally—though whether in the name of the party or in your own name I don't know. You did say, though, that it would go towards the Communist Party's election campaign.

MAZZARA: It must still exist, whether it was on my own account or the Party's.

PALAZZOLO: It won't still exist, because no doubt you've . . .

MAZZARA: Prove to me that I ever once went to Magaddino, or you, or anyone else.

PALAZZOLO: Tell me about the contracts in '58 when you were Councillor in charge of Public Works.

MAZZARA: You should ask the Mayor that sort of question, not me . . .

PALAZZOLO: No, you were in charge of Public Works . . .

VOICES: But how can you talk like that . . .
  —Because with you it's impossible to have . . .
  —You're not capable of . . .
  —Quiet! . . .
  —I can't go on shouting, you can believe it or not . . .
  —How can you have the face . . .

DANILO: May I ask you to express yourselves one at a time? Democratic people speak one at a time, and know how to listen too; otherwise no one can understand anything. Please, take it in turns to speak.

MAZZARA: I'll go back now to one or two things Doctor Barbara said. Doctor Barbara was not yet a member of the DC, and therefore I don't believe he took part in the election campaign of '46, and considering the age he must have been then I don't think he would have been capable of understanding certain things.

I have also heard it said that we won certain battles because a section of the mafia (I call them by their name, others call them 'the persons you refer to') were on our list, or working for our list. I genuinely know nothing about that. What's certain is that even though from time to time we have made a common front with other parties and other individuals, on our own lists we have never had a single mafioso.

BARBARA: I would like to present documents to prove what I'm saying, because I don't think I'm a fool—on the contrary.

In '46 I was twelve years old, and I think a boy of twelve is just at the age when he has an outstanding imagination, and certain things can remain branded on his mind.

MAZZARA: It'll be easy to refute you, simply by publishing earlier electoral lists—which we will do at once.

A COUNCIL OFFICIAL: Over recent years there has been stupendous progress.

GASPARE CASSARÀ: I'm a farm labourer, and I went to school up till the great age of . . . eleven! After school, out in the fields: my father needed me to go and dig the land. This 'stupendous progress' —I've never seen any sign of it! I started to dig at the age of eleven; at 14 I got my unemployment card; and till I was twenty-one I went and got it stamped regularly at the Labour Exchange. If this is 'stupendous progress' . . . The Government never took the slightest interest in whether I was a cripple, or whether I was ill, or unemployed, or dying of hunger—never the slightest interest. Then who was it went and told the Government as soon as I was twenty-one so they called me up for a soldier? (*Loud laughter and clapping*)

As for poverty, *I* know more about that than the *Ragioniere* or Barbara. *I* was the one who had to go out digging—he just fell into a job: he's never known what it's like to be starving with hunger!

So I had my medical in Palermo. What were my legs like? Fine. What were my arms like? Magnificent! Any teeth missing? No. Could I chew all right? (*Laughter*) And so I went for a soldier.

When I got out of the army and came back here, what did I find? The old mattock for digging—farming still in the very same miserable state as before. Once upon a time, all mankind used to dig with the mattock, in every corner of the world they had the wooden plough. Since then, though, things have been changing, there's been progress all over the place, even in Italy—even in many parts of Sicily: but at Castellammare I've seen no sign of any progress.

When Avv. Barbara was a student at University, they rented a farm up in the Ginestra country, and he used to go there for holidays, and I used to go there to earn my daily bread. Well, he used to tell me all kinds of stories; he used to go on about development, progress, all sorts of industries; he used to tell me about reafforestation schemes . . .

Reafforestation schemes! If a lad who was harvesting was to break the handle of his bill-hook—if he was to go round all the re-afforestation schemes of Castellammare, he wouldn't find enough wood even to make himself a new handle! (*Laughter and clapping*)

New industries? Not a sign of them. Land reform and redistribution? Nothing. Water—there's none.

VOICE: When it rains!

CASSARÀ: It's perfectly possible to bring water to Castellammare, there's plenty of good water—all running out to sea. The place is dying of thirst while the water runs out to sea. So much for this 'stupendous progress'!

In the old days at least there were one or two mills—now there aren't even those.

VOICE: They were busy making the Molitoria![1]

CASSARÀ: Ah yes, they were busy making the Molitoria!

VOICE: Forty-two million lire gobbled up.

VOICES: They gobbled it all up . . . it all disappeared . . .

CASSARÀ: Then they were supposed to be going to build a factory. What became of that?

There's the 'Foreign Legion', the so-called *Sicilmarmi*: I've a brother who works for them and he gets . . . eight hundred lire a day! Isn't that true? Isn't that true? (*Applause*)

When I came out of the army, I went and put my name down at the Labour Exchange. Unemployed for ten years—and the Labour Exchange never once sent me to any reafforestation scheme: because I never went to ask old so-and-so to pull strings for me.

Then I went to the 'Foreign Legion', to *Sicilmarmi* (and by the way, I'd be curious to know who owned it). At the age of twenty-four, I got a hundred lire an hour there! And I didn't get that job through the Labour Exchange, either: a friend got me in, and there was an understanding that they'd give me a rise after three months.

[1] The 'co-operative' mill through which a small group of mafiosi and friends of friends got hold of a vast Government subsidy: see pages 314–315. (Tr. note.)

Well, at the end of three months I present myself to the Management and I say to the *Ingegnere*: 'When am I getting my rise?'

'What's your name?'

'So-and-so.'

'All right, I'll look into it and let you know.'

I kept seeing him go past while I was working—every time, he just went straight past me.

So in the end I go and see him again: '*Ingegnere*, how about that business?'

'What business?'

I reminded him, since apparently he'd forgotten.

'I told you I'd let you know later.'

'But it *is* later,' I said: 'does later go on for ever?'

How could I manage on a hundred lire an hour? So then I went up to Milan, because I'd heard there was an economic miracle there. The minute I got there, though, the economic miracle turned into an economic crisis! (*Laughter and applause*)

Redundancy everywhere. They all told me: 'You got here too late.'

And so I came back here—and now I'm back to digging the land again.

If I'm not mistaken, ERAS was supposed to have tractors in the country. I don't know if the ERAS in Castellammare is the same as the Palermo one—I don't know if it works the same in Palermo as it does here in Castellammare, where the officials are just there in order to draw their salaries. I've had people say to me: 'Even if the fellow is drawing his salary and not doing any good whatever to the whole of humanity—what harm does it do you?' 'It may not look as though he's doing me any harm,' I say, 'but in fact he's getting paid for acting against the interests of the working man—I wouldn't mind them getting paid if they'd just keep quiet and do nothing.'

DANILO: How many ERAS officials are there?

CASSARÀ: I don't know exactly, but I think there are two anyway. One of them's Mattarella, the Minister's brother.

The subsidies for agriculture have been swallowed up by all sorts of people who don't work on the land at all—and now this fellow comes and gives me 'stupendous progress'! *I* haven't seen any signs of this 'stupendous progress'. As for the Castellammare fisheries—

hundreds of young men have had to leave the place because they couldn't even earn a bite of bread.[1] Is this your 'stupendous progress'?

VOICE: A stupendous progress in emigration—in thousands . . .

CASSARÀ: Exactly. Sometimes I think: 'The poorest fellow in all Italy must be me'—but then I look around a bit and I see plenty who are worse off. And you should just see how many of our fellow townsmen there are in Milan, and the kind of conditions they live in! I know Castellammare blokes in Milan who can't even come home because they haven't got the money for the fare.

Over and over again, people have said to me: 'Better vote for our fellow townsman, he'll take care of his own town.' 'The devil he will!' I think to myself: 'If it hadn't been for him taking care of us, what sort of a state would we be in now!' (*Laughter*)

VOICE: There's no life in a town where there's no work.

VOICE: You can't do a thing in the trade union in Castellammare, because the minute you move they've got their spies on you and the bosses hear of it at once, and because they're all hand in glove you won't find another job. Say one of us complains that we're not getting our rightful pay—they'll sack him, and there'll be ten, fifteen other people who've been coming there every day saying: 'Please take me on' . . . 'I'm out of work' . . . 'I've got children' . . . 'I've got a family to support.'

VOICE: In Castellammare there's hunger—Mattarella's town is the town of hunger.

VOICE: Here in Castellammare some men do ten hours' work for seven hours' pay—but if anyone says anything they just get sacked.

VOICE: People are scared: because suppose I go against a mafioso —naturally next morning I won't wake up alive.

VOICES: It's the truth, it's the truth.

VOICE: As I said, people are scared, because when there are three or four mafiosi in a town and twenty thousand poor people under them, the poor people still can't say anything because they only get their cows stolen or their houses burnt or their vines cut, and so

[1] Thanks to powerful protectors, the mafia has been allowed to ruin the fishing grounds all round the coast of Western Sicily by illegal trawling, dynamiting and poisoning. See Dolci's WASTE, Part II, no. V. (Tr. note.)

they're even worse off than before. (*Confused shouting: 'He's right'*—
'He's right'—*'And no one puts them in prison because they've got
powerful friends!'*)

How many people have been murdered, and the murderers never
found!

VOICE: There was one man murdered by the Church steps, and
two more on that corner where the kiosk is now. Three young men
aged between eighteen and twenty were murdered in the winter of
'48, some time around January. They were just poor lads, some of
the ones who used to go out collecting sparta grass in the mountains,
and they worked as farm labourers too. They were felled by bullets.
One was called Carmelo, Barbara or Barbuto. It happened about
nine in the evening.

The day before that, someone had fired on Bernardo Stabile,
Gaspare Magaddino's brother-in-law, just near here, on the corner
of Via Francesco Crispi where it meets Via Roma, only a little way
from his own house. He fell down and shammed dead. He got away
with practically nothing—he was only slightly injured.

The murderer of those three lads was never found.

VOICE: Leonardo Antonino was a livestock dealer, a nephew of the
mafioso Ferro Mario. He was murdered in 1960, on the ring road
above Castellammare, in the Madonna di Fatima district. It was
about eleven o'clock at night. They went to fetch him from his
house in the Case Nuove quarter. There were two of them. His
wife, who's gone to America now, saw them—but she declared she
didn't know them. They killed him with *lupara* shot and pistols.
The murderers were never found.

Ferro Mario himself had been murdered about a year earlier, in
his home. About eight in the evening, in front of his wife and his little
girl. That was in the summer of '59. The murderers were never
found.

VOICE: A plain clothes policeman, a Neapolitan who had only
recently come to Castellammare, was murdered in about 1950, one
morning while he was on duty with a *carabiniere*. I don't remember
his name—the *carabiniere's* name I do remember, though: Asta.
He was told to go away. They shot the policeman in the mouth. He
was found on the Castellammare–Trapani road, in the Madonna
delle Scale district, near the Belvedere. A few days earlier—he was

a man who talked freely, aloud, without fear—he'd said in the Square that he'd come to Castellammare to exterminate the mafia.

VOICE: Murderers never found.

VOICE: Also in the vicinity of the Belvedere, inside a ruined cottage—the one this side of the iron cross—they found the bodies of two lads of about twenty. At least a week after their murder. People on their way out to the fields noticed the smell, and called the Law. This double murder about a year after the policeman was killed.

VOICE: Murderers never found.

VOICE: The *carabiniere* Lance-Corporal di Vita was murdered in Via Guglielmo Marconi on the corner by the Three Stars Hotel, in '51 or '52.

VOICE: Murderers never found.

VOICE: In the Fraginese district, they murdered a man who used to get called 'Napuliuni' as an insult. That was about 1960 or '61. I remember it was in August, on Trappeto's feast day. He was in the same group as Magaddino, Mario Ferro, Buccellato, Bernardo Stabile and the rest.

VOICE: Murderers never found.

VOICE: Vito Caiozzo was murdered on Easter Saturday, in about 1949. It was only about eight days since he'd come out of prison after doing twenty years for murder. They shot him in the head, in broad daylight, on the Corso Garibaldi.

VOICE: Murderers never found.

VOICE: I remember another, a fellow called Vincenzo Mistretta, who was murdered there near the Belvedere, almost under St Joseph's Cross, about 1951. The murderers were never found. Before that, in '46 or '47, in the Castellaccio district, the two Constantini brothers from Castellammare were killed by *lupara* shot as they rode by on horses. They were fired on from behind a low wall. The murderers were never found then, either. And also around that time, about '48, a group of young men—about six or seven of them—were murdered in the Fraginesi district. It was in summer. Some shepherds found them, and informed their families and the Law, and the bodies were taken to the cemetery on a farm cart.

VOICE: Murderers never found.

VOICE: 'Gnazio Foderà and a friend of his whose name I don't remember—a good chap, a young man everybody knew, who just happened to be with him at the time (I think that's why they killed him too, to get rid of a witness)—they were murdered in about 1958, at Firriato, by *lupara* shot. 'Gnazio was a type who used to speak up freely if he had something to say. He was against the mafia.

They never even found the murderers of Giovannino Russo. He was killed in '49 or '50, at dusk, near the main crossroads, right in the middle of Castellammare.

VOICE: And there have been plenty more besides. The Customs Officer killed at Scopello; and a young man, Milillo, murdered near the San Bartolomeo river. These are just the ones we happen to remember. And the men responsible for all these murders have never been discovered. I don't think a single murderer has been found out since the war. I may be wrong—I'm not sure: but I believe they've got away with it every single time.

Meeting in Castellammare, 13 January 1966

(. . .)

DANILO: Would anyone like to speak?

BARBARA: I shall just avail myself of three minutes, and then go.
I hear you have been feeling unwell, and I am sorry about that:
let's hope it isn't due to last night's indigestion!

Yesterday when I spoke here I called you a foolish slave of the
Communist Party, and I should be happy if you could give me the
lie. I offer you this opportunity to do so. You say that you are seeking
truth, that you wish the truth (to use the exact terms of your leaflet)
to come out of the houses and flow through the squares and through
the streets. If the Communist Party has not put a muzzle on you,
you must answer me: if you answer, you will see me again tomorrow, and the next day too, and I shall be happy to keep you
company every day of this fake fast of yours.

DANILO: Pleasant company!

BARBARA: You are going to prove whether you are muzzled or
whether you are free to talk. Obviously I am suspending my judgement on your activities.

My question is this. I have incontrovertible, irrefutable, and
unequivocal proof of collaboration by the Communist Party at a
local level with the persons you have named as mafiosi. If you wish,
I will bring it to you here in the presence of everybody.

SORESI: Forgive my interrupting. You said: 'The persons you
have named as mafiosi.' Does this mean you yourself don't consider
them mafiosi?

BARBARA: My dear sir, there is a specially constituted body to
deal with these questions.

SORESI: But look, I'm a Christian Democrat too . . .

BARBARA: I'm not interested in the political colour, I'm not
interested, I'm not interested.

DANILO: One moment, please—one at a time. Let Signor Barbara
speak.

BARBARA: Thank you. I'm not interested in the colour.

SORESI: I'm sorry.

BARBARA: Not at all, not at all. I am happy to answer you. I'm not interested in the political colour: all of us in here are free citizens who have come to express our . . . our . . .

DANILO: Ideas.

BARBARA: Our ideas. I shall continue to regard these gentlemen as men of honour until such moment as the Magistrature, in its sovereignty and in its autonomy, shall pass judgement.

To continue, then; I have incontrovertible proof that the Communist Party, headed by the political Secretary of the local branch, Signor Mazzara, collaborated with those people named in your memorandum as mafiosi. Therefore, since I have these proofs—which you cannot deny because they are public deeds, resolutions by the Municipal Council, lists presented, visible collaboration between these men—this is a syllogism: you must admit that there is in Castellammare collusion between the mafia and the Communist Party. And if there is this collusion between the mafia and the Communist Party, why don't you come here and fast to condemn and brand this action of the Communist Party? This demagogic action which reveals itself not only at a local level but which is the position of the whole Communist Party, especially here in our own Region, in Sicily.

I would like you, therefore—if you really wish to prove to me that you are a lover of the truth—you must answer, and give me your own, independent, opinion. That is my request.

DANILO: Thank you.

First of all, I would say that as you start off by calling me a jackal, as you did yesterday, and then ask whether I am muzzled or not (muzzles are put on animals), while in a leaflet you have also called me a pig—this rather indicates the level of your argument. At a democratic level people don't use this kind of language. I remain unmoved, these words don't upset me at all: but I would advise you, in discussions with other people, not to call them things like pig or jackal, if your opinions and your cultural and moral position are of a different level. That's my first point.

My second: if you study the matter carefully for a month or two, you can't fail to recognize that in the post-war years the mafia, the bandits, and certain government politicians, were very, very closely interconnected electoral instruments, especially at certain periods and in certain areas. This is a fact which by now it's not too difficult to confirm; and any man in Castellammare who is not already perfectly well aware of these things ought, I think, to find out about them.

Point three: a direct answer to your question as to whether or not I am a slave of the Communist Party. I certainly didn't begin this study by going round beforehand asking one Communist or another for permission to do it. I was working on a book for a publisher who from the cultural point of view is perhaps the foremost publisher in Italy, and for whom I had already done other books. As in another book, *Waste*, I had tried to encourage analysis and auto-analysis of the waste of resources in the area, above all considering the low technical and cultural level of a large part of the population, so during the past year I have tried to discover, with the people, in depth, what could be another fundamental impediment to development: the obstacles to associative life. This was my orientation, this was my aim in conducting this study: to understand what links there were and what links were lacking between people; and also to fulfil an official invitation addressed to me by the Parliamentary Antimafia Commission. And I tried to get the information from all kinds of different backgrounds.

Point four: if you will bring me the local documents, I shall be very interested indeed to examine them, to go into the matter thoroughly and to authenticate them: the more detailed they are, the truer they are, the more grateful I will be to you.

BARBARA: If up till yesterday I might still have had some doubts, I have now received my confirmation that you are in bad faith: thank you for giving me that confirmation.

VITO GIACALONE: I was passing through Castellammare on my way to Trapani, and came in here to express my solidarity with our friend Danilo Dolci who is fighting a battle which, to my mind, has no party colour: the battle of the honest Sicilians. I had no idea I would come in on such a . . . dispute. As regards our Christian Democrat friends, I would like to offer them—I won't say a challenge, but an invitation: let's take advantage of this civil demonstration that's taking place here in Castellammare by inviting our Christian Democrat friends to a public debate. This would

10

make an important contribution to the search for truth: it's not enough to hurl abuse—in my opinion just flinging insults won't do.

I do not believe that Signor Barbara doesn't at least know Munna, the Mayor of Castellammare.[1] And Munna's dealings with mafiosi now in banishment—Signor Barbara isn't going to come and tell me they don't exist. The Regional Government subsidies that Munna has managed to get hold of by singular means—these aren't mere insinuations by Danilo Dolci. The foremost local representative of the Castellammare DC, as it happens, has business dealings with mafiosi. In Marsala, curiously enough, the same thing occurs.

The Communist peasants have always been on the opposite side: so far from their having connections or being in collusion with the mafia, it is they who have always been at the receiving end of the *lupara*! With anybody who is not quite . . . unprepared, it is possible for us to create a common front of honest men of all parties, in the Province of Trapani and throughout Sicily, to rid ourselves of the dishonest men and the mafiosi.

SORESI: I repeat, I am a Christian Democrat, even though my position may not be quite that of the Honourable Mattarella. I would like to ask a particular question: is it true that the mafia, which has always backed the parties with power, at a certain moment here in Castellammare altered course towards the right, towards the Liberals?

DANILO: I think first of all that it would be profoundly dishonest of us to say that the mafia sides exclusively with the Christian Democrats.

SORESI: I agree.

DANILO: Analysing the situation of many towns in Palermo Province, and others outside the Province, we find that many Christian Democrats have no connection at all with the mafia. I have stressed this fact, and I think it's obvious. Some people get their votes through the mafia, some by direct political methods, some through religious organizations, some through friends, and some through clientship systems unconnected with the mafia. The phenomenon is complex, and needs to be analysed with great care.

[1] See p. 210, no. V. (Tr.)

Besides this, we have noted that the mafia has collaborated on occasions with other government parties, such as the Liberals: everybody knows this. As for the Castellammare situation, I don't know all the details, having only studied certain aspects. For this reason, because I am aware of my ignorance, I am very glad that this should be discussed, so that our enquiry may be all the more accurate and thorough.

It must be recognized that there has on occasion been infiltration by mafiosi or other dubious people—there has been, and I believe there still is, infiltration even into the parties of the left: but if we take a general view, if we look at the phenomenon as a whole, then it is plainly obvious that the mafia has always fired on the left, that the mafia and the left have always been enemies. It is also obvious that mafia and banditry have been exploited for election purposes by particular groups; and that still, more than twenty years after the war, certain people and certain groups continue to make use of the mafia in order to guarantee themselves electoral strength. Forgive me for spelling it out like this, but I didn't want there to be any suspicion of partisanship.

FRANCO: If I remember them rightly, here are a few dates to bear in mind in connection with the bandits. In December '45, the day after Christmas, Giuliano attacks the *carabinieri* barracks at Bello-lampo; a few days later, he makes another assault on the *carabinieri* barracks at Grisí; in early January of '46, there follow the attacks on the *carabinieri* barracks of Pioppo, Borgetto, Montelepre, and a bloody ambush on a *carabinieri* lorry in Montelepre itself. This series of attacks against the State, under the flag of Separatism, (Giuliano attempts a series of sensational coups, including trying to take over Palermo Radio station,) continues until the beginning of February, and concludes with the attack on two van-loads of *carabinieri* on the Montelepre–Palermo road.

Between then and June '46, there are a number of executions of 'traitors', and a number of kidnappings, the most notorious being that of Gino Agnello.

Up till June '46, it is clear for anyone with eyes to see that Giuliano's activities take a certain very definite direction.

But at this point, about half way through '46, something happens which makes Giuliano change his tack. I would like to draw your attention to the questions written up on these posters here: '*What happened in the cottage on the Baglio di Parrini?*'[1] What meetings took place there, and who was present? Who was it that began at that moment to exercise a real political influence over Giuliano, in a certain definite direction?

It was from that moment that the remarkable series of murders of trades unionists began, giving the impression that a real criminal plan of attack had been launched against peasant organization, using the mafia and the bandits, with the aim of terrorizing the peasants who at that period had engaged in their great struggle for the re-distribution of land.

I quote from memory: between June and November 1946, Nunzio Passafiume is killed in Trabia, Giuseppe Camilleri in Naro, Gaetano Guarino in Favara, Castiglione and Girolamo Scaccia in Alia, and Nino Raia in Casteldaccia; in '47, Accurso Miraglia is killed in Sciacca, Macchiarella in Ficarazzi, and Salvia in Partinico; on the first of May you all know what happened at Portella della Ginestra;[2] in June, on the 22nd, bombs are thrown at the Camera del Lavoro rooms in Partinico (two dead and three injured), and other offices of left-wing parties are burnt in other towns of the area (here it is Giuliano operating); in Marsala, in November, Vittorio Pipitone, another trade unionist, is murdered; and early in '48 Epifanio di Puma of Petralia Soprana is also killed.

Between the middle of '46 and the end of '47, thirty representatives of the peasant movement are murdered (out of 41 between '45 and '65).

What had happened? In whose interests was it to halt the peasant movement? What promises were made to Giuliano to induce him to play this part? How and why, and under whose protection, was the mafia unleashed?

And remember: *not a single one of the murderers of these trades unionists has ever been discovered.* So much for the democratic State! So much for the protection of democracy!

SORESI: Undoubtedly, the mafioso is against the trade unionist: we've seen this in so many crimes.

Let me just add this: may democracy triumph, may truth triumph

---

[1] See S. Capria's statement, p. 339; also pp. 353–355, 1st, 3rd and 4th witnesses. (Tr.)   [2] See page 223. (Tr.)

in this Sicily of ours which needs the union of all parties, whatever their political commitment may be. (*Applause*)

VINCENZO LIGOTTI: These men who are cited as mafiosi in the texts of your Press conference in Rome, as reported by the Press— are you only calling them mafiosi, or has it been proved that they really are mafiosi?

DANILO: Ah, now that seems to me an intelligent question.

I propose that, taking Vincenzo's question as a starting point, we discuss whether we ought to wait till a man is defined as a mafioso by the Magistrature and the Police before we consider him such—or whether we ought to begin to consider him a mafioso when he behaves as a mafioso, when he talks and acts like a mafioso, when he lives as a mafioso.

LIGOTTI: These men referred to as mafiosi—isn't it possible that they're not? I'm too young to know, and maybe there are others who don't know. Are these men just called mafiosi by one particular group? Unless there's proof . . .

VOICE: We only have to open our eyes to see . . . the people around us, don't we?

VOICE: You can't just wait on the Magistrature before forming your judgement, if you see certain groups acting as mafiosi.

It's we ourselves who've got to make the first move, according to our own conscience: if the Police and Magistrature then come out in support of our conscience, so much the better.

VOICE: It could happen that one group defines as mafioso a person whom I don't consider mafioso. What guarantee is there in this case?

ROCCO GALATIOTO: Waiting on the verdict of the magistrature means virtually just marking time, and meanwhile allowing this sore to spread.

LIGOTTI: But what is our criterion for saying: this man is a mafioso?

GALATIOTO: It's something inside ourselves that makes us point to a man and say: he's a mafioso.

VOICE: They're considered mafiosi by public opinion.

VOICE: In my view the true mafiosi, the ones who really deserve the name, are people who by their presence compel you and me to do whatever suits them; men who take advantage of other people.

VOICE: With some, there's no doubt about whether they're mafiosi or not: they're recognized by everybody as capimafia or as mafiosi—and sometimes even they themselves like to be recognized as such.

VOICE: It can happen with some young men that while they're still young you can't be sure whether they are mafiosi; but then from their crimes, and from the kind of friends they have, you can soon tell.

If you go to Alcamo, though, and ask: 'After the war, who were the capimafia?' people know—and not just Communists and Socialists, either. They can point them out to you clearly.

VOICE: But we know what a state Italy was in after the war. Nobody goes around with 'I am a mafioso' written on his forehead.

DANILO: I think this is something we should consider really seriously. In '46, how was anyone to tell whether a person was a mafioso or not? How was Mattarella to know whether certain people were mafiosi or not?

VOICE: I can state that in Castellammare I don't know any mafiosi at all. Either we're all mafiosi, or there aren't any.

VOICE (*ironical*): How can you, of all people, say that in Castellammare either there aren't any mafiosi, or we're all mafiosi? (*Laughter and applause*) You of all people, knowing what you know, in public, for all these people to hear—*you* come here and say that in Castellammare either we're all scoundrels or else there aren't any scoundrels! And when they shot at you that time, what were they? Honest men? (*Confusion, shouting*)

VOICE: You ask, how was one to distinguish a mafioso after the war? Often a man is a mafioso by origin: his father was one, and his grandfather before that—so you could tell these ones were mafiosi from the very beginning.

CASSARÀ: I'd like to answer that other gentleman there.

I think I must be about the same age as that gentleman, perhaps a couple of years older—to be exact, I'm twenty-eight: and *I* can talk about the mafia! That gentleman said: 'How can someone tell if a man's a mafioso—does he have it written on his forehead?' Well, I'd like to ask him: 'I am a peasant: have I got it written on my forehead, that everyone can tell I'm a peasant? Wherever I go?' (*Prolonged and thunderous applause*)

If you're a peasant, people can see it, because you work on the land. And the mafioso—I can tell him, too, because he behaves as a mafioso: and I think mafia, in all its forms, means taking advantage of other people and using them for your own ends.

VOICE: But who do mafioso ever tell anything to? Who sees what they do, and where they meet?

CASSARÀ: I'll have to start again. I asked that gentleman whether I'm a peasant or not, whether I've got it written on my forehead. But anyone can *see* I'm a peasant! And in the same way anyone can see in Castellammare—it's elementary, even babies at nursery school can see—that the mafia exists. And it's also elementary knowledge in Castellammare who this same mafia is protected by. I've been digging the earth all my life—up till this very day I've always worked on the land, digging the earth, and everybody in Castellammare knows me. I've never studied, but I know from my own experience that, for instance, there's a difference between crime and mafia: crime means the ordinary type of thief—and may I say that crime is a lot less evil than the mafia, and the mafia as it exists in Castellammare is much more serious than ordinary crime. The ordinary criminal goes and steals one man's cow, and harms only one person: but the mafia harms everybody in Castellammare, and the whole area, as things stand at the moment—and so far there's been no serious effort anywhere to get rid of it.

Yesterday I was starting to say something about how they go to work on this reafforestation scheme. I'm not very good at expressing myself, so I'd like to make a comparison with a hen and its chickens: the capomafia being the hen, and the chickens being the children of the hen. (*Laughter*) Now these chickens (no, it's no laughing matter, I'm talking about things that really happen in Castellammare, serious things)—compared with the hen, these chickens feel very small; but compared with anyone not in this organization they feel very big. And the power is in the hands of these mafia gangs in the reafforestation schemes of Castellammare, like it is everywhere else —these are things that can't be hidden. I have clear proof: from the age of fourteen to the age of twenty-one, unemployed at the Labour Exchange, they never once gave me a job—because I'd never been to a mafioso to beg for work. Because that's what you have to do in Castellammare if you want a job. This isn't democracy!

A farm labourer, for instance, would go and have a word with one of the 'chickens', and the 'chicken' would go and have a word with the 'hen' (*laughter*): if the hen said Yes, then the fellow would be taken on and get a job digging. The 'chicken' was in charge, even though he was totally unqualified to be in charge of a reafforestation scheme—they're people who've never worked, who've never grown plants. It's tyranny—that's what I call mafia. And I haven't seen that written on anybody's forehead: I've found it written in my own conscience, my own experience—what little experience I've had, being a young man. They know nothing at all about plants, and that's a fact: shepherds, and people who've never even been into the country, not even for holidays! Even the people in charge. And there's proof of that, too: since the first trees were planted, how have they grown, these trees? All that money thrown away, and us Castellammare folk can't see that the slightest bit of good has come of all these schemes—because they weren't done properly.

They had to have a man to bring up the drinking water—he used to bring it up into the mountains on a mule (this was one of the 'chickens' too, the water-carrier); and while the 'hen' sat there in the cool, if the labourer who wasn't a hen nor a chicken was digging away and got thirsty and needed a drink, he'd go and ask the 'chicken', the foreman, and he'd answer (if you'll excuse the language) '*Porca la maiorca!* These damned workers, they're always thirsty—anyone would think they're crows the way they never stop drinking!' (*Laughter*)

Voice: It's fear that makes us hold back. We're afraid of the harm they could do to us and our families.

Meeting in Castellammare, 14 January 1966

DANILO: What we propose for today is this: Franco will draw a line down the middle of those big sheets of paper on the wall there, and then I'll begin by suggesting some of the characteristics of the old politician for him to write down in one column, and in the other column he'll write down the corresponding characteristics of the new politician—taking the word 'old' not, of course, in a historical sense but in the sense of 'outmoded': because obviously there existed centuries ago politicians far 'newer' than so many politicians today. If some of the comparisons seem somewhat obvious and repetitive, this is because our aim is to make things as clear as possible by looking at them from different angles.

Afterwards, we'll have a discussion to see whether everyone agrees with our list of characteristics, or not.

Do you think this is a good idea? Let's try, then.

THE 'OLD' POLITICIAN	THE 'NEW' POLITICIAN
commands by imposing	directs by identifying himself and developing with the group
centralizes power	stimulates and co-ordinates a variety of groups and personalities
secretive, lover of darkness	communicative, lover of light
rhetorical	simple and to the point
corrupter	educator
violent	non-violent
vindictive	generous, considers people's future
tends to join the side most likely to win	tends to take the side of the weak and oppressed

opportunist: changes tack according to more or less immediate advantage	sets his course according to his conscience—though continuing, with his own and other groups, to test the validity of his attitudes
intervenes with negative sanctions to block progress	joins in to try to encourage new research
uses intelligence, knowledge, and technical skills to impose himself on others	uses intelligence, knowledge, and technical skills to try and get the best out of himself and others
expert in double-dealing and intrigue; if loyal to anyone, only to his own closed group	direct, sincere, and open with everybody
has the qualities (adapted and refined to suit the time and place) of the man of war	above all constructive
enjoys and exploits his power, essentially an exploiter	works responsibly for others, essentially an improver
cultivates his own clientèle	stimulates and co-ordinates democratic groups
tries always to keep afloat, clings to power	tries to be humble enough to express the best in everybody
upholds and defends old structures	creates new structures
delegates power according to personal relationships	delegates power to whoever is most capable
his public actions and his work are aimed at reinforcing his own power	stimulates plans for development with the greatest possible participation by everybody

Now, shall we make comments and discuss these characteristics?—bearing in mind that today men cannot afford not to be 'political' men.

VOICE: The old politicians were concerned mainly with getting people gun licences, and seeing that contracts went to their friends, and favouring their own caucus, their clientèle.

VOICE: The old politician makes everything revolve round himself . . .

VOICE: . . . so much so that he used to be considered God.

VOICE: Things that everybody ought to know should be revealed to public opinion. If there isn't light in public words and deeds, then we're all in the dark.

VOICE: Each one of us ought to be allowed to know what's going on, and to be able to judge what's good and what's bad.

VOICE: The politician of the old mould corrupts people in order to get on. Like when we've seen *pasta* handed out in election campaigns, and flour, and five thousand lire notes to buy votes. That's what corruption means.

VOICE: The modern politician is an educator in that his job is to educate people's consciences, to give them a civic conscience; to broaden people's outlook.

VOICE: 'Violent' and 'vindictive' I would say mean much the same thing. For instance, if a man didn't give his vote to the old politician, if he disagreed with him, then the politician would probably take his revenge.

VOICE: I wouldn't call a man who goes in for that sort of thing a politician at all—what he is is an intriguer: he plays along with the various political currents, and as soon as he sees who's most likely to win—say it's Moro's party, for instance, then he'll start making eyes at Moro: if it's Fanfani, he'll try and play along with Fanfani in order to keep his seat, to keep the power in his own hands.

VOICE: For proof of this you only have to see how over the last twenty years certain Ministers have remained Ministers even though the Government itself has kept changing—often in Governments directly opposed to one another.

VOICE: The sort who wait to see which way the scales are going to tip and are ready to jump on the winning side at once.

VOICE: I think the aim of the old politician is to destroy other people's things in order to build up his own and his friends'. The new politician tries to co-operate with other people in building things for the good of everybody, in the light of the sun. For everybody, and making proper use of everybody.

VOICE: 'Double-dealing' means this sort of thing: when there was the referendum for Monarchy or Republic, there were some politicians who wouldn't commit themselves one way or the other till the last minute, till the very last speech of the campaign. In other words, if it's to be a Republic, I'm a Republican—but if the Monarchy wins, then I'm a Monarchist. Or another example: since a large part of present-day political life is characterized by the interplay of the various currents, the double-dealer speaks in half words—half a word to one current, another half to the other—so that he's always sure to be in with whichever side wins in the end.

VOICE: The old politician is constantly trying to keep afloat, like cork: in Sicilian we say '*si appatedda*'—he clings to power like a limpet clings to the rock.

VOICE: Kings used to hand on their kingdoms to their sons even if they were idiots.

VOICE: We all agree about what the new political man *ought* to be, and we agree we can't accept the old politician. But the problem is to see how to change from the old system to the new, how to put the new sort of politics into practice. I mean, I think this discussion needs to be wider.

VOICE: That's true, he's right.

DANILO: Our friend says: we all agree about the qualities of the new man, but the new man and his politics aren't yet to be found everywhere. The problem is, he says, to see how we can achieve this: we need to take a wider view of the problem. What would you say?

VOICE: I'll tell you the sort of thing I think is necessary in order to achieve the new sort of politics: I find myself, for example, in a certain situation. Well, I need to read about it in order to get a clear idea of what this situation really is; I need to get organized democratically in a party that's capable of appreciating the needs of the worker—but at the same time I mustn't trust blindly in any politician, even a left-wing one: you must follow what he does and check in case he makes mistakes, and correct him, and if necessary replace him.

We agree about the new sort of politics, but there's still ignorance, and there's still . . .

VOICE: . . . fear, too.

VOICE: Being a slave is worse than getting beaten . . .

(*A lot of people talk at the same time*)

DANILO: Let's hear what *he* has to say.

AN OLD MAN: Me—I'm not up to understanding this sort of thing.

DANILO: You've had experience . . .

OLD MAN: Yes, I've had experience, but not experience of political things. Each of us makes his own comments in his own mind.

DANILO: And what are your comments?

OLD MAN: I've plenty, but though I've got plenty there's not one I can say aloud.

DANILO: And what about you—you've got a white hair or two?

OLD MAN: What d'you expect *me* to say? I'm illiterate . . .

VOICE: For my part, I think anyone who hasn't got money is frightened.

VOICE: I'd like to say something about this fear. This so-called democracy we're supposed to have achieved—it's only a formal democracy, there's no real liberty.

VOICE: Because there's always the needy family, and at election time old so-and-so comes along to the house and offers them food or money, and so they vote for someone they really shouldn't vote for.

VOICE: We're all agreed on what this new politician ought to be, but how are we to get the new men, the new politics? In the first place, by being brave. The fear is real—the fear is real, and we've all known it to some extent. Unless a man is free from want, he won't be able even to express an idea. It is partly ignorance—but there are plenty of people who do have ideas but won't say anything because they're afraid—and the reason they're afraid is because they need work. The new structures don't exist yet, and the minute anyone rebels they start threatening him: 'We'll transfer you, we'll send you away, we'll chuck you out on to the street, into the gutter; we'll deport you.'

We've all been frightened, because we're poor. They still blackmail us by threats. It's written in the Italian Constitution that work is the right of everyone—not that we must go and beg a job off Minister So-and-So or Deputy Such-and-Such. Work is a sacred right: we shouldn't allow ourselves to become anybody's slaves—we should break with these mafia gangs. We've had enough of them. We've all been frightened, and I think in your consciences you'll all agree with me.

(*Cries of 'fear', 'subjection'*)

VOICE: Each of us depends on other people, and if a man talks in here, they'll hear of it outside.

DANILO: What do *you* say about fear?

VOICE: It's partly been conquered, but partly it still needs to be conquered.

VOICE: I agree there is fear—in fact a great deal of fear, among the poor of Sicily. A father of four or five children who has a job is frightened of getting the sack one day and so his children will be deprived of their daily bread: it's fear for the children, fear of not being able to feed them.

VOICE: I've got a family, and I'm afraid of getting the sack—and so I submit. It's a collective fear.

VOICE: To think of someone getting into power by using the mafia—it makes you sick . . .

VOICE: The corruption is real: in Castellammare at election time they've given away lorry-loads of *pasta*, medicines, second-hand clothes . . .

VOICE: It's not true!

DANILO: Let's hear what this gentleman has to say . . . what's your name?

VOICE: I don't know.

VOICE: Not only does he not know what his own name is—he doesn't know what he's saying.

DANILO: Please, we must keep the conversation respectful. Just a moment, one at a time. Let's hear the gentleman, let's hear what he has to say.

VOICE: All I have to say is that the sight of you makes me laugh.

DANILO: Laugh away, then, and tell us.

VOICE: No, that's all—I've nothing else to tell you.

VOICE: I state plainly that in Castellammare at election time they have distributed *pasta*. And heaps of money has been sent to Castellammare, but not a bit of it has been put to any proper use. These are things it's impossible to hide—who knows where a lot of that money ended up! And *pasta was* handed out for the elections.

If anyone says that's not true, let him put up his hand.

(*Nobody puts up a hand*)

DANILO: Well, then, I think he must be right.

VOICE: And I say there is no fear.

DANILO: In that case, how is it possible for things that have happened in front of thousands of people to be still kept dark?

A thing that's been going on in your own town for weeks, months, even years: a thing that everyone knows and everyone's seen—why won't people talk about it? What would *you* call their reason for not talking?

If something that's common knowledge can be admitted among two or three people, then why can't a thousand people admit it, or ten thousand—why doesn't everyone admit it?

Men are made for truth, and to deny the truth is to mutilate ourselves: telling lies makes us twisted—it's as if it twisted our ears, twisted our noses, and worse.

VOICE: I have the impression that we're disorientated. People have always voted according to a system of clientship, and practically never according to political conscience: that's always been my impression.

VOICE: With regard to what has already been said: people of my age, especially, who've seen so many election campaigns—we know they go round getting these votes with packets of *pasta*, and thousand lire notes, and suggestions, and all the other sorts of persuasion.

DANILO: But do they all do this?

VOICE: People still hesitate to speak because no one has yet succeeded in breaking the circle . . . what I'd call the circle of *omertà*, of fear: because when we go out of this place, outside they'll look askance at us, and there may well be reprisals.

Fear is still very strong, and some people's ideas are still very confused. If the truth is to come to the surface, in all honesty, loyal as I am to Castellammare, I have to admit that corruption has really been effectively used here, that votes have been got by dishonest tricks, either by exploiting people's ignorance, or with bribes of *pasta* or flour, or by intimidation, or by threats of sacking: this has happened among workers in town and country alike. And the parties that operated this corruption cannot, logically, be the parties of the left, because they are poor parties—everybody knows this. Neither the Socialists nor the Communists have used these methods. The Liberals and the Monarchists have to a certain extent: but the past master at it has been the DC.

And the mafia got going too—and how!

VOICE: To tell the truth, I don't know any mafiosi in Castellammare . . . personally.

VOICE: The gentleman there said that the Communist Party has never done electioneering with *pasta* and money etcetera, because it wasn't able to—but suppose it had been able to, would it have gone in for electioneering with *pasta*?

VOICE: Who knows if it mightn't . . .

VOICE: Many years ago even the Christian Democrats may have thought they wouldn't do it on principle, but then when the opportunity came along they did it.

VOICE: I wanted to answer what he said just now. Naturally the parties aren't abstractions—they're made up of men, and men are what they are, that's only natural; and so it's possible to find crooked people in all parties. I'm not a Communist myself, but I must point out something that's certainly true for this area at least: the sort of people who corrupt democratic life, who corrupt the civic life of a party, the sort who only go into it for what they can get out of it for themselves—those sort of people are very unlikely to go into the left-wing parties, because that's not where the prizes are to be had.

VOICE: Justice isn't a thing you have to go and look for somewhere else: justice begins on your own doorstep; we have to start by being honest ourselves, each one of us.

VOICE: The truth is that everyone's afraid, because maybe we haven't understood that democracy means government by the people—we haven't yet understood this clearly. People are still afraid of blackmail, of intimidation, afraid of losing a job, afraid of being transferred: this is the fact of the matter. The mafia exists, we all know that; and in this area it's in collusion with certain politicians—we all know that, and that's the truth . . .

VOICE: We must wait and see what the Magistrature says.

VOICE: I can see it's dark outside, I don't think there's any need for the Magistrature to tell me it's dark outside—I can see it's dark with my own eyes. I can see this smoke rising, I can see all these people in here having a civilized discussion—and so I say to myself: 'Here's smoke, and here's all these people having a civilized discussion'.—I don't need to wait for the Magistrature to point this out!

Christopher Columbus didn't wait for the Magistrature before he discovered America—he went ahead and discovered America, and the Magistrature heard about it afterwards.

VOICE: Nobody brought a lawsuit against Columbus for discovering America, though, whereas someone who's got twelve lawsuits against him is almost certain to be convicted. It's the Magistrature that decides everything.

LORENZO BARBERA[1]: We've got the Commune, the Municipal Council, the Local Administration: are we supposed to say, then, that since these bodies exist the citizens of Castellammare have absolutely no need to bother themselves about local problems? What business has the man in the street to wonder whether things are being done well or not? It's up to the Administration to take care of that! But d'you call that democratic?

Democratic institutions do gradually improve . . . take the Regional Government, for instance—they have responsibility for a large number of things: but if the Regional Government isn't doing its job properly, what do we say then? That it doesn't work, so it must be abolished? Not so fast—let's wait and see if we can't make it work, change it; let's first analyse why it's not working: let's try and give a hand ourselves, like responsible citizens, let's

---

[1] N.B.: Barbera, one of Dolci's colleagues from the Study Centre in Partanna: not to be confused with the Avv. M. Barbara who spoke at the earlier meetings. (Tr. note.)

see if we can't help it work better. Wouldn't you agree with this?

Each of us should responsibly make our own contribution, each have our say, and discuss things; and the results of our discussion will then be collected, and eventually it'll reach Rome. In Rome there's the Antimafia Commission, then there's a gap of a thousand kilometres or more, and here there's us—and the mafia. Well then? Isn't it our business to create a link across those thousand kilometres? Doesn't the question of the mafia concern us? And the collusion between mafia and politics? Isn't it up to us to ask first whether such and such a fact is true or not? Isn't it our business first to test the truth, to discuss the matter together, because it concerns *us* first and foremost? We can't just say: 'Now there's a Commission, an excellent Commission, with serious people, so we can all go to bed and leave it to them—we've no need to discuss it any more, we can forget it.' What can the Parliamentary Antimafia Commission do on its own? It is our duty to begin to shoulder responsibility ourselves. So many people have got themselves killed by trying to face up to these problems—trades unionists who've got themselves killed, simple folk and political men who've sacrificed their lives trying to see that right was done. And plenty of people living today have been, and are being, brave enough to stand up against evil—and yet we Sicilians still haven't managed to get together to discuss our problems and try and get to the bottom of them. But this attitude of 'keep your mouth shut' and 'mind your own business and I'll mind mine' won't get us anywhere—it's not in anyone's interests. If I've kept my mouth shut, if they bump me off no one'll know anything about it. But if we discuss everything of importance that happens to us, if we bring it into the open, out into the squares and on to the streets, then the situation will be different. We Sicilians have this responsibility—it's up to us to try and cut out everything that's rotten in our towns and in our country, to bring ourselves up to the level of civilization of other societies—or even higher; we must have the courage to rid ourselves of everything that is rotten and corrupt.

Voice: I think that things which concern the Magistrature and the Police and highly qualified bodies such as the Parliamentary

Commission of Enquiry into the Mafia should be left to *them* to judge. They are not within the scope of ordinary citizens: they are for more important bodies, more authoritative and better qualified bodies, to deal with. Therefore it is absurd for us citizens to meddle in these matters: let us leave judgement to them, let us await with Christian meekness the eventual verdict of the Magistrature and the Commission of Enquiry. As a citizen, I do not consider myself qualified to speak to the Antimafia Commission or to anyone else about problems which do not concern me. Therefore in my opinion it is useless to create this 'bridge', and I believe others will agree with me.

FRANCO: What you have just very clearly stated is important and also very dangerous: because in a sense what you are saying is that the Antimafia Commission and these bodies ought to be isolated. You say: 'These things aren't my business, they're not problems that concern me'—but what I'd say is this: if I go into the street and see a man beating up a little girl, thrashing her till she bleeds —am I supposed to think it's nothing to do with me because crimes like that are the business of the Magistrature? (*Thunderous applause*)

VOICE: In other words, that's an accusation: you want to accuse the Antimafia Commission of standing by and doing nothing—is that what you're saying?

FRANCO: Let me try and put it another way.

Look at this poster: *What democratic development plan have the government representatives of this area helped to initiate over the last twenty years?* Do you understand what this means?

VOICE: What's a development plan got to do with the Antimafia Commission?

CASSARÀ: I find myself here at this meeting in the company of some people of my own level of education, and others whose shoes I'm not even fit to polish—so I hope you'll excuse me speaking like this. Once upon a time I was in danger of my life (I want to tell you this story of mine as an example, because I think the comparison will mean something)—well, I was all on my own in North Italy, in a little shack, really miserable, and at the end of a week's work I didn't know what to do with myself to while away the time. Then along came two types I knew who I was always trying to shake off, but it didn't seem right to refuse them, and in any case I needed a bit of distraction. So they took me along to a Bar for a drink: really strong stuff like cognac; and I got in such a drunken state that if they hadn't got the doctor to me I wouldn't just have never got sober again—I'd have died of drink. (*Laughter*)

VOICE: What does this parable mean?

CASSARÀ: It means that certain young men who need jobs, and who in order to get those jobs had to have the help of the mafia and of certain people who've supported the mafia in order to get votes— these young men have come here now to speak against the meeting because they're still drunk. (*Applause*)

No, I haven't finished yet, and I don't want any clapping either: I say that to get them sober before they become alcoholics or die of drink, they need the doctor. (*Applause*)

He keeps talking about the independence of the Magistrature— how on earth does he explain the fact that from 1948 till now so many trials have been abandoned because of 'insufficient evidence'— over and over again—and, curiously enough, these are nearly always the trials that concern mafia elements?

VOICE: The only ones who never know anything are the so-called men with guts, the men of *omertà*[1]—in other words, the mafia or people in the power of the mafia; they're the ones who ought to speak up in public and don't.

VOICE: I don't even know what *omertà* means.

VOICE: In my opinion it means we've kept mum for centuries and centuries, and we still go on keeping mum, no matter what we've seen. As for you saying: I'm not qualified to play any part myself— it seems to me we're *all* qualified, even the humblest of us, the ones who've never had any schooling as well as the educated ones: we're all qualified to denounce these things when we're aware of them.

VOICE: New action by brave men can hasten on the time for a new kind of politics, a new life. Sooner or later, the mafia will disappear: times are changing and it's bound to go, and men will inevitably live in a more democratic world. But if we are intelligent and able, we can shorten the time this will take by fifteen or twenty

[1] See note p. 224. (Tr.)

years. If we have the intelligence and the seriousness to cut certain unhealthy ties and create new, healthy ones, then we can give a push which will hasten on by twenty years this too slow progress towards democratic life.

Meeting in Castellammare, 16 January 1966

(. . .)

LORENZO BARBERA: And now, let's discuss a point which seems particularly important to us. The Sicilian proverb says: '*Cu ioca sulu 'un perdi mai*'—'The man who plays alone never loses': let's have the opinion of each person, and see whether we agree with this proverb, and why, or whether we are against it, and why.

CASSARÀ: I disagree with the proverb.

BARBERA: Up till now people have generally thought it true.

CASSARÀ: If I really gave everything I could, if I did everything I'm capable of—little as it is—and if everyone else did the same, and we acted together, then I certainly wouldn't lose, and the others wouldn't lose either, and we'd reach the thing we're aiming at: real democracy.

VOICE: If I'm playing cards on my own, I'll always win; but if I find someone to play against, then it's only logical that I can lose too.

VOICE: I think this proverb was born from ignorance, and with the kind of life we live today we can't go on putting our faith in this proverb. I think it's madness to play on our own, because each of us needs to live with other people. It's absolutely untrue that if you play alone you always win. Men must co-operate.

VOICE: The question is this: us poor folk are slaves all over Sicily —we're asses, because we don't speak up. And since no one else speaks up, the mafioso is cock of the whole dunghill.

VOICE: How are the poor folk to live, though? It's only the office workers that get the pay-packet.

FRANCO: But to change this situation, is it better to act according to the old proverb 'The man who plays alone never loses'—or in some other way? I mean, isn't it possible that this situation was in fact created just *because* one man was playing alone here, and another alone there, and another on his own somewhere else?

VOICE: The government money has just been chucked away, thrown to the winds, thrown in the fire, instead of them using it to build factories.

VOICE: What's the point of one man playing cards on his own? That doesn't get anything done. And this gentleman wants factories: but how does he expect to get them? If everybody goes off on their own—one man to Italy, another abroad, another to dig the land, another into building, always on their own . . .

We're just not organized. I've come here every evening, seven days, and I haven't once heard anyone say that we should unite instead of going on we are like a flock of lost sheep wandering this way and that. And now this gentleman starts talking about factories—I don't think we'll ever get factories this way: this way we'll only go on having the mafia round our necks. (*Applause*)

DANILO: Is there anyone who does believe in the proverb? Is it possible—out of two or three hundred people crammed in here, only a handful believe in it?

VOICE: It's a dead proverb, it's had its day.

VOICE: The other day I saw a poster saying: 'The workers of the Tarantola firm are striking because two workers who joined a union to claim their rights have been sacked.' At the end, it called on the citizens of Castellammare to help these two unfortunates who'd lost their jobs (in fact they still haven't got them back). Yet not a single person, out of all of us packed in here, made a move to help them—not one. If we'd done this, we'd have lost a day's work maybe, but those two would have got their jobs back, and another time the firm wouldn't have sacked workers who want to join a union. (*Applause*)

VOICE: Ten years ago we organized a strike and a march down the *Corso* from the Labour Exchange to the Castellammare Police Station. How long is the *Corso*? Seven or eight hundred metres. And do you know how many people arrived at the Police Station? Six! This evening if you were to ask if we were all willing to go to the Superintendent to try and get him to do what we want—I promise you, the only ones who'd actually arrive there would be Danilo Dolci and one or two others.

A BLIND MAN: We must organize ourselves in common agreement to try and conquer dishonesty and encourage honesty, in the interests of everyone. No one can deprive us of the right to life. Every single person has the right to liberty, work, and freedom of thought. Anything that's discussed peaceably, systematically, and in a right frame of mind, is sure to turn out well. (*Applause*)

And not to be forced to swear: '*Porca l'oca*—what the hell am I to do now to get bread for my children?' My children go barefoot, I'm not ashamed to admit it. (*Applause*)

BARBERA: It's very often said that it's better to work on your own, rather than in company with others, because that way you get more done.

I'd like to ask this: is it always true that a man working on his own gets more done?

VOICE: In the field of work, it is true. In other fields, it would be better all being together, but . . . Here we are, all talking freely in here: but the minute we get outside we can't go on discussing things at all. In here it's all right, we look each other in the face and think: 'No one can touch us in here.' When we go out, though, no one dares say another word—starting with me!

VOICE: What we want is revolution.

VOICE: No—we've had enough of shooting, enough of murder!

VOICE: If I want fire and try to get somebody else to fetch it for me, he'll burn his hand and he won't bring me the fire. I've got to get the fire with my own hands—I've got to burn *my* hands if I want the fire.

VOICE: Tell me something: why is it that when we get outside we can't go on talking?

VOICE: I don't know.

VOICE: But you must answer me. If it was just a matter of one person talking, it's logical he can't talk; but when there are so many of us, then we're strong enough to talk, and we should be able to say what we like.

BARBERA: Lots of us have said we don't agree with the proverb. Doesn't this mean that we ought to organize, and discuss things intelligently amongst ourselves, and try and understand our needs, study them, and then see what can be done?

Somebody mentioned revolution. Today, to really change the situation we've got to *stop* shooting and killing: today, I believe, changing the situation means taking our affairs into our own hands—our work, our lives; it means starting to organize our lives ourselves.

VOICE: We can't go on playing alone any longer.

VOICE: The proverb may have been true up till now—but just because it was true that doesn't mean it's right.

VOICE: Poor me, I was fortunate—or unfortunate—enough to emigrate to Switzerland. (I've also been in North Italy: Como, Novara, Varese, etcetera.) And I can tell you that in Switzerland things are quite different.

The man who plays alone—in my opinion he doesn't lose *or* win: he just goes round and round seeing his own shadow. I think he doesn't either lose or win, and the present régime goes on unchanged.

VOICE: My friends, on our own we are powerless, now. All the way up the whole length of Italy, I take the next man's wallet, and he takes the next man's, and so on—all the way from Pantelleria right up to the Brenner Pass: too often we just prey off each other like this. And the Government, too—we've seen from the papers the scandals they've been involved in.

If we're on our own, every man for himself, we won't get anywhere. By not striking, we'll always be the losers: the Government isn't going to act willingly against its own interests and the interests of its supporters.

Replying to our friend about Switzerland: up there, if you go into a bar and pinch a glass, there's no need to have *carabinieri* to arrest you—the ordinary civilian will take you along to the prison himself —isn't that true? Here, though, when people see someone pinching something, they don't say a word, and this *omertà* is the foulest thing in the world.

So does this mean we're all to be cops? No it doesn't: it's just that all split up like this we're nothing but a rabble, whereas if everyone has a meeting they can each get some idea of things, and then they'll be able to judge whether a party is likely to do them good or harm. But with every man for himself, it's thank you very much, goodbye! I'm timid and don't say anything, you're timid and don't say anything—and so they do just as they please.

VOICE: Often proverbs contradict each other, they have different origins. For instance: 'Unity brings strength' but 'Work for yourself and you work for three'. Just because a thing is a proverb it doesn't mean it's right. As for the one we're discussing, I think the question to ask ourselves is this: is co-operation, is this brotherly relationship, right?

(. . .)

BARBERA: I think the new thing that has emerged in this—I don't know if any of you who've followed the discussions right from the first day have noticed the difference, the advance that's been made this week: now, without really noticing it, we've begun to talk more plainly about certain things, we're not so overawed by them; we've begun to make progress, and to be convinced that we are indeed men, every one of us.

And we've begun to realize that we've got to move forward together. Between neighbours, for example, it won't do just to discuss if the weather's good or bad—we must start discussing what are our common concerns, whether it be the street, or the sewage system, or work. And anything that touches one of our fellow men touches us too; every time a man's murdered, a part of us has been murdered, a part of humanity has been destroyed.

Each time we see any man touched, we ought to speak up immediately and say: 'No, sir! This matter concerns me personally.' I think, broadly speaking, we all agree about this.

But how do we set about becoming more and more united? We begin by discussing: 'What are your problems in this quarter?' 'What are our particular needs?' Well, we need so and so, such and such: all right, let's get together and try and solve our problems together. Between one district and another, between groups of workers in the same trade. And then why not have a whole town, say, or workers of all different categories meeting together, organizing, discussing, establishing clearly what needs doing so that they can then do it? And then, between neighbouring towns? There are so many interests in common between one region and another, between one nation and another. And we should begin to make use of the newspapers, those of us who can read a bit: we can broaden our experience through the papers, too. The world is big, and we ought to get to know it better and better, and try to become more and more united.

A good practical proposition would be to create in Castellammare itself a local organization which would allow as many people as possible to meet and discuss the town's problems. It's only right that now when we're beginning to discuss international politics, and questions such as whether or not we ought to go to the moon, we should also begin to unite and organize together to solve the problems of our own town.

We must break out of the closed circle wherever we possibly can.

VOICE: If so many of us young people are timid and don't talk, I'd say this isn't just timidity—there are plenty of us here who'd like to talk: it's fear, that's all. Because tomorrow, or this evening, or on our way out to work in the fields, there's always the thought that any minute a blast of *lupara* shot may strike us down.

Part Three

The Press Conference on Minister Mattarella, and the resulting trial

Our intention in organizing the Press conference of 22 September 1965 at the Rome Press Club was to try and get official verification of things that were already well known unofficially in Western Sicily and elsewhere—with all the practical consequences this verification would imply. In particular, we thought that on the one hand the Parliamentary Antimafia Commission would no longer be able to ignore the connection between the mafia and the foremost government politician of the area, and on the other hand an eventual trial would allow the documentation to be officially made public and circumstantiated.

Many Italian and foreign papers reported the conference prominently, and in the days that followed the Antimafia Commission did in fact set up a special sub-committee consisting of the Chairman, Senator Donato Pafundi, and the following Members of Parliament: Russo Spena (DC), Bergamasco (PLI), Morino (PSDI), and Assennato (PCI) (subsequently replaced by Spezzano). Again I was invited to attend the plenary discussion ('You are respectfully invited to testify before Parliamentary Commission Enquiry Mafia October thirteenth eighteen hours. Kindly wire confirmation. Chairman of Commission Pafundi'); and some twenty to thirty witnesses were heard.

Meanwhile proceedings were being instituted against me, Franco Alasia, and the editors of the left-wing papers—but only of the left-wing ones: *L'Unità*, *Paese Sera*, *L'Ora*—which had reported our conference prominently.

Bernardo Mattarella wrote to the Public Prosecutor in Rome that '. . . the contents of the so-called document are the ultimate manifestation of base political speculation . . . which ought to be classed with other variations on the same theme already executed by the same political faction of which Dolci is a tool'; for which reason 'the undersigned, though believing that a lawsuit shortens distances which ought to be maintained by contempt, formally sues'.

In the same way summonses for summary trial arrived one after the other following on actions brought by Calogero Volpe, Guido Anca Martinez, Giambrone Carmelo, Ganci Antonino, Giuseppe Munna—on his own behalf (he wrote to the Public Prosecutor: 'Having qualified in Law, the writer of this letter was called by the trust of the local Council to the office of Mayor of Castellammare del Golfo. The writer mafioso? It is preposterous!!! Could you imagine, dear sirs, a mafioso presiding over a local delegation of the DC?') and also on behalf of his late father Liborio Munna; and Michele Russo, Luigi Geraci, Francesco Guagenti, Pietro Venza, Vincenzo Messina.

At the hearing on 20th November 1965, the Court of Rome (IVth Penal Section[1]) adjourned the opening of the trial till 15th March 1966, to allow time for the co-ordination of the various actions, including two new suits brought by Mattarella and Volpe following the distribution of our leaflet (see page 250) in Castellammare del Golfo.

15th March 1966

The Presiding Judge is Dr Carlo Testi; the Public Prosecutor is Dr Pasquale Pedote. Mattarella's counsel are Giovanni Leone and Girolamo Bellavista. For Volpe, Girolamo Bellavista and Michele Mormino.

My counsel are Avv. Adolfo Gatti, Fausto Gullo, and Fausto Tarsitano; for Franco, Luigi Salerni, Giovanni Ozzo, Nino Sorgi.

Defending the newspapers are Avv. Nino Gaeta, Vinicio de Matteis, Fausto Fiore, Giuseppe Berlingeri.

After a wait of several hours while the Court deals with other trials, I am interrogated. Here is a summary of my answers:

In November '63, I explain, I received from the Parliamentary Antimafia Commission the following telegram: 'Parliamentary Commission Enquiry Maffia has decided to accept your informative

---

[1] Mattarella, Volpe, etc., were the plaintiffs suing for damages, but under Italian law libel is also a criminal offence, punishable by imprisonment. (Tr. note.)

declarations concerning Maffia phenomenon November thirteenth
'63 Palazzo Sapienza Corso Rinascimento Rome. Kindly wire confirmation Senate Republic Chairman of Commission Pafundi'.

Being invited thus to lay before the Commission all I knew
about the phenomenon of the mafia in the area in which I had been
studying, working and living for almost fifteen years, I could only
accept the invitation—which I did gladly—and try to collect as much
accurate evidence as possible. This meeting with the full Parliamentary Commission lasted for about two hours, and when the
Chairman, Pafundi, thanked me at the end of it, he asked me to
pursue these analyses further, and added that they might call on me
again. I could not but carry on with my documentation, as rigor-
ously as possible: and I had realized during the course of the meeting that the Commission would need some monographic contributions in order to have a basis of concrete information from which
to arrive at valid generalizations.

It was moreover essential to the work of our Study and Action
Centre that we and the people together should try to understand
exactly how progress was being hampered by the obstacles to
associative life, and how progress was being hampered by the
connection (varying from one case to another and from area to area)
between mafiosi and certain politicians.

I had no personal motive at all in concerning myself with Bernardo Mattarella and Calogero Volpe; with the diligent collaboration of Franco Alasia (author of one of the first studies on the emigration of Southerners to the North, *Milano–Corea*), I pursued this
investigation into the links between Mattarella and the mafiosi not
merely because this case was an important one in itself but because
it was in certain respects the standard pattern. Up to the time of the
Press conference we did not concern ourselves directly with Volpe
since his case was already plain enough.

At this point I am interrupted, with mocking sarcasm, by Avv.
Bellavista. I turn round to look at him: he was Calogero Vizzini's
lawyer, and Vincenzo Rimi's, and a close associate of Vanni Sacco.[1]

---

[1] Three of the most notorious capimafia (frequently referred to in the docu-
mentation on Mattarella at the end of Part One). Don Calò Vizzini was for years
Head of the mafia and in effect feudal overlord of Sicily. (Tr. note.)
  In Girolamo Bellavista's eyes, (*Arringhe*, Editrice Eloquentia—*ut verba*

His speech, which he tries to ornament with learned language, is ponderous. The Presiding Judge asks me to carry on.

The more serious material, I continue—for instance, the evidence of complicity between Mattarella and Giuliano—will be handed over later to the Parliamentary Antimafia Commission: but the material of a public nature, i.e. that which concerns events which generally took place in the presence of many people, besides being placed before the Antimafia Commission, was used publicly in order to ensure that the authorities responsible should take the necessary action to verify it. Besides, coming out into the open like this made us safer from the mafia, which prefers to keep to the shadows. At four o'clock one morning, in fact, when as usual I was on my way to work at the Study Centre, a car drew near us and we clearly saw a gun inside pointed in our direction. Perhaps it was only Franco's rapid action in getting between me and the car which dissuaded whoever was behind the gun; or perhaps (the window of the car was still shut at a distance of a few yards) they just meant to threaten, to intimidate us.

More loud laughter, another ponderous interruption by Avv. Bellavista, who seems really amused. Again the Presiding Judge asks me to carry on.

Meanwhile Giovanni Leone keeps up an incessant and often noisy commentary, even during the interrogation. I can't help thinking of the trial for the murder of Turiddu Carnevale[1] and the part Leone played in that.

I point out how of course Mattarella does not get votes only through the mafia; I describe how the electoral behaviour of the urban mafia differs from that of the rural mafia, and how the existence of the Antimafia Commission has imposed greater prudence on them recently; and I tell of the difficulty of obtaining information on this subject. I point out the necessity for collecting evidence from as wide a range as possible, beyond any party boundaries, and for collecting and comparing the preference votes for each election

maneant—) Calogero Vizzini was the 'charismatic father of his bounteously favoured citizens' in Villalba: 'smiling little township of the Nisseno where Li Causi incautiously broached the matter of the large latifundium'.

[1] A peasant leader murdered by the mafia in 1955 (their thirty-eighth trade unionist victim in less than ten years). Avv. Leone successfully defended the mafiosi accused of the murder. (Tr. note.)

in every Commune. I also point out that the Munna family are not strictly speaking true mafiosi but typical 'friends of friends', middle-men.

FRANCO ALASIA: I have heard Danilo Dolci's declaration; I confirm and agree with all he says.

I have lived in Sicily for eight years, and I have a Sicilian son. I am conscious of contributing through my work to the improvement of social relations in the Island. I believe that there needs to be a bridge between the people and the Parliamentary Antimafia Commission, between the people and the Court. I would like to describe an incident: I was talking to a policeman one day; when I left him, a peasant who I was very friendly with because I had taught him to read and write came up to me and said: 'Watch out— that fellow's a cop.' You see, that's what the Sicilian people so often think of the forces of law and order. And the people's faith in the organs of the State must be restored if the mafia is to be finally overcome. That is why I have worked on this study.

Massimo Ghiara, editor of *Unità*, specifies that he was not present at the Press conference but that he reported it in accordance with the right to publish news.

BERNARDO MATTARELLA (confirms the suit): I wish to state further and make quite clear that at no time have I solicited the votes of the mafia, nor have I ever collaborated with the forces of the mafia. On the contrary, the beginning of my activity in the political arena was in direct opposition to the forces of the mafia which in 1943, as is well known, had united in support of the Separatist movement which I consistently opposed; and may I add that I am proud of that battle. I did not even need the votes of the mafia, because I was starting out from a position of political solidity and popular consensus, having been active for two years in Catholic Action; at the age of thirteen I had been regional leader of the Young Catholics, and later of the men, and also Chairman of the diocesan council of Palermo. Finally, I would point out that I have always fought the phenomenon of the mafia not only at Political meetings but also in print, in '58 and in '63.

In '46 and '47 at the Regional and Parliamentary elections Giuliano and his band openly supported the movement for Sicilian Independence: so much so that the movement had outstanding electoral success in the Communes of Montelepre and Giardinello. Everybody knows that Giuliano's band was enrolled in EVIS, the Voluntary Army for Sicilian Independence.

I remember that in the local government election of '58 the DC had to fight against the civic list which united various political forces, among them the PCI, a list which had the open and definite support of the elements indicated in the dossier as mafiosi: I am referring to the elections in my birthplace, Castellammare del Golfo. A similar thing occurred in the 1960 elections, when the list headed by Antonino Barone, who had left the DC back in '51, was supported by the same elements as previously mentioned. I would further point out that in fact I consistently opposed the re-entry of Barone into the DC, both because he had gone out slamming the door, and because of his background.

In '63, at the most crucial period of the campaign, I did not hesitate, twenty-six or twenty-eight days before the actual election, to inveigh against the forces of the mafia at a public meeting in Alcamo, referring to them as backward, antisocial and unlawful, an obstacle to all reform. I also spoke upon the same theme in Castelvetrano at the time of the 1958 Parliamentary elections.

At the time when the Antimafia Commission was set up I was in office as Minister, and in the Cabinet I gave a favourable opinion on it; apart from that I have had no occasion to concern myself with the question.

Avv. SALERNI: Have you collaborated with the Antimafia Commission?

MATTARELLA: My collaboration has not been requested.

22nd March 1966

Another long wait while the Court is occupied with other trials. Ours begins at about one'oclock. Calogero Volpe is called.

PRESIDING JUDGE: Did you know Doctor Navarra?

CALOGERO VOLPE: Since '34, when I was attending the surgical clinic of Palermo University. I was an intern then, and Dr Navarra, who was already qualified, used to attend as a non-resident. I saw him again in '46 after I had come back to Sicily and made my entry into political life as a DC candidate. Then I saw him again at Corleone, where Navarra was Director of the hospital, because I was concerned with the building of a new hospital, which was completed a few months ago.

PRESIDING JUDGE: So you did have dealings with Navarra.

CALOGERO VOLPE: Naturally, naturally. Being concerned with the hospital I met him often.

PRESIDING JUDGE: Did you also know Vincenzo Collura, indicated as capomafia second in command to Navarra?

CALOGERO VOLPE: I learned of his existence from the newspapers.

PRESIDING JUDGE: You know what end Navarra came to?

CALOGERO VOLPE: Yes, he was killed, in '58 I think, together with another colleague, Dr Russo.

PRESIDING JUDGE: Were you aware of Dr Navarra's other activities?

CALOGERO VOLPE: Professional?

PRESIDING JUDGE: Not specifically.

CALOGERO VOLPE: No, I know nothing about any other activities of Dr Navarra.

PRESIDING JUDGE: You didn't know if he was a capomafia?

CALOGERO VOLPE: No, I did not.

PRESIDING JUDGE: Did you go to Corleone often?

CALOGERO VOLPE: Several times. In fact, I remember it was at Corleone that I held an election meeting in '46, in the municipal theatre: the meeting broke up noisily as soon as I made my position clear as opponent of the Communist Party and of the Separatist movement. There was an uproar, scuffles broke out, and I could not continue. That year in Corleone, if I remember rightly, I received about forty votes.

PRESIDING JUDGE: Did Navarra's faction in Corleone get the citizens to vote for you?

CALOGERO VOLPE: The people who voted for me in Corleone were the members of the DC, the members of the Pious Union of farm labourers, the priests, and the parish organizations.

PRESIDING JUDGE: Is it true that at Ficuzza a certain Vincenzo Catanzaro got votes for you?

CALOGERO VOLPE: It wasn't Catanzaro who procured votes for me at Ficuzza—it was my friend Salvatore Butera, director of the Forestry Office of Enna, and a native of Ficuzza; however that was only eleven votes.[1]

PRESIDING JUDGE: In the commune of Alia, were there capimafia among your electors?

CALOGERO VOLPE: I never went to Alia for rallies. I deny having had dealings with Don Botindari, with the Vallonis, and with the others mentioned in the extract which concerns me. May I point out that out of my sixty thousand preference votes in 1958, only thirty were from Alia; and the person who procured them for me was Dr Alfredo Sagona, a native of Alia. It was only in '63 that I had a meeting in Alia, organized by the then Secretary of the DC.

Dolci, or whoever was interviewed by him, says that there was a significant shift of votes in the '63 elections away from Mattarella and in my favour; but he is not aware that at least ten thousand of the additional votes I received since 1958 came from Palermo. The reason is absolutely simple, as I was assured by the various trades union organizers: perhaps remembering my activities as Under-Secretary to the Ministry of Transport, the railway men, and in particular those of the Palermo division, voted for me in a solid block—even those who did not hold the same political ideas as me.

AVV. GATTI: But how many railwaymen vote in Palermo?

CALOGERO VOLPE: I don't know. But the division of Palermo comprises the whole of Sicily, and the administrative offices are also in the capital.

AVV. GATTI: At the time of the elections, were you in the Government?

CALOGERO VOLPE: No, I had left the Government in '62, after having been Under-Secretary to the Ministry of Transport for two years.

AVV. LEONE: When did you begin your political career?

[1] Volpe ought to have added 'in '58'. In '63, his votes in this small community had in fact gone up to 112.

CALOGERO VOLPE: My father was a miner. As a Social Democrat he was on the local Council in Montedoro. Together with Don Giovanni Rizzo, now Archbishop of Rossano Calabro, he fought a victorious battle to get the crucifix into schools and public offices. My father then emigrated to America in 1921, where he continued to work as a miner, contracting silicosis and anthracosis. My father entrusted me to the care of the Salesians, and made sacrifices to enable me to study. I obtained a degree in Palermo, I was Assistant in Turin at the Obstetric clinic, then in Rome. Then in '43, before the invasion, I came back to Sicily in November, and founded the divisional branch of the DC in Caltanissetta.

AVV. LEONE: I would like the Honourable Volpe to explain what his attitude was towards the mafia.

CALOGERO VOLPE: I founded branches of my party, organizing associations of peasants and bricklayers, and DC co-operatives for obtaining grants of land: to such effect that eight thousand hectares of land was granted to the peasants. This was my battle against the feudal estate and that parasitic intermediarism that is identified in the mafia. Naturally, naturally. That was confirmed by a sentence in the Palermo Court of Appeal, following my action against Pompeo Colaianni.

I was the first to oppose Separatism,[1] a movement that was a receptacle for mafia elements. The battle was on two principles: against Separatism and against the Communist Party. At the 1950 DC Provincial Congress, a motion against the mafia was passed unanimously.

AVV. GATTI: Is it true that the witness was godfather to the son of Giuseppe Genco Russo?

---

[1] It is interesting to compare this with the deposition of Nicola Cipolla at the Colaianni–Volpe trial (n. 1291/51, Palermo, Vols. II–III, pp. 126–30), and that of Cesare Cigna (pp. 195–204).

NICOLA CIPOLLA: . . . I can state that during the first public demonstration after the liberation in 1944 (I cannot be exact as to which month it was), held in the Massimo Theatre in Palermo, and promoted by the movement for Sicilian Independence, I saw Calogero Vizzini on the stage beside the Hon. Volpe, as well as many other people I did not know.

Because I and other University students were disturbing the meeting, after having been asked once to desist by another group of young men who had come there to meet us, and having refused to comply, i.e. the said group having failed

CALOGERO VOLPE: No. Genco Russo has two sons: Salvatore, who has a degree in agriculture, and Vincenzo, and I did not stand as godfather or as marriage witness to either. It is true that I know them, but I have had no connection with them.

AVV. GATTI: Do you know Calogero Castiglione, Genco Russo's brother-in-law?

---

to 'dislodge' us, another group came up, among whom I recognized certain elements from my own town, Villalba; they were headed by the Hon. Volpe, who turned to me and said: 'You know me: what are we going to do?' And I answered back that I was only exercising my rights.

As there was now a confrontation between the two groups, the Police intervened and parted us.

CESARE CIGNA: . . . I was a notary in Mussomeli up till 1946.

I was on the Liberation Committee of Mussomeli after the fall of Fascism, and the members of the said Committee were all agreed on my nomination as Mayor, with the exception of Barcellona, who represented the Monarchists.

A first meeting took place in the house of Sorce Vincenzo, known as 'Nasca', at which I was urged to accept the office of Mayor. I declined, both because I had no particular desire for the office and because of professional commitments.

Subsequently another meeting took place, in the house of the registrar Giuseppe Giudice, who is today working in Milan; the meeting was arranged by the DC party—to be exact, by the Hon. Volpe, Giuseppe Genco Russo, Calogero Vizzini, Calogero Castiglione (known as 'Farfariello'), Scannella (whose first name I forget but who was at that time in business), others of Genco Russo's family, and others too whose names I do not remember: in all, there were about twelve to fifteen of them. This occurred after the American landings and before the appointment of the first Mayor.

The aforementioned persons, at the said meeting, urged me to co-operate with their administration of the Council. I refused my co-operation, both because of my political beliefs and because in the town these men did not stand for anything, their following consisting only of the other people involved in their misdoings, and those who complied with their wishes out of fear in so far as they were enforced with violence: in other words, I mean that the followers of the people I have named were the mafiosi and the *camorristi*.

Upon my refusing my co-operation, Volpe said: 'So you're asking for violence, then—you want blood to flow?'

. . . Since I had been apprised beforehand by the registrar Giudice of who was to attend this second meeting, I had thought it best to take the precaution of writing their names on a sheet of paper, which I handed to my landlord Nicolò Antonio Mingoia, advising him that in the event of my suffering any violence he should bear in mind that these were the people who had sent for me.

. . . Among the names on the sheet of paper which I left with my landlord was also the name of Volpe.

CALOGERO VOLPE: Yes. I was godfather at his daughter's christening. The little girl was born dystociac, and they say there that she was only born by the grace of God and with my help.

Avv. GATTI: Did you know Calogero Vizzini?

CALOGERO VOLPE: Yes. I got to know him in '38, just after I qualified. I spent a month in Villalba. I knew him then for professional reasons, as a doctor, that is; and subsequently I had further dealings with him on occasions, also for professional reasons. He became my opponent—political, not personal—in '46, which was when the DC first made a stand against Separatism. In '47 Vizzini supported the *Uomo Qualunque* Party candidate and in '48 the Liberal Party. In '53 Vizzini fell ill and died.

Avv. GATTI: In Delia, did you know Pietro Pittari, Michele Russo, Angelo Iannello, and Salvatore Lo Verde? Do you know if these men are mafiosi? (*Avv. Leone and others of the plaintiffs' counsel loudly oppose the question*) One doesn't bring legal actions if one is afraid of the evidence.

(*Further prolonged uproar*)

CALOGERO VOLPE: I do not remember knowing these people. I can't remember all the seven thousand people in Delia.

Avv. GATTI: So you deny any direct acquaintance?

CALOGERO VOLPE: I don't remember.

Avv. GATTI: And in Mazzarino, do you know Vincenzo Lo Presti, Ludovico Cinardo and Giuseppe Falzone?

Persistent excited shouting. Leone noisily opposes the question. I cannot help reflecting on the fact that this is the very man proposed by a large part of Italy as candidate for President of the Republic.[1]

Avv. GATTI: (*doggedly*) Don't bring actions, then, if you're afraid of the truth.

Avv. LEONE: These are tendentious questions. Counsel for the defence should indicate beforehand the witnesses they intend to call, they should present the list of witnesses.

[1] In June 1968 DC Senator Giovanni Leone became Prime Minister of the caretaker Government. (Tr. note.)
11*

Avv. GATTI: We are quite ready to present the lists of witnesses, but we would point out that we and you of the prosecution had previously agreed to present them at a later stage.

The Public Prosecutor requests that the Court disallow the question. Gatti, De Matteis and Gaeta request that the objection be overruled. After a brief consultation in the Council chamber, the Court allows Gatti's question, authorizing the parties to present the lists of witnesses.

CALOGERO VOLPE: I don't remember. I may have known Cinardi, if he's the secretary of the local branch of the Owner-farmers. Mazzarino has twenty-five thousand inhabitants.

Volpe likewise doesn't know if he knows Calogero Territo of Serradifalco, Arnone Viciu of Mussomeli. In Riesi he did know Francesco De Cristina[1] in that he was the father of Antonio, Secretary of the local DC branch; he denies having been visited by Genco Russo at his Montedoro estate. He recognizes himself in the centre of a photograph taken in Vallelunga during an election campaign.

Avv. GATTI: You don't recognize the man on your right here, and this other on your left, in the foreground?

CALOGERO VOLPE: No, I don't.[2]

Avv. TARSITANO (*reading*): At a public meeting in Villalba in '58, you said: 'I have come here to speak to the friends of the family, to the "friends of friends". I shall come back again a week after the elections, and we shall look each other in the eyes one by one to see who are the real friends and who are the traitors.'

CALOGERO VOLPE: It's not true. The man who declared that I pronounced those words was made to withdraw! In this very hall there was a trial for libel.

Avv. TARSITANO: We'll see. Were you intimate with Genco Russo?

---

[1] See pp. 360–361, witnesses 15 to 19. (Tr. note).

[2] They are, respectively, Giovanni Cammarata, wanted for two murders and later found murdered himself, and Salvatore Di Giovanni of Vallelunga, previously convicted and placed under special security measures.

CALOGERO VOLPE: I knew Genco Russo, a farmer, through my professional activities.

AVV. TARSITANO: You used to go around arm in arm with him? You kissed when you met? You embraced him? You had him to your house?

CALOGERO VOLPE: Naturally, naturally, of course I would have met him. Did he come to my house? Of course he did: everybody comes to the house of a politician.

AVV. TARSITANO: You haven't answered the rest of the question.

PRESIDING JUDGE: Did you hear?

CALOGERO VOLPE: What?

PRESIDING JUDGE: You used to embrace him, kiss him?

CALOGERO VOLPE: (*Nonplussed*) Mah! . . .

AVV. TARSITANO: Did you know that after the death of Calogero Vizzini, Genco Russo was held to be the head of the Sicilian mafia?

CALOGERO VOLPE: How should I know? I wasn't aware of that.

AVV. TARSITANO: Did Genco Russo campaign for you at elections?

CALOGERO VOLPE: I don't know. Politicians are in touch with the branch secretaries.

AVV. TARSITANO: In '46, did you take part in meetings with Calogero Vizzini?

CALOGERO VOLPE: I deny it. I attended meetings at Polizello, because I was concerned with the farm's being assigned to the National Ex-Servicemen's Organization, but I never met Calogero Vizzini there.

AVV. SALERNI: Have you co-operated with the Antimafia Commission?

CALOGERO VOLPE: The Commission has never asked me to.

AVV. SALERNI: Do you know Santo Volpe? Is he related to you?

CALOGERO VOLPE: Yes, he was my father's cousin. I met him in 1930 when he came over from the United States, where he had emigrated. I saw him again in 1950 in America.

AVV. SALERNI: Did you receive visits from Genco Russo by night?

CALOGERO VOLPE: By day politicians are visited by all kinds of people. Politicians don't receive anyone by night.

The Man Who Plays Alone

Avv. Gaeta: Whatever made you consider the news that Genco Russo attended your daughter's wedding libellous? The Court does not allow the question.

24th March 1966

According to the *Giornale di Sicilia*, Antonino Barone, now a Social Democrat Deputy in the Regional Assembly, 'today announced that he has filed a suit against the Honourable Bernardo Mattarella following on certain statements contained in the deposition made by the ex-Minister at the trial of Danilo Dolci; he has also made known the text of an application sent to the Presiding Judge of the IVth Penal Section of the Court of Rome, in which he asks to be heard as a witness . . . The application contains the following passage: "Contrary to the truth, the Honourable Mattarella has declared that in 1958 on the occasion of the local election in Castellammare the DC list was beaten by the civic list headed by me because, he alleges, the latter was openly supported by the mafia elements of that Commune; during the same hearing the Honourable Mattarella apparently declared that from 1950 onwards I attempted to re-enter the DC, and claimed that he opposed my re-entry because of my alleged mafia background . . ." '

26th March 1966

The lists of witnesses are filed in the Court Registry.

29th March 1966

Avvocato Michele Russo of Sciacca and Carmelo Giambrone of Valledolmo are heard: they confirm their suit, declaring themselves absolutely unconnected with the mafia. Particularly interesting are the following passages from the cross-examinations of Guido Anca Martinez, wine manufacturer of Marsala, and of Giuseppe Munna, Mayor of Castellammare del Golfo.

Presiding Judge: In document no. 13 of Dolci's and Alasia's dossier we read: 'In Marsala on various occasions at election rallies, the whole town could see Mattarella in the company of: Anca Martinez, considered by many people to be the brain of the Marsala mafia; Giuseppe Bua, mafioso of the big feudal estates, chairman of the *Bonomiana*, now in prison for criminal association, and whose son is a godson of Mattarella's; and Giuseppe Lo Presti, mafioso . . .' What have you to say about this, in so far as it concerns you?

GUIDO ANCA MARTINEZ: I confirm my suit. I deny the accusation of being the brain of the Marsala mafia.

AVV. SALERNI: Have you ever been in trouble with the Law?

GUIDO ANCA MARTINEZ: Only once, on the occasion of my call-up when I was involved in a judicial misadventure concerning the officer in charge of conscription.[1]

AVV. SALERNI: Does the witness remember anything about a trial for corruption and perjury?

GUIDO ANCA MARTINEZ: The affair dates back to forty-two years ago, and I don't remember.

AVV. SALERNI: Didn't you have anything to do with the division of the Genna-Spanò estate?[2]

Anca Martinez denies this: he was only concerned in a transaction between the Bishop and the Spanò family; he asserts that 'the mafia

[1] From *ABC* of 7 August 1960: 'One of these (governors of the '*Banco di Sicilia*') is now designated in the person of Guido Anca Martinez, a friend of Mattarella . . . acquitted through supervening amnesty of the following crimes: (1) house-breaking; (2) assault; (3) injuries; (4) causing bodily harm; (5) unlawful carrying of arms; (6) failure to declare arms. The crimes concerned were committed during the first Fascist period, on the occasion of punitive expeditions, but were so serious as to warrant prosecution by the Fascist authorities themselves.

'This is not all. Signor Anca Martinez, who is to represent the Region on the Board of Governors of the *Banco di Sicilia*, was sentenced on 11th June 1928 to six months and twenty-five days' penal servitude, as well as being debarred for a year from public office, for corruption of a public official.

'Subsequently Signor Anca Martinez was sentenced to one year and two months' penal servitude by the Court of Trapani for perjury. The sentence was revoked following an appeal "because the deed does not constitute a crime" . . . Similarly later, involved in legal proceedings over the purchase of contraband alcohol, he was acquitted on the curious grounds that: "the Law has been unable to obtain documentary proof, having failed to find the firm's account books, which appear to have been suppressed".'

[2] See page 338 (Vero Monti's statement). (Tr. note.)

had absolutely nothing to do with the business'; he admits that his wife acquired about thirty hectares of the estate.

Next comes the cross-examination of Giuseppe Munna.[1]

Avv. TARSITANO: The witness married the niece of Diego Plaja, at present detained in the Ucciardone prison for criminal association?

GIUSEPPE MUNNA: Yes, but my father-in-law himself has a clean record, he's an honest man.

Avv. TARSITANO: Do you know Vincenzo and Filippo Rimi, Salvatore Vitale, Frank Garofalo, Nino Buccellato?

GIUSEPPE MUNNA: I know Rimi, Salvatore Vitale, Nino Buccellato and Frank Garofalo in so far as they are citizens of the town where I was born and of which I am Mayor, but I deny ever having had any intimate acquaintance or friendship with them: on the contrary, some of them are in fact my political opponents.

Avv. TARSITANO: Have you had dealings with Gaspare and Giuseppe Magaddino?

GIUSEPPE MUNNA: I am a wine merchant, and I buy wine from whoever has it.

Avv. TARSITANO: But you belonged to the Molitoria co-operative?

GIUSEPPE MUNNA: I was only an ordinary member.

Avv. TARSITANO: Aren't you aware that the Molitoria obtained in the space of a few days a subsidy of forty-two million lire? That it was at the centre of a scandal?

GIUSEPPE MUNNA: It is true that I am still a member of the co-operative, and that in '61 the officer in charge of Public Works awarded a grant, as in the spirit of the law which provided for this; but the Chairman was Giuseppe Magaddino . . .

Avv. TARSITANO: The forty-two million were spent on purchasing old and unserviceable machines from Gaspare Magaddino. Do you know that?

GIUSEPPE MUNNA: I didn't have anything to do with administrative matters. I know nothing about it.

PRESIDING JUDGE: But how many members are there in this co-operative? Roughly. A hundred? Two hundred?

GIUSEPPE MUNNA: I think there are ten members.

[1] See page 210, no. V. (Tr. note.)

AVV. TARSITANO: Are you aware that the Molitoria had debts of almost fifty million lire to the *Banco di Sicilia* and to the firm of Magaddino?

GIUSEPPE MUNNA: I don't know. At the beginning I paid out a hundred thousand lire to join, and I've had no profit from it.

AVV. TARSITANO: Giuseppe Magaddino, formerly Chairman of this co-operative, has been arrested for criminal association and drug trafficking. You do know that?

The Court does not allow the question. Finally the witness recognizes, at the request of Avv. Tarsitano, a copy of the list of Christian Democrat candidates for the 1946 election in Castellammare, which includes the names of Mattarella (heading the list), Antonino Barone, Diego Plaja, and Giuseppe Munna. The document is added to the files.

Franco and I return to Partinico. Passing through Castellammare, after the local papers have published long reports on these last exchanges, we hear many protests: 'But how can Munna have the nerve to say he doesn't know the Rimis and Salvatore Vitale and Nino Buccellato well?' Others: 'But they were always together!' Others again: 'Giuseppe Munna, Vincenzo Rimi and Gaspare Magaddino were even fellow members of the same society, SIPAC.'

The protests get stronger and stronger and more and more concrete, until one day we find on our desk a copy of a document as interesting as it is unequivocal and it will be useful at this point to quote the essential part of it:

On 27th November 1952, Gaspare De Lisi of Partinico was found murdered in the Manca district of Partinico. Italiano Vincenzo and nine other men, among them Frank Coppola and Vincenzo Rimi, were charged with:

a: conspiring with criminal intent and making armed raids in the countryside around Partinico and neighbouring areas from June 1952 onwards;

b: conspiring together to cause the death by shooting of Gaspare De Lisi.

On pp. 32–35 of Vol. IV of the trial, we read this poetic piece of prose:

> To the examining Justice, section VII:
> Your Honour,
> Bewildered and grieved by the surprising imputations against our defendant Vincenzo Rimi, son of Filippo Rimi, in proof of his indisputable innocence . . . since he is accused of being a party to the murder of De Lisi on 27th November '52, although often it is impossible to give proof to the contrary, nevertheless when the Lord so wishes He can cause even the bird to leave traces of its flight. Thus my defendant has recollected that on 25th November a party was held in Castellammare to celebrate the name-day of Signora Caterina Vitale, the sister-in-law of Filippo Rimi, son of the accused; and that the said name-day was celebrated in a special manner, all the relatives being invited.
>   . . . On that same date the SIPAC, of which Vincenzo Rimi was a member, received the enclosed invitation for 28th November; and therefore on the evening preceding this meeting at the Savings Bank, i.e. on the 27th, the members of SIPAC held a meeting themselves.
>   The said meeting of the members was held in the SIPAC rooms and lasted from approximately 4 p.m. until approximately 10.30 p.m. The meeting was thus protracted for more than six hours in that it was necessary to examine the balance-sheet, and discuss the whole financial state of the Society, and examine the debits and credits, for the formulation of the future programme.
>   In case Your Honour should wish to verify the foregoing statements, we would request that the following persons be examined as witnesses:
>   Vitale Leonardo, member of SIPAC . . .
>   Rimi Filippo, member of SIPAC . . .
>   Plaja Diego, member of SIPAC . . .
>   Magaddino Gaspare, member of SIPAC . . .
>   Avv. Giuseppe Munna, member of SIPAC . . .
>   To sum up: on 27th November SIPAC received the enclosed letter from the Castellammare Savings Bank; the invitation was communicated to Rimi while he was in Castellammare celebrating . . .; on the preceding evening, i.e. the 27th, there was a meeting of all the

members, including Vincenzo Rimi; and the said meeting lasted from approximately 4.30 p.m. until approximately 10.30 p.m.

Your obedient servant,
Avv. Domenico Pugliese

From pp. 33–34, vol. III (examination of witnesses on 8th November '53 in Castellammare del Golfo):

DIEGO PLAJA: . . . (on 27th November) all of us members met, including Vincenzo Rimi, and we discussed the situation at length. The following day we went to the Bank to regularize our Society, and I believe Rimi also attended.

GASPARE MAGADDINO: I can testify that Vincenzo Rimi was present at the meeting of our society SIPAC. I remember clearly that on the following morning also, i.e. the 28th November '52, Vincenzo Rimi was present, together with his son Filippo, on the premises of the Bank.

Avv. GIUSEPPE MUNNA: I remember clearly that on 27th November '52 there was a meeting of the various members of SIPAC with the aim of putting the society itself in order, it being at that time in difficulties.

I remember clearly that Vincenzo Rimi also attended the said meeting, and discussed the said situation.

We make a note: at the next hearings our lawyers will present this document to the Court.

19th April 1966

Vito Messina[1] of Castellammare is cross-examined. He confirms the suit. A schoolmate of Joe Banana's, and business associate of Mancino's, he has 'always campaigned for Mattarella at elections': but he declares himself unconnected with the mafia.

The lawyers and the Public Prosecutor make various requests, including one that the original dossier be added to the files on the case.

[1] See in particular page 216, no. 8; and page 354, the second witness. (Tr. note.)

After a long consultation in the Council chamber, the Court
returns to announce its decision that it should acquire: a copy of
the original dossier presented by Dolci to the Antimafia Commission
in September '65, with the signed declarations; the evidence concerning the injured parties collected by the Commission itself on the
basis of the dossier; and the list of the people heard by the Commission in connection with the injured parties. It also ordains that
the Commission be asked to confirm that it did in fact send the two
telegrams quoted above (see pp. 299 and 301); and, in particular, to
verify the accused's claim to have been asked officially by the Commission to study the phenomenon of the mafia in Sicily and to present them with a written report.

17th May 1966

In reply to the Court's requests, the Parliamentary Antimafia
Commission has sent photostat copies of only the first fifty-seven
documents. One cannot see why they have chosen to send these and
not others (they could have sent only the fifty made public at the
Press conference—or more, including the very serious testimony of
the Rev. Don Caiozzo).

The texts of the telegrams are confirmed ('Parliamentary Commission . . . has decided to accept your informative declarations
concerning Mafia phenomenon . . . Pafundi'; and 'you are respectfully invited to testify before Parliamentary Commission . . .
Kindly wire confirmation . . . Pafundi'), and it is interesting to
compare these with the statement now sent by the same Pafundi
specifying that I had been given no official instructions: 'No official
instructions were given to Dolci by this Commission to enquire into
and report on the phenomenon of the mafia in Sicily, consequently
the statements and declarations which he caused to be delivered to
the Parliamentary Commission are to be attributed entirely to his
own personal initiative.'

I ask the Presiding Judge if I may clarify one or two points. On
22nd September, I explain, I had confined myself to presenting to
Signor Pafundi only the dossier containing the first fifty documents,
without revealing the names of the witnesses: I wanted the Com-

mission first to guarantee that these people would be protected as far as was possible. Not until the 13th October did the Commission ask me for the list of names. Within the next few days I handed over this list, and also the other documents concerning Mattarella and Volpe.

I also point out that I have never claimed that the Parliamentary Commission invested me with official powers to make inquiries of any sort: but they did several times ask me to bring to light whatever I knew about the phenomenon of the mafia in the area I lived in.

The Court has by now also received the documents relating to the action brought against us over the leaflet distributed in Castellammare in January. (There had already been an unsuccessful attempt to rush the trial through in Palermo: one or two headlines were already announcing DOLCI BEFORE THE LAW FOR DEFAMATION OF THE STATE.) Questioned about this, I refer them to the actual text of the leaflet, sufficiently clear in itself.

Next come rapid examinations of Luigi Geraci of Chiusa Sclafani; Pietro Venza and Vincenzo Messina of San Vito Lo Capo; Francesco Guagenti, cattle-stealer and tradesman of Caccamo: they confirm the suit. Guagenti points out that Caccamo is a devoutly Catholic town and therefore votes for Mattarella through the various Catholic organizations.[1]

Mattarella and Volpe are also questioned in connection with their suit over the leaflet. *Agenzia Italia* later reports: 'Mattarella again declared himself a proud adversary of the mafia. Volpe denied any connection whatsoever, even casual, with the Sicilian mafia.'

Antonino Ganci of San Giuseppe Iato, another of the plaintiffs, is unable to appear at the trial because a few days ago he was arrested for criminal association and kidnapping: naturally he too, in the accusation he filed before the Public Prosecutor on September 28th, 1965, complained that we had 'besmirched the good name of honest and industrious citizens, whose upright and blameless life is well known to all'.

---

[1] During this same period the capomafia of Caccamo, Panzeca, is in hiding, and the Police search the church of his brother the archpriest, described in document 49 of the dossier as 'brother of the capomafia in every respect'.

24th May 1966

At the end of the last hearing the Court had asked me to identify which testimonies in our dossier were signed, and to recognize the signatures of those that were. The list of seventeen names is added to the Court files.

Various requests are made by the lawyers on both sides, including a request by Gatti that the Court should also add to the files the whole collection of documents presented by us to the Antimafia Commission. Avv. Leone opposes this. After a private consultation, the Court:

a: admits as witnesses the authors of the seventeen signed declarations, plus a few others from the list of witnesses submitted by the accused;

b: admits eighteen witnesses to be selected from among those indicated by Mattarella's counsel;

c: admits six witnesses from among those indicated by Volpe.

. . . 'given that we do not consider it necessary, on the basis of the documents already available, to request further documentation from the Parliamentary Commission, *provided always that the accused shall have liberty to adduce or to indicate such further evidence as may be pertinent and useful in reaching a verdict'*.

The witnesses will be called at the expense of the parties.

Even a brief glance at the lists of witnesses is revealing: Mattarella's are for the most part 'big shots': they include two generals, six prefects, eight chiefs of police, three lieutenant-colonels, two magistrates, two *commendatori*, two prelates, three police superintendents, besides all the other inspectors, etc., who have mostly spent only a short time in the area while awaiting promotion. Our side are nearly all poor people who have known their home towns all their lives. Among those of our witnesses who are rejected are Don Giacomo Caiozzo, who for thirty years has been a priest in either Montelepre or Castellammare del Golfo; Professor Ross Waller, expert on Adult Education from the University of Manchester; Ilys Booker, expert in Community Development; Johan Galtung, Professor of Sociology at the University of Oslo and Director of the Institute of Sociology of Conflict: all of them (like Lorenzo Barbera of Partinico, expert in social development, and

Franco Alasia, neither of whom have ever been heard by the Anti-mafia Commission) singularly well qualified to speak on these problems and on the particular form they take in Western Sicily.

7th June 1966

PRESIDING JUDGE: You met Dolci and Alasia? You made declarations to them?

VITO FERRANTE: I am a humble clerk, I live in a small centre, Castellammare del Golfo, which is still dominated by *omertà* and fear. So I know what I'm up against, I know what I risk in making these declarations: but I mean to testify, because I am one of the people who believe in a better world.

I first met Danilo Dolci when he came to Castellammare to hold a conference at the Cultural Club. I had several conversations with him and his colleague Franco Alasia on questions concerning the mafia, and I told them what I knew.

PRESIDING JUDGE: These declarations of yours were transcribed by Dolci and Alasia?

VITO FERRANTE: Yes.

PRESIDING JUDGE: And you signed them?

VITO FERRANTE: Yes. After re-reading them, I signed. I was also called to testify on them before the Parliamentary Antimafia Commission.

PRESIDING JUDGE: The declarations attributed to you will now be read out. You will then say whether you confirm them.

VITO FERRANTE: All right. I would just like to point out the fact that I have no personal spite or resentment against anyone, nor in particular against the Honourable Mattarella.

One of the judges reads out the long declaration numbered 1-2-3: 'In the post-war period the whole town of Castellammare del Golfo used to see Bernardo Mattarella sitting about (even in public places such as the Café Navetta, the Café Russo, the Bar opposite the public gardens) with all the mafiosi of the area: the Rimis, the Plajas, the Magaddinos, the Buccellatos, and all the rest of them . . .'[1]

PRESIDING JUDGE: Is this what you said to Danilo Dolci?

[1] See page 207.

Vito Ferrante: Yes.

Avv. Bellavista: On whose recommendation were you appointed to the Registry office?

Avv. Tarsitano: What's that got to do with it?

Avv. Bellavista (*shouting*): I insist that the question be put.

Vito Ferrante: I was appointed on the recommendation of the Hon. Barone. There is no open competition, so in order to be appointed—in order to get any job at all—there was no other way but to seek a recommendation.

Presiding Judge: So you confirm the declarations? Have you anything else to say?

Vito Ferrante: What you read to me is exactly what I declared to Dolci and Alasia.

I would like to add one important fact.

Three days before the beginning of last April, Giacomo Catalano (who is now barman at the Café Russo, though he used to work at the Viviani Café, now called the Navetta) told me this: 'One evening,' he said, 'I was sent for, on the occasion of the christening of the son of Gaspare Magaddino's sister and Bernardo Stabile, and told to come to their house in Via Roma to cut up ice-cream. In those days the wooden ice-cream bucket was carried by two people on a pole over their shoulders, because it was so heavy. One of these carriers was called Settimo (he's now in a home in Calatafimi), and the other was Ciccio Vitale's father. When I got to Bernardo Stabile's house—it was dark by then—I was just about to start cutting up the ice-cream for the guests when I saw Vincenzo Rimi and his son go up-stairs, together with Bernardo Mattarella, Stellino the capomafia of Alcamo, Magaddino, Liborio Munna, Diego Plaja, the Bonventres: all the local mafia. After a while, Bernardo Stabile came downstairs and said to me: "Cut a bigger bit for Giuliano".'

Presiding Judge: When would this have taken place?

Vito Ferrante: About May '47. Catalano told me about it in the presence of Sciacchitano the whitewasher, too. And I reported this to Don Caiozzo as well as to Dolci and Alasia.

In fact, I remember clearly that Catalano spoke to me about it on two occasions: the second time, he was talking about it to Sciacchitano when I came along.

Catalano also told me that he noticed at the time, with a certain

amount of apprehension, a number of *carabinieri* in the neighbourhood. He was afraid there might be fighting, especially since he'd
heard a shot fired.

Around that time, Catalano also added, Giuliano had come into
the Bar several times for a coffee: and one day a *carabinieri* Inspector
had actually said to Catalano: 'Well! Did you see Giuliano?' To
which it seemed natural to Catalano to answer: 'Why don't you
arrest him then?' The Inspector replied: 'What—do you think
I'm mad?'

I myself also remember hearing one night around that same time
some commotion followed by a shot. The next day I heard that the
bandit Passatempo had been pursued by *carabinieri* while shifting
from the upper to the lower part of town.

Avv. BELLAVISTA: Which party does the witness belong to?
(*Strong protests by defence counsel. Even the Public Prosecutor objects
to the question.*)

The Court allows Bellavista's question.

VITO FERRANTE: I am a member of the Communist Party. And so?

To go back to what I was saying: the mafia gives votes in order to
have certain men in power; it gives in order to get. With my own
eyes I have seen Mattarella and the mafiosi going about town together, and I'm certainly not the only one: it happened in front of
everybody.

Next follows a series of questions and answers concerning the
electoral lists and the split between Mattarella and Barone.

Avv. TARSITANO: Are you aware that in the '63 elections there was
a drop in the Honourable Mattarella's votes?

VITO FERRANTE: Yes. After the clash between Barone and Mattarella, one section of the mafia stopped getting votes for Mattarella,
and in '63 about a thousand preference votes went to Volpe, even
though he'd never been to Castellammare: his canvassers recently
have been Giuseppe Magaddino and Diego Plaja, who are now in
prison for trafficking in drugs.

Avv. TARSITANO: Do you know anything about the two societies
IPAC and SIPAC?

VITO FERRANTE: I know their business was obtaining tunny

and mackerel for canning, and that among their members, besides Liborio and Giuseppe Munna, there were mafiosi like Plaja and Magaddino. There were also other people with clean records.

Avv. Gatti requests that the Court accept as witnesses Giacomo Catalano, Giovanni Sciacchitano, Settimo, Vitale, and Don Caiozzo. The Court reserves its decision.

Next follow, much more quickly, the depositions of Gianni Trapani, ex-Provincial Secretary of the Monarchist Party (for Mattarella), and of Leonardo Liggio, a Palermo bank official (for Volpe).

GIANNI TRAPANI : From things said by the most recent Christian Democrat Provincial Secretaries Occhipinti and Rolla, I understood that the Honourable Mattarella always professed and maintained on the part of the DC an attitude of clear opposition to the mafia. I am informed by my party colleagues, who know it through having followed the meetings of the other candidates in the '63 elections at which I myself was also a candidate, that the Honourable Mattarella at his meetings, and in particular at one in Trapani and another in Alcamo, took up a definite position against the mafia. Also with reference to the '58 elections I was informed that the Honourable Mattarella took the same attitude against the mafia : although I must point out that since on that occasion I was not myself a candidate it was only at Party headquarters that I obtained the information concerning the various candidates present in the area at the time.

I have known the Honourable Mattarella since 1930, since he used to frequent the office of my father, who was also a lawyer. From the time when I returned from being a prisoner of war and continued to exercise the legal profession, whether in the criminal sphere or in the sphere of application of precautionary measures, I have never been approached by the Honourable Mattarella for recommendations or anything else.

LEONARDO LIGGIO : In Corleone in '46 I attended one of Dr Volpe's meetings, which broke up in a far from orderly manner because Volpe had attacked the Separatists who at that time constituted q uite a powerful movement.

The Catholic organization supported Volpe and Gioa, and they in turn did not forget us.

I have two brothers, one of them, like myself, a bank employee, and the other an official in the judiciary: we are nothing to do with the bandit Liggio.

I was Mayor of Corleone from '61 to '64. During my administration the Honourable Mattarella saw to it that Corleone was linked up on the telephone with the outer districts, among them Ficuzza.

Ficuzza has about two hundred voters. Thanks to the concern of the Honourable Mattarella, a home was built at Ficuzza for the children of railway workers: a home which I then visited in the company of the Honourable Mattarella when he was Under-Secretary to the Ministry of Transport.

Dr Navarra was Corleone's Medical Officer of Health; he called himself a Christian Democrat, and if I remember rightly he was a member of the Party for a few years; but he never held any office, or took any part in the political life of the branch.[1]

Avv. Tarsitano exhibits a copy of the record of statements made by Diego Plaja, Gaspare Magaddino and Giuseppe Munna before the examining Justice in Palermo, 8th December 1953. This is placed in the Court files.

11th June 1966

Franco Alasia goes to Castellammare, accompanied by Nino Palermo, a friend and colleague; there he meets Vincenzo Di Gregorio, with whom he has the following conversation outside his carpenter's shop, No. 16 Via Segesta.

FRANCO: Do you know if Catalano the barman really did tell Vito Ferrante what he disclosed in Court in Rome?

DI GREGORIO: Certainly he did—a hundred per cent certain. He actually confirmed it to me. That morning, the day after Ferrante

---

[1] Doctor Navarra (see p. 305) was chairman of the *Bonomiana* of Corleone for several years. Michele Pantaleone in *Mafia e politica* (1962) stated that Navarra was Christian Democrat inspector for the branches of Mezzoiuso, Campofelice, Roccamena, Misilmeri, Bolognetta, Lercara, Godrano, and Marineo: and this has never been contradicted.

gave evidence in Rome, there was that article in the *Giornale di Sicilia*. I'd read the article, but when I met Catalano I pretended I hadn't. 'Here,' he says to me—'listen to what's happened . . .' But did you tell all that to Ferrante? I asked him. Yes, he did, he said. Well then, I said, why d'you want to go back on it now? If you weren't prepared to face up to things, why did you go and tell him?

There was an uproar. They went and called on him: 'What have you done, you wretch, you damned fool!' They made him deny the whole thing: but I knew the truth, because he'd already confirmed it to me that morning.

It's quite true. Ferrante didn't invent it.

These things happened all right. You see where we are now? This is where the bandit Passatempo hid, for three months. At first he was up in that house where the café is, about three hundred metres from here: then he moved down here. The owner of the house was arrested and taken off to Palermo. And who was it got him out of prison? It wasn't me, I can tell you that much! And these are well-known facts, they're common knowledge.

12th June 1966

The *Giornale di Sicilia* states in a despatch from Rome: 'Giacomo Catalano has retracted in a letter to the Court in Rome . . . he describes as "utterly without any foundation of truth" the events and the words attributed to him by Ferrante. He concludes the letter by stating that he is willing to put himself "at the Court's disposal in order to establish, if necessary, the truth of the matter".'

21st June 1966

The Presiding Judge reads the letter from Giacomo Catalano already reported in the *Giornale di Sicilia*. At this point Mattarella's defence exhibits the baptism certificate of Arcangela Stabile: she was indeed born on 6th May 1947 (five days after Portella della Ginestra), but she wasn't baptized till the 27th of July, not in May. I must admit I had been puzzled by one point in the evidence concerning the distinguished celebration over the little girl: would they really have had ice-cream at a party in Castellammare as early as the beginning of May? The certificate produced has settled that doubt at least.

But another worry of quite a different kind was looming. A few minutes before the hearing began, we learnt from our lawyer Fausto Gullo (having had only an indirect hint of it the day before) that he had prepared an application for amnesty on behalf of Franco and me.

But if the judges accepted this request, how could we carry on the argument in public? Hadn't we organized the Press conference for this very purpose? Wouldn't the newspapers announce that we were backing out? And what about the people who had put their faith in all we had been doing so far—what would they think of this? In the few minutes still left to us, Franco and I put these and other questions to him. Gullo, candid and smiling, argued thus: amnesty is a right which, now that it has been won in Parliament, it is one's duty to claim; a Court of law is not the most natural—or the only— place for a trial such as this which is fundamentally of a political nature; however, as long as a trial is in progress, it is supposed to be conducted in Court and not in the papers; besides, nothing will come of this—it is very unlikely that the judges will agree to grant an amnesty: but each of the plaintiffs, including the many who have not yet done so, will be obliged to grant leave to adduce evidence,[1] and the Court will have to recognize this; as for public opinion, even the less well-informed will soon understand anything they may not understand today, while the more knowledgeable understand quite well all the ins and outs of a legal duel.

Unconvinced, especially as we detected hints of uncertainty also in some of our lawyers who were just arriving, but having no confidence whatever in our own knowledge of legal processes (in fact thoroughly convinced of our own ignorance on the matter), trusting

---

[1] The amnesty of 4th June 1966 applied only to libel trials in which the plaintiffs had *not* granted the accused leave to adduce evidence.

(Under Italian libel law the accused is not necessarily allowed to try to establish in his defence that what he said is true and/or common knowledge. By applying for amnesty, Dolci's defence hoped to force the plaintiffs either to grant them leave to adduce evidence, or to drop the case—thereby appearing unwilling to face the evidence. (Tr. note.)

in the serenely authoritative competence of Gullo, and with the hearing already beginning, we gave in.

Everybody listens intently as Gullo speaks in his gentlemanly manner, without raising his voice, following the thread which leads him to the request for the application of the decree of amnesty. Leone and the other lawyers representing the civil parties to the action at first declare themselves opposed, but then one by one all grant leave on behalf of their clients, including Mattarella and Volpe in the matter of the leaflet distributed in Castellammare. The Public Prosecutor opposes Gullo's request, but asks that the Court accept the request of the parties who wish to grant leave to adduce evidence.

The Court withdraws: in the end, its conclusion is that since in effect all parties have now granted leave to adduce evidence, it rejects the request for amnesty. (Next day the headlines of most Italian newspapers announce in various ways: 'Danilo Dolci seeks amnesty but the judges refuse.')

General Luca is called to testify.

GENERAL LUCA: I confirm the position upon which I have been called to testify. I acknowledge as written by me to Bernardo Mattarella the letter dated 1st October '65 of which your Honour now shows me the photostat copy. I can state further that in 1949 when I was sent to Sicily as commander of the forces for the suppression of banditry, I found that the Service had only extremely modest means at its disposal, in fact they were practically non-existent, thus making my task most arduous, indeed impossible. Arms, ammunition, radio, transport, were all inadequate. By chance, I happened to meet in the Castellammare area the Honourable Mattarella, who was then Under-Secretary of State. I introduced myself, and in my official capacity drew his attention to the desperate plight of the forces of law and order which were then supposed to be suppressing banditry, a plight further aggravated by the fact that all activity and collaboration on the part of the Departmental Inspectorate of Public Security had ceased. I therefore begged the Honourable Mattarella to draw the attention of the appropriate quarters in Rome to the situation and to my urgent requirements.

He promised he would do what he could about it, but also urged me to take firm action against mafia and banditry.

Within about forty-five days I was sent all the equipment necessary for the carrying out of my task. I recollect that on that occasion I said to the Honourable Mattarella: 'Take care, now, in case they're after your skin, the mafia and the bandits.' And the Under-Secretary said the same to me.

Avv. DE MATTEIS: To what authority was General Luca responsible, at that time, as head of the forces for the repression of banditry?

GENERAL LUCA: Directly to the Minister for the Interior, Scelba.

Avv. DE MATTEIS: And the Honourable Mattarella was Under-Secretary to what?

GENERAL LUCA: To the Ministry of Transport, I think.

Avv. GAETA: Is it true that the witness, as he himself admitted in person in his statement as a witness at the Viterbo trial,[1] gave the bandit Pisciotta a testimonial for good service bearing the forged signature of Scelba which the latter publicly repudiated?

Counsel for Mattarella and Volpe object to the question, the Public Prosecutor objects, and the Court rejects it.

Avv. OZZO: Did you consider the frequent contacts you had with Pisciotta an effective weapon against banditry? Is it true that Pisciotta used to write to you addressing you as '*maestro*, doctor, friend'?

Mattarella's and Volpe's counsel object, the Public Prosecutor objects: the Court rejects the question.

Avv. GAETA: Why did you circulate a false version of the death of the bandit Giuliano? Do you confirm that your promotion to the rank of General happened after this? (*The usual opposition. Rejected 'because the question is absolutely irrelevant to the object of the trial and*

---

[1] The extraordinary mass trial in 1950–51 of the bandits of Salvatore Giuliano's band, including his cousin and lieutenant Pisciotta, accused of participation in the Portella della Ginestra massacre (see page 223). During the trial it became clear that certain police, *carabinieri*, and DC politicians were deeply involved, but the evidence has been suppressed ever since. (See 'Mafia and politics' by Michele Pantaleone.) (Tr. note.)

neither pertinent nor useful to its ends.') But how else are we to check the witness's reliability?[1]

[1] See also this extract from the judgement of the Viterbo Court (pp. 92 and 527):

'. . . Certain critical observations must also be made with regard even to two officers belonging to the bandit suppression forces: it is clear that the Court means to make explicit mention of the then Colonel Luca, and Captain Perenze . . .

'. . . The major contribution to Pisciotta's alibi was furnished by these two *carabinieri* officers who were with him from the end of June until several days after the death of Giuliano. It is plain to everybody that the Court expressly refers to the then Colonel Luca and Captain Perenze. The former sought to consolidate Pisciotta's alibi with regard to the X-ray, the latter with regard to the illness of the accused. Undoubtedly Luca was the more prudent of the two . . .'

See also the proceedings against Frank Garofalo and twenty others (pp. 149–150, vol. IV): '1965, 16th November, in Palermo, at Police H.Q. in the offices of the Mobile Squad. Before the undersigned officers appears *Salemi, Girolamo*, son of the late Calcedonio Salemi and the late Leonarda Lucania; born at Lercara Friddi 23rd March 1898, resident in Palermo, Via Vittorio Alfieri no. 14; who upon being questioned makes the following statement: I do not work, but live off the income from a property I own in Lercara Friddi, and am also supported by my sons who are in clerical jobs.

'After various ups and downs, after 1952 I began to associate with my cousin Salvatore Lucania, better known as Lucky Luciano, who at that time lived in Naples and often visited Palermo, staying at the Albergo Sole or at Hotel delle Palme.

'. . . I remember that during those years, i.e. from '53 to '58, when he came to Palermo Lucania used to meet Italo-Americans and other Palermitans held to be individuals belonging to the criminal underworld. Among these I recollect Giuseppe Genco Russo of Mussomeli. All the above named, as well as others whose names I do not remember, used to meet Lucania either at Hotel delle Palme or at the Albergo Sole but, I repeat, I parted company with Lucania whenever he was to meet the said persons, because I believe he himself did not trust me too much and thought I might pass on facts he did not want anyone else to know about. Besides, I was glad to disassociate myself because I had no wish to be involved in dubious business.

'With regard in particular to Giuseppe Genco Russo of Mussomeli, I remember him meeting Lucania both at the Albergo Sole and at Hotel delle Palme. However the pair of them always used to withdraw and I was never present to hear their discussions. I also remember that Genco Russo used to call Lucania "Don Turiddu".

'. . . In 1958 at Hotel delle Palme Lucania sent for me and told me with annoyance that he had received a request for money on the part of persons concerned with the election campaign of Senator Santi Savarino of Partinico. I also remember that Lucania was staying in the Albergo Sole and that, towards the end of May I think, he met the aforesaid Senator Santi Savarino and the *cara-*

Avv. De Matteis: Do you know and remember the names of the persons indicated by Pisciotta as the instigators of the massacre of Portella della Ginestra?

General Luca: I do not know whether Pisciotta mentioned names at the Viterbo trial. In an interview with him I tried to get the names of the murderers, but he did not tell me any.

Presiding Judge: But did you ask him for the names of the instigators?

General Luca: No . . .

Francesco Inturrisi: I have been Chief of Police of Palermo Province since 1st February 1965, and before that, from June '62, I was Chief of Police of the Province of Trapani. Before that, I was Deputy Chief in Palermo. In my professional capacity and with reference to the periods and the places in which I served, I can deny —indeed, I can positively declare that the Honourable Mattarella never applied to me, or to my office, in the interests of mafiosi.

Public Prosecutor: After Dolci's revelations, did you make any investigations on the persons indicated as mafiosi?

Chief Inturrisi: We did carry out certain investigations. In particular on two persons indicated in Dolci's dossier: we collected documents which we have passed on to the Antimafia Commission.

Avv. Ozzo: Did the investigations also concern Vincenzo Rimi of Alcamo?

Chief Inturrisi: As far as that particular person is concerned, there was no need for any investigations: I know perfectly well that Rimi is a mafioso.

Avv. Ozzo: Do you know Anca Martinez? Did you start any investigations on him?

Chief Inturrisi: I know Anca Martinez and his brothers, who are men of good repute in Marsala. No investigation has been carried out by my office on Anca Martinez.

---

binieri General Luca, at the Hotel delle Palme: for a certain length of time (I cannot specify exactly) these three conferred together, after which Lucania sent for me and handed me three hundred thousand lire, which I was to hand over (as I duly did) to a certain Colonel in the Medical Corps, whose name I do not remember exactly, who was concerned with Savarino's election campaign. I should add further that Lucania was somewhat annoyed by the said request and at having had to pay out such a sum in consequence.'

Avv. Ozzo shows the witness a photograph of Mattarella accompanied by several other people: 'Prominent among these is a well-known mafioso, do you recognize him?'

The Chief of Police recognizes, besides Mattarella, only Senator Maggi and a brother of Anca Martinez: 'I am not qualified to recognize any others.'

Avv. TARSITANO: What, you don't recognize a mafiosi as notorious as Vincenzo Martinez, who actually belongs to the Province of Trapani of which you have been Chief of Police?

CHIEF INTURRISI: I know of Martinez' little encounters with the law, but I am not acquainted with him personally.

28th June 1966

At this hearing the examinations are more rapid.

BARTOLOMEO VIVONA confirms that he collaborated with Ferrante and Varvara on a section of the document numbered 1–2–3, and confirms that he signed. He can personally testify that all those named and indicated there as mafiosi (a large proportion of them now under arrest) are men who were with Mattarella and canvassed for him at elections. He continues:

But at the '59 elections, one section of the mafia forces specified in the document supported Mattarella, and the other Barone. In the '63 elections one section continued to support Mattarella, but the other section backed Volpe instead of Barone: in '63 the Magaddinos and the Buccellatos backed Volpe.

All this is known to me personally, and it is also common knowledge among the citizens of Castellammare.

VARVARA ANTONINO: I am a local Councillor of Castellammare, elected on the Communist list. Concerning the document numbered 1–2–3 which has been read to me I can say that, in view of my age, I am only qualified to confirm matters regarding the political life of Mattarella from '59 onwards: subject to this qualification, I can confirm all that is said in the document.

In the '58, '59 and '63 elections, Mattarella's chief election campaigners were the Bonventres and the Fiordilinos. Barone's main backer was Magaddino.

. . . It is true that in '58 Barone stood in the local elections on the civic list which also included Communists and dissident Christian Democrats; in '59 he was active in Salvio Milazzo's party.

I myself have first-hand knowledge that during the elections the Bonventres and the Fiordilinos went round from house to house and also approached voters outside the polling stations just as they were going in to vote.

AGOSTINO MESSANA confirms document no. 8[1] when it is read to him; his statements were made on several occasions, and he signed. He adds:

For the elections the mafiosi handed out leaflets telling the people to give the preference vote to Mattarella: I know this because it went on quite openly, I could see it happening for myself, and also because since I was a Regional Deputy citizens of various political trends reported it to me with protests.

I would like to give just one example of how things work even within the same party. A few months ago Giuseppe La Monica, head of the DC group in Alcamo, reported to me that in June '64 on the occasion of the DC Provincial congress he was approached by Professor Di Bernardo and urged to vote for Mattarella in these words: 'If you want to live, vote for Mattarella. Remember your father is a Council employee, and you've got little brothers.'

PIERO PACE, member of the railwaymen's branch of CISL in Palermo, doesn't know what 'mafia' means—in his own words: 'I do not know the meaning of the word "mafia".'

From 1960 to '62 the Honourable Volpe took an active interest in us railwaymen, so much so that he was always willing to receive us, whatever the circumstances: with the result that in '63 we were delighted to be able to repay his interest and concern with our votes.

I wish to point out that the people who interested themselves on behalf of the Honourable Volpe were Salvatore Mitolo, Giuseppe Arcoleo and Michele Sacco, local Councillors: since Mitolo was elected a local Councillor with about six thousand votes and Arcoleo with four thousand, these two alone were sufficient to reach the preferential minimum, without counting the other preference votes which likewise went to Volpe.

I remember there were big rallies of DC adherents and railway workers and trade unionists, which the Honourable Volpe attended; on one occasion in Castelvetrano they waited for him patiently for four hours.

In Western Sicily there are about eight thousand railwaymen. I know that the Honourable Mattarella, too, was remembered by railway employees through having been Minister of Transport and Posts.

MICHELE SACCO: confirms the foregoing declaration by his colleague: Volpe showed 'timely concern' and took effective action towards solving the railwaymen's special problems 'even with personal sacrifice—indeed even when he was ill'. 'In the '63 elections we demonstrated our gratitude to Volpe by dispersing throughout Sicily to get votes for the 'Volpe–De Castillo' partnership, in conjunction with Catholic Action: the result was that the Honourable Volpe carried off about thirty thousand preference votes in the '63 elections.'

INSPECTOR SALVATORE GRIFASI: I have been in command of the Castellammare Station since July '58, and I can deny that the Honourable Mattarella ever asked me or my employees for favours towards mafiosi and other people of the area convicted of crimes. I have never seen the Honourable Mattarella in the company of mafiosi or elements considered as such. I have never declared that I was unable to act with regard to certain individuals because they were under political protection.

Whenever Mattarella comes to Castellammare he is greeted by everybody alike, regardless of their polical colour.

Summer 1966

Partinico. One of the witnesses rings up from a nearby town: 'I was going down the street when the son of the mafioso X spat at me.

What should I do?' He is tense, but bearing up well. I tell him with a smile that the same thing had already happened to me.

A week later, he rings again: they have spat at him again, and a few days before that someone openly warned and half threatened him.

Some go-betweens, to the father of a person who went to give evidence before the Parliamentary Antimafia Commission: 'Why doesn't your son retract, and mind his own business? Doesn't he realize he may lose his job? What's induced him to go against the big men, against the mafia? The big ones are big, and it's the small men who pay. There's nothing to be done against the mafia. The mafia doesn't forgive. Your son is young still. Something might happen to him.'

To another, also a witness at the Antimafia: 'You went and told tales to the Antimafia. You're a traitor. You'll all end up in prison, the whole lot of you. You watch out, because if you agree to go to Court in Rome the worst could happen to you.'

To another witness at the Antimafia: 'You shouldn't go and give evidence in Court. You ought to forgive.'
   'It's not a question of forgiving or not forgiving—personal things don't come into it. It's impossible to keep quiet any longer, because if we do we become responsible for whatever may happen . . .'
   'Well, we can come to some agreement . . .'

In Castellammare Franco again meets Di Gregorio who tells him: 'I met Settimo, the man who carried the ice-cream bucket to the famous christening that Ferrante told about in Court. He'd got leave from the old people's home in Calatafimi to come here for the local feast day. I asked him if he remembered the incident, and he did, and specified that Mattarella was also there on that occasion, and that (to use his own words) "the house was full of scoundrels".'

Another witness at the Antimafia is told: 'What's induced you to compromise yourself like this? If you'll say it's not true when you're called up to confirm before the Court, then they'll get you a job in Palermo with Vaselli.'

'In the town's main Bar, on the Piazza, you often see certain mafiosi who are supposed to be under special restrictions calmly sitting there up till ten or eleven at night. The *carabinieri* can see that they're out and about: aren't they supposed to be home by sunset? One of them goes to play lansquenet somewhere else in town: the *carabinieri* come in, they see him, but they just pretend not to notice anything.

'When people see this sort of thing going on they say: "Anti-mafia? That's a lot of nonsense!" People go by what they see with their own eyes here in town.

'Nowadays when I go out into the country, I have to be on my guard.'

'But what does your brother know about these things? It'll end up with the *carabinieri* coming to the house to get him. Something nasty could happen to him . . .'

A friend of ours having a coffee at a bar counter happens to find himself near a group of semi-mafiosi.

'Danilo's pushing things too far . . .'

'Nothing'll happen to him, he's well known.'

'Kennedy was well known too—a lot better known than Danilo . . .'

One man who had given evidence to the Antimafia Commission is suspended from his job. Others are finding it more difficult to get work now. One man is unable to find work at all in his own town. One person (he was only friendly from a distance, he hadn't even given evidence) is suddenly and mysteriously transferred to the North.

At least twice, by night, as I am walking along a poorly lit street, I see a car following me in a peculiar way until I come to where there are other people. Another time in a very quiet street a character I have never seen before drives past me and back again and presses me with heavy politeness to get into his car.

A young man who had spontaneously made us a declaration of considerable interest comes to us in tears: 'I can't go on with it. They're making my life impossible at home. When I go out my mother's so frightened for me that I'm afraid it may kill her. I've just got to retract.'

Another, a robust fellow who not so long ago had serenely talked to us about dealings between the mafia and his local politician, comes and tells us that if he is called by the Court he will commit suicide: he doesn't want to become a traitor[1] in the eyes of the people.

Franco (some time ago his door was forced open in his absence and his place ransacked: the visitors certainly weren't chicken thieves) from time to time is roused to anger, but then carries on with his work again, patient, diligent and meticulous.

No one has risked threatening the few really firm and resolute witnesses. And meanwhile many other people are opening up, and as things become clearer and they probe more deeply, they too become convinced.

11th October 1966

The trial in Rome reopens.

I cannot understand—perhaps because I'm not in the legal profession—why these hearings, in what is supposed to be a 'summary' trial, are held at such long and irregular intervals, and at such very odd times: on 27th June, for example, from one o'clock to 4.45; the same on 21st June; on 28th June (as today) from 4 p.m. onwards, in an absolutely empty Palace of Justice. What is certain is that this makes it more difficult for public opinion to follow the proceedings; and once people lose the thread, they lose interest. And so it happens that at a hearing as important as today's, only a handful of people are present.

LODOVICO CORRAO (formerly a prominent Christian Democrat official, now an Independent Deputy) is the first to be cross-questioned at length: he confirms his declaration, number 9 in the dossier,[2] and again describes how Leonardo Renda (who was a close friend and colleague of his) was murdered by Giuliano's bandits, as

---

[1] *Infame*—by breaking the code of *omertà*. (Tr. note.)
[2] See p. 217.

a scapegoat, for not having used his supposed influence with Mattarella and other fellow Christian Democrats to get them to keep their
promises to give the bandits protection in exchange for the votes
they had procured. Corrao also describes how when Superintendent
Carbonetto began his investigation of the murder along these lines
he was immediately transferred to Sardinia; all his findings to date,
including the deposition made by Corrao himself, disappeared from
the files; and Inspector General Messana issued instructions that
the aim of the investigations should thenceforth be to confirm the
hypothesis of a crime committed for profit.

Corrao again describes the very friendly terms Mattarella was on
with leading mafiosi of Alcamo such as Vincenzo Rimi and Giovanni
Stellino. Finally, in answer to a question by Avv. Tarsitano, he says
that from 1956 onwards attempts were made on his life.

VERO MONTI is questioned next: he confirms his declaration, no. 13,[1]
but specifies that Guido Anca Martinez is regarded in Marsala as
the brain behind the mafia organization with regard to the affair of
the Genna estate. He then tells the story of this transaction: in spite
of an official decree of expropriation on the estate, even after several
years two-thirds of the share-croppers had still not succeeded in
acquiring any of the land. Eventually it transpired that a large part o
the estate had been acquired by six members of the Bua family
(several of them well-known mafiosi); five members of the Scimemi
family (another family with a mafia background); Pellegrino Vittorio, Doctor to the *Bonomiana* (of which Giuseppe Bua was chairman) and ex-Mayor of Marsala; and the wife of Anca Martinez:
Martinez himself was supposed to have been acting in the affair on
behalf of the bishop who also had a claim on the estate.

The Presiding Judge now calls upon Salvatore Capria, a labourer
from Montelepre; his declaration, no. 15,[2] is read aloud, and he
confirms that he made it. When the Judge asks him when he made
the declaration, Capria at first doesn't understand the question, but
when the legal jargon is translated into ordinary language, he
answers: 'I reported to Dolci in '65. The things I spoke of happened in '46.'

[1] See p. 220.   [2] See pp. 221–222.

Avv. BELLAVISTA: Are you employed by Dolci? Do you work for him for pay?

SALVATORE CAPRIA: No, though I've known him a long time.

I should add that in February 1966 I told Dolci and Franco Alasia other things, too, which I also signed.

One day in '47 when I was working out in the Parrini district of Partinico, I saw a posh car draw up: it hooted three times, and out of the bushes where they'd been hiding came the bandits Giuliano, Peppino Passatempo, and Genovese. They went off in the direction of the village of Parrini. When I'd finished my work, I went up to the village to buy cigarettes, and I saw Rosario Candela armed with a Tommy-gun standing guard in the archway which led through into a big courtyard. That evening, about eleven o'clock, Candela (who is a cousin of my wife's) called at my house, and told us that Mattarella had come to Parrini to meet Giuliano, Passatempo and Genovese; he told us that things were going to go better from now on.

Also in 1947, Candela told me one evening that Mattarella had gone to Genovese's house, no. 60 Via Di Misa, where he'd also met Giuliano and Passatempo.

In March 1947, I was called by the barber Iacona into his house in Piazza Ventimiglia, and there I was asked by Passatempo to join their band; they were offering me a thousand lire a day. At that time us labourers were getting a hundred lire a day, and a loaf of bread cost a hundred lire. I was almost tempted to agree. But when Passatempo said to me: 'Don't worry, it's quite all right to join us because we've got Mattarella on our side, and Colonel Luca, and the Prince of Alliata, and Scelba,' then I refused, because I knew these were people you couldn't trust.

A few weeks after that, on the First of May 1947, there was the massacre of Portella della Ginestra, and then I realized why they'd been trying to recruit men.

One evening in January 1948 I saw that Inspector Calandra and Santucci were in Frank Mannino's[1] house, sitting at table and eating with them.

I didn't tell Dolci everything all at once, because it makes you scared—even now—to talk about these things.

[1] One of Giuliano's band. (Tr. note.)

GIUSEPPE LUMIA: I was Magistrate in Castellammare del Golfo from '48 to '58. I can deny that the Honourable Mattarella ever applied to me, in my official capacity, or interfered with police organization in favour of mafiosi.

I have never been subjected to pressure by any political party in favour of mafiosi.

SAVERIO FRASCA: I and many railway employees in the Department did indeed devote ourselves in '63 to achieving political victory for Volpe, even though the trade union organization of which I am head is not affiliated to the CISL.[1] We had a debt of gratitude: I know that many people even of different political parties voted for Volpe.

ANTONINO BUCCELLATO: I am on good, indeed friendly terms with Volpe, having also been chief of his private secretarial staff. In 1963 I gladly went to campaign for him in the provinces of Palermo and Trapani, and in Castellammare, my native town. As Under-Secretary to the Ministry of Transport Volpe concerned himself with the problems of the Railways; I, too, got in touch with the trades unionists to procure him votes.

Volpe's success in Castellammare in '63 was also partly due to my activity in certain spheres of the party and of the clergy.

I was secretary to the Honourable Mattarella from '57 to '58: I can affirm that he always issued directives to the effect that no interference should be practised either as regards the judicial authorities or as regards the police, and I can affirm that such directives were always scrupulously observed.

I remember that in '53 the Prefect Mastrobuono revealed to me the discontent of certain Sicilian elements, by which I took him to mean the mafiosi, who were complaining about the detachment and indifference of the Honourable Mattarella towards them.

In '53, I accompanied the Honourable Mattarella to Camporeale: I deny that Magaddino was present, or any others considered by us to be mafiosi.

NATALE GIAMMALVA acknowledges the following declaration to be

---

[1] The USFI is affiliated to the neo-Fascist CISNAL.

his, specifying: 'I had first-hand knowledge of the facts there reported.'

24

I remember very clearly that for the general election of '53 Bernardo Mattarella, then Under-Secretary, came to Camporeale: with him were a number of people in cars from Alcamo and Castellammare. They all got out at the electrical shed at the end of town, and came in a sort of procession up to the Piazza. With Mattarella, among others I don't know, were Gaspare Magaddino the mafioso bailiff of the Marchese estate, and a relative of Vincenzo Rimi.

The men who went to meet them were Pasquale Almerigo, who was Mayor at the time (later he was murdered); the old Vanni Sacco, undisputed capomafia of the area; Giuseppe and Benedetto Misuraca, Vanni Sacco's lieutenants and well known as criminals even then; Don Angelino Rizzuto, whom the police were unable to touch even though he was a notorious mafioso; and (if I remember rightly) also Nino Strada, who had been convicted for robbery with violence and criminal association in connection with Giuliano's band, and had then emigrated illegally and was later repatriated from America by Interpol. The majority of these mafiosi used to vote Liberal, but they were there to honour Mattarella—they were allies in government. Vanni Sacco and Rimi were intimate friends, on the closest terms. The old Vincenzo Rimi used to come here often to visit Vanni Sacco.

They all went up to the DC branch together; Vanni Sacco and Almerigo were closest to Mattarella, in the most respected position; but there were also a number of people who had just come to look on. Don Vincenzo Ferrante came along too with a group from Catholic Action, with flags, and there were also ordinary people there in good faith.

At this point occurred one of the most interesting incidents, I think, in the whole trial. Up stood Avv. Bellavista (I was able to watch him closely since he was no more than four metres away), and in his big confident voice he asked Giammalva, a small peasant: 'How could Vanni Sacco have been with Mattarella? Don't you know who

Vanni Sacco used to get votes for?' Giammalva, calm and precise, agreed that capomafia Vanni Sacco did indeed usually get votes for the Liberals: in fact, he remembered very well (and at this point I saw big drops of sweat appear on Bellavista's wide forehead as if we were in a Turkish bath) how on other occasions the dreaded Vanni Sacco had gone around town with none other than Avv. Bellavista himself; but it was also true that in local elections from '52 onwards Christian Democrats and Liberals had stood in coalition, which was the reason why Vanni Sacco had also honoured prominent Christian Democrats.

Avv. Bellavista subsided, grumbling that it wasn't 'in good taste' to make 'personal attacks'.

ALBERTO MANDRACCHIA: In September '65 I met Dolci, to whom I made the declaration just read,[1] which I confirm. I have direct personal knowledge of the facts there stated.

Concerning Avv. Russo of Sciacca, I can say that he is a nephew of Michele Russo who was in prison for a long time, and that he himself has been in trouble with the Law. But I read in the papers just recently that Russo declared at this trial that he had been acquitted.

18th October 1966

In addition to the requests for further witnesses presented by the lawyers of both sides, Avv. Leone asks that an article in *Specchio* (24th April '66) be added to the files, and also that Giuliano's sister Mariannina be called as a witness. The Court reserves its decision.

GAETANO D'ANDREA: The declaration, number 42,[2] which you have read to me is the one which I signed.

From the context of my interview with Dolci, at which other people were also present, it was clear that I was not speaking as an eye witness but reporting things well known to the population in general.

Avv. LEONE: In the declaration made to Dolci the witness says

[1] See pp. 226–227, no. 28.
[2] See page 230.

that on 12th April '55 during a ceremony in Alia, Mattarella was in
the company of a number of capimafia. Does the witness know if,
besides Mattarella, there were also present Cardinal Ruffini, the
departmental Head of Palermo Railways, and the chief Judge of the
Palermo Court of Appeal?

GAETANO D'ANDREA: At that time I was a correspondent on the
Palermo paper *L'Ora*; I was meant to be at the meeting, but because
of a series of hitches it was over by the time I arrived. But I made
enquiries, and was informed about the presence of the people mentioned in the letter I wrote to Dolci. I do not know whether the
departmental Head of Railways was there, but I do remember that
Cardinal Ruffini was.

I must point out that certain facts, because of their significance
and the weight they carried in the circumstances, made a more lasting impression on the people than other facts considered to be of
secondary importance: thus the presence of mafiosi at that public
ceremony remained more vividly in their memories than other
details. I should also point out that the ceremony took place on the
11th, not the 12th.

AVV. LEONE: Do you know whether a cousin of Mattarella's, Vito
Ricotti, treasurer at the Alia Savings Bank, concerned himself with
procuring votes for his relative in Parliament?

GAETANO D'ANDREA: I don't know. All I can say is that the Alia
Savings Bank gave credit to mafiosi and accepted bills backed by
them.

AVV. BELLAVISTA: The original page signed by you has several
corrections . . .

GAETANO D'ANDREA: The crossings-out were due to efforts to
perfect the text, and in any case were made before I signed.

AVV. MORRA: Does the witness belong to any party?

GAETANO D'ANDREA: To the Communist Party.

AVV. TARSITANO: In one of the previous hearings, the Honourable
Volpe declared that his preference votes in Alia were procured by
the family of Doctor Sagona. Can the witness tell us anything about
this gentleman?

GAETANO D'ANDREA: I don't know Doctor Alfredo Sagona personally. However I do know that he comes of a family of long-
standing mafia traditions, which was also involved in the Mori

investigations. One of Alfredo's brothers was indicated as a capo-mafia; another brother, who is now dead, was a priest.

PIETRO RESTIVO: I was Secretary of the DC in Gangi, which is about sixty kilometres from Alia. In Alia Volpe was received at the Nursery of which the Mother Superior is a compatriot of mine. Shortly before that the Honourable Volpe had held a political meeting in the DC branch.

Padre Botindari whom I met recently told me he had never seen Volpe.

MICHELANGELO MERCANTI: I entirely confirm the declarations just read to me, numbered 36 in the dossier,[1] as I have already confirmed them to the Antimafia Commission. I remember distinctly that during one of the post-war elections in Villafrati Mattarella attended the rallies surrounded on all sides by well-known local mafiosi.

PRESIDING JUDGE: In the dossier you gave names. Can you repeat them?

MICHELANGELO MERCANTI: Certainly. They were types like Antonino and Pietro Santomauro (who was later killed by *lupara*); his son Turi; Salvatore Spitalieri and Salvatore Badami . . .

PRESIDING JUDGE: Can you remember any particular circumstances?

MICHELANGELO MERCANTI: I remember that Mattarella was on friendly terms with all of them, and in one or two cases even affectionate terms.

Meanwhile in Villafrati there was a whole series of murders which went unpunished: the culprit was never found.

In Villafrati Mattarella gets a high proportion of preference votes.

INGEGNERE NICOLÒ RIZZO: I work in Palermo but whenever possible I return to Castellammare. I can state that never, while I have been in Castellammare, has the Honourable Mattarella been in the habit of frequenting the Catalano restaurant, still less of associating with mafia elements.

[1] See pp. 227–228.

I first stood as Christian Democrat candidate in '51, and was elected Deputy in one Regional Government. I had occasion to speak with Mattarella concerning the preparation of the lists, and I remember that he included only individuals of perfect moral rectitude. In Provincial congresses likewise the party and Mattarella further stressed their firm opposition to all that was not clearly moral, for the elevation of the electoral masses. I remember also that Corrao, in the 1956 congress, delivered a public eulogy on the Honourable Mattarella: nor am I aware that Corrao ever complained, all the time he was in the DC, of collusion between the DC and the mafia.

GIROLAMO BENINATI: I have known Mattarella since 1932. In '43 after the landings he came to greet his friends in Alcamo, where he had attended the Grammar school. At that time Mattarella was provincial director of Catholic Action. The DC was reconstituted, and in '48 I was appointed secretary, a post I still hold.

Out of family tradition I have always opposed the mafia. In this firm position I have always been backed up by the Honourable Mattarella who at a rally in '63 made a tough speech against the mafiosi.

Renda, who was also opposed to the mafia, likewise confided to me that Mattarella upheld him in this position.

Corrao never told me that Renda had informed him that he was being threatened by the mafia for failure to fulfil election promises. After Corrao's statement I approached my client Serafino Mancuso: he denied having voted for Mattarella, denied ever knowing him, and said that in fact in '65 he voted for Corrao.

GIACOMO ILARDO: I confirm the declaration numbered 38, 39[1] which has been read to me. I was a local Councillor in Lercara from '62 to '66, and I lived there continuously from '60 till '62. After that I lived in Termini Imerese, but often went to Lercara. I learned directly from Ferrara's miners that in the 1958 elections and subsequent ones their employer forced them to support Mattarella, on pain of losing their jobs.

Also present at the conversation I had with Dolci (with whom I

[1] See page 229.

had already collaborated in previous years on the studies published under the titles *Inchiesta a Palermo*[1] and *Spreco*[2]) were Gaetano Romano, the miner Ficarotta, and another miner: they also gave Dolci detailed declarations to this effect.

VINCENZO OCCHIPINTI: I have known the Honourable Mattarella since 1950. In 1951 I became DC Provincial secretary in Trapani. In accordance with the ideas of the Honourable Mattarella, whom I used to meet often, I always saw to it that the party maintained a firm attitude of detachment and intransigence towards the mafia: to the point of hesitating to have any dealings, even at election time, with individuals who, though not themselves unworthy, nevertheless had connections of some kind with the mafia.

In the Provincial Congresses of '51 and '56, Professor Calcara and Professor Marrone made speeches of firm intransigence against the phenomenon of the mafia, and the same theme was later re-echoed by the Honourable Mattarella.

BARTOLO GALLO: As a DC Provincial Secretary I was against the attempted re-entry of Nino Barone into the DC as proposed to me by the then Regional Secretary D'Angelo. I knew that my attitude was shared by the party, and in particular by the Honourable Mattarella.

Avv. TARSITANO: Were you chairman of the *Oceania* Society, with capital of one million lire?

BARTOLO GALLO: Yes, but not for long.

Avv. TARSITANO: Is it true that the *Oceania* Society acquired a fishing boat for the sum of three hundred and fifty million lire?

Mattarella's lawyers object. The Public Prosecutor suppresses this question in favour of another to be put by Avv. Tarsitano.

Avv. TARSITANO (*smiling*): Who are the working partners and who are the secret partners in the *Oceania* Society?

Mattarella's lawyers object. The Public Prosecutor observes that the Court can make its own enquiries to ascertain who are the working partners: as for the non-working partners, the question is irrelevant. The Court does not allow the question.

[1] *To Feed the Hungry* (1959).   [2] *Waste* (1963).

ARGANGELO CATALANO: For thirty years, up till five years ago, I ran a restaurant in Castellammare. I deny that the Honourable Mattarella ever frequented my premises.

Avv. Ozzo: Is it true that after the arrival of the Americans your premises had to be closed down for about three months?

ARGANGELO CATALANO: Yes, for contraband. It was the Allies who had my place closed, following a report by the then Mayor Padre Giacomo Caiozzo. But when the Prefect Superintendent took over the reins of the local administration, he ordered me to re-open.

GIUSEPPE PULEO confirms having signed the declaration no. 32, 33 which is read to him: he can confirm the section he knows about; the other part of the declaration was made by Stefano Venuti, who signed with him. When he has to talk about the capomafia Manzella, murdered a few years ago by means of a bomb, and other mafiosi still living in his town, Puleo is more than a little frightened.

Avvocato Bellavista and the Public Prosecutor then ask me to clarify certain details, which I do.

PIETRO LOMBARDO (*First Honorary President of the Court of Cassation*): I was born in Castellammare and I have known the Honourable Mattarella, who is younger than me, since he was little. I have always lived in Rome and usually return to my native town only in summer.

I have followed the political career of the Honourable Mattarella, and have met him often. I can affirm that, as far as is in my knowledge, he has always maintained an attitude of dignified and firm detachment from the world of the mafia.

I also knew the Honourable Mattarella's father, a good man who had no connection with the mafia, employed as agent by the Foderà family: and I deny that this was a mafia family or in any way suspected of having connections with the mafia.

Avv. TARSITANO: Doesn't the witness know that the bailiff and manager to the Foderà family was Gaspare Magaddino?

PIETRO LOMBARDO: I am not aware of that. I know that I used to hear rumours linking the name of Magaddino with the mafia.

ENZO CULICCHIA: I made the acquaintance of Dolci in March '65, on the occasion of a demonstration in Roccamena at which I was present, with others, in my capacity as Mayor.

I then met Dolci again at the Study Centre in Partinico, on his invitation: he was conducting an enquiry with a view to finding out whether there had been any collusion between the Honourable Mattarella and the mafia, and he asked me if I could furnish him with any information on the subject. I replied that not only was I not aware that the Honourable Deputy had any connections with the mafia, but that in fact I had constant proof to the contrary, the Honourable Mattarella having always, for as long as I have been in the DC party, endeavoured by his counsel to avert and prevent any infiltration into the party by elements in any way connected with the mafia.

AVV. TARSITANO: But didn't the questions and answers at the interview refer only to the situation in Partanna of which you had direct experience?

ENZO CULICCHIA: In Partanna and the whole Province.

AVV. TARSITANO: To your knowledge, what did Dolci say about Partanna at the Press conference and in the dossier?

ENZO CULICCHIA: I noticed that he said Mattarella hadn't received mafia votes in Partanna.

AVV. TARSITANO: Didn't you point out to Dolci, and subsequently on more than one occasion to Lorenzo Barbera (in charge of social work at the Study Centre), that the enquiry would be fairer and more useful if it referred not just to Mattarella but to all politicians of the area?

ENZO CULICCHIA: . . . I don't think so.

PUBLIC PROSECUTOR (*to Danilo Dolci*): Why didn't you get Culicchia to sign his declaration?

DANILO DOLCI: I asked him only about Partanna because I knew he didn't have close enough knowledge of other areas in the same Province—for instance, Castellammare, even though it is quite near. As for his reply concerning Partanna, I had no reason to doubt it, particularly as it was confirmed to me by other sources that mafia activity in Partanna was negligible. Culicchia was only very recently made DC Provincial Secretary.

I must point out, though, that not only did Culicchia say both to me and to Lorenzo Barbera that it would be opportune to extend the enquiry to cover the whole phenomenon of collusion between mafiosi and politicians, but, to make himself clearer, by way of an example he quoted three or four names of Christian Democrats in the Province of Trapani and Agrigento—I don't remember exactly which.

PUBLIC PROSECUTOR: Who did you get to sign, and when?

DANILO DOLCI: In general I was particularly careful about, and got people to sign, those declarations which by the nature of the facts they contained involved particular responsibility.

There were three cases in which I did not ask people to sign their declarations: out of faith in what they were saying, specially if it was not particularly significant; sometimes out of respect, in order not to offend people, even if their declarations were extremely serious (as in the case of Don Giacomo Caiozzo); and to enable people to talk about what they had to tell me as calmly and in as much detail as possible, specially when I wasn't sure whether they were prepared to undertake responsibility: if we were to be called to account for our work, then Franco Alasia and I were prepared to undertake responsibility for them. This also seemed to us the most educative way.

GAETANO ROMANO: I confirm the declarations you have read to me:[1] that is what I said to Dolci in a conversation in '65; also present then were Giacomo Ilardo (who signed with me), and Giusto Panepinto and Ficarotta (who signed their two declarations).[2]

Ficarotta and Panepinto, miners, also reported that Ferrara used to ask to see their voter's certificates, and took note of the section where they went to vote; and they said that for the General Election the Ferraras handed out slips with the names of the people to whom they were to give the preference votes: these names were marked with numbers which were arranged in a different way for each voter so that they could be identified. Being a baker, I am in contact with the miners: I have heard the same things repeated by many others, such as Giovanni Scimeca, Salvatore Dalanti, Giuseppe Milena, and others of Lercara, where I have lived since '54.

[1] See page 229, nos. 38, 39.   [2] See page 229, no. 40.

One of the judges slowly and clearly reads out declaration no. 4 in the dossier.[1]

SAVERIO MAZZARA confirms the declaration in all essentials, specifying that he was a direct witness of all the facts mentioned. His examination continues thus:

SAVERIO MAZZARA: . . . I have been Branch Secretary of the Communist Party in Castellammare for twenty years.

(*In answer to a question put by Mattarella's lawyers.*) Yes, in '46 I stood in the local elections on the civil list, which also included Dr Andrea Mancino and Vito Messina: on the rival list, the Christian Democrats', were Mattarella and Diego Plaja. In '58 I was candidate on the civic list with Vitale and Nino Barone. The disagreement between Barone and the DC, latent in '54, exploded in '58 after Barone had tried to get himself included on the DC list on condition that he would be appointed Mayor: when he broke off negotiations with the DC he was included on the civic list, and he was elected Mayor, and myself deputy Mayor, for about a year. After which, Barone having shown his wish to return to the DC, he got a minority vote and the Council was dissolved.

From '44 to '46 Barone was DC Mayor and I was Communist deputy Mayor, in coalition with the DC.

About 1960 I was elected Mayor in a second ballot with the votes of the civil list headed by Barone. I accepted, in view of the instability of the political situation, so that there wouldn't have to be a commissarial administration; I remained in office for a few months, until the budget was approved, after which I resigned. During my administration Magaddino was a local Councillor, but the Council was headed by the PCI.

AVV. BELLAVISTA: Is it true that the witness had bills of exchange paid by Gaspare and Giuseppe Magaddino, indicated as mafiosi?

SAVERIO MAZZARA: As I am chairman of a co-operative store and have commercial dealings with a very large number of people involving millions and millions of lire (for oil, wool, almonds, corn, cheese, and fruit and vegetables), it's quite probable.

GAETANO LA CORTE: What you have read to me[2] is what I declared to

[1] See page 212–213.   [2] Nos. 22, 23, page 224.

Dolci: I have first-hand knowledge of these things because I live in Ficuzza where Catanzaro is well known, under the nickname of *Borbone*. My wife and I spoke about this to Dolci and Alasia, knowing that they were doing a study on the subject.

When Zu Vincenzo Catanzaro procured votes for Barbaccia in 1958, Volpe only got a few votes; but in '63 when he procured them for Volpe, Volpe got practically all the votes.

Ficuzza is a district of Corleone where there have been so many murders by the mafia that people have lost count.

Biagio Adragna: The Honourable Mattarella was an intransigent opponent of the Separatist movement, which was supported by mafia forces.

On Easter Day 1948 a rally was held in the Piazza at Montelepre at which the speakers were the Honourable Bontade, Mattarella, and myself as a representative of cisl. The rally was particularly successful because the speakers laid great stress on the Christian Democrats' social reforms soundly inspired by Christian doctrine.

This hearing, begun in an empty Palace of Justice at 4.30 p.m., ends at the unusual hour of 8.30.

23rd November 1966

Giuseppe Migliore, Prefect of Palermo from 1955 to '58, and Alfredo Carrera, Prefect of Trapani from 1954 to '56, assure the Court that the Honourable Mattarella never exerted himself in favour of mafia elements. A similar assurance is given by Carlo Drago, Police Superintendent in Alcamo until 1952 and subsequently Deputy Chief of Police in Trapani until 1961: only occasionally did he see the Honourable Mattarella in conversation 'with Giovanni Stellino,[1] farmer and big wine dealer, rumoured in Alcamo to be a mafia element', but who during that period at least, continues the witness, was not in any trouble with the law.

Vincenzo Bivona, an elementary school teacher from Menfi, confirms his declaration, with a certain timidity and with confused attempts at clarification.

Giuseppe Di Palermo explains how, knowing us to be engaged on

[1] See declaration no. 9, page 217. (Tr.)

this study, he accompanied us to Ficuzza (a place of tragic significance) and was present during our conversation with the La
Cortes.

The two parties had agreed with the Court to present their requests
today, and to hand over additional documentary material of various
kinds. (Previously Volpe's lawyers had attached great importance to
presenting the sentences from trials decided in Volpe's favour
against individuals and newspapers that had accused him of being
in collusion with the mafia, and to the declarations they had succeeded in obtaining, following similar accusations, from Italo
Pietra (*Il Giorno*), Michele Pantaleone (*Espresso*), Felice Chilanti
(*Paese Sera*), Vittorio Nistico (*L'Ora*), Mario Tedeschi, Giano
Accame, Michele Melillo, and Ezio Calasciura.)

At this juncture, we can see only one way of breaking through finally
and being rid of all doubt. Since a breach has been made in the wall
of *omertà* and whoever wants to can now look through and begin to
get a clearer view of the situation, two things are necessary: first,
we must not hesitate to ask the Court to hear witnesses on the more
serious matters; and second, rather than go on asking the Antimafia
Commission, we must take it upon ourselves to present to the Court
copies of the documents so far presented exclusively to the Commission. Only in this way can the trial make a fundamental contribution towards ending one of the most grievous tangles in the history of post-war Italy.

Not without a certain civil emotion, Avv. Gatti explains the two
requests, underlining the necessity of allowing at least the more
important evidence to come out. It is worth reading carefully from
beginning to end the list of witnesses, with details, presented by
Avv. Gatti.

I

We the undersigned, counsel for Danilo Dolci and Franco Alasia,
in view of the fact that on 17th May of this year the Court of Rome,
Section IV, requested that Danilo Dolci acknowledge the signatures
of those who had signed the declarations contained in the dossier

passed on by the Antimafia Commission, thereby providing for their admission; and since, on the other hand, many other persons (in part already heard by the Antimafia Commission) made declarations contained in this dossier without their being requested to sign them, we ask that they be admitted as witnesses, in order that they may affirm that the contents of the aforesaid dossier and declarations correspond exactly to what they declared to Dolci and Alasia in the course of the interviews and conversations in which they took part.

In case they be required we append herewith particulars relating to the documentation (dossier) already in the Court's files [here follow particulars of thirty-one people].

II

We further request the admission of the following witnesses on the positions specified below (relative to Bernardo Mattarella and, in one or two cases, to other plaintiffs) [here follow particulars of fourteen people]:

The 1st, Don Giacomo Caiozzo, priest of Castellammare del Golfo

To state that he himself saw Bernardo Mattarella with Vincenzo Rimi in Alcamo, on cordial terms. He can also state that in Castellammare the Magaddinos, the Buccellatos, the Plajas, the Bonventres, and the Vitales campaigned for Bernardo Mattarella at elections. Further, that Police Lieutenant Verde, the magistrate Agrifoglio, and Avv. La Grutta, ex-vice-Prefect of Trapani, were subjected to pressure on the part of Bernardo Mattarella to favour his mafiosi friends.

Further, that Bernardo Mattarella attended a luncheon in New York at which all the American–Castellammarese mafia were also present, organized by the mafioso Spadaro, brother-in-law of Joe Bonanno.

He can state that the intermediary between Mattarella, Buccellato, and Magaddino was Liborio Munna.

And finally, how he knows that Bernardo Mattarella met the bandit Giuliano at Parrini before the massacre of Portella della Ginestra.

The 2nd, Gaspare Cassarà

To say that he himself observed the friendly relations between
Mattarella and individuals commonly known to be mafiosi: Diego
Plaja, Andrea Mancino, Cola Buccellato, Liborio Munna, Vito
Messina, Gaspare Magaddino, Tartamella, Giovanni Bonventre,
Bernardo Stabile; some of whom, when meeting them in the street,
Bernardo Mattarella used to embrace, and they would then go off
together to the Margherita Club or to the local DC headquarters.

To say also that Vito Messina was the ringleader of the group
that controlled the local Labour Exchange, and that he made himself
useful to herdsmen who were his friends by settling up with the
police matters such as trespass by their sheep or cows; that Messina
was a very active canvasser for Mattarella, promising jobs and
favours such as licences to carry arms for people who had difficulty
in obtaining them.

To say, further, that he himself saw Mattarella a number of
times in Alcamo embracing Vincenzo Rimi, and that he saw them at
lunch together in the company of Vito Bonventre, Antonino Buccellato, Andrea Mancino and Gaspare Magaddino in the Castellammare Motel.

To tell, finally, how from conversation with Frank Garofalo, on
whose farm he worked together with his father for over four years,
he learnt of the friendship between the said Garofalo and Mattarella.

The 3rd, Vincenzo Pisciotta

To tell of a meeting at Parrini between Bernardo Mattarella and
Giuliano in 1946, and another in Montelepre at the house of Giovanni Genovese, no. 60 Via Dimisa, in March 1947, before the
massacre of Portella della Ginestra.

The 4th, Benedetto Garofalo

To say that he saw with his own eyes Bernardo Mattarella arriving
at Parrini in a car in July 1946 to meet Salvatore Giuliano.

To say that he saw Mattarella in friendly conversation with Santo

Fleres, the capomafia of Partinico who was later murdered, and with the mafioso Gaspare Lo Medico, now in banishment.

The 5th, Avvocato Vito Varvaro

To confirm that the declarations numbered 8 and 9 in the Dolci dossier concern facts that are common knowledge in Alcamo.

To say also that he himself saw in Alcamo, during an election tour, Mattarella, Giovanni Stellino and Vincenzo Rimi at the head of a group of people.

The 6th, Professor Domenico Di Gaetano

To confirm that the documents numbered 8 and 9 in the Dolci dossier concern facts that are common knowledge in Alcamo.

To say also that in Alcamo and throughout the region of Trapani Giovanni Stellino and Vincenzo Rimi were notorious as big mafiosi.

The 7th, Grillo Biagio

To tell how on the occasion of a DC Provincial congress in Mazzara Bernardo Mattarella instructed him to report to Vincenzo Rimi on matters that related to previous dealings between the two.

The 8th, Giuseppe Benenati

To tell of the relations between Mattarella, Giovanni Stellino and Vincenzo Rimi, and of the election campaigning these two did for Mattarella, also through their associates.

To tell also of having seen on the night before the '58 election a large car marked 'Servizio di Stato' parked outside the house of Vincenzo Rimi's son Filippo, now in prison charged with murder.

The 9th, Cecilia De Simone

To tell of the continuous relations between Giovanni Stellino, Vincenzo Rimi and Mattarella; of the meetings in Stellino's house which took place even by day, and of those at night in Vincenzo Rimi's house.

To say also that Mattarella, Vincenzo Rimi and Giovanni Stellino, after a meeting at the time of the incident of the holding up of the Post, told her to pass on the news that the Post would leave again the next day, which duly happened.

To tell, finally, of a social gathering in public premises in Alcamo during which Vincenzo Rimi and Mattarella had a long and friendly conversation.

The 10th, Salvatore Taormina

To tell how he was sent for by Vincenzo Rimi and Giovanni Stellino who harboured grave resentment against the Honourable Girolamo Li Causi because a certain person—it later transpired that this was Mattarella—had informed them that the Honourable Girolamo Li Causi had reported them to the Police.

The 11th, Avvocato Paolo Della Rocca

To confirm the complete accuracy of the documentation concerning the relations between Mattarella and the mafia of Alcamo, and to say that this is trifling compared with other matters notorious in the town.

To give details about the circumstances and the persons that favoured the ascendancy of dangerous mafiosi like Rimi to such a degree that the Police and the *carabinieri* of Alcamo were powerless.

The 12th, Giovanni Abate

To tell of the propaganda activity carried out in Brancaccio on behalf of Mattarella by Gioacchino Caccamo, Filippo and Pietro Conte, and the son of Giovanni Alfano (all of old mafia families, all charged with criminal association).

To say also that Angelo Genova, of an old mafia family, asked him personally in 1963 to vote for Mattarella, describing him as a man from whom one could always obtain favours.

The 13th, Ignazio Fontana

To say that most of the votes for Mattarella, who was scarcely known in Villabate, were procured by local mafiosi such as: Anto-

nino Cottone, capomafia of Villabate, subsequently murdered,
father-in-law of Greco Salvatore who is now in prison; Giuseppe
Cottone, now in banishment, brother of the capomafia; Giovanni
Di Peri, an intimate associate of Cottone, at the moment in prison
for the blowing up of the *Giulietta* full of TNT in Villabate; Salvatore
Di Peri, now under special restrictions, and Antonino Vitale, known
as *Il Commendatore* (commonly regarded as the successor to Antonino Cottone), whom the witness himself saw with Mattarella, on
cordial terms, at the time of both the '48 and the '53 elections.

The *14th*, Onofrio Valenti[1]

To say that the relations between Mattarella and Vincenzo Rimi
were those of the candidate and his chief electoral henchman.

To say that he knows of the meal that took place at Spanò's, with
Mattarella, Barone, and mafia elements.

To give evidence about the contributions to Mattarella's election
campaign made by various bodies and organizations, banks, and
large industries such as Montecatini and Edison.

III

In connection with Calogero Volpe, we further request the admission of the following witnesses [here follow particulars of nineteen
people]:

The *1st*, Avvocato Cosimo D'Aura

To say that the chief mafiosi of Alia, such as Matteo Vallone and
his son, Paolo Castellana, Ditta Vincenzo, got votes mainly for Calogero Volpe and Bernardo Mattarella, intervening in person and
putting pressure on the voters with all their influence as capimafia.

The *2nd*, Francesco Lo Brutto

To say that on the occasion of the inauguration of the Mussumeli
Post Office, he saw that Volpe was received by (among others) Calogero Castiglione, a dangerous mafioso, and Vicio Arnone and Sorce

[1] See page 366. (Tr.)

(known as 'Nasca'), strong-arm men of Genco Russo. Meeting with
the latter in Piazza Manfredi in Mussumeli, Volpe went off with
him arm in arm. Genco Russo himself was at Volpe's side on the
balcony from which he made his speech. All the mafia of Mussumeli
used to be engaged during election campaigns in canvassing for
Volpe, handing out *pasta* or money, and themselves telling people to
vote for their candidate.

The 3rd, Salvatore Lanza

On the relationship between Genco Russo and Calogero Volpe.
The plaintiff attended mafia meetings in the house of Giuseppe Alfano with Castiglione and Sorce, Genco Russo himself also being
present; and he (Volpe) was called in the jargon of the 'family' first
of all '*u piccioteddu*'[1] and later 'the arm of Saint Francis'.[2]

The 4th, Pietro Guarnieri, and the 5th, Faustino Ingrao

To say that at successive political meetings in Montedoro Calogero Volpe never spoke against the mafia but actually acclaimed it,
affirming that 'in Sicily we all of us have the mafia spirit'. They are
also able to say that Volpe was in continuous collaboration with the
capimafia and the mafiosi of the area, as a member of the 'family'.
Finally they can declare that in Montedoro they often saw Calogero Volpe embrace and kiss Genco Russo, who was often accompanied by Vicio Arnone, Calogero Castiglione, Alfredo Falletta and
Felice Angiolella. And that several times they saw Calogero Vizzini
himself come to Montedoro to visit Volpe.

The 6th, Antonino Cimino

He can state that during an election rally held by Volpe in Delia,
Volpe had at his side Pietro Pittari, later arrested for criminal
association, Michele Russo, sentenced for criminal association, and
Salvatore Lo Verde, a criminal agent later murdered.

[1] An affectionate diminutive of *picciotto*, one of 'the boys'. (Tr. note.)
[2] i.e. someone who intercedes for people and grants favours such as getting
them out of prison. (Tr. note.)

The 7th, Ferdinando Dolce

He will say that Volpe sought the support of the mafia and was backed by them, and that in '46 when Volpe addressed a meeting in Delia from the balcony of the DC headquarters he saw beside him Angelo Iannello, a greatly feared mafioso who was murdered a few years later.

The 8th, Gaetano Virga

He can state that in Mazzarino Calogero Volpe obtains votes through the mafia, and that he saw the plaintiff at a gathering in the sacristy of the mother church which was also attended by capomafia Giuseppe Falzone, and Lodovico Cinardo, a mafioso connected with various estate bailiffs.

The 9th, Francesco Ferreri

To say that in the '63 election Volpe's posters were taken round Mazzarino by a son of Cicco Di Cristina, the capomafia of Riesi at present in banishment.

The 10th, Giuseppe Medicea

To say that Volpe's big election campaigners in Mazzarino were Lodovico Cinardo, legally cautioned, and Vincenzo Lo Presti, nephew of the capomafia Beppe Falzone. These were the men who put up the posters for Volpe and handed out the facsimiles.

The 11th, Salvatore Speziale

That when Calogero Volpe came to hold a meeting in Serradifalco, he arrived in town accompanied by Genco Russo.

The 12th, Liborio Butera

He will say that every time Calogero Volpe came to Serradifalco, he embraced and kissed, in public, the local capomafia Calogero

Territo, Salvatore Pace, and Viciu Arnone, a mafioso from Mussumeli, and that these and other mafiosi did electioneering on behalf of the plaintiff.

The 13th, Immordino Liborio

He can affirm that in Villalba, in the course of an election rally, Volpe declared that he had come to talk to the 'friends of the family' and added that he would return a week after the elections for a little intimate gathering of the 'friends of the family', when they would 'look each other in the eyes one by one to see who were the true friends and who the enemies'.

(We exhibit the accompanying declaration signed by seventy citizens of Villalba.)

The 14th, Francesco Marchese, State lawyer of Caltanissetta

He can tell of a conversation with Avv. Matteo Sanfilippo who declared to him that in one of the elections before 1963 Volpe paid Genco Russo ten million lire to support him as a Parliamentary candidate.

The 15th, Filippo Di Bilio, and the 16th, Gaspare Abisso

That in Riesi the canvassing for Volpe was done by Francesco Di Cristina, capomafia of the area, by his son Giuseppe, by Marazzotta Gaetano who is now in banishment, by Giuseppe Cammarata, sentenced for criminal association, and by Calogero Giambarresi, also recently banished; that when Di Cristina and Volpe met they embraced and kissed one another as close friends; and that the mafiosi even tried to make the people of Riesi vote for Volpe by means of threats and force of arms.

The 17th, Calogero Culisano, and the 18th, Vicenzo Carrubba

That Di Cristina of Riesi and Calogero Volpe were on the most affectionate terms; that in order to compel the people of Riesi to vote for Volpe these persons used to accompany him through the streets and stand with him on the balcony when he spoke; they organized celebrations in his honour, and drove out with large numbers of cars to meet him as he entered town.

The 19th, Gaetano Lo Manlio

That the whole of the Sicilian mafia attended the funeral of Ciccio Di Cristina, including Genco Russo himself; and that Di Cristina had been charged with criminal association and kidnapping.

That when Calogero Volpe spoke to Di Cristina he used to call him 'Zu Ciccu' or addressed him as '*Vossia*'.[1]

[Here follows the request for witnesses relative to the other plaintiffs besides Mattarella and Volpe.]

Avv. Gatti—also on behalf of his colleagues Fausto Gullo, Fausto Tarsitano, Giovanni Ozzo, and Luigi Salerni—hands over the new list of witnesses, precise and detailed this time because previously several of the most important witnesses were rejected 'because of the generality of their positions'; and he also hands over a copy of the dossier hitherto shown only to the Commission.

Avv. Leone briefly opposes both requests ('this is an attempt to obstruct the course of justice: they are attempting to prolong the trial indefinitely'), and hopes to be able to expound the position of his client in full at the next hearing, before the Court makes any decision on the matter. His tone, and that of his colleagues, is belligerent: who knows with what zeal and with what resources they will oppose us at the next hearing.

4th December 1966

Sunday. Franco goes out with his family on a trip to Castellammare, and there he meets someone who tells him:

'It's already known here that the trial's practically over. And it's already known that Padre Caiozzo isn't going to be called to give evidence in Court.'

'How do you mean—"it's already known"? How can anyone "know" yet?' replies Franco. 'They're just bluffing. We'll know on

[1] These denote familiarity and respect. (Tr. note.)

Friday: I don't believe it's possible for the trial to be suddenly cut
off like that—a few more will be questioned, at least.'

9th December 1966

The lawyers exhibit various documents and written requests.

No. No battle. In almost subdued tones, Avv. Leone has his say
in just a few minutes: the Court, he repeats, should not admit either
the copy of the dossier hitherto withheld, or further witnesses;
counsel for the other plaintiffs equally rapidly come to the same
conclusion.

The Public Prosecutor opposes 'any evidence concerning the
dealings Mattarella had (*sic*) with Giuliano and his associates';
he opposes the admission of the new dossier ('the documents they
wish to introduce are not those concerning which the action was
brought.'); as for our request for new witnesses to be heard, the gist
of what he says is: all of them, no—some, yes; and in fact he names
about ten of them.

Avv. Fausto Gullo perseveres, among other things insisting:

. . . It seems absurd to deny the right to a full enquiry. It is
impossible to go on feigning ignorance of the real situation in Sicily.
I need only remind you of one outstanding fact: the innumerable
trials begun in Sicily to ascertain responsibility for countless murders of trades unionists, invariably either closed by dismissal of the
case, or ending in acquittal on grounds of insufficient evidence. Not
one out of all these trials has ever found anyone guilty. It is obvious,
then, that there is a phenomenon of *omertà* which compels witnesses
to evasion or silence, thus impeding the due course of justice.

Now, exceptionally, we have witnesses who have made up their
minds to speak, to reveal circumstances and names. There is no need
for me to tell you how much this determination is costing some of
them in terms of anxiety and apprehension. In the name of what
insidious procedural subtlety are you prepared to turn them away?

From Avv. Leone's reply:

The parties to the action, having sufficient information already,
do not consider any further verifications appropriate. The trial

cannot and should not exceed its proper limits: its business is not to confront general problems but only to deal with the personal problems.

. . . Our task here is not to defend society, but only our own good name. If Dolci had not publicized at a Press conference matters reported by him to the Antimafia Commission, we would not have taken any steps, but would respectfully have waited for the Commission to accomplish its lofty task and announce its judgement to Parliament.

The judges withdraw to make their decision. After two hours in the Council chamber, they reject all Gatti's and Gullo's requests, approving instead the proposals of Avv. Leone.

Partinico, January 1967

To the Presiding Judge and other judges of the IVth Penal Section of the Court of Rome.

Your Honours,

As I have already told you, I have never had any grounds for personal animosity towards Bernardo Mattarella, Calogero Volpe, or the other people who have brought this case against me. For many years now I have been engaged, together with a group of experts, in work for social and economic development in Sicily, and for this reason I welcomed the invitation from the Parliamentary Antimafia Commission and handed over to them the results of our enquiries. Our aim in disclosing through a Press conference the most public part of our information (the less extensive and less serious part) was, I repeat, to facilitate and expedite effective action: to make the public aware of exactly how the mafia is involved in Sicilian politics, exactly how its underground violence has succeeded in becoming so powerful. It is obvious that the mafia can never be overcome without a full, general, and public denunciation of its every facet and its every connection that will really paralyse it, render it impotent, and defeat it finally.

With the opening of the trial, it seemed to me that two new things of a certain historical importance had happened: first, that a Court of law had been made responsible for the most important and most fruitful investigation in the struggle against the mafia, i.e. the investigation into the connection between mafia and politics; and second, that witnesses had shaken off the traditional fear of mafia vengeance and were reporting in public on facts that up till then had generally been whispered only within little groups of close friends.

As the trial proceeded, it became plainly necessary to complete investigations into certain circumstances already to some extent revealed, and to investigate fresh circumstances indicated bit by bit as the witnesses gave their evidence: and for this purpose to call authoritative witnesses who had direct knowledge of the basic facts at issue. This was the reason why my defending counsel, at the hearing on 23rd November, availed himself of the leave granted by the Court in its order of the 24th May, and gave notice of further evidence.

The Court, however, in its decision of 9th December, refused to accept copies of the other relevant documents which I had handed to the Parliamentary Antimafia Commission (60 concerning Mattarella and 35 Volpe), and refused to hear a single additional witness, even on a matter as palpably serious as this. This refusal was in fact contrary to the Court's own previously stated intentions. Perhaps the Court considered it already had sufficient evidence on which to base a judgement, but I believe that this decision has made it impossible to penetrate further into the phenomenon of the mafia, and in particular into its links with politics.

To see the matter as a whole, I think certain questions need to be asked. Is it true that the Antimafia Commission has in effect suspended its work on verifying the allegations about Mattarella and Volpe precisely because the matter is now *sub judice*? If the Court now refuses to hear fundamental evidence, how can it take up a definite position about information of which the most essential part is in the sole possession of the Antimafia Commission? And that is not all: in a conversation I had (in the absence of the Minister Taviani) with the Under-Secretary for Home Affairs, the Honourable Leonetto Amadei, to whom I showed certain serious documents in my possession, (the Head of the Italian Police, Prefect Vicari, was also present during part of the conversation,) I was told—as I had expected—that since a trial was in progress, the proper place to produce these documents was the Court itself. Could that statement have been mistaken?

Since I believe that a trial should be a common search for the truth, (though with the parties involved no doubt having different responsibilities,) my conscience will not allow me to share responsibility for an incomplete enquiry into a matter which for so many people has been, and still is, a matter of life and death. I therefore intend to take no further part in the proceedings, and have formally requested my valiant and able counsel—even though this request means they will have certain legal perplexities to contend with—not to take any further part in my defence unless I authorize it.

Those who have begun to break the silence of fear—and as long as I am still alive I shall be with them—will find other ways: I have no doubt at all that somehow or other the truth will out.

I know that the mafiosi and their friends, and those who out of fear or self-interest take their side, will say—as they have said before —that in doing this we are seeking to evade justice. This is not true, since we have all along requested a full and, if possible, swift ascertainment of the whole truth: unlike those who, openly or otherwise, have so obstinately resisted our requests for further evidence; and in any case it is obvious that judgement will be given just the same in our absence.

This step is forced upon me by my first-hand knowledge of the great harm that has been done, and is still being done today, by the mafia-clientship system—(and *that* is what is in the dock at this trial, let there be no mistake about it)—oppressing and humiliating whole areas where it flourishes; and by the conviction that no progress can be made towards a new life, in Sicily or anywhere in the world, as long as these basic problems are evaded.

I have agreed on the above with Franco Alasia.

Yours faithfully,

Danilo Dolci

In agreement with Danilo Dolci's assessment of the situation and with his decision, I shall abstain from taking any further part in the proceedings. I have formally requested my valiant counsel to consider their task completed.

Franco Alasia

January–May 1967

Whenever I meet non-mafiosi fishermen and peasants of Castellammare, I find they all have the same constant and deep preoccupation—briefly: what's going to happen to Vito Ferrante and Don Caiozzo and the others who have spoken out? Seeing that in Rome they want to cover up the sun, what can be done to prevent Mattarella and the mafia taking their revenge on them?

I learn from the papers (in general they have seen the point of our protest) that the Court of Rome, having appointed two official lawyers, is completing the examination of the few remaining witnesses: they all consider Mattarella and Volpe to be above any . . .; nobody saw anything; two of our witnesses who before had collaborated with us openly and in detail assert that they have never seen us, not even from a distance.

Meanwhile the scandal of the *Banco di Sicilia*[1] breaks out: Carlo Bazan, the former Chairman, is imprisoned; Gaetano Baldacci evades arrest in Beirut; Onofrio Valenti, DC Administrative Secretary of the Province, who had given us very important declarations and detailed confirmation of our records, is found dead in his study, killed by a pistol shot (the talk is of suicide caused by the banks' refusal of further credit to his industry); at the opening of the campaign for the Regional election of 11th June, those closest to DC Secretary Rumor on the platform in Palermo are Mattarella, Volpe, Gioa and Lima.

---

[1] Sicily's main bank and one of the biggest in Italy. At the preliminary investigation of this case (summer 1967), the ex-Chairman Bazan was accused (with others) of misappropriating millions of lire of the Bank's funds and other public money—using it for political purposes, for bribery etc. (Gaetano Baldacci, one of Italy's leading journalists, was accused of accepting large sums of money for not revealing what he knew of goings-on at the Bank). Practically the whole Sicilian Establishment was implicated; but the cases against many of them—particularly the politicians—were dismissed, on the usual grounds of 'insufficient evidence' etc. Those acquitted included the ex-Mayor of Palermo, Salvo Lima, who had been receiving a salary from the Bank for more than ten years after ceasing to work for it. Doubts were voiced about the impartiality of even the Palermo Attorney General (who has family connections with Mattarella).

Summer 1968: Bazan is still awaiting trial; Lima is now a Deputy in the Italian Parliament. (Tr. note.)

22nd June 1967

In New York (where I hear that in official Italian circles here quite as much is known about the subject as in Italy), as I am about to set off for South America to attend courses for the training of new social workers, I read in *Il Tempo*, just arrived from Rome, under the headline *Sentenced to two years for libelling Mattarella*, the following report:

The 'hunger-striker' from Trieste, accused of libelling the ex-Minister for Foreign Trade, the Honourable Bernardo Mattarella, and the present Under-Secretary to the Ministry of Health, the Honourable Calogero Volpe, has been sentenced to two years' imprisonment and a fine of 250,000 lire; the sentence is, however, suspended.

The writer is also to pay 3,500,000 lire costs, and 1,500,000 lire in reparation. Compensation for damages to Mattarella and Volpe will be repaid separately.

The judges of the IVth Section of the Court, headed by Dr Carlo Testi, were much harsher than the Public Prosecutor, Dr Pasquale Pedote, who in his final statement (which concluded with the request for a sentence of one year's imprisonment) had stressed Dolci's standing, as well as his very grave error in having deliberately committed libel by making public the results of an inquiry into the Sicilian mafia. In his reply yesterday, Pedote urged that the Court should also take into account the aggravating circumstances of excessive publication by means of the Press.

Speaking in defence of Dolci and of Franco Alasia (one of the 'hunger-striker's' colleagues sentenced to one year and seven months) were Avv. Mario Pittaluga and Avv. Gabriella Niccolai, officially appointed at the request of the Court . . .